THE POSTAL SERVICE
GUIDE TO
U.S. STAMPS

UPDATED STAMP VALUES

30TH EDITION

UNITED STATES
POSTAL SERVICE®

HarperResource
An Imprint of HarperCollins*Publishers*

HarperCollins books may be purchased for educational, business, or sales
promotional use. For information please write: Special Markets Department,
HarperCollins Publishers Inc., 10 East 53rd Street, New York, NY 10022.

Printed in the United States of America.

Library of Congress Cataloging-in-Publication Data has been applied for.

ISBN 0-06-052825-7

03 04 05 06 07 v/QWT 10 9 8 7 6 5 4 3 2 1

Table of Contents

A Nation of Firsts

The United States has long been a nation of firsts. Philosophers, scientists, educators, activists, musicians, writers, jurists, and hosts of others have contributed to the ever-growing list of American breakthroughs. Political barriers have fallen as greater opportunities have become available to all Americans; doctors and scientists have dealt with terrible diseases through careful research and consummate skill; and new technologies have transformed the country and the world in ways that our predecessors never could have foreseen.

Many of these firsts are chronicled on U.S. postage stamps, from the earliest American issuances to today's colorful commemoratives and definitives. In 2003, the U.S. Postal Service continued this tradition with a stamp program honoring a wide variety of firsts in American life, including the first African-American justice on the U.S. Supreme Court, the first National Wildlife Refuge, and the Wright brothers' amazing first flight near Kitty Hawk, North Carolina. Philatelists know that key events in our nation's history are destined to be memorialized on stamps, and that older issuances can serve as important reminders of our common heritage as Americans. Decades from now, these stamps will endure not only as a record of the subjects that interested us at the dawn of the 21st century, but also as a fascinating tribute to the people and events that have made the United States a true nation of firsts.

Background: Orville and Wilbur Wright test a glider as a kite, 1901. Courtesy of Special Collections and Archives, Wright State University.

An Adventure in Miniature

Collecting stamps as a hobby brings a world of adventure and learning to people of all ages. This year, the U.S. Postal Service issues its second prestige booklet (*Old Glory*) and honors a diverse array of people, events, and subjects, including—to name just a few individuals—author Zora Neale Hurston, activist Cesar E. Chavez, artist Mary Cassatt, and legendary jurist Thurgood Marshall. Without a big investment, you can visit picturesque lighthouses or a wildlife refuge, celebrate Ohio statehood, or commemorate the Louisiana Purchase. Stamp collecting puts the world at your fingertips. For ideas about how to start your own adventure, read on!

WHAT IS PHILATELY?

The word *philately* (*fi-latt'-eh-lee*) means the study of stamps and other postal materials. Stamp collectors are sometimes called philatelists.

HOW DO I START COLLECTING STAMPS?

You can start by simply saving stamps from letters, packages, and postcards. Or, start your collection by choosing one or two favorite subjects. Then, collect stamps that fit your theme—art, history, sports, transportation, science, or animals, for example. This is called topical or thematic stamp collecting.

WILL IT COST ME A LOT TO START A COLLECTION?

No. Start with used stamps and a few inexpensive accessories (such as a small album and a package of stamp hinges), and you can have a great time on a limited budget.

WHAT KINDS OF STAMPS ARE THERE?

There are a number of different types of stamps. Their purposes can be described as commemorative, definitive, or special; their formats can be in sheets, booklets, or coils.

- **Definitive stamps** (also called "regular issues") are the most common type of postage stamps. They feature everything from animals to the American flag or historic vehicles. They tend to be fairly small (generally less than an inch square), with denominations (the face value printed on the stamp) from one cent to many dollars. They are printed in large quantities, often more than once, and tend to be available for several years.

- **Commemorative stamps** are usually larger and more colorful than definitives. They are printed in smaller quantities and typically are printed only once. They remain on sale for a limited period of time, generally about a year. They are issued for specific rates, most often the prime letter rate. They honor, or commemorate, important people, events, or subjects, all of which reflect some aspect of American culture.

- **Special stamps** supplement the regular issues and tend to be larger and more colorful. They may be reprinted, but tend to remain on sale for only the life of the specific rate for which they are issued. These include Love stamps, Holiday Celebration stamps, international rate stamps, Priority Mail and Express Mail stamps.

- **Sheet stamps** are printed as large press sheets, then trimmed into smaller units called panes, most of which measure less than eight by ten inches. Panes generally contain twenty stamps, but may contain up to a hundred or as few as one stamp; smaller commemorative panes, with fewer than ten stamps, are often called souvenir sheets, depending on their purpose. Individual stamps tend to have perfs (perforations) or die-cut edges (generally with a wavy pattern) on all sides.

- **Booklet stamps** generally contain twenty stamps and may contain separate panes of stamps in a small folder or may be issued in a flat unit designed to be folded into a booklet by the customer. Most individual booklet stamps have at least one straight edge (no perfs or die-cuts) and sometimes two adjacent straight edges.

- **Coil stamps** are issued in rolls. Customers often buy them in rolls of a hundred stamps; business mailers can buy them in rolls of up to ten thousand stamps.

HOW DO I REMOVE STAMPS FROM ENVELOPES?

If you wish, you can save whole envelopes with stamps on them. These are called "covers." Collecting entire envelopes reflects a specialty called "postal history." It's a good idea to save the whole envelope if there's something special about the address or return address (famous places or people, for example), or the postmark (a date or location of some historic significance).

If you want to remove stamps from envelopes, it pays to be careful. The best way to remove stamps from envelopes is to soak them. Here's how:

1. Tear or cut off the upper right-hand corner of the envelope, leaving enough margin around the stamps to ensure they aren't damaged.
2. Place it, stamp side down, in a small pan of warm (not hot) water. If the stamp is affixed to a piece of colored envelope, use colder water; it may take longer, but any dyes from the paper are less likely to run and discolor the stamp. After a few minutes, the stamp should sink to the bottom. Remove the envelope piece from the water as soon as the stamp is off.
3. Wait a few more minutes for any remaining gum to dislodge from the stamp. The newer self-adhesive gums tend to take a bit longer.
4. Lift the stamp out. If you use your fingers, be sure your hands are clean, since oil from your skin can hasten discoloration of the stamps over time. Tongs—a stamp-collecting tool resembling tweezers—can be used to minimize contact. Wet stamps are delicate and should be handled carefully.
5. Place the stamp between two paper towels and put a heavy object, such as a book, on top. This will keep the stamp from curling as it dries. Leave the stamp there overnight.
6. If the stamp shows signs of remaining adhesive, even after lengthy soaking, dry it face down on a single paper towel with nothing touching the back. If necessary, it can be flattened after it's dried; otherwise, it may stick to surfaces when drying.

HOW DO I COLLECT FIRST DAY COVERS?

The fastest way to get a First Day cover is to buy the stamp yourself (it will usually go on sale the day after the first day of issue), attach it to your own envelope (or cover), and send it to the first day post office for cancellation. You can submit up to fifty envelopes, up to thirty days after the stamp's issue date. Here's how:

1. Write your address in the lower right-hand corner of each first day envelope, at least 5/8 inch from the bottom. Leave plenty of room for the stamp(s) and cancellation. Use a peel-off label if you prefer.
2. Insert a piece of cardboard (about as thick as a postcard) into each envelope. You can tuck the flap in or seal the envelope.
3. Affix your stamp(s) to your first day envelope(s).
4. Put your first day envelope(s) inside another, larger envelope and mail it to "Customer-Affixed Envelopes" in care of the postmaster of the first day city. Your envelopes will be canceled and returned.

Or, you can purchase a plain envelope with the stamp(s) already affixed and canceled. These are now sold directly by mail order through the U.S. Postal Service.

I WANT TO ARRANGE MY STAMPS IN AN ALBUM. WHAT KIND OF ALBUM SHOULD I BUY?

Some stamp albums feature specific categories with pictures of the stamps that should appear on each page. You may want to select one with loose-leaf pages so you can add pages as your collection grows. Personal computers can help you design your own pages, featuring your collection in a totally personalized manner. Software programs can help you with stamp-album pages, and common page-design programs can help you customize any design.

A stock book is an album with plastic or paper pockets on each page. There are no pictures of any stamps, so you can organize the stock book in any way. These books are especially useful for holding duplicate stamps, stamps for trading, and stamps that you've saved but haven't yet had time to put in the album containing your permanent collection.

HOW DO I PUT A STAMP IN THE ALBUM?

It's best to use a stamp hinge—a small strip of thin material (often glassine) with gum on one side. Unlike tape or glue (which should *never* be used), hinges let you peel the stamp off the page without damaging it. Hinges come either folded or unfolded.

Alternatively, stamp mounts can be used instead of a hinge. Stamp mounts are small, clear plastic sleeves that cover the entire stamp. Mounts are more expensive than hinges, but they protect stamps from air, dirt, and moisture. Hinges are fine for used stamps (stamps without adhesive that you've removed from mail), but mounts offer better protection for mint stamps (new stamps with adhesive, such as those you buy from the post office).

IS THERE ANYTHING ELSE I NEED?

Here's a list of other materials and accessories you may find helpful:

- **Glassine envelopes** are made of a special thin, see-through paper that protects stamps from grease and air. You can use them to keep stamps until you put them in your album.
- A **stamp catalog** is a reference book (like this book) with illustrations to help you identify stamps. It also lists the values of used and unused (mint) stamps.
- A **magnifying glass** (or **loupe**) helps you examine stamps by making them appear larger. Sometimes it's important to examine certain details of stamps more closely.
- A **perforation gauge** measures perforations along the edges of stamps. Sometimes the size and number of perfs are needed to identify stamps.
- A **watermark tray** (and **watermark fluid**) help make watermarks on stamps more visible. A watermark is a design or pattern that is pressed into some stamp paper during manufacturing.

HOW CAN I TELL WHAT A STAMP IS WORTH?

Ask yourself two questions: "How rare is it?" and "What condition is it in?" The price listed in a stamp catalog gives you some idea of how rare it is. However, the stamp may sell at more or less than the catalog price, depending on its condition. Always try to find stamps in the best possible condition.

HOW SHOULD I JUDGE THE CONDITION OF A STAMP?

Stamp dealers put stamps into categories according to their condition. A stamp in mint condition is the same as when purchased from the post office. An unused stamp has no cancellation but may not have any gum on the back. Mint stamps

Superb

Very Fine

Fine

Good

Light Cancel—Very Fine

Medium Cancel—Fine

Heavy Cancel

are usually worth more than unused stamps. Hinge marks on mint stamps can reduce value, which is why the use of stamp mounts is recommended for mint stamps.

You can begin to judge the condition of a stamp by examining the front of it. Are the colors bright or faded? Is the stamp clean, dirty, or stained? Is the stamp torn or creased? Torn stamps are not considered "collectible," but you may want to keep an example as a space filler until you get a better copy.

Are all the perforations intact? Has the stamp been canceled? A stamp with a light cancellation is in better condition than one with heavy marks across it.

Is the stamp design centered on the paper, crooked, or off to one side? Centering can range from "superb" (perfectly centered on the stamp) to "good" (the design on at least one side is marred somewhat by the perfs). Anything less would be graded "fair" or "poor" and, like torn copies, should be saved only as space fillers. Centering varies widely on older stamps; modern production techniques make it unlikely that copies with less than "fine" centering could be found.

Now look at the back of the stamp. Is there a thin spot in the paper? If so, it may have been caused by careless removal from a hinge or envelope.

The values listed in this book are for used and unused stamps in "very fine" condition that may have been hinged.

WHERE ELSE CAN I FIND STAMPS?
Check the classified ads in philatelic newspapers and magazines at your local library. Some publications are listed under "periodicals" in this book, and most will

Ornate
Chorus Frog

USA
37

send you a free sample copy on request. There are also a number of stamp-related sites on the Internet, which can be accessed through most search programs and services.

WHAT OTHER STAMP MATERIALS CAN I COLLECT?

Postal stationery products have the stamp design printed and/or embossed (with an impressed or raised image) directly on them.

- **Stamped envelopes** were first issued in the United States in 1853. More than five hundred million of them are printed each year.
- **Stamped cards** (also called *postal cards*) were first issued in 1873. Several different stamped card designs are issued each year.
- **Aerogrammes** (also called **air letters**) are designed to be letters and envelopes all in one. They are specially stamped, marked for folding, and gummed for sealing.

Other philatelic collectibles include:

- **Plate numbers** (including **plate blocks**) appear on or adjacent to stamps. These are most common on sheet stamps. Plate blocks are the group of stamps which have the printing plate numbers in the adjoining selvage—or margin (usually in the corner of the pane). On coils, these numbers appear in the margins of the stamps themselves, and collectors may save a **plate number strip** of two or more stamps with the number on the center stamp. On booklets, the plate numbers usually appear on the booklet "tab" by which the panes are affixed to the booklet cover.

- **Booklet panes** are panes of stamps affixed in, or as part of, a thin folder to form a booklet. With self-adhesive stamps, a newer convertible booklet format has been created, so that the stamps, liner, and booklet are all one unit. Usually, collectors of booklet panes save the entire pane or the entire booklet.

- **Marginal blocks** (including **copyright blocks**) feature marginal inscriptions other than the plate numbers. The most common is the copyright block, which features the copyright symbol ©, copyright date, and U.S. Postal Service information. All U.S. stamp designs since 1978 are copyrighted.
- **First Day Covers** (FDCs) are envelopes bearing new stamps

that are postmarked on the first day of sale. For each new postal issue, the U.S. Postal Service generally selects one location, usually related to the stamp subject, as the place for the first day dedication ceremony and the first day postmark.

- **First day ceremony programs** are given to persons who attend first day ceremonies. They contain a list of participants, information on the stamp subject, and the actual stamp attached and postmarked.

American Commemorative Panels are pages that contain photos or steel engravings, mint condition stamps, and subject-related text about a new stamp issue.

American Commemorative Collection features commemorative stamps on specially designed album pages with protective mounts.

American Commemorative Cancellations are specially tinted color pages featuring technical and text information about the stamp subject and a stamp(s) canceled with the First Day of Issue cancellation.

ARE THERE ANY STAMP GROUPS I CAN JOIN?

Yes! Stamp clubs can be a great source for new stamps and stamp-collecting advice. These clubs often meet at schools, libraries, and community centers. Ask your local postmaster or librarian for the locations of stamp clubs in your area and other contact information. You may also refer to the listing under Organizations in this book.

2003 Issues
U.S. Postage Stamps & Postal Stationery

Black Heritage: Thurgood Marshall. The first African American to serve as a justice on the U.S. Supreme Court and as the nation's solicitor general, Thurgood Marshall was known for his commitment to defending constitutional rights and affirmative action.
Date of Issue: January 7, 2003
Place of Issue: Washington, DC

Lunar New Year: Year of the Ram. This stamp celebrating the Year of the Ram is the eleventh issuance in the Lunar New Year series.
Date of Issue: January 15, 2003
Place of Issue: Chicago, IL

Literary Arts: Zora Neale Hurston. Novelist, folklorist, and anthropologist Zora Neale Hurston was a central figure in the Harlem Renaissance.
Date of Issue: January 24, 2003
Place of Issue: Eatonville, FL

Ohio Statehood. In honor of the 200th anniversary of Ohio's statehood, the stamp features a photograph taken near the first permanent settlement in what was once known as the Northwest Territory.
Date of Issue: March 1, 2003
Place of Issue: Chillicothe, OH

Pelican Island National Wildlife Refuge. This stamp celebrates the centennial of the creation of Pelican Island National Wildlife Refuge, which marked the beginning of the National Wildlife Refuge System. Today, the system encompasses more than 93 million acres across more than 570 refuges and wetland management districts in every state and U.S. territory.
Date of Issue: March 14, 2003
Place of Issue: Sebastian, FL

American Filmmaking: Behind the Scenes. This pane of ten stamps honors all of those highly skilled men and women who work behind the scenes to create American movie magic.

Date of Issue: February 25, 2003
Place of Issue: Beverly Hills, CA

Old Glory Prestige Booklet. The American flag has appeared on many kinds of patriotic ephemera. These five stamps appear in a commemorative prestige booklet.

Date of Issue: April 3, 2003
Place of Issue: New York, NY

Cesar E. Chavez. Civil rights leader Cesar E. Chavez, founder of the United Farm Workers of America, was a tireless advocate for nonviolent social change. He led the first successful farm workers union in American history, achieving fair wages, medical coverage, pension benefits, and other rights and protections for farm workers.

Date of Issue: April 23, 2003
Place of Issue: Los Angeles, CA

Louisiana Purchase. Often referred to as the greatest real estate deal in history, the Louisiana Purchase doubled the size of the United States. This stamp commemorates the bicentennial of the Louisiana Purchase, and its role in opening the heartland of the continent to American exploration and settlement.

Date of Issue: April 30, 2003
Place of Issue: New Orleans, LA

First Flight. This souvenir sheet commemorates the centennial of the Wright brothers' first controlled, powered airplane flight on December 17, 1903.

Date of Issue: May 22, 2003
Place of Issue: Dayton, OH and Kill Devil Hills, NC

Legends of Hollywood: Audrey Hepburn. A film star, fashion icon, and humanitarian, Audrey Hepburn appeared in nearly 30 films.

Date of Issue: June 11, 2003
Place of Issue: Los Angeles, CA

Southeastern Lighthouses. These five landmarks along the southeastern coast of the United States typify the beauty and history of the nation's lighthouses.

Date of Issue: June 13, 2003
Place of Issue: Tybee Island, GA

ARCTIC TUNDRA

FIFTH IN A SERIES

N A T U R E   O F   A M E R I C A

Nature of America: Arctic Tundra. Coldest of the North American ecosystems, the arctic tundra is a vast treeless region stretching across northern Alaska and Canada. The stamp pane depicts a tundra scene in autumn.
Date of Issue: July 2, 2003
Place of Issue: Fairbanks, AK

Korean War Veterans Memorial. Located on the National Mall in Washington, D.C., the memorial recognizes the sacrifices of those who served in the Korean conflict.
Date of Issue: July 27, 2003
Place of Issue: Washington, DC

District of Columbia. This stamp commemorates the District of Columbia and the dynamic city within its boundaries—Washington—which serves not only as the nation's capital but as home to more than a half million residents.
Date of Issue: Fall 2003
Place of Issue: Washington, DC

American Treasures: Mary Cassatt.
Four paintings by Mary Cassatt, the only American artist ever invited to exhibit with the French Impressionists, make up the third issuance in the American Treasures series.
Date of Issue: **August 7, 2003**
Place of Issue: **Columbus, OH**

Early Football Heroes.
Four great figures from the early days of football—Walter Camp, Ernie Nevers, Red Grange, and Bronko Nagurski—are celebrated for their contributions to the sport.
Date of Issue: **August 8, 2003**
Place of Issue: **South Bend, IN**

Roy Acuff.
This stamp honors Roy Acuff, often called the King of Country Music, on the centenary of his birth. Acuff helped turn the Grand Ole Opry into the nation's foremost country music institution, and he helped make Nashville the country music capital of America.
Date of Issue: **September 13, 2003**
Place of Issue: **Nashville, TN**

Reptiles and Amphibians. These five stamps feature two amphibians and three reptiles native to the United States: the scarlet kingsnake, the blue-spotted salamander, the reticulate collared lizard, the ornate chorus frog, and the ornate box turtle.

Date of Issue: October 7, 2003
Place of Issue: San Diego, CA

Holiday Music Makers. These colorful stamps feature whimsical Santas and fanciful reindeer as reminders of the joys of the season.

Date of Issue: October 23, 2003
Place of Issue: New York, NY

Definitive, Rate Change, and Semipostals

American Clock. This 10-cent definitive stamp, second in the American Design series, features a detail of a banjo clock made in Massachusetts early in the 19th century.
Date of Issue: January 24, 2003
Place of Issue: Tucson, AZ

Nurturing Love Stamped Envelope. This envelope, the sixth to feature a Love theme, depicts a gardener watering plants that create a leafy heart with their curving stems.
Date of Issue: January 25, 2003
Place of Issue: Tucson, AZ

Special Olympics. This stamp honors the competitors, coaches, and volunteers who bring joy and dedication to the Special Olympics.
Date of Issue: February 13, 2003
Place of Issue: Chicago, IL

Wisdom. This $1 stamp features a stylized treatment of a detail from the relief sculpture *Wisdom, with Light and Sound* at Rockefeller Center in New York City.
Date of Issue: February 28, 2003
Place of Issue: Biloxi, MS

University of Ohio Postal Card. The U.S. Postal Service commemorates the 200th anniversary of the founding of Ohio University with the issuance of this stamped card in the Historic Preservation series.
Date of Issue: October 2003
Place of Issue: Athens, Ohio

Tiffany Lamp. The third stamp in the American Design series evokes the work of Louis Comfort Tiffany (1848-1933), one of the greatest designers of glass in his era.
Date of Issue: March 1, 2003
Place of Issue: Biloxi, MS

Purple Heart. With this stamp, the U.S. Postal Service honors the courage and sacrifices of the men and women who serve in the U.S. military.
Date of Issue: May 30, 2003
Place of Issue: Mount Vernon, VA

Stop Family Violence. This semipostal will allow every American to contribute to a nationwide fight against domestic violence.
Date of Issue: November 15, 2003
Place of Issue: Denver, CO

American Eagle. This First-Class presorted stamp features an artistic rendering of a detail of the Great Seal of the United States.
Date of Issue: June 26, 2003
Place of Issue: Santa Clara, CA

Snowy Egret. This first-class definitive stamp features an artistic rendering of a snowy egret. Admired for its graceful plumage, the snowy egret is considered one of the most beautiful American birds.
Date of Issue: October 24, 2003
Place of Issue: New York, NY

Explanation of Catalog Prices

The United States Postal Service sells only the commemoratives and special issues released during the past few years. Current postal stationery and regular issues remain on sale for longer periods of time. Prices in this book are called "catalog prices" by stamp collectors. Collectors use catalog prices as guidelines when buying or trading stamps. **It is important to remember the prices are simply guidelines to the stamp values. Stamp condition is very important in determining the actual value of a stamp.**

Prices are Estimated
Listed prices are estimates of how much you can expect to pay for a stamp from a dealer. **A 20-cent minimum valuation has been established that represents a fair-market price to have a dealer locate and provide a single stamp to a customer. Dealers may charge** less per stamp to provide a group **of such stamps, and may charge less for such a single stamp. Similarly, a $1.00 minimum has been established for First Day Covers (FDCs).** If you sell a stamp to a dealer, he or she may offer you much less than the catalog price. Dealers pay based on their interest in owning a particular stamp. If they already have a full supply, they may only buy additional stamps at a low price.

Condition Affects Value
The catalog prices are given for unused (mint) stamps and used (canceled) stamps that have been hinged and are in "very fine" condition. Stamps in "superb" condition that have never been hinged may cost more than the listed price. Stamps in less than "fine" condition may cost less.

The prices for used stamps are based on a light cancellation; a heavy cancellation lessens a stamp's value. Canceled stamps may be worth more than uncanceled stamps. This happens if the cancellation is of a special type or for a significant date. Therefore, it is important to study an envelope before removing a stamp and discarding its "cover." Additional information about and examples of stamp conditions can be found in the Introduction to this book.

Sample Listing

				Un	U	PB/LP/PNC	#	FDC	Q(M)
3069	32¢	Georgia O'Keefe	05/23/96	.65	.20	2.75	(4)	1.25	156

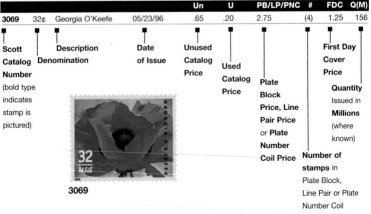

Scott Catalog Number (bold type indicates stamp is pictured)

Description Denomination

Date of Issue

Unused Catalog Price

Used Catalog Price

Plate Block Price, Line Pair Price or **Plate Number** Coil Price

First Day Cover Price

Quantity Issued in **Millions** (where known)

Number of **stamps** in Plate Block, Line Pair or Plate Number Coil

3069

Understanding the Listings

◼ Prices in **regular type** for single unused and used stamps are taken from the *Scott 2003 Specialized Catalogue of U.S. Stamps & Covers,* whose editors have based these prices on **actual retail values** as they found them in the marketplace. The Scott numbering system for stamps is used in this book. Prices quoted for unused and used stamps are for "very fine" condition, except where "very fine" is not available.

◼ Stamp values in *italic* generally refer to items difficult to value accurately.

◼ A dash (—) in a value column means the item is known to exist but information is insufficient for establishing a value.

◼ The stamp listings contain a number of additions designated "*a,*" "*b,*" "*c,*" etc. These represent recognized variations of stamps as well as errors. These listings are as complete as space permits.

Occasionally, a new stamp or major variation may be inserted by the catalog editors into a series or sequence where it was not originally anticipated. These additions are identified by capital letters "*A,*" "*B*" and so forth. For example, a new stamp which logically belonged between 1044 and 1045 is designated 1044A, even though it is entirely different from 1044. The insertion was preferable to a complete renumbering of the series.

◼ Prices for Plate Blocks, First Day Covers, American Commemorative Panels and Souvenir Pages are taken from *Scott 2003 Specialized Catalogue of U.S. Stamps & Covers.*

Sample Variation Listing

			Un	U	PB/LP/PNC	#	FDC	Q(M)
2281	25¢ Honeybee	09/02/88	.45	.20	3.00	(3)	1.25	
a	Imperf. pair		50.00					
b	Black omitted		60.00	—				
d	Pair, imperf. between		1,000.00					

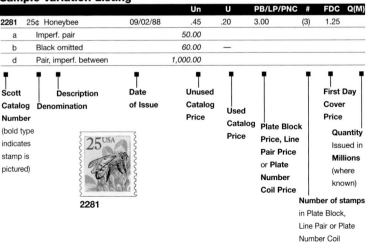

Scott Catalog Number (bold type indicates stamp is pictured)

Description / Denomination

Date of Issue

Unused Catalog Price

Used Catalog Price

Plate Block Price, Line Pair Price or **Plate Number** Coil Price

First Day Cover Price

Quantity Issued in **Millions** (where known)

Number of stamps in Plate Block, Line Pair or Plate Number Coil

2281

Commemorative and Definitive Stamps

1847-1875

1
2

3
4

5
11

14
17

12

Issues of 1847

**Thin, Bluish Wove Paper,
July 1, Imperf., Unwmkd.**

		Un	U
1	5¢ Benjamin Franklin	6,250.00	575.00
a	5¢ dark brown	7,000.00	625.00
b	5¢ orange brown	8,000.00	850.00
c	5¢ red orange	12,500.00	6,000.00
	Pen cancel		290.00
	Double transfer of top and bottom frame lines		725.00
	Double transfer of top, bottom and left frame lines and numerals		3,000.00
2	10¢ George Washington	27,500.00	1,400.00
	Pen cancel		700.00
	Vertical line through second "F" of "OFFICE"	—	1,900.00
	With "stick pin" in tie, or with "harelip"	—	1,900.00
	Double transfer in lower right "X," or of left and bottom frame lines	—	2,000.00
	Double transfer in "POST OFFICE"	—	2,500.00

**Issues of 1875, Reproductions
of 1 and 2, Bluish Paper, Without Gum**

		Un	U
3	5¢ Franklin	750.00	—
4	10¢ Washington	950.00	—

5¢. On the originals, the left side of the white shirt frill touches the oval on a level with the top of the "F" of "Five." On the reproductions, it touches the oval on a level with the top of the figure "5."

10¢. On the originals, line of coat points to "T" of TEN and right line of coat points between "T" and "S" of CENTS.

On the reproductions left, line of coat points to right tip of "X" and right line of coat points to center of "S" of CENTS.

On the reproductions, the eyes have a sleepy look, the line of the mouth is straighter, and in the curl of hair near the left cheek is a strong black dot, while the originals have only a faint one.

Issues of 1851-57, Imperf.

		Un	U
5	1¢ Franklin, type I	200,000.00	45,000.00
5A	1¢ blue, type Ib	16,000.00	6,250.00
	#6-9: Franklin (5), 1851		
6	1¢ blue, type Ia	37,500.00	10,000.00
7	1¢ blue, type II	1,200.00	160.00
	Cracked plate	1,450.00	375.00
8	1¢ blue, type III	12,500.00	3,000.00
8A	1¢ blue, type IIIa	4,500.00	1,100.00
9	1¢ blue, type IV	750.00	125.00
	Triple transfer, one inverted	900.00	175.00

Issues of 1851-57

#10-11, 25-26a all had plates on which at least four outer frame lines (and usually much more) were recut, adding to their value.

		Un	U
10	3¢ orange brown Washington, type I (11)	3,250.00	100.00
	3¢ copper brown	3,750.00	250.00
	On part-India paper	—	500.00
11	3¢ Washington, type I	240.00	11.00
	3¢ deep claret	325.00	19.00
	Double transfer, "GENTS" for "CENTS"	375.00	50.00
12	5¢ Jefferson, type I	19,000.00	1,000.00
13	10¢ green Washington, type I (14)	15,000.00	800.00
14	10¢ green, type II	4,500.00	210.00
15	10¢ Washington, type III	4,500.00	210.00
16	10¢ green, type IV (14)	27,500.00	1,600.00
17	12¢ Washington	5,250.00	325.00

Issues of 1857-61, Perf. 15.5
(Issued in 1857 except #18, 27, 28A, 29, 30, 30A, 35, 36b, 37, 38, 39)

#18-24: Franklin (5)

		Un	U
18	1¢ blue, type I	2,000.00	600.00
19	1¢ blue, type Ia	22,500.00	6,500.00
20	1¢ blue, type II	1,100.00	250.00
21	1¢ blue, type III	12,500.00	2,200.00
22	1¢ blue, type IIIa	2,000.00	500.00
23	1¢ blue, type IV	8,500.00	700.00
24	1¢ blue, type V	175.00	40.00
	"Curl" on shoulder	240.00	67.50
	"Earring" below ear	600.00	95.00
	Long double "curl" in hair	300.00	80.00
b	Laid paper	—	

#25-26a: Washington (11)

		Un	U
25	3¢ rose, type I	2,500.00	90.00
	Major cracked plate	4,000.00	550.00
26	3¢ dull red, type II	75.00	7.50
	3¢ brownish carmine	150.00	18.00
	3¢ claret	170.00	23.00
	Left or right frame line double	110.00	17.50
	Cracked plate	750.00	250.00
26a	3¢ dull red, type IIa	225.00	60.00
	Double transfer	325.00	130.00
	Left frame line double	—	150.00

5
Bust of Benjamin Franklin.

Detail of **#7, 20** Type II

Lower scrollwork incomplete (lacks little balls and lower plume ornaments). Side ornaments are complete.

Detail of **#9, 23** Type IV

Similar to Type II, but outer lines recut top, bottom or both.

Detail of **#5, 18, 40** Type I

Has curved, unbroken lines outside labels. Scrollwork is substantially complete at top, forms little balls at bottom.

Detail of **#8, 21** Type III

Outer lines broken in the middle. Side ornaments are substantially complete.

Detail of **#8A, 22** Type IIIa

Outer lines broken top or bottom but not both.

Detail of **#24** Type V

Similar to Type III of 1851-57 but with side ornaments partly cut away.

Detail of **#6, 19** Type Ia

Same as Type I at bottom but top ornaments and outer line partly cut away. Lower scrollwork is complete.

Detail of **#5a** Type Ib

Lower scrollwork is incomplete, the little balls are not so clear.

3¢ Washington Types I-IIa, Series 1851-1857, 1857-1861, 1875

10
Bust of George Washington

Detail of **#10, 11, 25, 41**
Type I

There is an outer frame line at top and bottom.

Detail of **#26**
Type II

The outer frame line has been removed at top and bottom. The side frame lines were recut so as to be continuous from the top to the bottom of the plate.

Detail of **#26a**
Type IIa

The side frame lines extended only to the bottom of the stamp design.

5¢ Jefferson Types I-II, Series 1851-1857, 1857-1861

12
Portrait of
Thomas Jefferson

Detail of **#12, 27-29**
Type I

There are projections on all four sides.

Detail of **#30-30a**
Type II

The projections at top and bottom are partly cut away.

10¢ Washington Types I-IV, Series 1851-1857, 1857-1861, 1875

15
Portrait of
George Washington

Detail of **#14, 32**
Type II

The design is complete at the top. The outer line at the bottom is broken in the middle. The shells are partly cut away.

Detail of **#16, 34** Type IV

The outer lines have been recut at top or bottom or both. Types I, II, III and IV have complete ornaments at the sides of the stamps and three pearls at each outer edge of the bottom panel.

Detail of **#13, 31, 43**
Type I

The "shells" at the lower corners are practically complete. The outer line below the label is very nearly complete. The outer lines are broken above the middle of the top label and the "X" in each upper corner.

Detail of **#15, 33**
Type III

The outer lines are broken above the top label and the "X" numerals. The outer line at the bottom and the shells are partly cut away, as in Type II.

Detail of
#35
Type V

(Two typical examples.)

Side ornaments slightly cut away. Outer lines complete at top except over right "X." Outer lines complete at bottom and shells nearly so.

1857-1875

	Issues of 1857-61	Un	U
	Perf. 15.5		
	#27-29: Jefferson (12)		
27	5¢ brick red, type I	*27,500.00*	1,400.00
28	5¢ red brown, type I	5,000.00	800.00
b	5¢ brt. red brn., type I	5,500.00	1,000.00
28A	5¢ Indian red, type I	*32,500.00*	3,000.00
29	5¢ brown, type I	2,500.00	350.00
	Defective transfer	—	—
30	5¢ orange brown, type II	1,200.00	1,100.00
30A	5¢ brown, type II (30)	2,000.00	300.00
b	Printed on both sides	*4,500.00*	*4,750.00*
	#31-35: Washington (15)		
31	10¢ green, type I	17,500.00	900.00
32	10¢ green, type II	5,250.00	275.00
33	10¢ green, type III	5,250.00	275.00
	"Curl" on forehead		
	or in left "X"	—	350.00
34	10¢ green, type IV	*32,500.00*	2,250.00
35	10¢ green, type V	275.00	65.00
	Small "curl" on forehead	325.00	77.50
	"Curl" in "e" or		
	"t" of "Cents"	350.00	90.00
	Plate I Outer frame lines complete		
36	12¢ blk. Washington		
	(17), plate I	1,400.00	260.00
	Triple transfer	1,700.00	—
36b	12¢ black, plate III	750.00	180.00
	Vertical line		
	through rosette	925.00	260.00
37	24¢ gray lilac	1,600.00	350.00
a	24¢ gray	1,600.00	350.00
38	30¢ orange Franklin	1,900.00	450.00
	Recut at bottom	2,200.00	575.00
39	90¢ blue Washington	2,900.00	*7,000.00*
	Double transfer		
	at top or bottom	3,100.00	—
	Pen cancel		2,250.00

Note: Beware of forged cancellations of #39. Genuine cancellations are rare

	Issues of 1875	Un	U
	Government Reprints, White Paper		
	Without Gum, Perf. 12		
40	1¢ bright blue Franklin (5)	*625.00*	
41	3¢ scarlet Wash. (11)	*3,250.00*	
42	5¢ orange brown		
	Jefferson (30)	*1,250.00*	
43	10¢ blue green		
	Washington (14)	*3,000.00*	
44	12¢ greenish black		
	Washington (17)	*3,500.00*	
45	24¢ blackish violet		
	Washington (37)	*3,500.00*	
46	30¢ yellow orange		
	Franklin (38)	*3,500.00*	
47	90¢ deep blue		
	Washington (39)	*4,500.00*	
48-54	Not assigned		
	Issue of 1861, Thin,		
	Semi-Transparent Paper		
	#55-62 are no longer considered postage stamps. Many experts consider them to be essays and/or trial color proofs.		
62B	10¢ dark green		
	Washington (58)	*7,000.00*	1,000.00

30

37

38

39

40

62B

63   64   65   67

68   69   70   71

72   73   77

Details

Issues of 1861-62, 1861-66, 1867 and 1875

Detail of **#63, 86, 92**

There is a dash in 63, 86 and 92 added under the tip of the ornament at the right of the numeral in upper left corner.

Detail of **#67, 75, 80, 95**

There is a leaf in 67, 75, 80 and 95 added to the foliated ornaments at each corner.

Detail of **#69, 85E, 90, 97**

In 69, 85E, 90 and 97, ovals and scrolls have been added at the corners.

Detail of **#64-66, 74, 79, 82-83, 85, 85C, 88, 94**

In 64-66, 74, 79, 82-83, 85, 85C, 88 and 94, ornaments at corners have been enlarged and end in a small ball.

Detail of **#68, 85D, 89, 96**

There is an outer line in 68, 85D, 89 and 96 cut below the stars and an outer line added to the ornaments above them.

Detail of **#72, 101**

In 72 and 101, parallel lines form an angle above the ribbon containing "U.S. Postage"; between these lines a row of dashes has been added, along with a point of color to the apex of the lower line.

Issues of 1861-1862		Un	U
Perf. 12			
63	1¢ blue Franklin	325.00	32.50
	Double transfer	—	45.00
	Dot in "U"	350.00	37.50
a	1¢ ultramarine	750.00	275.00
b	1¢ dark blue	650.00	90.00
c	Laid paper	—	—
d	Vert. pair,		
	imperf. horizontally		—
e	Printed on both sides	—	2,500.00
64	3¢ pink Washington	8,000.00	800.00
a	3¢ pigeon blood pink	19,000.00	3,500.00
b	3¢ rose pink	575.00	150.00
65	3¢ rose Washington	130.00	2.50
	Cracked plate	—	—
	Double transfer	150.00	5.50
b	Laid paper	—	—
d	Vertical pair,		
	imperf. horizontally	3,500.00	750.00
e	Printed on both sides	10,000.00	2,750.00
f	Double impression		6,000.00
66	3¢ lake Washington is considered		
	a Trial Color Proof		
67	5¢ buff Jefferson	21,000.00	800.00
68	10¢ yellow green		
	Washington	850.00	50.00
	10¢ deep yellow green		
	on thin paper	1,000.00	60.00
	Double transfer	925.00	55.00
a	10¢ dark green	900.00	62.50
b	Vert. pair,		
	imperf. horizontally		3,500.00
69	12¢ blk. Washington	1,400.00	100.00
	12¢ intense black	1,450.00	115.00
	Double transfer of top		
	or bottom frame line	1,500.00	130.00
	Double transfer of top		
	and bottom frame lines	1,550.00	135.00
70	24¢ red lilac		
	Washington	2,250.00	190.00
	Scratch under "A"		
	of "POSTAGE"		—
a	24¢ brown lilac	1,750.00	140.00
b	24¢ steel blue	9,000.00	725.00
c	24¢ violet	10,000.00	1,300.00
d	24¢ grayish lilac	3,750.00	1,500.00
71	30¢ orange Franklin	1,750.00	160.00
a	Printed on both sides		—
72	90¢ bl. Washington	3,000.00	425.00
a	90¢ pale blue	2,750.00	425.00
b	90¢ dark blue	3,250.00	550.00
Issues of 1861-66			
73	2¢ blk. Andrew Jackson	375.00	50.00
	Double transfer	425.00	55.00
	Major double transfer of top		
	left corner and "POSTAGE"		12,500.00
	Cracked plate	—	—

Issues of 1861-1866		Un	U
Perf. 12			
	#74 3¢ scarlet Washington was not regularly		
	issued and is considered a Trial Color Proof.		
75	5¢ red brown		
	Jefferson (67)	4,750.00	475.00
76	5¢ brown Jefferson (67)	1,300.00	120.00
a	5¢ dark brown	1,450.00	175.00
	Double transfer of top		
	or bottom frame line	1,400.00	130.00
77	15¢ blk. Lincoln	2,250.00	160.00
	Double transfer	2,350.00	170.00
78	24¢ lilac Washington (70)	1,350.00	110.00
a	24¢ grayish lilac	1,350.00	110.00
b	24¢ gray	1,350.00	110.00
c	24¢ blackish violet	30,000.00	2,500.00
d	Printed on both sides		3,500.00
Grills on U.S. Stamps			
	Between 1867 and 1870, postage stamps		
	were embossed with pyramid-shaped grills		
	that absorbed cancellation ink to prevent		
	reuse of canceled stamps.		
Issues of 1867, With Grills			
Grills A, B and with C: Points Up			
A. Grill Covers Entire Stamp			
79	3¢ rose Washington (56)	5,250.00	1,200.00
b	Printed on both sides		—
80	5¢ brown Jefferson (57)	—	130,000.00
a	5¢ dark brown		130,000.00
81	30¢ orange Franklin (61)		60,000.00
B. Grill about 18 x 15mm			
82	3¢ rose Washington (56)		175,000.00
C. Grill about 13 x 16mm			
83	3¢ rose Washington (56)	5,250.00	1,000.00
	Double grill	6,500.00	2,300.00
Grills, D, Z, E, F with Points Down			
D. Grill about 12 x 14mm			
84	2¢ black Jackson (73)	15,000.00	3,500.00
85	3¢ rose Washington (56)	6,500.00	1,000.00
	Split grill		1,100.00
Z. Grill about 11 x 14mm			
85A	1¢ blue Franklin (55)		935,000.00
85B	2¢ black Jackson (73)	7,500.00	1,200.00
	Double transfer	8,000.00	1,250.00
85C	3¢ rose Washington (56)	12,500.00	3,250.00
	Double grill	14,000.00	
85D	10¢ grn. Washington (58)		90,000.00
85E	12¢ blk. Washington (59)	11,000.00	1,600.00
	Double transfer		
	of top frame line		1,700.00
85F	15¢ black Lincoln (77)		220,000.00
E. Grill about 11 x 13mm			
86	1¢ blue Franklin (55)	3,000.00	450.00
a	1¢ dull blue	3,000.00	425.00
	Double grill	—	575.00
	Split grill	3,100.00	500.00

1867-1875

	Issues of 1867	Un	U
	With Grills, Perf. 12		
87	2¢ black Jackson (73)	1,500.00	150.00
	2¢ intense black	1,600.00	190.00
	Double grill	—	—
	Double transfer	1,600.00	165.00
88	3¢ rose Washington (65)	850.00	22.50
a	3¢ lake red	925.00	25.00
	Double grill	—	—
	Very thin paper	875.00	25.00
89	10¢ grn. Washington (68)	5,000.00	300.00
	Double grill	6,400.00	500.00
90	12¢ blk. Washington (69)	4,750.00	350.00
	Double transfer of top		
	or bottom frame line	5,000.00	375.00
91	15¢ black Lincoln (77)	9,500.00	625.00
	Double grill	—	950.00
	F. Grill about 9 x 13mm		
92	1¢ blue Franklin (63)	1,000.00	200.00
	Double transfer	1,050.00	240.00
	Double grill	—	370.00
93	2¢ black Jackson (73)	475.00	50.00
	Double grill	—	180.00
	Very thin paper	525.00	57.50
94	3¢ red Washington (65)	375.00	7.50
a	3¢ rose	375.00	7.50
	Double grill		—
	End roller grill		350.00
	Quadruple split grill	675.00	130.00
c	Vertical pair,		
	imperf. horizontally	1,100.00	
d	Printed on both sides	2,250.00	
95	5¢ brown Jefferson (67)	3,250.00	750.00
a	5¢ black brown	3,500.00	950.00
96	10¢ yellow green		
	Washington (68)	2,750.00	200.00
a	10¢ dark green	2,750.00	200.00
	Double transfer	—	—
	Quadruple split grill		625.00
97	12¢ blk. Washington (69)	2,900.00	225.00
	Double transfer of top		
	or bottom frame line	3,250.00	240.00
	Triple grill		—
98	15¢ black Lincoln (77)	3,250.00	300.00
	Double transfer of		
	upper right corner	—	—
	Double grill	—	450.00
	Quadruple split grill	4,000.00	625.00
99	24¢ gray lilac		
	Washington (70)	6,000.00	900.00
100	30¢ orange Franklin (71)	6,000.00	750.00
	Double grill	8,250.00	1,600.00
101	90¢ bl. Washington (72)	11,000.00	1,500.00
	Double grill	15,000.00	

	Issues of 1875	Un	U
	Reissue of 1861-1866 Issues,		
	Without Grill, Perf. 12		
102	1¢ blue Franklin (63)	800.00	1,100.00
103	2¢ black Jackson (73)	3,500.00	5,000.00
104	3¢ brown red		
	Washington (65)	3,750.00	6,250.00
105	5¢ brown Jefferson (67)	3,000.00	2,900.00
106	10¢ grn. Washington (68)	3,250.00	12,500.00
107	12¢ blk. Washington (69)	4,500.00	6,500.00
108	15¢ black Lincoln (77)	4,500.00	9,000.00
109	24¢ deep violet		
	Washington (70)	5,500.00	10,000.00
110	30¢ brownish orange		
	Franklin (71)	5,500.00	12,500.00
111	90¢ bl. Washington (72)	6,500.00	50,000.00
	Issues of 1869, With Grill,		
	Hardware Paper		
	G. Grill about 9.5 x 9mm		
112	1¢ buff Franklin (63)	800.00	160.00
	Double grill	1,200.00	340.00
b	Without grill	6,000.00	
113	2¢ br. Post Horse and		
	Rider	750.00	75.00
	Split grill	900.00	100.00
	Double transfer		95.00
114	3¢ Locomotive	300.00	18.00
	Triple grill	—	—
	Sextuple grill	—	3,250.00
	Gray paper		95.00
a	Without grill	1,250.00	
115	6¢ Washington	3,000.00	210.00
	Quadruple split grill	—	825.00
116	10¢ Shield and Eagle	2,250.00	140.00
	End roller grill	—	—
117	12¢ S.S. Adriatic	2,500.00	150.00
	Split grill	3,000.00	165.00
118	15¢ Landing of Columbus,		
	type I	8,000.00	650.00
119	15¢ type II (118)	3,500.00	250.00
b	Center inverted	275,000.00	17,000.00
c	Center double, one inverted		35,000.00
120	24¢ Declaration of		
	Independence	7,500.00	750.00
b	Center inverted	275,000.00	18,000.00
121	30¢ Shield, Eagle		
	and Flags	7,500.00	550.00
	Double grill	—	1,100.00
b	Flags inverted	210,000.00	70,000.00
122	90¢ Lincoln	9,750.00	2,500.00
	Split grill	—	—
	Issues of 1875, Reissue of 1869 Issue,		
	Without Grill, Hard White Paper, Perf. 12		
123	1¢ buff (112)	500.00	325.00
124	2¢ brown (113)	700.00	475.00
125	3¢ blue (114)	5,500.00	20,000.00
126	6¢ blue (115)	1,900.00	2,100.00

112   113   114

115   116   117

118   120

121   122

Details

15¢ Landing of Columbus, Types I-III, Series 1869-1875

Detail of **#118** Type I
Picture unframed.

Detail of **#119** Type II
Picture framed.

#129 Type III
Same as Type I but
without fringe of
brown shading lines
around central
vignette.

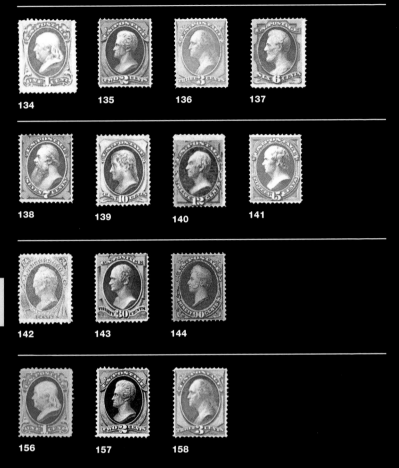

134   135   136   137

138   139   140   141

142   143   144

156   157   158

Details

Detail of #134, 145

Detail of #135, 146

Detail of #136, 147

Detail of #156, 167, 182, 192

Detail of #157, 168, 178, 180, 183, 193

Detail of #158, 169, 184, 194

1¢. In the pearl at the left of the numeral "1" there is a small crescent.

2¢. Under the scroll at the left of "U.S." there is a small diagonal line. This mark seldom shows clearly.

3¢. The under part of the upper tail of the left ribbon is heavily shaded.

Issues of 1875		Un	U
127	10¢ yellow (116)	2,100.00	1,750.00
128	12¢ green (117)	2,750.00	2,750.00
129	15¢ brown and blue,		
	type III (118)	2,000.00	1,150.00
a	Imperf. horizontally	4,000.00	7,000
130	24¢ grn. & violet (120)	2,250.00	1,600.00
131	30¢ bl. & carmine (121)	3,000.00	2,500.00
132	90¢ car. & black (122)	5,000.00	5,500.00
	Issue of 1880, Reissue of 1869,		
	Soft Porous Paper		
133	1¢ buff (112)	325.00	200.00
a	1¢ brown orange,		
	issued without gum	240.00	175.00
	Issues of 1870-71		
	With Grill, White Wove Paper,		
	No Secret Marks		
	H. Grill about 10 x 12mm		
134	1¢ Franklin	2,100.00	140.00
	End roller grill		650.00
135	2¢ Jackson	1,200.00	70.00
136	3¢ Washington	725.00	20.00
	Cracked plate	—	90.00
137	6¢ Lincoln	4,500.00	525.00
	Double grill	—	900.00
138	7¢ Edwin M. Stanton	3,250.00	425.00
139	10¢ Jefferson	5,000.00	650.00
140	12¢ Henry Clay	22,500.00	3,000.00
141	15¢ Daniel Webster	5,750.00	1,200.00
142	24¢ Gen. Winfield Scott	—	6,250.00
143	30¢ Alexander Hamilton	15,000.00	2,500.00
144	90¢ Commodore Perry	14,000.00	1,700.00
	Split grill		1,750.00

Issues of 1870-71		Un	U
Without Grill, White Wove Paper,			
No Secret Marks			
145	1¢ ultra. Franklin (134)	500.00	15.00
146	2¢ red brn. Jackson (135)	325.00	9.00
147	3¢ grn. Washington (136)	300.00	1.50
148	6¢ carmine Lincoln (137)	725.00	25.00
	6¢ violet carmine	750.00	30.00
149	7¢ verm. Stanton (138)	900.00	90.00
150	10¢ brown Jefferson (139)	825.00	20.00
151	12¢ dull violet Clay (140)	1,900.00	160.00
152	15¢ brt. or. Webster (141)	2,100.00	160.00
153	24¢ purple Scott (142)	1,600.00	140.00
154	30¢ black Hamilton (143)	5,500.00	190.00
155	90¢ carmine Perry (144)	4,250.00	300.00
Issues of 1873, Without Grill,			
White Wove Paper, Thin to Thick,			
Secret Marks			
156	1¢ ultra. Franklin	250.00	3.75
	Paper with silk fibers	—	25.00
f	Imperf. pair	—	550.00
157	2¢ br. Jackson	375.00	17.50
	Double paper	500.00	35.00
c	With grill	1,850.00	750.00
158	3¢ gr. Washington	130.00	.60
	olive green	375.00	15.00
	Cracked plate	—	32.50

Alice Paul (1885-1977)

A woman of exceptional energy and strong convictions, Alice Paul became the 20th century heir to the women's right-to-vote movement organized in the 1800s by Susan B. Anthony and Elizabeth Cady Stanton. After several years in England, where she was jailed three times for suffragist agitation, Paul returned to the United States resolved to use more militant tactics in bringing the vote to women. Imprisoned after organizing protests and marches, she went on a hunger strike; her treatment during this period elicited great public outrage. Overcoming resistance from Congress and President Woodrow Wilson, her tactics finally succeeded, and in 1920 the 19th Amendment, insuring a woman's right to vote, became part of the U.S. Constitution. Paul continued her efforts on behalf of women by drafting and introducing an equal rights amendment before Congress in 1923, which failed to pass. Over the years she would successfully lobby for the inclusion of references to gender equality in the U.S. Civil Rights Act of 1964 and in the preamble to the United Nations charter. In 1995, the U.S. Postal Service issued a stamp honoring Paul's leadership in the crusade for women's rights as part of the Great Americans series. ■

1873-1879

Issues of 1873		Un	U
Without Grill, White Wove Paper, Thin to Thick, Secret Marks			
159	6¢ dull pk. Lincoln	425.00	17.50
b	With grill	1,800.00	
160	7¢ or. verm. Stanton	1,250.00	80.00
	Ribbed paper	—	95.00
161	10¢ br. Jefferson	700.00	18.00
162	12¢ bl. vio. Clay	2,000.00	95.00
163	15¢ yel. or. Webster	2,100.00	110.00
a	With grill	5,250.00	
164	24¢ pur. Scott		—
165	30¢ gray blk. Hamilton	2,750.00	100.00
166	90¢ rose carm. Perry	2,750.00	250.00

Issues of 1875, Special Printing, Hard, White Wove Paper, Without Gum, Secret Marks

Although perforated, these stamps were usually cut apart with scissors. As a result, the perforations are often much mutilated and the design is frequently damaged.

167	1¢ ultra. Franklin (156)	12,500.00	
168	2¢ dk. br. Jackson (157)	5,750.00	
169	3¢ blue green Washington (158)	15,000.00	—
170	6¢ dull rose Lincoln (159)	14,500.00	
171	7¢ reddish vermilion Stanton (160)	3,250.00	
172	10¢ pale brown Jefferson (161)	14,500.00	
173	12¢ dark vio. Clay (162)	4,750.00	

Issues of 1875		Un	U
174	15¢ bright orange Webster (163)	14,500.00	
175	24¢ dull pur. Scott (142)	3,250.00	5,000.00
176	30¢ greenish black Hamilton (143)	12,000.00	
177	90¢ vio. car. Perry (144)	14,000.00	
Regular Issue, Yellowish Wove Paper			
178	2¢ verm. Jackson (157)	400.00	10.00
c	With grill	750.00	
179	5¢ Zachary Taylor, June	575.00	20.00
	Cracked plate	—	170.00
	Double paper	650.00	
	Paper with silk fibers	—	32.50
c	With grill	3,000.00	
Special Printing, Hard, White Wove Paper, Without Gum			
180	2¢ carmine vermilion Jackson (157)	35,000.00	
181	5¢ br. bl. Taylor (179)	75,000.00	
Issues of 1879, Soft, Porous Paper, Thin to Thick, Perf. 12			
182	1¢ dark ultramarine Franklin (156)	300.00	3.50
183	2¢ verm. Jackson (157)	130.00	3.00
a	Double impression	—	—

Ernest E. Just (1883-1941)

A great American research scientist and professor, Ernest E. Just was the first recipient of the Spingarn Medal, which was awarded to him in 1915 by the National Association for the Advancement of Colored People (NAACP). This award "to the man or woman of African descent and American citizenship, who shall have made the highest achievement during the preceding year or years in any honorable field of human endeavor" brought international recognition to the young scientist from Charleston, South Carolina. A distinguished scholar, Just graduated *magna cum laude* from Dartmouth College in June 1907 and joined the faculty at Howard University the following fall. In 1916, after a year's leave from teaching, Just earned his Ph.D. in zoology at the University of Chicago, again graduating *magna cum laude*. In the 1920s and 1930s, Just was increasingly torn between his teaching duties and his desire to concentrate on research. He was one of the first Americans invited to do research at the Kaiser Wilhelm Institute for Biology in Berlin-Dahlem, then considered one of the best research labs in the world. Just died in 1941 in Washington, D.C., where he is buried. The U.S. Postal Service honored him in 1996 with a stamp in the Black Heritage series. ■

159 160 161 162 163

179

Details

Detail of #137, 148

Detail of #138, 149

Detail of #139, 150, 187

Detail of #159, 170, 186, 195

6¢. The first four vertical lines of the shading in the lower part of the left ribbon have been strengthened.

Detail of #160, 171, 196

7¢. Two small semi-circles are drawn around the ends of the lines that outline the ball in the lower righthand corner.

Detail of #161, 172, 188, 197

10¢. There is a small semi-circle in the scroll at the right end of the upper label.

Detail of #140, 151

Detail of #141, 152

Detail of #143, 154, 165, 176

Detail of #162, 173, 198

12¢. The balls of the figure "2" are crescent-shaped.

Detail of #163, 174, 189, 199

15¢. In the lower part of the triangle in the upper left corner two lines have been made heavier, forming a "V." This mark can be found on some of the Continental and American (1879) printings, but not all stamps show it.

Detail of #190

30¢. In the "S" of "CENTS," the vertical spike across the middle section of the letter has been broadened.

37

205   206   207   208

209   210   211   212

219   220   221   222   223   224

225   226   227   228   229

Details

Issues of 1881-1882, Re-engravings of 1873 Designs

Detail of **#206**

1¢. Upper vertical lines have been deepened, creating a solid effect in parts of background. Upper arabesques shaded.

Detail of **#207**

3¢. Shading at sides of central oval is half its previous width A short horizontal dash has been cut below the "TS" of "CENTS."

Detail of **#209**

10¢. Has four vertical lines instead of five between left side of oval and edge of the shield. Horizontal lines in lower part of background strengthened.

Detail of **#208**

6¢. Has three vertical lines instead of four between the edge of the panel and the outside of the stamp.

Issues of 1879	Un	U
184 3¢ grn. Washington (158)	100.00	.60
Double transfer	—	—
Short transfer	—	6.00
185 5¢ blue Taylor (179)	500.00	12.00
186 6¢ pink Lincoln (159)	1,000.00	20.00
187 10¢ brown Jefferson		
(139) (no secret mark)	2,750.00	25.00
188 10¢ brown Jefferson		
(161) (with secret mark)	1,900.00	25.00
black brown	2,100.00	37.50
Double transfer		45.00
189 15¢ red or. Webster (163)	350.00	22.50
190 30¢ full blk. Hamilton (143)	1,100.00	55.00
191 90¢ carmine Perry (144)	2,250.00	275.00
Issues of 1880, Special Printing,		
Soft Porous Paper, Without Gum, Perf. 12		
192 1¢ dark ultramarine		
Franklin (156)	27,500.00	
193 2¢ blk. br. Jackson (157)	15,000.00	
194 3¢ blue green		
Washington (158)	50,000.00	
195 6¢ dull rose		
Lincoln (159)	25,000.00	
196 7¢ scarlet vermilion		
Stanton (160)	4,500.00	
197 10¢ deep brown		
Jefferson (161)	30,000.00	
198 12¢ blk. pur. Clay (162)	8,000.00	
199 15¢ or. Webster (163)	27,500.00	
200 24¢ dk. vio. Scott (142)	7,500.00	
201 30¢ greenish black		
Hamilton (143)	18,000.00	
202 90¢ dull carmine		
Perry (144)	25,000.00	
203 2¢ scarlet vermilion		
Jackson (157)	55,000.00	
204 5¢ dp. bl. Taylor (179)	85,000.00	
Issues of 1882, Perf. 12		
205 5¢ Garfield, Apr. 10	300.00	9.00
Special Printing, Soft Porous		
Paper, Without Gum, Perf. 12		
205C 5¢ gray brown		
Garfield (205)	40,000.00	
Issues of 1881-82, Designs		
of 1873 Re-engraved		
206 1¢ Franklin, Aug. 1881	85.00	.90
Double transfer	110.00	6.00
207 3¢ Washington,		
July 16, 1881	85.00	.55
Double transfer	—	12.00
Cracked plate	—	
208 6¢ Lincoln, June 1882	550.00	80.00
a 6¢ deep brown red	525.00	110.00
209 10¢ Jefferson, Apr. 1882	160.00	6.00
10¢ pur. or. olive brown	175.00	6.50
b 10¢ black brown	1,000.00	150.00

Issues of 1883	Un	U
210 2¢ Washington, Oct. 1	50.00	.60
Double transfer	55.00	2.25
211 4¢ Jackson, Oct. 1	300.00	17.50
Cracked plate	—	
Special Printing, Soft Porous Paper, Perf. 12		
211B 2¢ pale red brown		
Washington (210)	450.00	—
c Horizontal pair,		
imperf. between	1,900.00	
211D 4¢ deep blue green		
Jackson (211) no gum	35,000.00	
Issues of 1887, Perf. 12		
212 1¢ Franklin, June	110.00	1.75
Double transfer		—
213 2¢ green Washington		
(210), Sept. 10	50.00	.40
Double transfer	—	3.25
b Printed on both sides		—
214 3¢ vermilion Washington		
(207), Oct. 3	80.00	60.00
Issues of 1888, Perf. 12		
215 4¢ carmine		
Jackson (211), Nov.	225.00	20.00
216 5¢ indigo		
Garfield (205), Feb.	250.00	14.00
217 30¢ orange brown		
Hamilton (165), Jan.	450.00	110.00
218 90¢ pur. Perry (166),		
Feb.	1,300.00	250.00
Issues of 1890-93, Perf. 12		
219 1¢ Franklin, Feb. 22, 1890	27.50	.60
Double transfer	—	—
219D 2¢ lake Washington		
(220), Feb. 22, 1890	250.00	1.10
Double transfer	—	—
220 2¢ Washington, 1890	22.50	.55
Double transfer	—	3.25
a Cap on left "2"	125.00	2.50
c Cap on both "2s"	550.00	20.00
221 3¢ Jackson, Feb. 22, 1890	80.00	7.50
222 4¢ Lincoln, June 2, 1890	90.00	2.75
Double transfer	105.00	—
223 5¢ Grant, June 2, 1890	80.00	2.75
Double transfer	100.00	3.25
224 6¢ Garfield, Feb. 22, 1890	85.00	20.00
225 8¢ Sherman, Mar. 21, 1893	60.00	13.00
226 10¢ Webster,		
Feb. 22, 1890	190.00	3.50
Double transfer	—	—
227 15¢ Clay, Feb. 22, 1890	250.00	20.00
Double transfer	—	—
Triple transfer	—	
228 30¢ Jefferson,		
Feb. 22, 1890	400.00	30.00
Double transfer	—	—
229 90¢ Perry, Feb. 22, 1890	600.00	125.00
Short transfer at bottom	—	—

Issues of 1893		Un	U	PB	#	FDC	Q(M)
Columbian Exposition Issue, Printed by The American Bank Note Co., Perf. 12							
230	1¢ Columbus in Sight of Land 01/02/93	22.50	.40	310.00	(6)	*6,000.00*	449
	Double transfer	27.50	.75				
	Cracked plate	90.00					
231	2¢ Landing of Columbus 01/02/93	21.00	.30	250.00	(6)	*11,000.00*	1,464
	Double transfer	26.00	.35				
	Triple transfer	62.50	—				
	Quadruple transfer	95.00					
	Broken hat on third						
	figure left of Columbus	65.00	.45				
	Broken frame line	22.50	.35				
	Recut frame lines	22.50	—				
	Cracked plate	87.50	—				
232	3¢ *Santa Maria*, Flagship 01/02/93	60.00	15.00	725.00	(6)	*10,000.00*	12
	Double transfer	80.00	—				
233	4¢ ultramarine, Fleet 01/02/93	87.50	7.50	1,050.00	(6)	*15,000.00*	19
a	4¢ blue (error)	*19,000.00*	*15,000.00*	*87,500.00*	(4)		
	Double transfer	125.00	—				
234	5¢ Columbus Soliciting						
	Aid from Queen Isabella 01/02/93	95.00	8.00	1,400.00	(6)	*25,000*	35
	Double transfer	145.00	—				
235	6¢ Columbus Welcomed						
	at Barcelona 01/02/93	85.00	22.50			*20,000.00*	5
a	6¢ red violet	85.00	22.50	1,175.00	(6)		
	Double transfer	110.00	30.00				
236	8¢ Columbus Restored to Favor 03/93	75.00	11.00	825.00	(6)		11
	Double transfer	87.50	—				
237	10¢ Columbus						
	Presenting Natives 01/02/93	140.00	8.00	3,350.00	(6)	*30,000.00*	17
	Double transfer	180.00	12.50				
	Triple transfer	—					
238	15¢ Columbus						
	Announcing His Discovery 01/02/93	240.00	65.00	*3,750.00*	(6)		2
	Double transfer	—	—				
239	30¢ Columbus at La Rábida 01/02/93	300.00	85.00	*8,500.00*	(6)		0.6
240	50¢ Recall of Columbus 01/02/93	600.00	160.00	*14,000.00*	(6)		0.2
	Double transfer	—	—				
	Triple transfer	—	—				
241	$1 Queen Isabella						
	Pledging Her Jewels 01/02/93	1,300.00	650.00	*47,500.00*	(6)		0.05
	Double transfer	—	—				
242	$2 Columbus in Chains 01/02/93	1,400.00	600.00	*67,500.00*	(6)	*60,000.00*	0.05
243	$3 Columbus Describing						
	His Third Voyage 01/02/93	2,100.00	1,100.00				0.03
a	$3 olive green	2,100.00	1,100.00	*85,000.00*	(6)		
244	$4 Queen Isabella and						
	Columbus 01/02/93	2,900.00	1,350.00				0.03
a	$4 rose carmine	2,900.00	1,350.00	*250,000.00*	(6)		
245	$5 Portrait of Columbus 01/02/93	3,250.00	1,700.00	*190,000.00*	(6)		0.03

230

231

232

233

234

235

236

237

238

239

240

241

242

243

244

245

246   248   253

254   255   256

257   258   259

Details

2¢ Washington Types I-III, Series 1894-1898

Triangle of **#248-50, 265** Type I

Horizontal lines of uniform thickness run across the triangle.

Triangle of **#251, 266** Type II

Horizontal lines cross the triangle, but are thinner within than without.

Triangle of **#252, 267, 279B-279Be** Type III

The horizontal lines do not cross the double frame lines of the triangle.

Issues of 1894		Un	U	PB	#
Unwmkd., Perf. 12					

Bureau Issues Starting in 1894 and continuing until 1979, the Bureau of Engraving and Printing in Washington produced all U.S. postage stamps except #909-21, 1335, 1355, 1410-18 and 1789. Beginning in 1979, security printers in addition to the Bureau of Engraving and Printing started producing postage stamps under contract with the U.S. Postal Service.

#	Description	Date	Un	U	PB	#
246	1¢ Franklin	10/94	32.50	4.50	425.00	(6)
	Double transfer		40.00	5.50		
247	1¢ blue Franklin (246)	11/94	67.50	2.25	850.00	(6)
	Double transfer		—	3.75		
248	2¢ pink Washington, type I	10/94	27.50	3.25	275.00	(6)
	Double transfer		—	—		
249	2¢ carmine lake, type I (248)	10/94	150.00	3.00	2,100.00	(6)
	Double transfer		—	3.50		
250	2¢ carmine, type I (248)		30.00	1.20		
a	2¢ rose		30.00	2.25		
b	2¢ scarlet		30.00	.45	375.00	(6)
	Double transfer		—	3.25		
c	Vertical pair, imperf. horizontally		*4,500.00*			
d	Horizontal pair, imperf. between		*2,000.00*			
251	2¢ carmine, type II (248)		300.00	6.00	3,250.00	(6)
252	2¢ carmine, type III (248)		120.00	6.00		
a	2¢ scarlet		120.00	6.00	1,750.00	(6)
b	Horizontal pair, imperf. vertically		*1,500.00*			
c	Horizontal pair, imperf. between		*1,750.00*			
253	3¢ Jackson	09/94	110.00	9.00	1,350.00	(6)
254	4¢ Lincoln	09/94	150.00	4.25	1,900.00	(6)
255	5¢ Grant	09/94	110.00	6.00	1,200.00	(6)
	Worn plate, diagonal lines missing in oval background		110.00	4.50		
	Double transfer		135.00	6.50		
c	Vertical pair, imperf. horiz.		*2,750.00*			
256	6¢ Garfield	07/94	175.00	22.50	2,750.00	(6)
a	Vertical pair, imperf. horizontally		*1,600.00*		*14,000.00*	(6)
257	8¢ Sherman	03/94	140.00	16.00	1,850.00	(6)
258	10¢ Webster	09/94	275.00	11.00	3,100.00	(6)
	Double transfer		325.00	12.50		
259	15¢ Clay	10/94	300.00	55.00	4,750.00	(6)

			Un	U	PB	#
	Issues of 1894					
260	50¢ Jefferson	11/94	550.00	120.00	*10,000.00*	(6)
261	$1 Perry, type I	11/94	1,000.00	350.00	*17,500.00*	(6)
261A	$1 black Perry, type II (261)	11/94	2,300.00	700.00	*27,500.00*	(6)
262	$2 James Madison	12/94	3,100.00	1,100.00	*42,500.00*	(6)
263	$5 John Marshall	12/94	5,000.00	2,250.00	*22,500.00*	(3)
	Issues of 1895, Wmkd. (191), Perf. 12					
264	1¢ blue Franklin (246)	04/95	6.50	.50	225.00	(6)
265	2¢ carmine Washington,					
	type I (248)	05/95	30.00	1.75	400.00	(6)
	Double transfer		45.00	5.25		
266	2¢ carmine, type II (248)		30.00	3.50	425.00	(6)
267	2¢ carmine, type III (248)		5.50	.25	190.00	(6)
268	3¢ purple Jackson (253)	10/95	37.50	1.40	675.00	(6)
	Double transfer		45.00	3.25		
269	4¢ dark brown Lincoln (254)	06/95	40.00	2.00	725.00	(6)
	Double transfer		45.00	3.25		
270	5¢ chocolate Grant (255)	06/11/95	37.50	2.25	625.00	(6)
	Double transfer		45.00	3.50		
	Worn plate, diagonal lines					
	missing in oval background		40.00	2.75		
271	6¢ dull brown Garfield (256)	08/95	95.00	5.00	2,400.00	(6)
	Very thin paper		105.00	5.00		
a	Wmkd. USIR		*10,000.00*	*7,500.00*		
272	8¢ violet brown Sherman (257)	07/95	65.00	1.60	900.00	(6)
	Double transfer		80.00	3.00		
a	Wmkd. USIR		*5,000.00*	750.00	*20,000.00*	(3)
273	10¢ dark green Webster (258)	06/95	95.00	1.60	1,700.00	(6)
	Double transfer		120.00	3.60		
274	15¢ dark blue Clay (259)	09/95	225.00	10.00	3,500.00	(6)
275	50¢ orange Jefferson (260)	11/95	300.00	22.50	6,000.00	(6)
a	50¢ red orange		325.00	27.50	6,000.00	(6)
276	$1 black Perry, type I (261)	08/95	650.00	80.00	*14,000.00*	(6)
276A	$1 black Perry, type II (261)	08/95	1,300.00	175.00	*25,000.00*	(6)
277	$2 bright blue Madison (262)	08/95	1,100.00	350.00		
a	$2 dark blue		1,100.00	350.00	*21,000.00*	(6)
278	$5 dark green Marshall (263)	08/95	2,400.00	500.00	*75,000.00*	(6)

Visit us online at The Postal Store at www.usps.com

or call 1-800-STAMP-24

260

261

262

263

277

Watermark 191
Double-line
"USPS" in
capital letters;
detail at right.

Details

$1 Perry, Types I-II, Series 1894

Detail of **#261, 276**
Type I

The circles enclosing
$1 are broken.

Detail of **#261A, 276A**
Type I

The circles enclosing
$1 are complete.

	Issues of 1898-1900		Un	U	PB	#	FDC	Q(M)
	Wmkd. (191), Perf. 12							
279	1¢ deep grn. Franklin (246)	01/98	9.00	.40	175.00	(6)		
	Double transfer		12.00	1.00				
279B	2¢ red Washington, type III (248)	01/98	9.00	.40	200.00	(6)		
c	2¢ rose carmine, type III		250.00	75.00	2,900.00	(6)		
d	2¢ orange red, type III		10.00	.35	220.00	(6)		
e	Booklet pane of 6	04/16/00	425.00	900.00				
f	2¢ carmine, type IV		10.00	.30	220.00	(6)		
g	2¢ pink, type IV		11.00	.45	240.00	(6)		
h	2¢ vermillion, type IV		10.00	.30	220.00	(6)		
i	2¢ brown orange, type IV		*100.00*	*6.00*	*425.00*	(3)		
280	4¢ rose brn. Lincoln (254)	10/98	30.00	1.10				
a	4¢ lilac brown		30.00	1.10				
b	4¢ orange brown		30.00	1.10	625.00	(6)		
	Extra frame line at top		50.00	4.25				
281	5¢ dark blue Grant (255)	03/98	35.00	1.00	625.00	(6)		
	Double transfer		45.00	2.25				
	Worn plate, diagonal lines missing in oval background		40.00	1.25				
282	6¢ lake Garfield (256)	12/98	45.00	2.75	850.00	(6)		
	Double transfer		57.50	3.75				
a	6¢ purple lake		60.00	4.00	1,050.00	(6)		
282C	10¢ brown Webster (258), type I	11/98	180.00	2.75	2,400.00	(6)		
	Double transfer		200.00	4.50				
283	10¢ orange brown Webster (258), type II		125.00	2.50	1,700.00	(6)		
284	15¢ olive grn. Clay (259)	11/98	160.00	8.75	2,100.00	(6)		
	Issues of 1898, Trans-Mississippi Exposition Issue							
285	1¢ Jacques Marquette on the Mississippi	06/17/98	30.00	6.50	325.00	(6)	*12,500.00*	71
	Double transfer		40.00	7.50				
286	2¢ Farming in the West	06/17/98	27.50	1.75	300.00	(6)	*9,500.00*	160
	Double transfer		42.50	2.75				
	Worn plate		30.00	2.10				
287	4¢ Indian Hunting Buffalo	06/17/98	150.00	24.00	1,500.00	(6)	*27,500.00*	5
288	5¢ John Charles Frémont on the Rocky Mountains	06/17/98	140.00	21.00	1,400.00	(6)	*17,500.00*	8
289	8¢ Troops Guarding Wagon Train	06/17/98	180.00	42.50	2,900.00	(6)	*20,000*	3
a	Vertical pair, imperf. horizontally		*22,500.00*		*75,000.00*	(4)		
290	10¢ Hardships of Emigration	06/17/98	180.00	27.50	3,250.00	(6)	*27,500.00*	5
291	50¢ Western Mining Prospector	06/17/98	700.00	190.00	*26,000.00*	(6)	*30,000.00*	0.5
292	$1 Western Cattle in Storm	06/17/98	1,250.00	550.00	*50,000.00*	(6)	—	0.06
293	$2 Mississippi River Bridge	06/17/98	2,100.00	1,000.00	*150,000.00*	(6)		0.06

282C

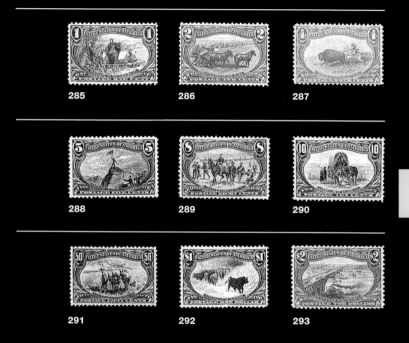

285 **286** **287**

288 **289** **290**

291 **292** **293**

Details

10¢ Webster Types I-II, Series 1898

Detail of **#282C**
Type I

The tips of the foliate ornaments do not impinge on the white curved line below "TEN CENTS."

Detail of **#283**
Type II

The tips of the ornaments break the curved line below the "E" of "TEN" and the "T" of "CENTS."

	Issues of 1906-1908		Un	U	PB/LP	#	FDC	Q(M)
	Imperf. (All issued in 1908 except #314)							
314	1¢ bl. grn. Franklin (300)	10/02/06	18.00	15.00	170.00	(6)		
314A	4¢ brown Grant (303)	04/08	45,000.00	40,000.00				
	#314A was issued imperforated, but all copies were privately perforated at the sides.							
315	5¢ blue Lincoln (304)	05/12/08	250.00	*600.00*	2,600.00	(6)		
	Coil Stamps, Perf. 12 Horizontally							
316	1¢ bl. grn. pair Franklin (300)	02/18/08	*115,000.00*	—	190,000.00	(2)		
317	5¢ blue pair Lincoln (304)	02/24/08	*15,000.00*	—	*32,500.00*	(2)		
	Coil Stamp, Perf. 12 Vertically							
318	1¢ bl. grn. pair Franklin (300)	07/31/08	14,000.00	—	*21,500.00*	(2)		
	Issues of 1903, Perf. 12							
319	2¢ Washington	11/12/03	6.00	.25	110.00	(6)		
a	2¢ lake, type I		—	—				
b	2¢ carmine rose, type I		8.00	.40	150.00	(6)		
c	2¢ scarlet, type I		6.00	.30	110.00	(6)		
d	Vertical pair, imperf. horizontally		*6,000.00*					
e	Vertical pair, imperf. between		*1,750.00*					
f	2¢ lake, type II		8.00	.25	250.00	(6)		
g	Booklet pane of 6, carmine, type I	12/03/03	120.00	*250.00*				
h	Booklet pane of 6, carmine, type II		350.00					
i	2¢ carmine, type II		75.00	*50.00*				
j	2¢ carmine rose, type II		50.00	.75	1,000.00	(6)		
k	2¢ scarlet, type II		50.00	.45	1,000.00	(6)		
m	Booklet pane of 6, lake		—					
n	Booklet pane of 6, carmine rose		200.00	*300.00*				
p	Booklet pane of 6, scarlet		180.00	*290.00*				
q	Booklet pane of 6, lake		225.00	*450.00*				
	Issues of 1906, Washington (319), Imperf.							
320	2¢ carmine	10/02/06	17.50	14.00	200.00	(6)		
	Double transfer		25.00	17.50				
a	2¢ lake, die II		47.50	40.00	725.00	(6)		
b	2¢ scarlet		18.00	12.50	200.00	(6)		
c	2¢ carmine rose, type I		55.00	40.00				
d	2¢ carmine, type II		300.00					
	Issues of 1908, Coil Stamp (319), Perf. 12 Horizontally							
321	2¢ carmine pair, type I	02/18/08	*125,000.00*		—			
	Coil Stamp, Perf. 12 Vertically							
322	2¢ carmine pair, type II	07/31/08	12,000.00	—	*15,500.00*	(2)		
	Issues of 1904, Louisiana Purchase Exposition Issue, Perf. 12							
323	1¢ Robert R. Livingston	04/30/04	30.00	4.00	275.00	(6)	*6,000.00*	80
	Diagonal line through left "1"		50.00	11.00				
324	2¢ Thomas Jefferson	04/30/04	27.50	1.75	275.00	(6)	*4,750.00*	193
325	3¢ James Monroe	04/30/04	90.00	30.00	950.00	(6)	*5,000.00*	5
326	5¢ William McKinley	04/30/04	95.00	25.00	1,000.00	(6)	*22,500.00*	7
327	10¢ Map of Louisiana Purchase	04/30/04	180.00	30.00	2,250.00	(6)	*24,000.00*	4
	Issues of 1907, Jamestown Exposition Issue, Wmkd. (191), Perf. 12							
328	1¢ Captain John Smith	04/26/07	30.00	4.00	275.00	(6)	*6,000.00*	78
	Double transfer		35.00	5.00				
329	2¢ Founding of Jamestown, 1607	04/26/07	35.00	3.50	375.00	(6)	*9,000.00*	149
330	5¢ Pocahontas	04/26/07	135.00	27.50	2,600.00	(6)		

319

323   324

325   326   327

328   329   330

Details

2¢ Washington Die I-II, Series 1903

Detail of #319a, 319b, 319g Die I   Detail of #319c, 319f, 319h, 319i Die II

331   332   333   334

335   336   337   338

339   340   341   342

Details

3¢ Washington Types I-IV, Series 1908-1919

Detail of **#333, 345, 359, 376, 389, 394, 426, 445, 456, 464, 483, 493, 501-01b**
Type I

Top line of toga rope is weak and rope shading lines are thin. Fifth line from left is missing. Line between lips is thin.

Detail of **#484, 494, 502, 541** Type II

Top line of toga rope is strong and rope shading lines are heavy and complete. Line between lips is heavy.

Detail of **#529**
Type I

Top row of toga rope is strong but fifth shading line is missing as in Type I. Toga button center shading line consists of two dashes, central dot. "P," "O" of "POSTAGE" are separated by line of color.

Detail of **#530, 535**
Type IV

Top rope shading lines are complete. Second, fourth toga button shading lines are broken in middle, third line is continuous with dot in center. "P," "O" of "POSTAGE" are joined.

Issues of 1908-1909		Un	U	PB/LP	#
Wmkd. (191) Perf. 12 (All issued in 1908 except #336, 338-42, 345-47)					
331	1¢ Franklin	12/08	7.25	.25	77.50	(6)
	Double transfer		9.50	.60		
a	Booklet pane of 6	12/02/08	160.00	*140.00*		
b	"China Clay" paper		*1,000.00*			
332	2¢ Washington	11/08	6.75	.25	70.00	(6)
	Double transfer		12.50	—		
	Cracked plate		—	—		
a	Booklet pane of 6	11/16/08	135.00	*130.00*		
333	3¢ Washington, type I	12/08	35.00	2.50	375.00	(6)
a	"China Clay" paper		*1,000.00*		9,000.00	(6)
334	4¢ Washington	12/08	42.50	1.00	425.00	(6)
	Double transfer		55.00	—		
a	"China Clay" paper		*1,300.00*			
335	5¢ Washington	12/08	52.50	2.00	550.00	(6)
a	"China Clay" paper		*1,000.00*			
336	6¢ Washington	01/09	65.00	5.00	750.00	(6)
a	"China Clay" paper		*750.00*			
337	8¢ Washington	12/08	50.00	2.50	500.00	(6)
	Double transfer		57.50	—		
a	"China Clay" paper		*1,000.00*			
338	10¢ Washington	01/09	70.00	1.40	800.00	(6)
a	"China Clay" paper		*1,000.00*			
339	13¢ Washington	01/09	42.50	19.00	500.00	(6)
	Line through "TAG" of "POSTAGE"		70.00	—		
a	"China Clay" paper		*1,000.00*			
340	15¢ Washington	01/09	70.00	5.50	650.00	(6)
a	"China Clay" paper		*1,000.00*			
341	50¢ Washington	01/13/09	350.00	20.00	*7,000.00*	(6)
342	$1 Washington	01/29/09	525.00	90.00	*16,000.00*	(6)
	Imperf.					
343	1¢ green Franklin (331)	12/08	5.00	4.50	47.50	(6)
	Double transfer		11.00	7.00		
344	2¢ carmine Washington (332)	12/10/08	6.00	3.00	77.50	(6)
	Double transfer		12.50	4.00		
	Foreign entry, design of 1¢		*1,250.00*	—		
	#345-47: Washington (333-35)					
345	3¢ deep violet, type I	1809	11.50	20.00	155.00	(6)
	Double transfer		22.50	—		
346	4¢ orange brown	02/25/09	19.00	22.50	175.00	(6)
	Double transfer		37.50	—		
347	5¢ blue	02/25/09	36.00	35.00	275.00	(6)
	Cracked plate		—			
	Issues of 1908-10, Coil Stamps, Perf. 12 Horizontally					
	#350-51, 354-56: Washington (Designs of 334-35, 338)					
348	1¢ green Franklin (331)	12/29/08	37.50	22.50	290.00	(2)
349	2¢ carmine Washington (332)	01/09	80.00	12.50	550.00	(2)
	Foreign entry, design of 1¢		—	*1,750.00*		
350	4¢ orange brown	08/15/10	170.00	125.00	1,250.00	(2)
351	5¢ blue	01/09	180.00	160.00	1,250.00	(2)
	Issues of 1909, Coil Stamps, Perf. 12 Vertically					
352	1¢ green Franklin (331)	01/09	95.00	47.50	750.00	(2)
	Double transfer		—	—		

	Issues of 1909		Un	U	PB/LP	#	FDC	Q(M)
	Coil Stamps, Perf. 12 Vertically							
353	2¢ carmine Washington (332)	01/12/09	95.00	12.50	750.00	(2)		
354	4¢ orange brown	02/23/09	220.00	85.00	1,500.00	(2)		
355	5¢ blue	02/23/09	230.00	120.00	1,500.00	(2)		
356	10¢ yellow	01/07/09	2,750.00	1,250.00	13,000.00	(2)		
	Bluish Paper, Perf. 12, #359-66: Washington (Designs of 333-40)							
357	1¢ green Franklin (331)	02/16/09	90.00	100.00	1,000.00	(6)		
358	2¢ carmine Washington (332)	02/16/09	85.00	100.00	975.00	(6)		
	Double transfer		—					
359	3¢ deep violet, type I	1909	2,000.00	2,500.00	22,500.00	(6)		
360	4¢ orange brown	1909	24,000.00		110,000.00	(4)		
361	5¢ blue	1909	5,000.00	12,500.00	60,000.00	(6)		
362	6¢ red orange	1909	1,500.00	5,000.00	16,000.00	(6)		
363	8¢ olive green	1909	26,000.00		115,000.00	(3)		
364	10¢ yellow	1909	1,800.00	5,500.00	32,500.00	(6)		
365	13¢ blue green	1909	3,000.00	2,250.00	30,000.00	(6)		
366	15¢ pale ultramarine	1909	1,450.00	11,000.00	11,000.00	(6)		
	Lincoln Memorial Issue, Wmkd. (191)							
367	2¢ Bust of Abraham Lincoln	02/12/09	5.50	1.75	150.00	(6)	500.00	148
	Double transfer		7.50	2.50				
	Imperf.							
368	2¢ carmine (367)	02/12/09	21.00	20.00	180.00	(6)	12,500.00	1
	Double transfer		42.50	27.50				
	Bluish Paper							
369	2¢ carmine (367)	02/09	210.00	260.00	2,900.00	(6)		0.6
	Alaska-Yukon Pacific Exposition Issue							
370	2¢ Willam H. Seward	06/01/09	8.75	2.00	200.00	(6)	3,000.00	153
	Double transfer		10.50	4.50				
	Imperf.							
371	2¢ carmine (370)	06/09	24.00	22.50	220.00	(6)		0.5
	Double transfer		37.50	27.50				
	Hudson-Fulton Celebration Issue, Wmkd. (191)							
372	2¢ Half Moon & Clermont	09/25/09	12.50	4.50	280.00	(6)	750.00	73
	Double transfer		15.00	4.75				
	Imperf.							
373	2¢ carmine (372)	09/25/09	27.50	25.00	240.00	(6)	7,000.00	0.2
	Double transfer		42.50	30.00				
	Issues of 1910-11, Wmkd. (190) #376-82: Washington (Designs of 333-38, 340)							
374	1¢ green Franklin (331)	11/23/10	6.75	.25	77.50	(6)		
	Double transfer		13.50	—				
	Cracked plate		—	—				
a	Booklet pane of 6	10/07/10	175.00	125.00				
375	2¢ carmine Washington (332)	11/23/10	6.75	.25	85.00	(6)		
	Cracked plate		—	—				
	Double transfer		11.50	—				
	Foreign entry, design of 1¢		—	1,000.00				
a	Booklet pane of 6	11/30/10	95.00	95.00				
b	2¢ lake		425.00					
376	3¢ deep violet, type I	01/16/11	20.00	1.75	210.00	(6)		

367

370

372

USPS

Watermark 190
Single-line
"USPS"
in capital letters;
detail at right.

1912-1915

	Issues of 1914-1915		Un	U	PB/LP	#
	Perf. 10					
401	1¢ green (397)	12/14	25.00	5.50	340.00	(6)
402	2¢ carmine (398)	01/15	75.00	1.50	1,950.00	(6)
403	5¢ blue (399)	02/15	175.00	15.00	4,000.00	(6)
404	10¢ irabge (400)	07/15	900.00	62.50	12,500.00	(6)
	Issues of 1912-14, Wmkd. (190), Perf. 12					
405	1¢ green	02/12	7.00	.20	95.00	(6)
	Cracked plate		14.50	—		
	Double transfer		8.50	—		
a	Vertical pair, imperf. horizontally		1,500.00	—		
b	Booklet pane of 6	02/08/12	60.00	50.00		
406	2¢ carmine, type I	02/12	7.00	.20	105.00	(6)
	Double transfer		9.00	—		
a	Booklet pane of 6	02/08/12	60.00	65.00		
b	Double impression		—			
c	2¢ lake		1,500.00	—		
407	7¢ black	04/14	80.00	11.00	1,200.00	(6)
	Imperf. #408-13: Washington (Designs of 405-6)					
408	1¢ green	03/12	1.10	.65	18.00	(6)
	Double transfer		2.40	1.00		
	Cracked plate		—	—		
409	2¢ carmine, type I	02/12	1.30	.65	35.00	(6)
	Cracked plate		14.00	—		
	Coil Stamps, Perf. 8.5 Horizontally					
410	1¢ green	03/12	6.00	4.25	30.00	(2)
	Double transfer		—	—		
411	2¢ carmine, type I	03/12	10.00	3.75	55.00	(2)
	Double transfer		12.50	—		
	Coil Stamps, Perf. 8.5 Vertically					
412	1¢ green	03/18/12	25.00	5.50	120.00	(2)
413	2¢ carmine, type I	03/12	50.00	1.25	280.00	(2)
	Double transfer		52.50	—		
	Perf. 12					
414	8¢ Franklin	02/12	45.00	1.25	475.00	(6)
415	9¢ Franklin	04/14	55.00	12.50	650.00	(6)
416	10¢ Franklin	01/12	45.00	.40	500.00	(6)

Visit us online at The Postal Store at www.usps.com

or call 1-800-STAMP-24

405   406   407   414   415   416

2¢ Washington, Types I-VII, Series 1912-1921

Detail of **#406-06a, 411, 413, 425-25e, 442, 444, 449, 453, 461, 463-63a, 482, 499-99f** Type I

One shading line in first curve of ribbon above left "2" and one in second curve of ribbon above right "2." Toga button has only a faint outline. Top line of toga rope, from button to front of the throat, is very faint. Shading lines of face end in the front of the ear, with little or no joining, to form lock of hair.

Detail of **#482a, 500** Type Ia

Similar to Type I but all lines are shorter.

Detail of **#454, 487, 491, 539** Type II

Shading lines in ribbons as in Type I. Toga button, rope and rope shading lines are heavy. Shading lines of face at lock of hair end in strong vertical curved line.

Detail of **#450, 455, 488, 492, 540, 546** Type III

Two lines of shading in curves of ribbons.

Detail of **#526, 532** Type IV

Top line of toga rope is broken. Toga button shading lines form "DID." Line of color in left "2" is very thin and usually broken.

Detail of **#527, 533** Type V

Top line of toga rope is complete. Toga button has five verticle shading lines. Line of color in left "2" is very thin and usually broken. Nose shading dots are as shown.

Detail of **#528, 534** Type Va

Same as Type V except third row from bottom of nose shading dots has four dots instead of six. Overall height of design is 1/3mm shorter than Type V.

Detail of **#528A, 534A** Type VI

Generally same as Type V except line of color in left "2" is very heavy.

Detail of **#528B, 534B** Type VII

Line of color in left "2" is continuous, clearly defined and heavier than in Type V or Va but not as heavy as Type VI. An additional vertical row of dots has been added to upper lip. Numerous additional dots appear in hair at top of head.

417   418

419   420

421   423

434

After 1915 (from 1916 to date),
all postage stamps, except #519 and 832b,
are on unwatermarked paper.

	Issues of 1912-1914		Un	U	PB	#
417	12¢ Franklin	04/14	50.00	4.25	625.00	(6)
	Double transfer		55.00	—		
	Triple transfer		72.50	—		
418	15¢ Franklin	02/12	85.00	3.50	850.00	(6)
	Double transfer		—	—		
419	20¢ Franklin	04/14	200.00	15.00	2,000.00	(6)
420	30¢ Franklin	04/14	125.00	15.00	1,450.00	(6)
421	50¢ Franklin	08/14	425.00	17.50	10,00.00	(6)
	Wmkd. (191)					
422	50¢ Franklin (421)	02/12/12	250.00	15.00	4,750.00	(6)
423	$1 Franklin	02/12/12	525.00	60.00	12,000.00	(6)
	Double transfer		550.00	—		
	Issues of 1914-1915, Wmkd. (190), Perf. 10 #424-30: Wash. (Designs of 405-06, 333-36, 407)					
424	1¢ green	09/05/14	2.50	.20	42.50	(6)
	Cracked plate		—	—		
	Double transfer		4.75	—		
	Experimental precancel, New Orleans		—			
c	Vertical pair, imperf. horizontally		1,750.00	1,500.00		
d	Booklet pane of 6		5.25	3.25		
e	As "d", imperf.		1,600.00			
425	2¢ rose red, type I	09/05/14	2.30	.20	27.50	(6)
	Cracked plate		9.50	—		
	Double transfer		—	—		
e	Booklet pane of 6	01/06/14	17.50	17.50		
426	3¢ deep violet, type I	09/18/14	15.00	1.25	175.00	(6)
427	4¢ brown	09/07/14	35.00	.50	475.00	(6)
	Double transfer		45.00	—		
428	5¢ blue	09/14/14	35.00	.50	390.00	(6)
429	6¢ red orange	09/28/14	50.00	1.40	525.00	(6)
430	7¢ black	09/10/14	90.00	4.00	950.00	(6)
	#431-33, 435, 437-40: Franklin (414-21, 423)					
431	8¢ pale olive green	09/26/14	36.00	2.00	550.00	(6)
	Double impression		—			
432	9¢ salmon red	10/06/14	50.00	7.50	700.00	(6)
433	10¢ orange yellow	09/09/14	47.50	.50	825.00	(6)
434	11¢ Franklin	08/11/15	25.00	7.50	240.00	(6)
435	12¢ claret brown	09/10/14	27.50	4.00	290.00	(6)
	Double transfer		35.00	—		
	Triple transfer		40.00	—		
a	12¢ copper red		30.00	5.00	325.00	(6)
436	Not assigned					
437	15¢ gray	09/16/14	135.00	7.25	1,125.00	(6)
438	20¢ ultramarine	09/19/14	220.00	4.00	3,250.00	(6)
439	30¢ orange red	09/19/14	260.00	16.00	4,100.00	(6)
440	50¢ violet	12/10/15	575.00	16.00	15,000.00	(6)

1914-1917

	Issues of 1914		Un	U	PB/LP	#
	Coil Stamps, Perf. 10 Horizontally #441-59: Wash.					
	(Designs of 405-06, 333-35; Flat Press, 18.5-19 x 22mm)					
441	1¢ green	11/14/14	1.00	1.00	8.00	(2)
442	2¢ carmine, type I	07/22/14	10.00	6.00	60.00	(2)
	Coil Stamps, Perf. 10 Vertically					
443	1¢ green	05/29/14	25.00	5.00	155.00	(2)
444	2¢ carmine, type I	04/25/14	40.00	1.50	300.00	(2)
445	3¢ violet, type I	12/18/14	225.00	125.00	1,300.00	(2)
446	4¢ brown	10/02/14	125.00	42.50	750.00	(2)
447	5¢ blue	07/30/14	45.00	27.50	260.00	(2)
	Issues of 1915-1916, Coil Stamps, Perf. 10 Horizontally					
	(Rotary Press, Designs 18.5-19 x 22.5mm)					
448	1¢ green	12/12/15	6.00	3.25	40.00	(2)
449	2¢ red, type I	12/05/15	2,600.00	600.00	*15,000*	(2)
450	2¢ carmine, type III	02/16	10.00	4.00	80.00	(2)
451	Not assigned					
	Issues of 1914-1916, Coil Stamps, Perf. 10 Vertically (Rotary Press, Designs 19.5 20 x 22mm)					
452	1¢ green	11/11/14	10.00	2.00	75.00	(2)
453	2¢ carmine rose, type I	07/03/14	150.00	5.00	725.00	(2)
	Cracked plate		—	—		
454	2¢ red, type II	06/15	82.50	10.00	425.00	(2)
455	2¢ carmine, type III	12/15	8.50	1.00	50.00	(2)
456	3¢ violet, type I	02/02/16	240.00	90.00	1,250.00	(2)
457	4¢ brown	02/18/16	25.00	17.50	150.00	(2)
	Cracked plate		35.00	—		
458	5¢ blue	03/09/16	30.00	17.50	180.00	(2)
	Issue of 1914, Horizontal Coil Stamp, Imperf.					
459	2¢ carmine, type I	06/30/14	240.00	*1,100.00*	1,000.00	(2)
	Issues of 1915, Wmkd. (191), Perf. 10					
460	$1 violet black Franklin (423)	02/08/15	850.00	100.00	*12,000.00*	(6)
	Double transfer		900.00	—		
	Perf. 11					
461	2¢ pale carmine red Washington					
	(406), type I	06/17/15	150.00	*275.00*	*1,500.00*	(6)
	Privately perforated copies of #409 have been made to resemble 461.					
	Issues of 1916-1917, Unwmkd., Perf. 10 #462-69: Wash. (Designs of 405-06, 333-36, 407)					
462	1¢ green	09/27/16	7.00	.35	160.00	(6)
	Experimental precancel, Springfield, MA,					
	or New Orleans, LA			10.00		
a	Booklet pane of 6	10/15/16	9.50	*8.00*		
463	2¢ carmine, type I	09/25/16	4.50	.25	130.00	(6)
	Experimental precancel, Springfield, MA			22.50		
	Double transfer		6.50	—		
a	Booklet pane of 6	10/08/16	95.00	*65.00*		
464	3¢ violet, type I	11/11/16	75.00	14.00	1,350.00	(6)
	Double transfer in "CENTS"		*90.00*	—		
465	4¢ orange brown	10/07/16	45.00	1.80	650.00	(6)
466	5¢ blue	10/17/16	75.00	1.80	950.00	(6)
	Experimental precancel, Springfield, MA			175.00		
467	5¢ carmine (error in plate of 2¢)		550.00	*750.00*		
468	6¢ red orange	10/10/16	95.00	7.50	1,350.00	(6)
	Experimental precancel, Springfield, MA			175.00		
469	7¢ black	10/10/16	130.00	12.50	1,350.00	(6)
	Experimental precancel, Springfield, MA			175.00		

Issues of 1916-1917		Un	U	PB/LP	#	FDC
#470-78: Franklin (Designs of 414-16, 434, 417-21, 423)						
470	8¢ olive green	11/13/16	60.00	7.00	600.00	(6)	
	Experimental precancel, Springfield, MA			165.00			
471	9¢ salmon red	11/16/16	60.00	16.00	750.00	(6)	
472	10¢ orange yellow	10/17/16	110.00	1.75	1,350.00	(6)	
473	11¢ dark green	11/16/16	40.00	18.00	360.00	(6)	
	Experimental precancel, Springfield, MA			575.00			
474	12¢ claret brown	10/10/16	55.00	6.50	625.00	(6)	
	Double transfer		65.00	6.50			
	Triple transfer		77.50	9.50			
475	15¢ gray	11/16/16	200.00	14.00	3,000.00	(6)	
476	20¢ light ultramarine	12/05/16	250.00	15.00	3,600.00	(6)	
476A	30¢ orange red		3,750.00	—	40,000	(6)	
477	50¢ light violet	03/02/17	1,100.00	70.00	57,500.00	(6)	
478	$1 violet black	12/22/16	800.00	20.00	13,000.00	(6)	
	Double transfer		825.00	25.00			
479	$2 dark blue Madison (312)	03/22/17	275.00	40.00	4,000.00	(6)	
480	$5 light green Marshall (313)	03/22/17	225.00	40.00	3,100.00	(6)	
Issues of 1916-1917, Imperf.						
#481-96: Washington (Designs of 405-06, 333-35)						
481	1¢ green	11/16	1.00	.65	13.00	(6)	
	Double transfer		2.50	1.50			
482	2¢ carmine, type I	12/08/16	1.40	1.25	22.50	(6)	
482A	2¢ deep rose, type Ia			37,500.00			
483	3¢ violet, type I	10/13/17	13.00	7.50	115.00	(6)	
	Double transfer		17.50	—			
484	3¢ violet, type II		10.00	5.00	87.50	(6)	
	Double transfer		12.50	—			
485	5¢ carmine (error in plate of 2¢)	03/17	12,000.00		130.00	(6)	
Issues of 1916-1922, Coil Stamps, Perf. 10 Horizontally						
486	1¢ green	01/18	.90	.40	4.75	(2)	
	Double transfer		2.25	—			
487	2¢ carmine, type II	11/15/16	13.50	4.00	105.00	(2)	
488	2¢ carmine, type III	1919	2.50	1.75	20.00	(2)	
	Cracked plate		12.00	7.50			
489	3¢ violet, type I	10/10/17	5.00	1.50	32.50	(2)	
Coil Stamps, Perf. 10 Vertically						
490	1¢ green	11/17/16	.55	.25	3.50	(2)	
	Cracked plate (horizontal)		7.50	—			
	Cracked plate (vertical) retouched		9.00	—			
	Rosette crack		60.00	—			
491	2¢ carmine, type II	11/17/16	2,200.00	750.00	12,000.00	(2)	
492	2¢ carmine, type III		9.50	.35	55.00	(2)	
493	3¢ violet, type I	07/23/17	16.00	3.00	110.00	(2)	
494	3¢ violet, type II	02/04/18	10.00	1.10	75.00	(2)	
495	4¢ orange brown	04/15/17	10.00	4.00	75.00	(2)	
	Cracked plate		25.00	—			
496	5¢ blue	01/15/19	3.50	1.00	30.00	(2)	
497	10¢ orange yellow						
	Franklin (416)	01/31/22	20.00	11.00	140.00	(2)	4,500.00

517

523

524

	Issues of 1917		Un	U	PB	#	FDC	Q(M)
	Wmkd. (191), Perf. 11							
517	50¢ red violet	05/17	67.50	.60	1,600.00	(6)		
b	Vertical pair, imperf. between							
	and at bottom		—	*6,000.00*				
c	Perf. 10, top or bottom			*10,000.00*				
518	$1 violet brown	05/17	52.50	1.50	1,300.00	(6)		
b	$1 deep brown		*1,800.00*	*1,050.00*				
519	2¢ carm. Washington (332)	10/10/17	450.00	*1,100.00*	2,700.00	(6)		
	Privately perforated copies of #344 have been made to resemble #519.							
520-22	Not assigned							
	Issues of 1918, Unwmkd.							
523	$2 Franklin	08/19/18	600.00	230.00	*12,000.00*	(8)		
524	$5 Franklin	08/19/18	200.00	35.00	4,000.00	(8)		
	Issues of 1918-1920 #525-35: Washington (Designs of 405-06, 333)							
525	1¢ gray green	12/18	2.50	.90	22.50	(6)		
	1¢ Emerald		3.50	1.25				
a	1¢ dark green		5.00	1.75				
c	Horizontal pair, imperf. between		100.00					
d	Double impression		40.00	30.00				
526	2¢ carmine, type IV	03/06/20	27.50	4.00	240.00	(6)	*800.00*	
	Gash on forehead		40.00	—				
	Malformed "2" at left		37.50	6.00				
527	2¢ carmine, type V	03/20/20	20.00	1.25	165.00	(6)		
	Line through "2" and "EN"		30.00	—				
a	Double impression		65.00	12.50				
b	Vertical pair, imperf. horizontally		*600.00*					
c	Horizontal pair, imperf. vertically		*1,000.00*	—				
528	2¢ carmine, type Va	05/04/20	9.50	.40	82.50	(6)		
c	Double impression		27.50					
g	Vertical pair, imperf. between		*3,500.00*					
528A	2¢ carmine, type VI	06/24/20	52.50	1.75	425.00	(6)		
d	Double impression		160.00	—				
f	Vertical pair, imperf. horizontally		—					
h	Vertical pair, imperf. between		*1,000.00*					
528B	2¢ carmine, type VII	11/03/20	22.50	.75	175.00	(6)		
	Retouched on cheek		400.00	—				
e	Double impression		70.00					
529	3¢ violet, type III	03/18	3.25	.40	57.50	(6)		
a	Double impression		40.00	—				
b	Printed on both sides		*1,500.00*					
530	3¢ purple, type IV		1.80	.30	18.00	(6)		
	"Blister" under "U.S."		4.75	—				
	Recut under "U.S."		4.75	—				
a	Double impression		30.00	7.00				
b	Printed on both sides		*350.00*					
	Imperf.							
531	1¢ green	01/19	9.50	8.00	85.00	(6)		
532	2¢ carmine rose, type IV	03/20	40.00	27.50	325.00	(6)		
533	2¢ carmine, type V	05/04/20	110.00	80.00	1,050.00	(6)		
534	2¢ carmine, type Va	05/25/20	11.00	7.00	105.00	(6)		
534A	2¢ carmine, type VI	07/26/20	45.00	25.00	375.00	(6)		
534B	2¢ carmine, type VII	12/02/20	2,100.00	1,250.00	*17,000.00*	(6)		
535	3¢ violet, type IV	1918	9.00	5.00	75.00	(6)		
a	Double impression		90.00	—				
	Issues of 1919, Perf. 12.5							
536	1¢ gray green							
	Washington (405)	08/15/19	22.50	20.00	200.00	(6)		
a	Horizontal pair, imperf. vertically		*900.00*					

	Issues of 1919		Un	U	PB	#	FDC	Q(M)
	Perf. 11							
537	3¢ Allied Victory	03/03/19	9.00	3.25	105.00	(6)	*750.00*	100
	Double transfer		—	—				
a	deep red violet		*1,400.00*	*2,000.00*	10,000.00	(6)		
b	light reddish violet		9.00	3.00	105.00	(6)		
c	red violet		50.00	12.00				
	Issues of 1919, George Washington, Unwmkd., Perf. 11 x 10							
538	1¢ green	06/19	11.00	8.50	110.00	(4)		
	Double transfer		17.50	—				
a	Vertical pair, imperf. horizontally		50.00	*100.00*	900.00	(4)		
539	2¢ carmine rose, type II		2,750.00	*4,750.00*	*17,500.00*	(4)		
540	2¢ carmine rose, type III	06/14/19	13.00	8.50	55.00	(4)		
	Double transfer		22.50	—				
a	Vertical pair, imperf. horizontally		50.00	*100.00*	1,000.00	(4)		
b	Horizontal pair, imperf. vertically		*1,250.00*					
541	3¢ violet, type II	06/19	45.00	30.00	360.00	(4)		
	Issue of 1920, Perf. 10 x 11							
542	1¢ green	05/26/20	14.00	1.10	165.00	(6)	*1,750.00*	
	Issues of 1921, Perf. 10							
543	1¢ green	05/21	.50	.30	14.00	(4)		
	Double transfer			—				
	Triple transfer		—	—				
a	Horizontal pair, imperf. between		*1,750.00*					
	Issue of 1922, Perf. 11							
544	1¢ green		*18,000.00*	*3,500.00*				
	Issues of 1921							
545	1¢ green	05/21	190.00	175.00	1,100.00	(4)		
546	2¢ carmine rose, type III	05/21	125.00	*160.00*	775.00	(4)		
	Recut in hair		140.00	*185.00*				
a	Perf. 10 at left		*6,500.00*	*10,000.00*				
	Issue of 1920							
547	$2 Franklin	11/01/20	175.00	40.00	4,000.00	(8)		
	Pilgrim Tercentenary Issue							
548	1¢ The *Mayflower*	12/21/20	4.50	2.25	47.50	(6)	*900.00*	138
	Double transfer		—	—				
549	2¢ Landing of the Pilgrims	12/21/20	6.50	1.60	65.00	(6)	*700.00*	196
550	5¢ Signing of the Compact	12/21/20	45.00	12.50	450.00	(6)		11
	Issues of 1922-1925 (See also #581-91, 594-606, 622-23, 631-42, 658-79, 684-87, 692-701, 723)							
551	½¢ Nathan Hale	04/04/25	.20	.20	5.75	(6)	17.50	(4)
	"Cap" on fraction bar		.75	.20				
552	1¢ Franklin	01/17/23	1.50	.20	22.50	(6)	25.00	(2)
	Double transfer		3.50	—				
a	Booklet pane of 6	08/11/23	6.00	*2.00*				
553	1½¢ Warren G. Harding	03/19/25	2.50	.20	27.50	(6)	30.00	(2)
554	2¢ Washington	01/15/23	1.30	.20	20.00	(6)	37.50	
	Double transfer		2.50	.80				
a	Horizontal pair, imperf. vertically		*300.00*					
b	Vertical pair, imperf. horizontally		*4,000.00*					
c	Booklet pane of 6	02/10/23	6.75	*2.00*				
d	Perf. 10 at top or bottom		*7,000.00*	*5,000.00*				
555	3¢ Lincoln	02/12/23	17.50	1.25	170.00	(6)	35.00	
556	4¢ Martha Washington	01/15/23	19.00	.35	170.00	(6)	60.00	
a	Vertical pair, imperf. horizontally		*10,500.00*					
b	Perf. 10, top or bottom		*3,000.00*	*10,000.00*				
557	5¢ Theodore Roosevelt	10/27/22	19.00	.25	190.00	(6)	*125.00*	
a	Imperf., pair		*1,400.00*					
b	Horizontal pair, imperf. vertically		—					
c	Perf. 10, top or bottom		—	*4,000.00*				

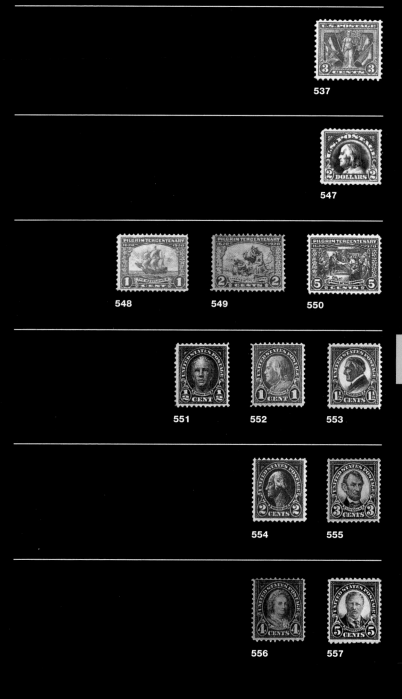

537

547

548

549

550

551

552

553

554

555

556

557

558   559   560

561   562   563

564   565   566

567   568   569

570   571   572

573

Issues of 1922-1923			Un	U	PB	#	FDC
Perf. 11							
558	6¢ Garfield	11/20/22	35.00	.85	400.00	(6)	225.00
	Double transfer		55.00	2.00			
	Same, recut		55.00	2.00			
559	7¢ McKinley	05/01/23	9.00	.65	75.00	(6)	175.00
	Double transfer		—	—			
560	8¢ Grant	05/01/23	50.00	.75	575.00	(6)	175.00
	Double transfer		—	—			
561	9¢ Jefferson	01/15/23	14.00	1.10	170.00	(6)	175.00
	Double transfer		—	—			
562	10¢ Monroe	01/15/23	17.50	.30	200.00	(6)	175.00
a	Vertical pair, imperf. horizontally		2,250.00				
b	Imperf., pair		1,500.00				
c	Perf. 10 at top or bottom			5,000.00			
563	11¢ Rutherford B. Hayes	10/04/22	1.40	.50	27.50	(6)	600.00
a	11¢ light bluish green		1.40	.50			
d	Imperf., pair			17,500.00			
564	12¢ Grover Cleveland	03/20/23	6.00	.30	80.00	(6)	175.00
a	Horizontal pair, imperf. vertically		1,750.00				
565	14¢ American Indian	05/01/23	4.00	.85	50.00	(6)	400.00
	Double transfer		—	—			
566	15¢ Statue of Liberty	11/11/22	21.00	.25	275.00	(6)	550.00
567	20¢ Golden Gate	05/01/23	20.00	.25	250.00	(6)	500.00
a	Horizontal pair, imperf. vertically		1,500.00				
568	25¢ Niagara Falls	11/11/22	18.00	.60	240.00	(6)	650.00
b	Vertical pair, imperf. horizontally		2,000.00				
c	Perf. 10 at one side		5,000.00	11,500.00			
569	30¢ Buffalo	03/20/23	32.50	.50	240.00	(6)	850.00
	Double transfer		55.00	—			
570	50¢ Arlington Amphitheater	11/11/22	52.50	.30	600.00	(6)	1,250.00
571	$1 Lincoln Memorial	02/12/23	42.50	.55	300.00	(6)	7,000.00
	Double transfer		90.00	1.50			
572	$2 U.S. Capitol	03/20/23	85.00	9.00	650.00	(6)	15,000.00
573	$5 Head of Freedom,						
	Capitol Dome	03/20/23	140.00	15.00	1,900.00	(8)	25,000.00
a	Carmine lake and dark blue		200.00	17.50	2,400.00	(8)	
574	Not assigned						
Issues of 1923-1925, Imperf.							
575	1¢ green Franklin (552)	03/20/23	7.00	5.00	70.00	(6)	
576	1½¢ yel. brn. Harding (553)	04/04/25	1.40	1.50	20.00	(6)	45.00
577	2¢ carmine Washington (554)		1.50	1.25	25.00	(6)	
Issues of 1923, Perf. 11 x 10							
578	1¢ green Franklin (552)	1923	95.00	160.00	800.00	(4)	
579	2¢ carmine Washington (554)	1923	85.00	140.00	600.00	(4)	
	Recut in eye		110.00	150.00			
Issues of 1923-1926, Perf. 10 (See also #551-73, 622-23, 631-42, 658-79, 684-87, 692-701, 723)							
580	Not assigned						
581	1¢ green Franklin (552)	04/21/23	11.00	.65	120.00	(4)	6,000.00
582	1½¢ brn. Harding (553)	03/19/25	5.50	.60	45.00	(4)	40.00
	Pair with full horiz. gutter between		160.00				
583	2¢ carm. Wash. (554)	04/14/24	3.00	.25	35.00	(4)	
a	Booklet pane of 6	08/27/26	90.00	50.00			1,800.00
584	3¢ violet Lincoln (555)	08/01/25	32.50	2.75	260.00	(4)	55.00
585	4¢ yellow brown Martha						
	Washington (556)	03/25	19.00	.55	230.00	(4)	55.00
586	5¢ blue T. Roosevelt (557)	12/24	19.00	.30	225.00	(4)	57.50
587	6¢ red orange Garfield (558)	03/25	9.25	.50	105.00	(4)	60.00
588	7¢ black McKinley (559)	05/29/26	13.50	6.25	125.00	(4)	70.00

1923-1929

	Issues of 1925-1926		Un	U	PB/LP	#	FDC	Q(M)
	Perf. 11 x 10							
589	8¢ olive grn. Grant (560)	05/29/26	30.00	4.00	240.00	(4)	72.50	
590	9¢ rose Jefferson (561)	05/29/26	6.00	2.25	55.00	(4)	72.50	
591	10¢ orange Monroe (562)	06/08/25	72.50	.40	475.00	(4)	95.00	
592-93	Not assigned							
	Issues of 1923, Perf. 11							
594	1¢ green Franklin (552), design 19.75 x 22.25mm	1923	19,000.00	6,500.00				
595	2¢ carmine Washington (554), design 19.75 x 22.25mm	1923	300.00	325.00	2,100.00	(4)		
596	1¢ green Franklin (552), design 19.25 x 22.5mm	1923		115,000.00				
	Issues of 1923-1929, Coil Stamps, Perf. 10 Vertically							
597	1¢ green Franklin (552)	07/18/23	.30	.20	2.25	(2)	600.00	
	Gripper cracks or double transfer		2.60	1.00				
598	1½¢ brown Harding (553)	03/19/25	1.00	.20	4.75	(2)	60.00	
599	2¢ carmine Washington (554), type I	01/23	.40	.20	2.30	(2)	1,500.00	
	Double transfer		1.90	1.00				
	Gripper cracks		2.30	2.00				
599A	2¢ carmine Washington (554), type II	03/29	125.00	11.00	675.00	(2)		
600	3¢ violet Lincoln (555)	05/10/24	7.25	.20	25.00	(2)	80.00	
601	4¢ yellow brown M. Washington (556)	08/05/23	4.50	.35	30.00	(2)		
602	5¢ dark blue T. Roosevelt (557)	03/05/24	1.75	.20	10.00	(2)	85.00	
603	10¢ orange Monroe (562)	12/01/24	4.00	.20	26.50	(2)	100.00	
	Coil Stamps, Perf. 10 Horizontally							
604	1¢ yel. grn. Franklin (552)	07/19/24	.35	.20	3.75	(2)	90.00	
605	1½¢ yel. brn. Harding (553)	05/09/25	.35	.20	3.50	(2)	70.00	
606	2¢ carmine Washington (554)	12/31/23	.35	.20	2.60	(2)	125.00	
607-09	Not assigned							
	Issues of 1923, Harding Memorial Issue, Perf. 11							
610	2¢ blk. Warren Gamaliel Harding	09/01/23	.65	.25	20.00	(6)	30.00	1,459
	Double transfer		1.75	.50				
a	Horizontal pair, imperf. vertically		2,000.00					
	Imperf.							
611	2¢ blk. Harding (610)	11/15/23	6.25	4.00	70.00	(6)	90.00	0.8
	Perf. 10							
612	2¢ blk. Harding (610)	09/12/23	17.50	1.75	300.00	(4)	100.00	100
	Perf. 11							
613	2¢ black Harding (610)	1923		37,500.00				
	Issues of 1924, Huguenot-Walloon Tercentary Issue, May 1							
614	1¢ Ship *Nieu Nederland*	01/05/24	2.75	3.25	40.00	(6)	40.00	51
615	2¢ Walloons' Landing at Fort Orange (Albany)	01/05/24	5.50	2.25	55.00	(6)	55.00	78
	Double transfer		12.00	3.50				
616	5¢ Huguenot Monument to Jan Ribault at Duval County, Florida	01/05/24	22.50	13.00	225.00	(6)	80.00	6

599   610

614   615   616

Details

2¢ Washington, Types I-II, Series 1923-1929

Detail of **#599, 634**
Type I

No heavy hair lines at top
center of head.

Detail of **#599A, 634A**
Type II

Three heavy hair lines at
top center of head.

	Issues of 1927-1931		Un	U	PB/LB	#	FDC	Q(M)
	Perf. 11 x 10.5							
638	6¢ red orange Garfield (558)	07/27/27	2.10	.20	14.00	(4)	57.50	
	Pair with full vert. gutter between		*200.00*					
639	7¢ black McKinley (559)	03/24/27	2.10	.20	14.00	(4)	57.50	
a	Vertical pair, imperf.							
	between		*300.00*	100.00				
640	8¢ olive green Grant (560)	06/10/27	2.10	.20	14.00	(4)	62.50	
641	9¢ orange red Jefferson (561)	1931	2.10	.20	13.00	(4)	72.50	
642	10¢ orange Monroe (562)	02/03/27	3.50	.20	20.00	(4)	90.00	
	Double transfer		—	—				
	Perf. 11							
643	2¢ Vermont Sesquicentennial	08/03/27	1.40	.80	37.50	(6)	6.00	40
644	2¢ Burgoyne at Saratoga	08/03/27	3.75	2.10	32.50	(6)	12.50	26
	Issues of 1928							
645	2¢ Valley Forge	05/26/28	1.05	.50	25.00	(6)	4.00	101
	Perf. 11 x 10.5							
646	2¢ Battle of Monmouth/							
	Molly Pitcher	10/20/28	1.10	1.10	35.00	(4)	15.00	10
	Wide spacing, vertical pair		50.00	—				
	Hawaii Sesquicentennial Issue							
647	2¢ Washington (554)	08/13/28	5.00	4.50	135.00	(4)	15.00	6
	Wide spacing, vertical pair		100.00					
648	5¢ Theodore Roosevelt (557)	08/13/28	14.50	13.50	275.00	(4)	22.50	1
	Aeronautics Conference Issue, Perf. 11							
649	2¢ Wright Airplane	12/12/28	1.25	.80	10.00	(6)	7.00	51
650	5¢ Globe and Airplane	12/12/28	5.25	3.25	47.50	(6)	10.00	10
	Plate flaw "prairie dog"		27.50	12.50				
	Issues of 1929							
651	2¢ George Rogers Clark	02/25/29	.65	.50	9.50	(6)	6.00	17
	Double transfer		4.25	2.25				
652	Not assigned							
	Perf. 11 x 10.5							
653	½¢ olive brown							
	Nathan Hale (551)	5/25/29	.20	.20	1.60	(4)	27.50	
	Electric Light's Golden Jubilee Issue, Perf. 11							
654	2¢ Thomas Edison's First Lamp	06/05/29	.70	.70	22.50	(6)	10.00	32
	Perf. 11 x 10.5							
655	2¢ carmine rose (654)	06/11/29	.65	.20	35.00	(4)	80.00	210
	Coil Stamp, Perf. 10 Vertically							
656	2¢ carmine rose (654)	06/11/29	14.00	1.75	75.00	(2)	90.00	133
	Perf. 11							
657	2¢ Sullivan Expedition	06/17/29	.70	.60	22.50	(6)	4.00	51
a	2¢ lake		350.00	—				

643

644

645

646

647

648

649

650

651

654

657

1930-1932

	Issues of 1930		Un	U	PB	#	FDC	Q(M)
	Perf. 11							
688	2¢ Battle of Braddock's Field	07/09/30	1.00	.85	30.00	(6)	4.00	26
689	2¢ Gen. von Steuben	09/17/30	.55	.55	20.00	(6)	4.00	66
a	Imperf., pair		2,750.00		12,500.00	(6)		
	Issues of 1931							
690	2¢ General Pulaski	01/16/31	.30	.25	10.00	(6)	4.00	97
691	Not assigned							
	Perf. 11 x 10.5 (See also #551-73, 575-79, 581-91, 594-606, 622-23, 631-42, 658-79, 684-87, 723)							
692	11¢ light bl. Hayes (563)	09/04/31	2.60	.20	14.00	(4)	100.00	
	Retouched forehead		20.00	1.00				
693	12¢ brown violet Cleveland (564)	08/25/31	5.50	.20	25.00	(4)	100.00	
694	13¢ yellow green Harrison (622)	09/04/31	2.00	.20	14.00	(4)	100.00	
695	14¢ dark blue American Indian (565)	09/08/31	3.75	.25	26.00	(4)	100.00	
696	15¢ gray Statue of Liberty (566)	08/27/31	8.00	.20	37.50	(4)	125.00	
	Perf. 10.5 x 11							
697	17¢ black Wilson (623)	07/25/31	4.50	.20	31.50	(4)	2,750.00	
698	20¢ carmine rose Golden Gate (567)	09/08/31	8.25	.20	37.50	(4)	325.00	
	Double transfer		20.00	—				
699	25¢ blue green Niagara Falls (568)	07/25/31	8.50	.20	45.00	(4)	2,000.00	
700	30¢ brown Buffalo (569)	09/08/31	16.00	.20	67.50	(4)	300.00	
	Cracked plate		26.00	.85				
701	50¢ lilac Arlington Amphitheater (570)	09/04/31	37.50	.20	180.00	(4)	425.00	
	Perf. 11							
702	2¢ "The Greatest Mother"	05/21/31	.25	.20	1.90	(4)	3.00	99
a	Red cross omitted		40,000.00					
703	2¢ Yorktown	10/19/31	.40	.25	2.25	(4)	3.50	25
a	2¢ lake and black		4.50	.75				
b	2¢ dark lake and black		450.00		2,250.00	(4)		
c	Pair, imperf. vertically		5,000.00		—	(6)		
	Issues of 1932, Washington Bicentennial Issue, Perf. 11 x 10.5							
704	½¢ Portrait by Charles W. Peale	01/01/32	.20	.20	6.00	(4)	5.00 (4)	88
	Broken circle		.75	.20				
705	1¢ Bust by Jean Antoine Houdon	01/01/32	.20	.20	4.50	(4)	4.00 (2)	1,266
706	1½¢ Portrait by Charles W. Peale	01/01/32	.40	.20	15.00	(4)	4.00 (2)	305
707	2¢ Portrait by Gilbert Stuart	01/01/32	.20	.20	1.50	(4)	4.00	4,222
	Gripper cracks		1.75	.65				
708	3¢ Portrait by Charles W. Peale	01/01/32	.55	.20	17.50	(4)	4.00	456
709	4¢ Portrait by Charles P. Polk	01/01/32	.25	.20	5.50	(4)	4.00	151
	Broken bottom frame line		1.50	.50				
710	5¢ Portrait by Charles W. Peale	01/01/32	1.60	.20	16.50	(4)	4.00	171
	Cracked plate		5.25	1.10				
711	6¢ Portrait by John Trumbull	01/01/32	3.25	.20	52.50	(4)	4.00	112
712	7¢ Portrait by John Trumbull	01/01/32	.25	.20	9.00	(4)	4.00	83
713	8¢ Portrait by Charles B.J.F. Saint Memin	01/01/32	2.75	.50	50.00	(4)	4.50	97
	Pair, full vert. gutter between		—					
714	9¢ Portrait by W. Williams	01/01/32	2.40	.20	35.00	(4)	4.50	76
715	10¢ Portrait by Gilbert Stuart	01/01/32	10.00	.20	90.00	(4)	4.50	147

688
689
690

702
703

704
705
706

707
708
709

710
711
712

713
714
715

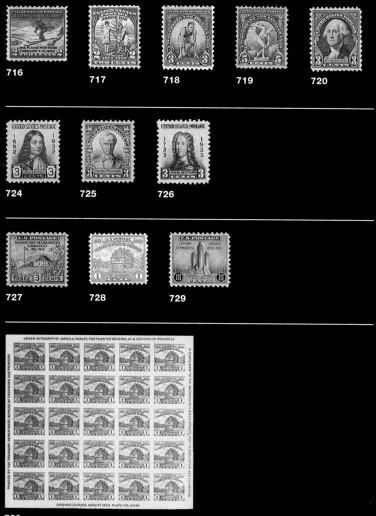

716

717

718

719

720

724

725

726

727

728

729

730

731

732

733

734

	Issues of 1932		Un	U	PB/LP	#	FDC	Q(M)
	Olympic Winter Games Issue, Perf. 11							
716	2¢ Ski Jumper	01/25/32	.40	.20	10.00	(6)	6.00	51
	Recut		3.50	1.50				
	Colored "snowball"		25.00	5.00				
	Perf. 11 x 10.5							
717	2¢ Arbor Day	04/22/32	.20	.20	6.00	(4)	4.00	100
	Olympic Summer Games Issue, Perf. 11 x 10.5							
718	3¢ Runner at Starting Mark	06/15/32	1.40	.20	11.50	(4)	6.00	168
	Gripper cracks		4.25	.75				
719	5¢ Myron's Discobolus	06/15/32	2.20	.20	20.00	(4)	8.00	53
	Gripper cracks		4.25	1.00				
720	3¢ Washington	06/16/32	.20	.20	1.30	(4)	7.50	
	Pair with full vertical or horizontal gutter between		200.00					
	Recut lines on face		2.00	.75				
b	Booklet pane of 6	07/25/32	40.00	7.50			100.00	
c	Vertical pair, imperf. between		1,250.00	1,250.00				
	Coil Stamp, Perf. 10 Vertically							
721	3¢ deep violet (720)	06/24/32	2.75	.20	10.00	(2)	15.00	
	Recut lines around eyes		—	—				
	Coil Stamp, Perf. 10 Horizontally							
722	3¢ deep violet (720)	10/12/32	1.50	.35	6.25	(2)	15.00	
	Coil Stamp, Perf. 10 Vertically (See also #551-73, 575-79, 581-91, 594-606, 622-23, 631-42, 684-87, 692-701)							
723	6¢ deep orange Garfield (558)	08/18/32	11.00	.30	60.00	(2)	15.00	
	Perf. 11							
724	3¢ William Penn	10/24/32	.30	.20	8.00	(6)	3.25	49
a	Vertical pair, imperf. horizontally		—					
725	3¢ Daniel Webster	10/24/32	.30	.25	16.50	(6)	3.25	49
	Issues of 1933							
726	3¢ Georgia Settlement	02/12/33	.30	.20	10.00	(6)	3.25	61
	Perf. 10.5 x 11							
727	3¢ Peace of 1783	04/19/33	.20	.20	3.75	(4)	3.50	73
	Century of Progress Issue							
728	1¢ Restoration of Fort Dearborn	05/25/33	.20	.20	1.90	(4)	3.00 (3)	348
	Gripper cracks		2.00	—				
729	3¢ Federal Building at Chicago	05/25/33	.20	.20	2.25	(4)	3.00	480
	American Philatelic Society Issue Souvenir Sheets, Without Gum, Imperf.							
730	1¢ sheet of 25 (728)	08/25/33	27.50	27.50			100.00	0.4
a	Single stamp from sheet		.75	.50			3.25 (3)	11
731	3¢ sheet of 25 (729)	08/25/33	25.00	25.00			100.00	0.4
a	Single stamp from sheet		.65	.50			3.25	11
	Perf. 10.5 x 11							
732	3¢ National Recovery Act	08/15/33	.20	.20	1.50	(4)	3.25	1,978
	Gripper cracks		1.50	—				
	Recut at right		2.00					
	Perf. 11							
733	3¢ Byrd Antarctic Expedition II	10/09/33	.50	.50	12.00	(6)	10.00	5
	Double transfer		2.75	1.00				
734	5¢ General Tadeusz Kosciuszko	10/13/33	.55	.25	27.50	(6)	4.50	45
a	Horizontal pair, imperf. vertically		2,250.00	25,000.00	(8)			

	Issues of 1934		Un	U	PB	#	FDC	Q(M)
	National Stamp Exhibition Issue Souvenir Sheet, Without Gum, Imperf.							
735	3¢ Byrd sheet of 6 (733)	02/10/34	12.50	10.00			40.00	0.8
a	Single stamp from sheet		2.00	1.65			5.00	4
	Perf. 11							
736	3¢ Maryland Tercentenary	03/23/34	.20	.20	6.00	(6)	1.60	46
	Double transfer		—	—				
	Mothers of America Issue, Perf. 11 x 10.5							
737	3¢ Portrait of his Mother,							
	by James A. McNeill Whistler	05/02/34	.20	.20	.95	(4)	1.60	193
	Perf. 11							
738	3¢ deep violet (737)	05/02/34	.20	.20	4.25	(6)	1.60	15
739	3¢ Wisconsin Tercentenary	07/07/34	.20	.20	2.90	(6)	1.10	64
a	Vert. pair, imperf. horizontally		350.00					
b	Horiz. pair, imperf. vertically		525.00		2,000.00	(6)		
	National Parks Issue, Unwmkd.							
740	1¢ El Capitan, Yosemite							
	(California)	07/16/34	.20	.20	1.00	(6)	2.25	84
	Recut		1.50	.50				
a	Vertical pair, imperf.							
	horizontally, with gum		1,300.00					
741	2¢ Grand Canyon (Arizona)	07/24/34	.20	.20	1.25	(6)	2.25	74v
	Double transfer		1.25	—				
a	Vertical pair, imperf.							
	horizontally, with gum		475.00					
b	Horizontal pair, imperf.							
	vertically, with gum		600.00					
742	3¢ Mt. Rainier, and Mirror Lake,							
	(Washington)	08/03/34	.20	.20	1.75	(6)	2.50	95
a	Vertical pair, imperf.							
	horizontally, with gum		700.00					
743	4¢ Cliff Palace, Mesa Verde							
	(Colorado)	09/25/34	.35	.40	7.00	(6)	2.25	19
a	Vertical pair, imperf.							
	horizontally, with gum		1,000.00					
744	5¢ Old Faithful, Yellowstone							
	(Wyoming)	07/30/34	.70	.65	8.75	(6)	2.25	30
a	Horizontal pair, imperf.							
	vertically, with gum		600.00					
745	6¢ Crater Lake (Oregon)	09/05/34	1.10	.85	15.00	(6)	3.00	16
746	7¢ Great Head, Acadia							
	Park (Maine)	10/02/34	.60	.75	10.00	(6)	3.00	15
a	Horizontal pair, imperf.							
	vertically, with gum		725.00					
747	8¢ Great White Throne,							
	Zion Park (Utah)	09/18/34	1.60	1.50	15.00	(6)	3.25	15
748	9¢ Glacier National Park							
	(Montana)	08/27/34	1.50	.65	15.00	(6)	3.50	17
749	10¢ Great Smoky Mountains							
	(North Carolina)	10/08/34	3.00	1.25	22.50	(6)	6.00	18
	American Philatelic Society Issue Souvenir Sheet, Imperf.							
750	3¢ sheet of 6 (742)	08/28/34	30.00	27.50			40.00	0.5
a	Single stamp from sheet		3.50	3.25			3.25	3
	Trans-Mississippi Philatelic Exposition Issue Souvenir Sheet							
751	1¢ sheet of 6 (740)	10/10/34	12.50	12.50			35.00	0.7
a	Single stamp from sheet		1.40	1.60			3.25 (3)	4

735

736

737

739

740

741

742

743

744

745

746

747

748

749

750

751

Examples of Special Printing Position Blocks

Gutter Block 752

Centerline Block 754

Line Block 756

Arrow Block 763

Cross-Gutter Block 768

Issues of 1935			Un	U	PB	#	FDC	Q(M)
Special Printing (#752-71), Without Gum, Perf. 10.5 x 11								
752	3¢ violet Peace of 1783 (727)	03/15/35	.20	.20	22.50	(4)	5.00	3
	Perf. 11							
753	3¢ blue Byrd Expedition II (733)	03/15/35	.50	.45	17.50	(6)	6.00	2
	Imperf.							
754	3¢ dp. vio. Whistler's Mother (737)	03/15/35	.60	.60	16.00	(6)	6.00	2
755	3¢ deep violet Wisconsin (739)	03/15/35	.60	.60	16.00	(6)	6.00	2
756	1¢ green Yosemite (740)	03/15/35	.20	.20	5.00	(6)	6.00	3
757	2¢ red Grand Canyon (741)	03/15/35	.25	.25	5.75	(6)	6.00	3
	Double transfer		—					
758	3¢ deep violet Mt. Rainier (742)	03/15/35	.50	.45	14.00	(6)	6.00	2
759	4¢ brown Mesa Verde (743)	03/15/35	.95	.95	20.00	(6)	6.50	2
760	5¢ blue Yellowstone (744)	03/15/35	1.50	1.30	25.00	(6)	6.50	2
	Double transfer		—					
761	6¢ dark blue Crater Lake (745)	03/15/35	2.40	2.10	37.50	(6)	6.50	2
762	7¢ black Acadia (746)	03/15/35	1.50	1.40	30.00	(6)	6.50	2
	Double transfer		—					
763	8¢ sage green Zion (747)	03/15/35	1.60	1.50	37.50	(6)	7.50	2
764	9¢ red orange Glacier (748)	03/15/35	1.90	1.65	42.50	(6)	7.50	2
765	10¢ gray black Smoky Mts. (749)	03/15/35	3.75	3.25	50.00	(6)	7.50	2
766	1¢ yellow grn. (728), pane of 25	03/15/35	25.00	25.00			250.00	0.1
a	Single stamp from pane		.70	.50			5.50 (3)	2
767	3¢ violet (729), pane of 25	03/15/35	23.50	23.50			250.00	0.09
a	Single stamp from pane		.60	.50			5.50	2
768	3¢ dark blue (733), pane of 6	03/15/35	20.00	15.00			250.00	0.3
a	Single stamp from pane		2.80	2.40			6.50	2
769	1¢ green (740), pane of 6	03/15/35	12.50	11.00			250.00	0.3
a	Single stamp from pane		1.85	1.80			4.00	2
770	3¢ deep violet (742), pane of 6	03/15/35	30.00	24.00			250.00	0.2
a	Single stamp from pane		3.25	3.10			5.00	1
771	16¢ dark blue Great Seal of U.S.	03/15/35	2.40	2.40	50.00	(6)	12.50	1
	For perforate variety, see #CE2.							

A number of position pieces can be collected from the panes or sheets of the 1935 Special Printing issues, including horizontal and vertical gutter (#752, 766-70) or line (#753-65, 771) blocks of four (HG/L and VG/L), arrow-and-guideline blocks of four (AGL) and crossed-gutter or centerline blocks of four (CG/L). Pairs sell for half the price of blocks of four. Arrow-and-guideline blocks are top or bottom only.

	HG/L	VG/L	AGL	CG/L		HG/L	VG/L	AGL	CG/L
752	5.75	9.50		50.00	762	4.25	3.75	8.25	14.00
753	2.25	25.00	52.50	67.50	763	3.75	4.75	11.00	17.50
754	1.75	1.40	3.00	7.25	764	5.00	4.50	10.50	22.50
755	1.75	1.40	3.00	7.25	765	9.00	10.50	24.00	30.00
756	.45	.55	1.25	3.00	766	5.50	7.00		15.00
757	.70	.55	1.25	3.50	767	5.25	6.75		15.00
758	1.40	1.25	2.75	5.25	768	7.50	9.00		20.00
759	2.75	2.25	4.75	8.50	769	6.00	9.00		15.00
760	3.50	4.25	9.00	15.00	770	12.50	11.00		30.00
761	6.50	5.50	12.50	20.00	771	6.50	5.50	12.50	60.00

785   786   787

788   789

790   791   792

793   794

795   796   798   799

800   801   802

	Issues of 1936-1937		Un	U	PB	#	FDC	Q(M)
	Army Issue, Perf. 11 x 10.5							
785	1¢ George Washington, Nathanael Greene and Mount Vernon	12/15/36	.20	.20	.85	(4)	6.00	105
	Pair with full vertical gutter between		—					
786	2¢ Andrew Jackson, Winfield Scott and The Hermitage	01/15/37	.20	.20	.85	(4)	6.00	94
787	3¢ Generals Sherman, Grant and Sheridan	02/18/37	.20	.20	1.25	(4)	6.00	88
788	4¢ Generals Robert E. Lee and "Stonewall" Jackson and Stratford Hall	03/23/37	.30	.20	8.00	(4)	6.00	36
789	5¢ U.S. Military Academy at West Point	05/26/37	.60	.25	8.50	(4)	6.00	37
	Navy Issue							
790	1¢ John Paul Jones, John Barry, *Bon Homme Richard* and *Lexington*	12/15/36	.20	.20	.85	(4)	6.00	105
791	2¢ Stephen Decatur, Thomas MacDonough and *Saratoga*	01/15/37	.20	.20	.75	(4)	6.00	92
792	3¢ David G. Farragut and David D. Porter, *Hartford* and *Powhatan*	02/18/37	.20	.20	1.00	(4)	6.00	93
793	4¢ Admirals William T. Sampson, George Dewey and Winfield S. Schley	03/23/37	.30	.20	8.50	(4)	6.00	35
794	5¢ Seal of U.S. Naval Academy and Naval Cadets	05/26/37	.60	.25	8.50	(4)	6.00	37
	Issues of 1937							
795	3¢ Northwest Territory Ordinance	07/13/37	.20	.20	1.10	(4)	7.00	85
	Perf. 11							
796	5¢ Virginia Dare and Parents	08/18/37	.20	.20	6.50	(6)	9.00	25
	Society of Philatelic Americans Issue Souvenir Sheet, Imperf.							
797	10¢ blue green (749)	08/26/37	.60	.40			8.00	5
	Perf. 11 x 10.5							
798	3¢ Constitution Sesquicentennial	09/17/37	.20	.20	1.00	(4)	8.00	100
	Territorial Issues, Perf. 10.5 x 11							
799	3¢ Hawaii	10/18/37	.20	.20	1.25	(4)	10.00	78
	Perf. 11 x 10.5							
800	3¢ Alaska	11/12/37	.20	.20	1.25	(4)	8.00	77
	Pair with full gutter between		—					
801	3¢ Puerto Rico	11/25/37	.20	.20	1.25	(4)	8.00	81
802	3¢ Virgin Islands	12/15/37	.20	.20	1.25	(4)	8.00	76
	Pair with full vertical gutter between	275.00						

1938-1939

	Issues of 1938-1939		Un	U	PB	#	FDC
	Presidential Issue, Perf. 11 x 10.5 (#804b, 806b, 807a issued in 1939, 832b in 1951, 832c in 1954, rest in 1938; see also 839-51)						
803	½¢ Benjamin Franklin	05/19/38	.20	.20	.40	(4)	3.00
804	1¢ George Washington	04/25/38	.20	.20	.25	(4)	3.00
	Pair with full vertical gutter between		160.00	—			
b	Booklet pane of 6	01/27/39	2.00	.50			
805	1½¢ Martha Washington	05/05/38	.20	.20	.20	(4)	3.00
	Pair with full horizontal gutter between		175.00				
b	Horizontal pair, imperf. between		160.00	25.00			
806	2¢ John Adams	06/03/38	.20	.20	.30	(4)	3.00
	Recut at top of head		3.00	1.50			
b	Booklet pane of 6	01/27/39	4.75	.85			15.00
807	3¢ Thomas Jefferson	06/16/38	.20	.20	.25	(4)	3.00
a	Booklet pane of 6	01/27/39	8.50	2.00			17.50
b	Horizontal pair, imperf. between		1,500.00	—			
c	Imperf., pair		2,500.00				
808	4¢ James Madison	07/01/38	.75	.20	3.50	(4)	3.00
809	4½¢ The White House	07/11/38	.20	.20	1.50	(4)	3.00
810	5¢ James Monroe	07/21/38	.20	.20	1.00	(4)	3.00
811	6¢ John Quincy Adams	07/28/38	.20	.20	1.00	(4)	3.00
812	7¢ Andrew Jackson	08/04/38	.25	.20	1.25	(4)	3.00
813	8¢ Martin Van Buren	08/11/38	.30	.20	1.40	(4)	3.00
814	9¢ William H. Harrison	08/18/38	.30	.20	1.40	(4)	3.00
	Pair with full vertical gutter between		—				
815	10¢ John Tyler	09/02/38	.25	.20	1.25	(4)	3.00
816	11¢ James K. Polk	09/08/38	.65	.20	3.00	(4)	5.00
817	12¢ Zachary Taylor	09/14/38	.90	.20	4.00	(4)	5.00
818	13¢ Millard Fillmore	09/22/38	1.25	.20	6.50	(4)	5.00
819	14¢ Franklin Pierce	10/06/38	.90	.20	4.50	(4)	5.00
820	15¢ James Buchanan	10/13/38	.40	.20	1.90	(4)	5.00
821	16¢ Abraham Lincoln	10/20/38	.90	.25	5.00	(4)	6.00
822	17¢ Andrew Johnson	10/27/38	.85	.20	4.50	(4)	6.00
823	18¢ Ulysses S. Grant	11/03/38	1.75	.20	8.75	(4)	6.00
824	19¢ Rutherford B. Hayes	11/10/38	1.25	.35	6.25	(4)	6.00
825	20¢ James A. Garfield	11/10/38	.70	.20	3.50	(4)	7.00
826	21¢ Chester A. Arthur	11/22/38	1.25	.20	7.00	(4)	7.00
827	22¢ Grover Cleveland	11/22/38	1.00	.40	9.50	(4)	8.00
828	24¢ Benjamin Harrison	12/02/38	3.50	.20	17.00	(4)	8.00
829	25¢ William McKinley	12/02/38	.60	.20	3.00	(4)	8.00
830	30¢ Theodore Roosevelt	12/08/38	3.50	.20	16.00	(4)	9.00
831	50¢ William Howard Taft	12/08/38	5.00	.20	22.50	(4)	12.50

803   804   805   806   807

808   809   810   811   812

813   814   815   816   817

818   819   820   821   822

823   824   825   826   827

828   829   830   831

832   833   834

835   836   837   838

852   853   854

855   856

858

857

	Issues of 1938-1954		Un	U	PB/LP	#	FDC	Q(M)
	Perf. 11							
832	$1 Woodrow Wilson	08/29/38	6.75	.20	31.50	(4)	50.00	
a	Vertical pair, imperf. horizontally		1,600.00					
b	Watermarked "USIR" (1951)		220.00	65.00	—	(4)		
c	$1 red violet and black	08/31/54	6.00	.20	30.00	(4)	25.00	
d	As "c," vert. pair, imperf. horiz.		1,500.00					
e	Vertical pair, imperf. between		2,750.00					
f	As "c," vert. pair, imperf. between		8,500.00					
833	$2 Warren G. Harding	09/29/38	20.00	3.75	95.00	(4)	100.00	
834	$5 Calvin Coolidge	11/17/38	95.00	3.00	425.00	(4)	150.00	
a	$5 red, brown and black		3,000.00	7,000.00				
	Issues of 1938, Perf. 11 x 10.5							
835	3¢ Constitution Ratification	06/21/38	.25	.20	3.50	(4)	15.00	73
	Perf. 11							
836	3¢ Swedish-Finnish Tercentenary	06/27/38	.20	.20	2.50	(6)	15.00	59
	Perf. 11 x 10.5							
837	3¢ Northwest Territory	07/15/38	.20	.20	7.50	(4)	15.00	66
838	3¢ Iowa Territorial Centennial	08/24/38	.20	.20	5.25	(4)	15.00	47
	Pair with full vertical gutter between		—					
	Issues of 1938-39, Coil Stamps, Perf. 10 Vertically							
839	1¢ green Washington (804)	01/20/39	.30	.20	1.40	(2)	4.75	
840	1½¢ bister brn.							
	Martha Washington (805)	01/20/39	.30	.20	1.50	(2)	4.75	
841	2¢ rose carmine							
	John Adams (806)	01/20/39	.40	.20	1.75	(2)	4.75	
842	3¢ deep violet Jefferson (807)	01/20/39	.50	.20	2.00	(2)	4.75	
	Gripper cracks		—					
	Thin, translucent paper		2.50	—				
843	4¢ red violet Madison (808)	01/20/39	7.50	.40	27.50	(2)	5.00	
844	4½¢ dark gray							
	White House (809)	01/20/38	.70	.40	5.00	(2)	5.00	
845	5¢ bright blue Monroe (810)	01/20/39	5.00	.35	27.50	(2)	5.00	
846	6¢ red orange							
	John Quincy Adams (811)	01/20/39	1.10	.20	7.50	(2)	6.50	
847	10¢ brown red Tyler (815)	01/20/39	11.00	.50	42.50	(2)	9.00	
	Coil Stamps, Perf. 10 Horizontally							
848	1¢ green Washington (804)	01/27/39	.85	.20	2.75	(2)	5.00	
849	1½¢ bister brn.							
	Martha Washington (805)	01/27/39	1.25	.30	4.50	(2)	5.00	
850	2¢ rose carmine							
	John Adams (806)	01/27/39	2.50	.40	6.50	(2)	5.00	
851	3¢ deep violet Jefferson (807)	01/27/39	2.25	.35	6.25	(2)	5.50	
	Perf. 10.5 x 11							
852	3¢ Golden Gate Exposition	02/18/39	.20	.20	1.25	(4)	15.00	114
853	3¢ New York World's Fair	04/01/39	.20	.20	1.75	(4)	15.00	102
	Perf. 11							
854	3¢ Washington's Inauguration	04/30/39	.40	.20	3.50	(6)	15.00	73
	Perf. 11 x 10.5							
855	3¢ Baseball	06/12/39	1.75	.20	7.50	(4)	35.00	81
	Perf. 11							
856	3¢ Panama Canal	08/15/39	.25	.20	3.00	(6)	17.50	68
	Perf. 10.5 x 11							
857	3¢ Printing	09/25/39	.20	.20	1.00	(4)	15.00	71
	Perf. 11 x 10.5							
858	3¢ 50th Anniversary of Statehood (Montana, North Dakota, South Dakota, Washington)	11/02/39	.20	.20	1.10	(4)	12.50	67

1940

	Issues of 1940		Un	U	PB	#	FDC	Q(M)
	Famous Americans Issue, Perf. 10.5 x 11							
	Authors							
859	1¢ Washington Irving	01/29/40	.20	.20	.95	(4)	3.00	56
860	2¢ James Fenimore Cooper	01/29/40	.20	.20	.95	(4)	3.00	53
861	3¢ Ralph Waldo Emerson	02/05/40	.20	.20	1.25	(4)	3.00	53
862	5¢ Louisa May Alcott	02/05/40	.30	.20	8.25	(4)	4.00	22
863	10¢ Samuel L. Clemens							
	(Mark Twain)	02/13/40	1.65	1.20	32.50	(4)	8.00	13
	Poets							
864	1¢ Henry W. Longfellow	02/16/40	.20	.20	1.75	(4)	3.00	52
865	2¢ John Greenleaf Whittier	02/16/40	.20	.20	1.75	(4)	3.00	52
866	3¢ James Russell Lowell	02/20/40	.20	.20	2.25	(4)	3.00	52
867	5¢ Walt Whitman	02/20/40	.35	.20	9.00	(4)	4.00	22
868	10¢ James Whitcomb Riley	02/24/40	1.75	1.25	30.00	(4)	6.00	12
	Educators							
869	1¢ Horace Mann	03/14/40	.20	.20	1.90	(4)	3.00	52
870	2¢ Mark Hopkins	03/14/40	.20	.20	1.25	(4)	3.00	52
871	3¢ Charles W. Eliot	03/28/40	.20	.20	2.25	(4)	3.00	52
872	5¢ Frances E. Willard	03/28/40	.40	.20	9.00	(4)	4.00	21
873	10¢ Booker T. Washington	04/07/40	1.25	1.10	25.00	(4)	10.00	14
	Scientists							
874	1¢ John James Audubon	04/08/40	.20	.20	.95	(4)	3.00	59
875	2¢ Dr. Crawford W. Long	04/08/40	.20	.20	.95	(4)	3.00	58
876	3¢ Luther Burbank	04/17/40	.20	.20	1.10	(4)	3.00	58
877	5¢ Dr. Walter Reed	04/17/40	.25	.20	5.00	(4)	4.00	24
878	10¢ Jane Addams	04/26/40	1.10	.85	16.00	(4)	6.00	15
	Composers							
879	1¢ Stephen Collins Foster	05/03/40	.20	.20	1.00	(4)	3.00	57
880	2¢ John Philip Sousa	05/03/40	.20	.20	1.00	(4)	3.00	58
881	3¢ Victor Herbert	05/13/40	.20	.20	1.10	(4)	3.00	56
882	5¢ Edward A. MacDowell	05/13/40	.40	.20	9.25	(4)	4.00	21
883	10¢ Ethelbert Nevin	06/10/40	3.75	1.35	32.50	(4)	6.00	13
	Artists							
884	1¢ Gilbert Charles Stuart	09/05/40	.20	.20	1.00	(4)	3.00	54
885	2¢ James A. McNeill Whistler	09/05/40	.20	.20	.95	(4)	3.00	54
886	3¢ Augustus Saint-Gaudens	09/16/40	.20	.20	1.00	(4)	3.00	55
887	5¢ Daniel Chester French	09/16/40	.50	.20	8.00	(4)	4.00	22
888	10¢ Frederic Remington	09/30/40	1.75	1.25	20.00	(4)	6.00	14
	Inventors							
889	1¢ Eli Whitney	10/07/40	.20	.20	1.90	(4)	3.00	48
890	2¢ Samuel F.B. Morse	10/07/40	.20	.20	1.10	(4)	3.00	54
891	3¢ Cyrus Hall McCormick	10/14/40	.25	.20	1.75	(4)	3.00	54
892	5¢ Elias Howe	10/14/40	1.10	.30	12.50	(4)	4.00	20
893	10¢ Alexander Graham Bell	10/28/40	11.00	2.00	65.00	(4)	8.00	14

859

860

861

862

863

864

865

866

867

868

869

870

871

872

873

874

875

876

877

878

879

880

881

882

883

884

885

886

887

888

889

890

891

892

893

894

895

896

898

897

899

900

901

903

904

902

905

906

907

908

	Issues of 1940		Un	U	PB	#	FDC	Q(M)
894	3¢ Pony Express	04/03/40	.25	.20	2.75	(4)	9.00	46
	Perf. 10.5 x 11							
895	3¢ Pan American Union	04/14/40	.20	.20	2.75	(4)	7.00	48
	Perf. 11 x 10.5							
896	3¢ Idaho Statehood	07/03/40	.20	.20	1.75	(4)	7.00	51
	Perf. 10.5 x 11							
897	3¢ Wyoming Statehood	07/10/40	.20	.20	1.50	(4)	7.00	50
	Perf. 11 x 10.5							
898	3¢ Coronado Expedition	09/07/40	.20	.20	1.50	(4)	7.00	61
	National Defense Issue							
899	1¢ Statue of Liberty	10/16/40	.20	.20	.45	(4)	4.25	
	Cracked plate		3.00					
	Gripper cracks		3.00					
a	Vertical pair, imperf. between		650.00	—				
b	Horizontal pair, imperf. between		35.00	—				
	Pair with full vertical gutter between		200.00					
900	2¢ 90mm Antiaircraft Gun	10/16/40	.20	.20	.45	(4)	4.25	
a	Horizontal pair, imperf. between		40.00	—				
	Pair with full vertical gutter between		275.00					
901	3¢ Torch of Enlightenment	10/16/40	.20	.20	.60	(4)	4.25	
a	Horizontal pair, imperf. between		27.50	—				
	Pair with full vertical gutter between		—					
	Perf. 10.5 x 11							
902	3¢ Thirteenth Amendment	10/20/40	.20	.20	3.00	(4)	10.00	44
	Issue of 1941, Perf. 11 x 10.5							
903	3¢ Vermont Statehood	03/04/41	.20	.20	1.75	(4)	9.50	55
	Issues of 1942							
904	3¢ Kentucky Statehood	06/01/42	.20	.20	1.10	(4)	5.50	64
905	3¢ Win the War	07/04/42	.20	.20	.40	(4)	5.50	
	Pair with full vertical or horizontal gutter between		175.00					
b	3¢ purple		—	—				
906	5¢ Chinese Resistance	07/07/42	.85	.20	9.00	(4)	12.00	21
	Issues of 1943							
907	2¢ Allied Nations	01/14/43	.20	.20	.30	(4)	5.50	1,700
	Pair with full vertical or horizontal gutter between		225.00					
908	1¢ Four Freedoms	02/12/43	.20	.20	.60	(4)	5.50	1,200

927

928

929

930

931

932

933

934

935

936

937

938

939

940

941

942

943

944

945

946

947

	Issues of 1945, Perf. 11 x 10.5		Un	U	PB	#	FDC	Q(M)
927	3¢ Florida Statehood	03/03/45	.20	.20	.50	(4)	5.50	62
928	5¢ United Nations Conference	04/25/45	.20	.20	.45	(4)	5.00	76
	Perf. 10.5 x 11							
929	3¢ Iwo Jima (Marines)	07/11/45	.20	.20	.45	(4)	10.00	137
	Issues of 1945-1946, Franklin D. Roosevelt Issue, Perf. 11 x 10.5							
930	1¢ Roosevelt and Hyde Park Residence	07/26/45	.20	.20	.20	(4)	3.50	128
931	2¢ Roosevelt and "The Little White House" at Warm Springs, Ga.	08/24/45	.20	.20	.35	(4)	3.50	67
932	3¢ Roosevelt and White House	06/27/45	.20	.20	.35	(4)	3.50	134
933	5¢ Roosevelt, Map of Western Hemisphere and Four Freedoms	01/30/46	.20	.20	.45	(4)	3.50	76
934	3¢ Army, Sept. 28	09/28/45	.20	.20	.45	(4)	6.00	128
935	3¢ Navy	10/27/45	.20	.20	.45	(4)	6.00	136
936	3¢ Coast Guard	11/10/45	.20	.20	.45	(4)	6.00	112
937	3¢ Alfred E. Smith	11/26/45	.20	.20	.40	(4)	2.50	309
	Pair with full vertical gutter between	—						
938	3¢ Texas Statehood	12/29/45	.20	.20	.40	(4)	4.00	171
	Issues of 1946							
939	3¢ Merchant Marine	02/26/46	.20	.20	.45	(4)	5.00	136
940	3¢ Veterans of World War II	05/09/46	.20	.20	.40	(4)	4.00	260
941	3¢ Tennessee Statehood	06/01/46	.20	.20	.45	(4)	2.50	132
942	3¢ Iowa Statehood	08/03/46	.20	.20	.35	(4)	2.50	132
943	3¢ Smithsonian Institution	08/10/46	.20	.20	.35	(4)	2.50	139
944	3¢ Kearny Expedition	10/16/46	.20	.20	.30	(4)	2.50	115
	Issues of 1947, Perf. 10.5 x 11							
945	3¢ Thomas A. Edison	02/11/47	.20	.20	.35	(4)	4.25	157
	Perf. 11 x 10.5							
946	3¢ Joseph Pulitzer	04/10/47	.20	.20	.35	(4)	1.50	120
947	3¢ Postage Stamps Centenary	05/17/47	.20	.20	.30	(4)	1.50	127

Luis Muñoz Marín (1898-1980)

An author, editor, and politician, Luis Muñoz Marín is one of the most beloved figures in Puerto Rican history. He was born in San Juan in 1898, but spent much of his boyhood in Washington, D.C., where his father was stationed in a diplomatic post. After his father's death in 1916, Muñoz Marín got a job with the island's new resident commissioner in Washington, D.C. He also began publishing poems and essays and founded a literary journal, *La Revista de Indias* ("*Review of the Indies*"). In 1926, he returned to his native Puerto Rico, where he edited a newspaper founded by his father. He invited First Lady Eleanor Roosevelt to the island and escorted her to its historic sites as well as its slums. In 1948, Muñoz Marín became the first governor of Puerto Rico to be elected by popular vote rather than appointed by Washington officials. He served four four-year terms, always working for social and economic progress, and in 1963, he received the U.S. Presidential Medal of Freedom. He died in San Juan in 1980. ■

968

969

970

971

972

973

974

975

976

977

978

979

980

981

982

983

984

985

986

987

988

	Issues of 1948		Un	U	PB	#	FDC	Q(M)
968	3¢ Poultry Industry	09/09/48	.20	.20	.40	(4)	1.50	53
	Perf. 10.5 x 11							
969	3¢ Gold Star Mothers	09/21/48	.20	.20	.40	(4)	1.50	77
	Perf. 11 x 10.5							
970	3¢ Fort Kearny	09/22/48	.20	.20	.40	(4)	1.50	58
971	3¢ Volunteer Firemen	10/04/48	.20	.20	.50	(4)	7.00	56
972	3¢ Indian Centennial	10/15/48	.20	.20	.45	(4)	1.00	58
973	3¢ Rough Riders	10/27/48	.20	.20	.45	(4)	1.00	54
974	3¢ Juliette Gordon Low	10/29/48	.20	.20	.40	(4)	6.00	64
	Perf. 10.5 x 11							
975	3¢ Will Rogers	11/04/48	.20	.20	.45	(4)	1.50	67
976	3¢ Fort Bliss	11/05/48	.20	.20	1.00	(4)	2.00	65
	Perf. 11 x 10.5							
977	3¢ Moina Michael	11/09/48	.20	.20	.45	(4)	1.00	64
978	3¢ Gettysburg Address	11/19/48	.20	.20	.50	(4)	1.75	63
	Perf. 10.5 x 11							
979	3¢ American Turners	11/20/48	.20	.20	.30	(4)	1.25	62
980	3¢ Joel Chandler Harris	12/09/48	.20	.20	.55	(4)	1.25	57
	Issues of 1949, Perf. 11 x 10.5							
981	3¢ Minnesota Territory	03/03/49	.20	.20	.30	(4)	1.50	99
982	3¢ Washington and Lee University	04/12/49	.20	.20	.30	(4)	1.50	105
983	3¢ Puerto Rico Election	04/27/49	.20	.20	.30	(4)	2.00	109
984	3¢ Annapolis Tercentenary	05/23/49	.20	.20	.30	(4)	2.00	107
985	3¢ Grand Army of the Republic	08/29/49	.20	.20	.30	(4)	2.00	117
	Perf. 10.5 x 11							
986	3¢ Edgar Allan Poe	10/07/49	.20	.20	.45	(4)	2.00	123
	Thin outer frame line at top, inner frame line missing		6.00					
	Issues of 1950, Perf. 11 x 10.5							
987	3¢ American Bankers	01/03/50	.20	.20	.35	(4)	2.00	131
	Perf. 10.5 x 11							
988	3¢ Samuel Gompers	01/27/50	.20	.20	.30	(4)	1.00	128

Jim Thorpe (1886-1953)

"Sir, you are the greatest athlete in the world." King Gustav V made that pronouncement at the 1912 Olympic Games in Sweden as he awarded gold medals for the pentathlon and decathlon events to Jim Thorpe, the first person ever to win both events at a single Olympics. The accolade would be repeated during the rest of the century and even after his death in 1953 by news and sports organizations. In 1999 the U.S. House of Representatives designated him America's Athlete of the Century. Of Native-American heritage, Thorpe's Indian name meant "Bright Path," which aptly predicted his athletic career. The same year of his Olympic success, he led his Carlisle Indian School football team to a national collegiate championship. He went on to play six years of major league baseball, simultaneously leading the Canton Bulldogs, an early professional football team, to three world championships. In 1920 he became the first president of the American Professional Football Association (later the National Football League). The Postal Service issued stamps in 1984 and 1998 in his honor. ■

008

1009

1010

1011

012

1013

1014

015

1016

1017

018

1019

1020

021

1022

1023

024

1025

1026

	Issues of 1952		Un	U	PB	#	FDC	Q(M)
1008	3¢ NATO	04/04/52	.20	.20	.30	(4)	1.00	2,900
1009	3¢ Grand Coulee Dam	05/15/52	.20	.20	.30	(4)	1.00	115
1010	3¢ Arrival of Lafayette	06/13/52	.20	.20	.45	(4)	1.00	113
	Perf. 10.5 x 11							
1011	3¢ Mt. Rushmore Memorial	08/11/52	.20	.20	.35	(4)	1.00	116
	Perf. 11 x 10.5							
1012	3¢ Engineering	09/06/52	.20	.20	.30	(4)	1.00	114
1013	3¢ Service Women	09/11/52	.20	.20	.30	(4)	1.25	124
1014	3¢ Gutenberg Bible	09/30/52	.20	.20	.30	(4)	1.00	116
1015	3¢ Newspaper Boys	10/04/52	.20	.20	.30	(4)	1.00	115
1016	3¢ International Red Cross	11/21/52	.20	.20	.30	(4)	1.50	136
	Issues of 1953							
1017	3¢ National Guard	02/23/53	.20	.20	.30	(4)	1.00	115
1018	3¢ Ohio Statehood	03/02/53	.20	.20	.45	(4)	1.00	119
1019	3¢ Washington Territory	03/02/53	.20	.20	.30	(4)	1.00	114
1020	3¢ Louisiana Purchase	04/30/53	.20	.20	.50	(4)	1.00	114
1021	5¢ Opening of Japan	07/14/53	.20	.20	.65	(4)	1.25	89
1022	3¢ American Bar Association	08/24/53	.20	.20	.30	(4)	5.00	115
1023	3¢ Sagamore Hill	09/14/53	.20	.20	.35	(4)	1.00	116
1024	3¢ Future Farmers	10/13/53	.20	.20	.30	(4)	1.00	115
1025	3¢ Trucking Industry	10/27/53	.20	.20	.30	(4)	1.25	124
1026	3¢ General George S. Patton, Jr.	11/11/53	.20	.20	.40	(4)	1.50	115
1027	3¢ New York City	11/20/53	.20	.20	.35	(4)	1.00	116
1028	3¢ Gadsden Purchase	12/30/53	.20	.20	.30	(4)	1.00	116
	Issue of 1954							
1029	3¢ Columbia University	01/04/54	.20	.20	.30	(4)	1.00	119

American Commemorative Collections Binder

You'll find this binder is a great way to keep your panels and sheets in mint condition.

Item #880600–American Commemorative Collections Binder $21.95

To order, call **1-800 STAMP-24** or
visit us online at **www.usps.com**

1045

1046

1047

1048

1049

1050

1051

1052

1053

Issues of 1955-1968			Un	U	PB/LP	#	FDC
Perf. 11 x 10.5							
1045	12¢ Benjamin Harrison	06/06/59	.35	.20	1.50	(4)	1.25
a	Tagged	1968	.35	.20	4.00	(4)	25.00
1046	15¢ John Jay	12/12/58	.60	.20	3.00	(4)	1.25
a	Tagged	07/06/66	1.10	.50	13.00	(4)	20.00
Perf. 10.5 x 11							
1047	20¢ Monticello	04/13/56	.40	.20	1.75	(4)	1.25
Perf. 11 x 10.5							
1048	25¢ Paul Revere	04/18/58	1.10	.75	4.75	(4)	1.25
1049	30¢ Robert E. Lee	09/21/55	.70	.20	4.00	(4)	
a	Wet printing	09/21/55	1.10	.75	5.00	(4)	2.00
1050	40¢ John Marshall	04/58	1.50	.20	7.50	(4)	
a	Wet printing	09/24/55	2.25	.25	12.50	(4)	2.00
1051	50¢ Susan B. Anthony	04/58	1.50	.20	7.00	(4)	
a	Wet printing	08/25/55	1.75	.20	11.00	(4)	6.00
1052	$1 Patrick Henry	10/58	4.50	.20	19.00	(4)	
a	Wet printing	10/07/55	5.25	1.00	22.50	(4)	10.00
Perf. 11							
1053	$5 Alexander Hamilton	03/19/56	65.00	6.75	280.00	(4)	65.00
Issues of 1954-1980, Coil Stamps, Perf. 10 Vertically							
1054	1¢ dark green Washington (1031)	08/57	.20	.20	1.00	(2)	
b	Imperf., pair		2,500.00	—			
c	Wet printing	10/08/54	.35	.20	1.75	(2)	1.00
Coil Stamp, Perf. 10 Horizontally							
1054A	1¼¢ turquoise Palace of the Governors (1031A)	06/17/60	.20	.20	2.25	(2)	1.00
Coil Stamps, Perf. 10 Vertically							
1055	2¢ rose carmine Jefferson (1033)	05/57	.35	.20	.80	(2)	
a	Tagged	05/06/68	.20	.20	.75	(2)	11.00
b	Imperf., pair (Bureau precanceled)			550.00			
c	As "a," imperf., pair		600.00				
d	Wet printing	10/22/54	.40	.20	3.50	(2)	1.00
1056	2½¢ gray blue Bunker Hill (1034)	09/09/59	.25	.25	3.50	(2)	2.00
1057	3¢ deep violet Statue of Liberty (1035)	10/56	.35	.20	.80	(2)	
a	Imperf., pair		1,750.00	—	2,750.00	(2)	
b	Tagged	06/26/67	1.00	.50	25.00	(2)	
c	Wet printing	07/20/54	.35	.20	2.75	(2)	1.00
1058	4¢ red violet Lincoln (1036)	07/31/58	.50	.20	2.50	(2)	1.00
a	Imperf., pair		120.00	120.00	200.00	(2)	
b	Wet printing (Bureau precanceled)		27.50	.50	375.00	(2)	
Coil Stamp, Perf. 10 Horizontally							
1059	4¼¢ blue green The Hermitage (1037)	05/01/59	1.50	1.20	14.00	(2)	1.75
Coil Stamp, Perf. 10 Vertically							
1059A	25¢ green Revere (1048)	02/25/65	.50	.30	2.00	(2)	1.25
b	Tagged	04/03/73	.80	.20	3.25	(2)	14.00
	Dull finish gum	1980	1.25		5.00	(2)	
c	Imperf., pair		55.00		100.00	(2)	

1073

1074

1075

1076

1077

1078

1079

1080

1081

1082

1083

1084

1085

	Issues of 1956		Un	U	PB	#	FDC	Q(M)
1073	3¢ Benjamin Franklin	01/17/56	.20	.20	.40	(4)	1.00	129
	Perf. 11 x 10.5							
1074	3¢ Booker T. Washington	04/05/56	.20	.20	.30	(4)	1.50	121
	Fifth International Philatelic Exhibition Issues Souvenir Sheet, Imperf.							
1075	Statue of Liberty Sheet of 2 stamps							
	(1035, 1041)	04/28/56	2.00	2.00			5.00	3
a	3¢ (1035), single stamp from sheet		.80	.80				
b	8¢ (1041), single stamp from sheet		1.00	1.00				
	Perf. 11 x 10.5							
1076	3¢ New York Coliseum and							
	Columbus Monument	04/30/56	.20	.20	.30	(4)	1.00	120
	Wildlife Conservation Issue							
1077	3¢ Wild Turkey	05/05/56	.20	.20	.35	(4)	1.50	123
1078	3¢ Pronghorn Antelope	06/22/56	.20	.20	.35	(4)	1.50	123
1079	3¢ King Salmon	11/09/56	.20	.20	.35	(4)	1.50	109
	Perf. 10.5 x 11							
1080	3¢ Pure Food and Drug Laws	06/27/56	.20	.20	.50	(4)	1.00	113
	Perf. 11 x 10.5							
1081	3¢ Wheatland	08/05/56	.20	.20	.30	(4)	1.00	125
	Perf. 10.5 x 11							
1082	3¢ Labor Day	09/03/56	.20	.20	.30	(4)	1.00	118
	Perf. 11 x 10.5							
1083	3¢ Nassau Hall	09/22/56	.20	.20	.50	(4)	1.00	122
	Perf. 10.5 x 11							
1084	3¢ Devils Tower	09/24/56	.20	.20	.30	(4)	1.00	118
	Pair with full horizontal gutter between		—					
	Perf. 11 x 10.5							
1085	3¢ Children's Stamp	12/15/56	.20	.20	.30	(4)	1.00	101

Emily Bissell
Crusader Against Tuberculosis
USA 15c

Emily Bissell (1861-1948)

Emily Bissell, a devoted and innovative social worker, is best known for introducing the Christmas Seal to America. Born into a prominent Wilmington, Delaware, family, she soon recognized the needs of the less fortunate. In 1889, she established the West End Reading Room, which provided Wilmington's first free kindergarten and playground. In 1907 when her cousin asked her to raise funds to maintain a tuberculosis sanatorium in Wilmington, she agreed. She knew about the success in Denmark of Christmas stamp sales to aid in fighting tuberculosis and decided to try that idea. The Red Cross gave her permission to use its symbol on the small red seal she designed, and by enlisting the help of a Philadelphia newspaper, she raised $3,000. Her success resulted in a nationwide campaign in 1908, when sales of a stamp designed by noted illustrator Howard Pyle raised $100,000. Emily Bissell continued her work in the anti-tuberculosis movement for the rest of her life. ■

1109

1110

1111

1112

1113

1114

1115

1116

1117

1118

1119

1120

1121

1122

1123

1124

1125

1126

1127

1128

1129

1130

1131

	Issues of 1958		Un	U	PB	#	FDC	Q(M)
	Perf. 10.5 x 11							
1109	3¢ Mackinac Bridge	06/25/58	.20	.20	.30	(4)	1.00	107
	Champion of Liberty Issue							
1110	4¢ Bust of Simon Bolivar on							
	Medal	07/24/58	.20	.20	.35	(4)	1.25	115
	Perf. 11							
1111	8¢ Bust of Bolivar on Medal	07/24/58	.20	.20	1.25	(4)	1.25	39
	Plate block of four, ocher # only		—					
	Perf. 11 x 10.5							
1112	4¢ Atlantic Cable	08/15/58	.20	.20	.35	(4)	1.00	114
	Issues of 1958-1959, Abraham Lincoln Sesquicentennial Issue, Perf. 10.5 x 11							
1113	1¢ Portrait by George Healy	02/12/59	.20	.20	.25	(4)	1.00	120
1114	3¢ Sculptured Head by							
	Gutzon Borglum	02/27/59	.20	.20	.40	(4)	1.00	91
	Perf. 11 x 10.5							
1115	4¢ Lincoln and Stephen Douglas							
	Debating, by Joseph							
	Boggs Beale	08/27/58	.20	.20	.45	(4)	1.00	114
1116	4¢ Statue in Lincoln Memorial							
	by Daniel Chester French	05/30/59	.20	.20	.40	(4)	1.00	126
	Champion of Liberty Issue, Perf. 10.5 x 11							
1117	4¢ Bust of Lajos Kossuth on							
	Medal	09/19/58	.20	.20	.30	(4)	1.25	120
	Perf. 11							
1118	8¢ Bust of Kossuth on Medal	09/19/58	.20	.20	1.10	(4)	1.25	44
	Perf. 10.5 x 11							
1119	4¢ Freedom of the Press	09/22/58	.20	.20	.30	(4)	1.00	118
	Perf. 11 x 10.5							
1120	4¢ Overland Mail	10/10/58	.20	.20	.30	(4)	1.00	125
	Perf. 10.5 x 11							
1121	4¢ Noah Webster	10/16/58	.20	.20	.35	(4)	1.00	114
	Perf. 11							
1122	4¢ Forest Conservation	10/27/58	.20	.20	.30	(4)	1.00	156
	Perf. 11 x 10.5							
1123	4¢ Fort Duquesne	11/25/58	.20	.20	.35	(4)	1.00	124
	Issues of 1959							
1124	4¢ Oregon Statehood	02/14/59	.20	.20	.30	(4)	1.00	120
	Champion of Liberty Issue, Perf. 10.5 x 11							
1125	4¢ Bust of José de San Martin							
	on Medal	02/25/59	.20	.20	.30	(4)	1.25	133
a	Horizontal pair, imperf. between		1,500.00					
	Perf. 11							
1126	8¢ Bust of San Martin							
	on Medal	02/25/59	.20	.20	.90	(4)	1.25	45
	Perf. 10.5 x 11							
1127	4¢ NATO	04/01/59	.20	.20	.30	(4)	1.00	122
	Perf. 11 x 10.5							
1128	4¢ Arctic Explorations	04/06/59	.20	.20	.40	(4)	1.00	131
1129	8¢ World Peace Through							
	World Trade	04/20/59	.20	.20	.85	(4)	1.00	47
1130	4¢ Silver Centennial	06/08/59	.20	.20	.30	(4)	1.00	123
	Perf. 11							
1131	4¢ St. Lawrence Seaway	06/26/59	.20	.20	.35	(4)	1.25	126
	Pair with full horizontal gutter between		—					

1960

1152

1153

1154

1155

1156

1157

1158

1159

1160

1161

1162

1163

1164

1165

1166

1167

1168

1169

1170

1171

1172

1173

Issues of 1960		Un	U	PB	#	FDC	Q(M)
Perf. 11 x 10.5							
1152 4¢ American Woman	06/02/60	.20	.20	.30	(4)	1.25	111
Perf. 11							
1153 4¢ 50-Star Flag	07/04/60	.20	.20	.30	(4)	1.00	153
Perf. 11 x 10.5							
1154 4¢ Pony Express	07/19/60	.20	.20	.45	(4)	1.50	120
Perf. 10.5 x 11							
1155 4¢ Employ the Handicapped	08/28/60	.20	.20	.30	(4)	1.50	118
1156 4¢ 5th World Forestry Congress	08/29/60	.20	.20	.30	(4)	1.00	118
Perf. 11							
1157 4¢ Mexican Independence	09/16/60	.20	.20	.30	(4)	1.00	112
1158 4¢ U.S.-Japan Treaty	09/28/60	.20	.20	.35	(4)	1.00	125
Champion of Liberty Issue, Paderewski, Perf. 10.5 x 11							
1159 4¢ Bust of Ignacy Jan Paderewski							
on Medal	10/08/60	.20	.20	.30	(4)	1.25	120
Perf. 11							
1160 8¢ Bust of Paderewski							
on Medal	10/08/60	.20	.20	.90	(4)	1.25	43
Perf. 10.5 x 11							
1161 4¢ Sen. Robert A. Taft							
Memorial	10/10/60	.20	.20	.45	(4)	1.00	107
Perf. 11 x 10.5							
1162 4¢ Wheels of Freedom	10/15/60	.20	.20	.30	(4)	1.00	110
Perf. 11							
1163 4¢ Boys' Clubs of America	10/18/60	.20	.20	.30	(4)	1.00	124
1164 4¢ First Automated Post Office	10/20/60	.20	.20	.30	(4)	1.00	124
Champion of Liberty Issue, Perf. 10.5 x 11							
1165 4¢ Bust of Gustaf Mannerheim							
on Medal	10/26/60	.20	.20	.30	(4)	1.25	125
Perf. 11							
1166 8¢ Bust of Mannerheim							
on Medal	10/26/60	.20	.20	.80	(4)	1.25	42
1167 4¢ Camp Fire Girls	11/01/60	.20	.20	.40	(4)	2.50	116
Champion of Liberty Issue, Perf. 10.5 x 11							
1168 4¢ Bust of Giusseppe Garibaldi							
on Medal	11/02/60	.20	.20	.30	(4)	1.25	126
Perf. 11							
1169 8¢ Bust of Garibaldi on Medal	11/02/60	.20	.20	.85	(4)	1.25	43
Perf. 10.5 x 11							
1170 4¢ Sen. Walter F. George							
Memorial	11/05/60	.20	.20	.35	(4)	1.00	124
1171 4¢ Andrew Carnegie	11/25/60	.20	.20	.35	(4)	1.00	120
1172 4¢ John Foster Dulles Memorial	12/06/60	.20	.20	.35	(4)	1.00	117
Perf. 11 x 10.5							
1173 4¢ Echo I-Communications							
for Peace	12/15/60	.20	.20	.65	(4)	2.50	124

	Issues of 1961		Un	U	PB	#	FDC	Q(M)
	Champion of Liberty Issue, Perf. 10.5 x 11							
1174	4¢ Bust of Gandhi on Medal	01/26/61	.20	.20	.30	(4)	1.25	113
	Perf. 11							
1175	8¢ Bust of Gandhi on Medal	01/26/61	.20	.20	1.00	(4)	1.25	42
1176	4¢ Range Conservation	02/02/61	.20	.20	.40	(4)	1.00	111
	Perf. 10.5 x 11							
1177	4¢ Horace Greeley	02/03/61	.20	.20	.30	(4)	1.00	99
	Issues of 1961-1965, Civil War Centennial Issue, Perf. 11 x 10.5							
1178	4¢ Fort Sumter	04/12/61	.20	.20	.90	(4)	3.75	101
1179	4¢ Shiloh	04/07/62	.20	.20	.75	(4)	3.75	125
	Perf. 11							
1180	5¢ Gettysburg	07/01/63	.20	.20	.85	(4)	3.75	80
1181	5¢ The Wilderness	05/05/64	.20	.20	.60	(4)	3.75	125
1182	5¢ Appomattox	04/09/65	.25	.20	1.20	(4)	3.75	113
a	Horizontal pair, imperf. vertically		4,500.00					
1183	4¢ Kansas Statehood	05/10/61	.20	.20	.35	(4)	1.00	106
	Perf. 11 x 10.5							
1184	4¢ Sen. George W. Norris	07/11/61	.20	.20	.40	(4)	1.00	111
1185	4¢ Naval Aviation	08/20/61	.20	.20	.35	(4)	1.00	117
	Pair with full vertical gutter between		150.00					
	Perf. 10.5 x 11							
1186	4¢ Workmen's Compensation	09/04/61	.20	.20	.35	(4)	1.00	121
	With plate # inverted				.60	(4)		
	Perf. 11							
1187	4¢ Frederic Remington	10/04/61	.20	.20	.40	(4)	1.25	112
	Perf. 10.5 x 11							
1188	4¢ Republic of China	10/10/61	.20	.20	.45	(4)	5.50	111
1189	4¢ Naismith-Basketball	11/06/61	.20	.20	.50	(4)	6.50	109
	Perf. 11							
1190	4¢ Nursing	12/28/61	.20	.20	.50	(4)	10.00	145
	Issues of 1962							
1191	4¢ New Mexico Statehood	01/06/62	.20	.20	.30	(4)	1.50	113
1192	4¢ Arizona Statehood	02/14/62	.20	.20	.30	(4)	1.50	122
1193	4¢ Project Mercury	02/20/62	.20	.20	.35	(4)	3.00	289
1194	4¢ Malaria Eradication	03/30/62	.20	.20	.30	(4)	1.00	120
	Perf. 10.5 x 11							
1195	4¢ Charles Evans Hughes	04/11/62	.20	.20	.30	(4)	1.00	125

Visit us online at The Postal Store at www.usps.com

or call 1-800-STAMP-24

1174

1175

1176

1177

1178

1179

1180

1181

1183

1182

1184

1185

1186

1187

1188

1189

1190

1191

1192

1193

1194

1195

1962-1963

1196

1197

1198

1199

1200

1201

1202

1203

1204

1205

1206

1207

1208

1209

1213

1230

1231

1232

1233

1234

Issues of 1962		Un	U	PB/LP	#	FDC	Q(M)
Perf. 11							
1196 4¢ Seattle World's Fair	04/25/62	.20	.20	.30	(4)	1.00	147
1197 4¢ Louisiana Statehood	04/30/62	.20	.20	.50	(4)	1.00	119
Perf. 11 x 10.5							
1198 4¢ Homestead Act	05/20/62	.20	.20	.30	(4)	1.00	123
1199 4¢ Girl Scout Jubilee	07/24/62	.20	.20	.30	(4)	5.25	127
Pair with full vertical gutter between		250.00					
1200 4¢ Sen. Brien McMahon	07/28/62	.20	.20	.35	(4)	1.00	131
1201 4¢ Apprenticeship	08/31/62	.20	.20	.30	(4)	1.00	120
Perf. 11							
1202 4¢ Sam Rayburn	09/16/62	.20	.20	.30	(4)	1.50	121
1203 4¢ Dag Hammarskjold	10/23/62	.20	.20	.30	(4)	1.00	121
1204 4¢ black, brown and yellow (yellow inverted), Dag Hammarskjold, special printing	11/16/62	.20	.20	1.10	(4)	5.00	40
Christmas Issue							
1205 4¢ Wreath and Candles	11/01/62	.20	.20	.30	(4)	1.10	862
1206 4¢ Higher Education	11/14/62	.20	.20	.35	(4)	1.25	120
1207 4¢ Winslow Homer	12/15/62	.20	.20	.45	(4)	1.25	118
a Horizontal pair, imperf. between		6,750.00					
Issues of 1963-1966							
1208 5¢ Flag over White House	01/09/63	.20	.20	.40	(4)	1.00	
Pair with full horizontal gutter between		—					
a Tagged	08/25/66	.20	.20	2.00	(4)	25.00	
b Horizontal pair, imperf. between		1,500.00					
Issues of 1962-1966, Perf. 11 x 10.5							
1209 1¢ Andrew Jackson	03/22/63	.20	.20	.20	(4)	1.00	
Pair with full vertical gutter between		—					
a Tagged	07/06/66	.20	.20	.40	(4)	25.00	
1210-12 Not assigned							
1213 5¢ George Washington	11/23/62	.20	.20	.40	(4)	1.00	
a Booklet pane of 5 + label		3.00	2.00			4.00	
b Tagged	10/28/63	.50	.20	4.50	(4)	25.00	
c As "a," tagged	10/28/63	2.00	1.50			100.00	
1214-24 Not assigned							
Coil Stamps, Perf. 10 Vertically							
1225 1¢ green Jackson (1209)	05/31/63	.20	.20	2.00	(2)	1.00	
a Tagged	07/06/66	.20	.20	.75	(2)	15.00	
1226-28 Not assigned							
1229 5¢ dark blue gray Washington (1213)	11/23/62	1.10	.20	3.50	(2)	1.00	
a Tagged	10/28/63	1.40	.20	6.50	(2)	25.00	
b Imperf., pair		450.00		1,250.00	(2)		
Issues of 1963, Perf. 11							
1230 5¢ Carolina Charter	04/06/63	.20	.20	.40	(4)	1.00	130
1231 5¢ Food for Peace-Freedom from Hunger	06/04/63	.20	.20	.40	(4)	1.00	136
1232 5¢ West Virginia Statehood	06/20/63	.20	.20	.40	(4)	1.00	138
1233 5¢ Emancipation Proclamation	08/16/63	.20	.20	.50	(4)	1.75	132
1234 5¢ Alliance for Progress	08/17/63	.20	.20	.40	(4)	1.00	136

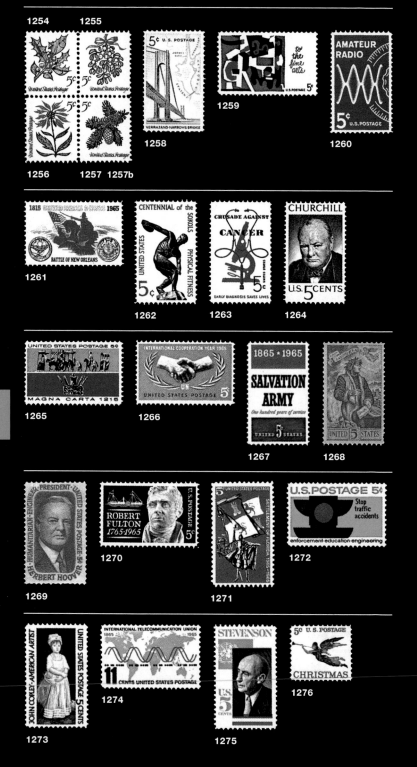

1254   1255

1256   1257 1257b

1258

1259

1260

1261

1262   1263   1264

1265   1266

1267   1268

1269

1270

1271   1272

1273

1274

1275

1276

	Issues of 1964		Un	U	PB	#	FDC	Q(M)
	Christmas Issue, Perf. 11							
1254	5¢ Holly	11/09/64	.25	.20			1.00	352
a	Tagged		.60	.50				
1255	5¢ Mistletoe	11/09/64	.25	.20			1.00	352
a	Tagged		.60	.50				
1256	5¢ Poinsettia	11/09/64	.25	.20			1.00	352
a	Tagged		.60	.50				
1257	5¢ Sprig of Conifer	11/09/64	.25	.20			1.00	352
a	Tagged		.60	.50				
b	Block of four, #1254-57		1.00	1.00	1.10	(4)	3.00	
c	As "b," tagged		2.50	2.25			57.50	
	Perf. 10.5 x 11							
1258	5¢ Verrazano-Narrows Bridge	11/21/64	.20	.20	.45	(4)	1.00	120
	Perf. 11							
1259	5¢ Fine Arts	12/02/64	.20	.20	.40	(4)	1.00	126
	Perf. 10.5 x 11							
1260	5¢ Amateur Radio	12/15/64	.20	.20	.60	(4)	5.00	122
	Issues of 1965, Perf. 11							
1261	5¢ Battle of New Orleans	01/08/65	.20	.20	.60	(4)	1.00	116
1262	5¢ Physical Fitness-Sokol	02/15/65	.20	.20	.50	(4)	1.25	115
1263	5¢ Crusade Against Cancer	04/01/65	.20	.20	.40	(4)	2.50	120
	Perf. 10.5 x 11							
1264	5¢ Winston Churchill Memorial	05/13/65	.20	.20	.40	(4)	1.25	125
	Perf. 11							
1265	5¢ Magna Carta	06/15/65	.20	.20	.40	(4)	1.00	120
	Corner block of four, black PB# omitted		—					
1266	5¢ International Cooperation							
	Year-United Nations	06/26/65	.20	.20	.40	(4)	1.00	115
1267	5¢ Salvation Army	07/02/65	.20	.20	.40	(4)	2.00	116
	Perf. 10.5 x 11							
1268	5¢ Dante Alighieri	07/17/65	.20	.20	.40	(4)	1.00	115
1269	5¢ President Herbert Hoover							
	Memorial	08/10/65	.20	.20	.45	(4)	1.00	115
	Perf. 11							
1270	5¢ Robert Fulton	08/19/65	.20	.20	.40	(4)	1.00	116
1271	5¢ Florida Settlement	08/28/65	.20	.20	.45	(4)	1.00	117
a	Yellow omitted		350.00					
1272	5¢ Traffic Safety	09/03/65	.20	.20	.45	(4)	1.00	114
1273	5¢ John Singleton Copley	09/17/65	.20	.20	.50	(4)	1.00	115
1274	11¢ International							
	Telecommunication Union	10/06/65	.35	.20	2.25	(4)	1.10	27
1275	5¢ Adlai E. Stevenson Memorial	10/23/65	.20	.20	.40	(4)	1.00	128
	Christmas Issue							
1276	5¢ Angel with Trumpet							
	(1840 Weather Vane)	11/02/65	.20	.20	.40	(4)	1.00	1,140
a	Tagged	11/15/65	.75	.25	5.50	(4)	42.50	
1277	Not assigned							

1294 **1295** **1305**

1306 **1307**

1310

1308 **1309**

1311

1314

1312 **1313**

	Issues of 1966-1973		Un	U	PB/LP	#	FDC	Q(M)
	Perf. 11 x 10.5, 10.5 x 11							
1294	$1 Eugene O'Neill	10/16/67	2.25	.20	10.00	(4)	6.00	
a	Tagged	04/03/73	1.65	.20	6.75	(4)	35.00	
1295	$5 John Bassett Moore	12/03/66	9.50	2.25	40.00	(4)	40.00	
a	Tagged	04/03/73	8.00	2.00	32.50	(4)	80.00	
1296	Not assigned							
	Issues of 1967-1975, Coil Stamps, Perf. 10 Horizontally							
1297	3¢ violet Parkman (1281)	11/04/75	.20	.20	.45	(2)	1.00	
a	Imperf., pair		30.00		55.00	(2)		
b	Untagged (Bureau precanceled)			.20				
c	As "b," imperf., pair			6.00	25.00	(2)		
1298	6¢ Franklin D. Roosevelt (1284)	12/28/67	.20	.20	1.10	(2)	1.00	
a	Imperf., pair		2,250.00					
b	Tagging omitted		3.00					
	Issues of 1966-1981, Coil Stamps, Perf. 10 Vertically (See also #1279-96)							
1299	1¢ green Jefferson (1278)	01/12/68	.20	.20	.25	(2)	1.00	
a	Untagged (Bureau precanceled)			.20				
b	Imperf., pair		30.00	—	60.00	(2)		
1300-02	Not assigned							
1303	4¢ blk. Lincoln (1282)	05/28/66	.20	.20	.75	(2)	1.00	
a	Untagged (Bureau precanceled)			.20				
b	Imperf., pair		900.00		1,900.00	(2)		
1304	5¢ bl. Washington (1283)	09/08/66	.20	.20	.40	(2)	1.00	
a	Untagged (Bureau precanceled)			.20				
b	Imperf., pair		175.00		400.00	(2)		
e	As "a," imperf. pair			375.00	850.00	(2)		
1304C	5¢ redrawn (1283B)	1981	.20	.20	1.25	(2)		
d	Imperf., pair		750.00					
1305	6¢ gray brown Roosevelt	02/28/68	.20	.20	.55	(2)	1.00	
a	Imperf., pair		75.00		130.00	(2)		
b	Untagged (Bureau precanceled)			.20				
1305E	15¢ magenta, Type I (1288)	06/14/78	.25	.20	1.10	(2)	1.00	
	Dull finish gum		.60		3.50	(2)		
f	Untagged (Bureau precanceled)			.30				
g	Imperf., pair		30.00		75.00	(2)		
h	Pair, imperf. between		200.00		550.00	(2)		
i	Type II, dull gum		.60	.20	2.75	(2)		
j	Type II, dull gum, imperf., pair		85.00		290.00	(2)		
1305C	$1 dull purple Eugene O'Neill (1294)	01/12/73	2.00	.40	5.50	(2)	4.00	
d	Imperf., pair		2,250.00		4,000.00	(2)		
	Issues of 1966, Perf. 11							
1306	5¢ Migratory Bird Treaty	03/16/66	.20	.20	.40	(4)	1.75	117
1307	5¢ Humane Treatment of Animals	04/09/66	.20	.20	.40	(4)	1.25	117
1308	5¢ Indiana Statehood	04/16/66	.20	.20	.50	(4)	1.00	124
1309	5¢ American Circus	05/02/66	.20	.20	.50	(4)	2.00	131
	Sixth International Philatelic Exhibition Issue							
1310	5¢ Stamped Cover	05/21/66	.20	.20	.40	(4)	1.00	122
	Souvenir Sheet, Imperf.							
1311	5¢ Stamped Cover (1310) and Washington, D.C., Scene	05/23/66	.20	.20			1.10	15
	Perf. 11							
1312	5¢ The Bill of Rights	07/01/66	.20	.20	.45	(4)	1.75	114
	Perf. 10.5 x 11							
1313	5¢ Poland's Millennium	07/30/66	.20	.20	.45	(4)	1.25	128
	Perf. 11							
1314	5¢ National Park Service	08/25/66	.20	.20	.45	(4)	1.00	120
a	Tagged	08/26/66	.30	.25	2.00	(4)	30.00	

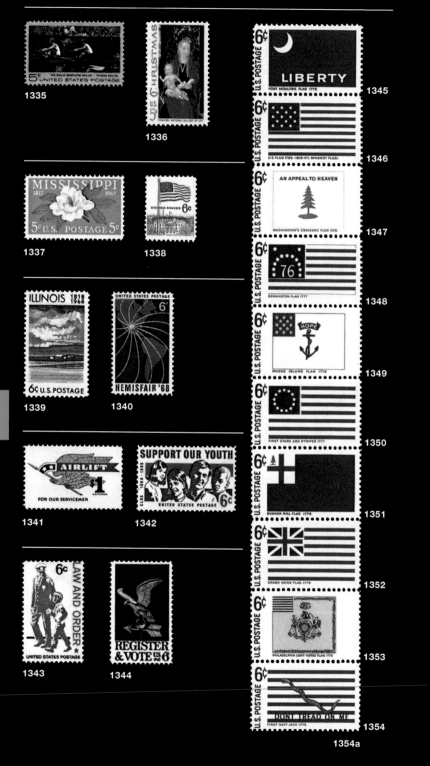

1335

1336

1337

1338

1339

1340

1341

1342

1343

1344

1345

1346

1347

1348

1349

1350

1351

1352

1353

1354

1354a

Issues of 1967		Un	U	PB	#	FDC	Q(M)
Perf. 12							
1335 5¢ Thomas Eakins	11/02/67	.20	.20	.50	(4)	1.25	114
Christmas Issue, Perf. 11							
1336 5¢ Madonna and Child,							
by Hans Memling	11/06/67	.20	.20	.40	(4)	1.25	1,209
a Tagging omitted		5.00	—				
1337 5¢ Mississippi Statehood	12/11/67	.20	.20	.60	(4)	1.00	113
a Tagging omitted		6.00	—				
Issues of 1968-1971							
1338 6¢ Flag over White House							
(design 19 x 22mm)	01/24/68	.20	.20	.45	(4)	1.00	
k Vertical pair, imperf. between		550.00					
m Tagging omitted		4.00	—				
Coil Stamp, Perf. 10 Vertically							
1338A 6¢ dk bl, rd and grn (1338)	05/30/69	.20	.20	.30	(2)	1.00	
b Imperf., pair		500.00					
q Tagging omitted		8.50	—				
Perf. 11 x 10.5							
1338D 6¢ dark blue, red and green							
(1338, design 18.25 x 21mm)	08/07/70	.20	.20	2.60	(20)	1.00	
e Horizontal pair, imperf. between		175.00					
n Tagging omitted		5.00	—				
1338F 8¢ dk bl, rd and slt grn (1338)	05/10/71	.20	.20	3.00	(20)	1.00	
i Imperf., vertical pair		45.00					
j Horizontal pair, imperf. between		55.00					
o Tagging omitted		6.50	—				
Coil Stamp, Perf. 10 Vertically							
1338G 8¢ dk bl, rd and slt grn (1338)	05/10/71	.20	.20	.40	(2)	1.00	
h Imperf., pair		55.00					
r Tagging omitted		6.00	—				
Issues of 1968, Perf. 11							
1339 6¢ Illinois Statehood	02/12/68	.20	.20	.50	(4)	1.00	141
1340 6¢ HemisFair '68	03/30/68	.20	.20	.50	(4)	1.00	144
a White omitted		1,250.00					
1341 $1 Airlift	04/04/68	2.00	1.25	9.00	(4)	7.00	
Pair with full horizontal gutter between			—				
1342 6¢ Support Our Youth-Elks	05/01/68	.20	.20	.50	(4)	1.00	147
a Tagging omitted		7.50	—				
1343 6¢ Law and Order	05/17/68	.20	.20	.50	(4)	2.00	130
1344 6¢ Register and Vote	06/27/68	.20	.20	.50	(4)	1.00	159
Historic Flag Issue							
1345 6¢ Ft. Moultrie Flag, 1776	07/04/68	.40	.25			3.00	23
1346 6¢ Ft. McHenry (U.S.)							
Flag, 1795-1818	07/04/68	.30	.25			3.00	23
1347 6¢ Washington's							
Cruisers Flag, 1775	07/04/68	.25	.25			3.00	23
1348 6¢ Bennington Flag, 1777	07/04/68	.25	.25			3.00	23
1349 6¢ Rhode Island Flag, 1775	07/04/68	.25	.25			3.00	23
1350 6¢ First Stars and							
Stripes, 1777	07/04/68	.25	.25			3.00	23
1351 6¢ Bunker Hill Flag, 1775	07/04/68	.25	.25			3.00	23
1352 6¢ Grand Union Flag, 1776	07/04/68	.25	.25			3.00	23
1353 6¢ Philadelphia Light Horse							
Flag, 1775	07/04/68	.25	.25			3.00	23
1354 6¢ First Navy Jack, 1775	07/04/68	.25	.25			3.00	23
a Strip of 10, #1345-54		2.75	3.25	6.50	(20)	17.50	

1378   1379   1379a

1380

1381   1382

1383

1384

1384 Precancel

1385

1386

1387   1388

1391

AMERICAN BALD EAGLE : AFRICAN ELEPHANT HERD

HAIDA CEREMONIAL CANOE : THE AGE OF REPTILES

	Issues of 1969		Un	U	PB	#	FDC	Q(M)
	Botanical Congress Issue, Perf. 11							
1376	6¢ Douglas Fir (Northwest)	08/23/69	.35	.20			1.50	40
1377	6¢ Lady's Slipper (Northeast)	08/23/69	.35	.20			1.50	40
1378	6¢ Ocotillo (Southwest)	08/23/69	.35	.20			1.50	40
1379	6¢ Franklinia (Southeast)	08/23/69	.35	.20			1.50	40
a	Block of 4, #1376-79		1.50	2.50	1.75	(4)	5.00	
	Perf. 10.5 x 11							
1380	6¢ Dartmouth College Case	09/22/69	.20	.20	.50	(4)	1.00	130
	Perf. 11							
1381	6¢ Professional Baseball	09/24/69	.65	.20	3.00	(4)	12.00	131
a	Black omitted		1,100.00					
1382	6¢ Intercollegiate Football	09/26/69	.20	.20	.85	(4)	6.50	139
1383	6¢ Dwight D. Eisenhower	10/14/69	.20	.20	.50	(4)	1.00	151
	Christmas Issue, Perf. 11 x 10.5							
1384	6¢ Winter Sunday in							
	Norway, Maine	11/03/69	.20	.20	1.40	(10)	1.25	1,710
	Precanceled		.50	.20				
b	Imperf., pair		1,000.00					
c	Light green omitted		22.50					
d	Light green and yellow omitted		950.00	—				
e	Yellow omitted		2,250.00					
f	Tagging omitted		5.00	—				

Precanceled versions issued on an experimental basis in four cities whose names appear on the stamps: Atlanta, GA; Baltimore, MD; Memphis, TN; and New Haven, CT.

	Perf. 11							
1385	6¢ Hope for the Crippled	11/20/69	.20	.20	.50	(4)	1.25	128
1386	6¢ William M. Harnett	12/03/69	.20	.20	.55	(4)	1.00	146
	Issues of 1970, Natural History Issue							
1387	6¢ American Bald Eagle	05/06/70	.20	.20			1.50	50
1388	6¢ African Elephant Herd	05/06/70	.20	.20			1.50	50
1389	6¢ Tlingit Chief in							
	Haida Ceremonial Canoe	05/06/70	.20	.20			1.50	50
1390	6¢ Brontosaurus, Stegosaurus							
	and Allosaurus from							
	Jurassic Period	05/06/70	.20	.20			1.50	50
a	Block of 4, #1387-90		.55	.80	.70	(4)	4.00	
1391	6¢ Maine Statehood	07/09/70	.20	.20	.50	(4)	1.50	172
	Perf. 11 x 10.5							
1392	6¢ Wildlife Conservation	07/20/70	.20	.20	.50	(4)	1.00	142

Visit us online at The Postal Store at www.usps.com

or call 1-800-STAMP-24

1414   1414a

1415   1416

1417   1418   1418b

1419

1420

1421   1422   1422a

1425

1426

1423   1424

1427   1428

1429   1430   1430a

Issues of 1970		Un	U	PB	#	FDC	Q(M)
Christmas Issue, Perf. 10.5 x 11							
1414 6¢ Nativity, by Lorenzo Lotto	11/05/70	.20	.20	1.10	(8)	1.25	639*
a Precanceled		.20	.20	1.90	(8)	7.50	358
b Black omitted		550.00					
c As "a," blue omitted		1,500.00					
d Type II		.20	.20	2.75	(8)		
e Type II, precanceled		.25	.20	4.00	(8)		
#1414a-18a were furnished to 68 cities. Unused prices are for copies with gum and used prices are for copies with or without gum but with an additional cancellation. *Includes #1414a.							
Perf. 11 x 10.5							
1415 6¢ Tin and Cast-iron Locomotive	11/05/70	.30	.20			1.50	122
a Precanceled		.75	.20				110
b Black omitted		2,500.00					
1416 6¢ Toy Horse on Wheels	11/05/70	.30	.20			1.50	122
a Precanceled		.75	.20				110
b Black omitted		2,500.00					
c Imperf., pair			4,000.00				
1417 6¢ Mechanical Tricycle	11/05/70	.30	.20			1.50	122
a Precanceled		.75	.20				110
b Black omitted		2,500.00					
1418 6¢ Doll Carriage	11/05/70	.30	.20			1.50	122
a Precanceled		.75	.20				110
b Block of 4, #1415-18		1.25	1.75	3.00	(8)	5.50	
c Block of 4, #1415a-18a		3.25	3.75	6.25	(8)	15.00	
d Black omitted		2,500.00					
Perf. 11							
1419 6¢ United Nations	11/20/70	.20	.20	.50	(4)	1.00	128
Pair with full horizontal gutter between		—					
1420 6¢ Landing of the Pilgrims	11/21/70	.20	.20	.50	(4)	1.00	130
a Orange and yellow omitted		900.00					
Disabled American Veterans and Servicemen Issue							
1421 6¢ Disabled American Veterans Emblem	11/24/70	.20	.20			2.00	67
1422 6¢ U.S. Servicemen	11/24/70	.20	.20			2.00	67
a Attached pair, #1421-22		.30	.40	1.00	(4)	3.00	
Issues of 1971							
1423 6¢ American Wool Industry	01/19/71	.20	.20	.50	(4)	1.00	136
a Tagging omitted		11.00	—				
1424 6¢ Gen. Douglas MacArthur	01/26/71	.20	.20	.50	(4)	1.50	135
1425 6¢ Blood Donor	03/12/71	.20	.20	.50	(4)	1.00	131
a Tagging omitted		11.00	—				
Perf. 11 x 10.5							
1426 8¢ Missouri Statehood	05/08/71	.20	.20	2.00	(12)	1.00	161
Wildlife Conservation Issue, Perf. 11							
1427 8¢ Trout	06/12/71	.20	.20			1.25	44
1428 8¢ Alligator	06/12/71	.20	.20			1.25	44
1429 8¢ Polar Bear and Cubs	06/12/71	.20	.20			1.25	44
1430 8¢ California Condor	06/12/71	.20	.20			1.25	44
a Block of 4, #1427-30			.80	1.00	.90	(4)	3.00
b As "a," light green and dark green omitted from #1427-28		4,500.00					
c As "a," red omitted from #1427, 1429-30		7,500.00					

1446   1447

1448   1449

1450   1451   1451a

1452

1453

1454

1455

1456   1457

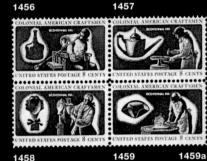

1458   1459   1459a

1460   1461   1462

1463

	Issues of 1972		Un	U	PB	#	FDC	Q(M)
1446	8¢ Sidney Lanier	02/03/72	.20	.20	.65	(4)	1.00	137
a	Tagging omitted		15.00					
	Perf. 10.5 x 11							
1447	8¢ Peace Corps	02/11/72	.20	.20	1.00	(6)	1.00	150
a	Tagging omitted		5.00					
	National Parks Centennial Issue (See also #C84)							
1448	2¢ Ship at Sea	04/05/72	.20	.20				43
1449	2¢ Cape Hatteras Lighthouse	04/05/72	.20	.20				43
1450	2¢ Laughing Gulls on Driftwood	04/05/72	.20	.20				43
1451	2¢ Laughing Gulls and Dune	04/05/72	.20	.20				43
a	Block of 4, #1448-51		.25	.45	.50	(4)	2.00	
b	As "a," black omitted		2,250.00					
1452	6¢ Performance at Wolf Trap Farm, Shouse Pavilion	06/26/72	.20	.20	.55	(4)	1.00	104
a	Tagging omitted		11.00					
1453	8¢ Old Faithful, Yellowstone	03/01/72	.20	.20	.70	(4)	1.00	164
a	Tagging omitted		15.00					
1454	15¢ View of Mount McKinley in Alaska	07/28/72	.30	.20	1.30	(4)	1.00	54

Note: Beginning with this National Parks Centennial issue, the USPS began to offer stamp collectors first day cancellations affixed to 8" x 101/2" souvenir pages. The pages are similar to the stamp announcements that have appeared on Post Office bulletin boards beginning with Scott #1132. See "Souvenir Pages" listed in the back of this book (see Table of Contents)

1455	8¢ Family Planning	03/18/72	.20	.20	.65	(4)	1.00	153
a	Yellow omitted		1,250.00					
c	Dark brown missing		9,500.00					
d	Tagging omitted		—					
	American Bicentennial Issue, Perf. 11 x 10.5							
1456	8¢ Glass Blower	07/04/72	.20	.20			1.00	50
1457	8¢ Silversmith	07/04/72	.20	.20			1.00	50
1458	8¢ Wigmaker	07/04/72	.20	.20			1.00	50
1459	8¢ Hatter	07/04/72	.20	.20			1.00	50
a	Block of 4, #1456-59		.65	.90	.80	(4)	2.50	
	Olympic Games Issue, (See also #C85)							
1460	6¢ Bicycling and Olympic Rings	08/17/72	.20	.20	1.25	(10)	1.00	67
	Cylinder flaw (broken red ring)		10.00					
1461	8¢ Bobsledding and Olympic Rings	08/17/72	.20	.20	1.60	(10)	1.00	180
a	Tagging omitted		7.50					
1462	15¢ Running and Olympic Rings	08/17/72	.30	.20	3.00	(10)	1.00	46
1463	8¢ Parent Teachers Association	09/15/72	.20	.20	.65	(4)	1.00	180

1484

1485

1486

1487

Copernicus
1473 – 1973

1488

| U.S. POSTAL SERVICE 8¢ | U.S. POSTAL SERVICE 8¢ | U.S. POSTAL SERVICE 8¢ | U.S. POSTAL SERVICE 8¢ | U.S. POSTAL SERVICE 8¢ |

1489   1490   1491   1492   1493

| Nearly 27 billion U.S. stamps are sold yearly to carry your letters to every corner of the world. | Mail is picked up from nearly a third of a million local collection boxes, as well as your mailbox. | More than 87 billion letters and packages are handled yearly—almost 300 million every delivery day. | The People in your Postal Service handle and deliver more than 500 million packages yearly. | Thousands of machines, buildings, and vehicles must be operated and maintained to keep your mail moving. |
| People Serving You | People Serving You | People Serving You | People Serving You | People Serving You |

| U.S. POSTAL SERVICE 8¢ | U.S. POSTAL SERVICE 8¢ | U.S. POSTAL SERVICE 8¢ | U.S. POSTAL SERVICE 8¢ | U.S. POSTAL SERVICE 8¢ |

1494   1495   1496   1497   1498

| The skill of sorting mail manually is still vital to delivery of your mail. | Employees use modern, high-speed equipment to sort and process huge volumes of mail in central locations. | Thirteen billion pounds of mail are handled yearly by postal employees as they speed your letters and packages. | Our customers include 54 million urban and 12 million rural families, plus 9 million businesses. | Employees cover 4 million miles each delivery day to bring mail to your home or business. |
| People Serving You | People Serving You | People Serving You | People Serving You | People Serving You |

Issues of 1973		Un	U	PB	#	FDC	Q(M)
American Arts Issue, Perf. 11							
1484 8¢ George Gershwin and Scene							
from "Porgy and Bess"	02/28/73	.20	.20	1.75	(12)	1.00	139
a Vertical pair, imperf. horizontally		240.00					
1485 8¢ Robinson Jeffers, Man and Children							
of Carmel with Burro	08/13/73	.20	.20	1.75	(12)	1.00	128
a Vertical pair, imperf. horizontally		250.00					
1486 8¢ Henry Ossawa Tanner,							
Palette and Rainbow	09/10/73	.20	.20	1.75	(12)	2.50	146
1487 8¢ Willa Cather, Pioneer Family							
and Covered Wagon	09/20/73	.20	.20	1.75	(12)	1.00	140
a Vertical pair, imperf. horizontally		275.00					
1488 8¢ Nicolaus Copernicus	04/23/73	.20	.20	.65	(4)	1.25	159
a Orange omitted		1,000.00					
b Black omitted		900.00					
Postal Service Employees Issue, Perf. 10.5 x 11							
1489 8¢ Stamp Counter	04/30/73	.20	.20			1.00	49
1490 8¢ Mail Collection	04/30/73	.20	.20			1.00	49
1491 8¢ Letter Facing on Conveyor	04/30/73	.20	.20			1.00	49
1492 8¢ Parcel Post Sorting	04/30/73	.20	.20			1.00	49
1493 8¢ Mail Canceling	04/30/73	.20	.20			1.00	49
1494 8¢ Manual Letter Routing	04/30/73	.20	.20			1.00	49
1495 8¢ Electronic Letter Routing	04/30/73	.20	.20			1.00	49
1496 8¢ Loading Mail on Truck	04/30/73	.20	.20			1.00	49
1497 8¢ Mail Carrier	04/30/73	.20	.20			1.00	49
1498 8¢ Rural Mail Delivery	04/30/73	.20	.20			1.00	49
a Strip of 10, #1489-98		1.75	2.00	3.25	(20)	5.00	
b As "a," tagging omitted		—					

#1489-98 were the first United States postage stamps to have printing on the back.

(See also 1559-62.)

Mary Lyon (1797-1849)

Mary Lyon, educator and founder of Mount Holyoke Female Seminary (now Mount Holyoke College), was raised in rural western Massachusetts. She was taught basic domestic skills such as baking, spinning, and weaving by her mother, and attended the village one-room school for her formal education. At the age of 17, she was teaching children in summer schools. Lyon used a $37 inheritance from her father, plus her earnings from teaching and weaving, to continue her education. She attended various academies where educators "talked to ladies as if they had brains." She was introduced to advanced subjects and current ideas. A stimulating teacher, she introduced novel classroom activities such as coloring maps and class discussions of current events. In 1834 she began promoting her ideas about a school for women. She publicized her plan and raised the first thousand dollars—she called this the cornerstone of the institution—from interested women. In 1837 the Mount Holyoke Female Seminary opened with eighty students. Lyon served as principal and teacher until her death twelve years later. ∎

	Issues of 1973		Un	U	PB	#	FDC	Q(M)
	Perf. 11							
1499	8¢ Harry S. Truman	05/08/73	.20	.20	.65	(4)	1.25	157
	Progress in Electronics Issue, (See also #C86)							
1500	6¢ Marconi's Spark							
	Coil and Gap	07/10/73	.20	.20	.55	(4)	1.00	53
1501	8¢ Transistors and Printed							
	Circuit Board	07/10/73	.20	.20	.70	(4)	1.00	160
a	Black omitted		450.00					
b	Tan and lilac omitted		1,250.00					
1502	15¢ Microphone, Speaker, Vacuum							
	Tube, TV Camera Tube	07/10/73	.30	.20	1.30	(4)	1.00	39
a	Black omitted		1,350.00					
1503	8¢ Lyndon B. Johnson	08/27/73	.20	.20	1.90	(12)	1.00	153
a	Horizontal pair, imperf. vertically		350.00					
	Issues of 1973-1974, Rural America Issue							
1504	8¢ Angus and Longhorn Cattle,							
	by F.C. Murphy	10/05/73	.20	.20	.65	(4)	1.00	146
a	Green and red brown omitted		950.00					
b	Vertical pair, imperf. between			—				
1505	10¢ Chautauqua Tent and							
	Buggies	08/06/74	.20	.20	.85	(4)	1.00	151
1506	10¢ Wheat Fields and Train	08/16/74	.20	.20	.85	(4)	1.00	141
a	Black and blue omitted		750.00					
	Issues of 1973, Christmas Issue, Perf. 10.5 x 11							
1507	8¢ Small Cowper Madonna,							
	by Raphael	11/07/73	.20	.20	1.75	(12)	1.00	885
	Pair with full vertical gutter between		—					
1508	8¢ Christmas Tree in							
	Needlepoint	11/07/73	.20	.20	1.75	(12)	1.00	940
	Pair with full horizontal gutter between		—					
a	Vertical pair, imperf. between		300.00					
	Issues of 1973-1974, Perf. 11 x 10.5							
1509	10¢ 50-Star and							
	13-Star Flags	12/08/73	.20	.20	4.25	(20)	1.00	
a	Horizontal pair, imperf. between		50.00	—				
b	Blue omitted		175.00	—				
c	Imperf., pair		950.00					
d	Horizontal pair, imperf. vertically		1,000.00					
e	Tagging omitted		9.00					
1510	10¢ Jefferson Memorial	12/14/73	.20	.20	.85	(4)	1.00	
a	Untagged (Bureau precanceled)			.20				
b	Booklet pane of 5 + label		1.65	.90			2.25	
c	Booklet pane of 8		1.65	1.00			2.50	
d	Booklet pane of 6	08/05/74	5.25	1.75			3.00	
e	Vertical pair, imperf. horizontally		525.00					
f	Vertical pair, imperf. between		—					
g	Tagging omitted		5.00					

1499

1500   **1501**   **1502**

1503

1504   **1505**   **1506**

1509

1510

1507   **1508**

	Issues of 1974		Un	U	PB	#	FDC	Q(M)
	Mineral Heritage Issue, Perf. 11							
1538	10¢ Petrified Wood	06/13/74	.20	.20			1.00	42
a	Light blue and yellow omitted		—					
1539	10¢ Tourmaline	06/13/74	.20	.20			1.00	42
a	Light blue omitted		—					
b	Black and purple omitted		—					
1540	10¢ Amethyst	06/13/74	.20	.20			1.00	42
a	Light blue and yellow omitted		—					
1541	10¢ Rhodochrosite	06/13/74	.20	.20			1.00	42
a	Block of 4, #1538-41		.80	.90	.90	(4)	2.75	
b	As "a," light blue and yellow omitted		1,900.00					
c	Light blue omitted		—					
d	Black and red omitted		—					
1542	10¢ First Kentucky Settlement-Ft. Harrod	06/15/74	.20	.20	.85	(4)	1.00	156
a	Dull black omitted		750.00					
b	Green, black and blue omitted		3,000.00					
c	Green omitted		—					
d	Green and black omitted		—					
e	Tagging omitted		—					
	American Bicentennial Issue, First Continental Congress							
1543	10¢ Carpenters' Hall	07/04/74	.20	.20			1.00	49
1544	10¢ "We Ask but for Peace, Liberty and Safety"	07/04/74	.20	.20			1.00	49
1545	10¢ "Deriving Their Just Powers from the Consent of the Governed"	07/04/74	.20	.20			1.00	49
1546	10¢ Independence Hall	07/04/74	.20	.20			1.00	49
a	Block of 4, #1543-46		.80	.90	.90	(4)	2.75	
1547	10¢ Energy Conservation	09/23/74	.20	.20	.85	(4)	1.00	149
a	Blue and orange omitted		850.00					
b	Orange and green omitted		600.00					
c	Green omitted		825.00					
	American Folklore Issue							
1548	10¢ Headless Horseman and Ichabod Crane	10/10/74	.20	.20	.85	(4)	1.25	157
1549	10¢ Retarded Children	10/12/74	.20	.20	.85	(4)	1.00	150
a	Tagging omitted		7.50					
	Christmas Issue, Perf. 10.5 x 11							
1550	10¢ Angel from Perussis Altarpiece	10/23/74	.20	.20	2.10	(10)	1.00	835
	Perf. 11 x 10.5							
1551	10¢ "The Road-Winter," by Currier and Ives	10/23/74	.20	.20	2.50	(12)	1.00	883
a	Buff omitted		35.00					
	Precanceled Self-Adhesive, Imperf.							
1552	10¢ Dove Weather Vane atop Mount Vernon	11/15/74	.20	.20	4.25	(20)	1.50	213
	Issues of 1975, American Arts Issue, Perf. 10.5 x 11							
1553	10¢ Benjamin West, Self-Portrait	02/10/75	.20	.20	2.10	(10)	1.00	157
	Perf. 11							
1554	10¢ Paul Laurence Dunbar and Lamp	05/01/75	.20	.20	2.10	(10)	1.50	146
a	Imperf., pair		1,300.00					
1555	10¢ D.W. Griffith and Motion-Picture Camera	05/27/75	.20	.20	.85	(4)	1.00	149
a	Brown omitted		625.00					

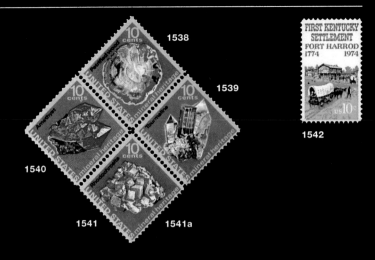

1538

1539

1540

1541 1541a

FIRST KENTUCKY
SETTLEMENT
FORT HARROD
1774 1974

1542

1543 1544

1545 1546 1546a

1547

1548

1549 1550

Retarded Children
Can Be Helped

1551

1552

Benjamin West
American artist
10 cents U.S. postage

1553

Paul Laurence
Dunbar
American poet
10 cents U.S. postage

1554

1555

1556

1557

1558

1559

1560

1561

YOUTHFUL HEROINE
On the dark night of April 26, 1777, 16-year-old Sybil Ludington rode her horse "Star" alone through the Connecticut countryside rallying her father's militia to repel a raid by the British on Danbury.

GALLANT SOLDIER
The conspicuously courageous actions of black foot soldier Salem Poor at the Battle of Bunker Hill on June 17, 1775, earned him citations for his bravery and leadership ability.

FINANCIAL HERO
Businessman and broker Haym Salomon was responsible for raising most of the money needed to finance the American Revolution and later to save the new nation from collapse.

1562

1563

FINANCIAL HERO
Businessman and broker Haym Salomon was responsible for raising most of the money needed to finance the American Revolution and later to save the new nation from collapse.

1564

1565   1566   1569

1567   1568   1568a

1570   1570a

	Issues of 1975		Un	U	PB	#	FDC	Q(M)
	Space Issues, Perf. 11							
1556	10¢ Pioneer 10 Passing							
	Jupiter	02/28/75	.20	.20	.85	(4)	1.25	174
a	Red and yellow omitted		1,400.00					
b	Blue omitted		950.00					
c	Tagging omitted		9.00					
1557	10¢ Mariner 10, Venus							
	and Mercury	04/04/75	.20	.20	.85	(4)	1.25	159
a	Red omitted		450.00					
b	Ultramarine and bister omitted		2,000.00					
c	Tagging omitted		9.00					
1558	10¢ Collective Bargaining	03/13/75	.20	.20	1.75	(8)	1.00	153
	Imperfs. of #1558 exist from printer's waste							
	American Bicentennial Issue Perf. 11 x 10.5							
1559	8¢ Sybil Ludington							
	Riding Horse	03/25/75	.20	.20	1.50	(10)	1.00	63
a	Back inscription omitted		210.00					
1560	10¢ Salem Poor Carrying							
	Musket	03/25/75	.20	.20	2.10	(10)	1.50	158
a	Back inscription omitted		210.00					
1561	10¢ Haym Salomon							
	Figuring Accounts	03/25/75	.20	.20	2.10	(10)	1.00	167
a	Back inscription omitted		210.00					
b	Red omitted		250.00					
1562	18¢ Peter Francisco							
	Shouldering Cannon	03/25/75	.35	.20	3.60	(10)	1.00	45
	Battle of Lexington & Concord, Perf. 11							
1563	10¢ "Birth of Liberty,"							
	by Henry Sandham	04/19/75	.20	.20	2.50	(12)	1.00	144
a	Vertical pair, imperf. horizontally		425.00					
	Battle of Bunker Hill							
1564	10¢ "Battle of Bunker							
	Hill," by John Trumbull	06/17/75	.20	.20	2.50	(12)	1.00	140
	Military Uniforms							
1565	10¢ Soldier with Flintlock							
	Musket, Uniform Button	07/04/75	.20	.20			1.00	45
1566	10¢ Sailor with Grappling							
	Hook, First Navy Jack, 1775	07/04/75	.20	.20			1.00	45
1567	10¢ Marine with Musket,							
	Full-Rigged Ship	07/04/75	.20	.20			1.00	45
1568	10¢ Militiaman with							
	Musket, Powder Horn	07/04/75	.20	.20			1.00	45
a	Block of 4, #1565-68		.85	.90	2.50	(12)	2.50	
	Apollo Soyuz Space Issue							
1569	10¢ Apollo and Soyuz							
	after Link-up and Earth	07/15/75	.20	.20			3.00	81
	Pair with full horizontal gutter between		—					
1570	10¢ Spacecraft before Link-up,							
	Earth and Project Emblem	07/15/75	.20	.20			3.00	81
a	Attached pair, #1569-70		.45	.40	2.50	(12)		
b	As "a," tagging omitted		30.00	—				
c	As "a," vertical pair,							
	imperf. horizontally		1,750.00					

1975-1981

	Issues of 1975		Un	U	PB	#	FDC	Q(M)
	Perf. 11 x 10.5							
1571	10¢ International Women's Year	08/26/75	.20	.20	1.30	(6)	1.00	146
	Postal Service Bicentennial Issue							
1572	10¢ Stagecoach and							
	Trailer Truck	09/03/75	.20	.20			1.00	42
1573	10¢ Old and New Locomotives	09/03/75	.20	.20			1.00	42
1574	10¢ Early Mail Plane and Jet	09/03/75	.20	.20			1.00	42
1575	10¢ Satellite for Mailgrams	09/03/75	.20	.20			1.00	42
a	Block of 4, #1572-75		.85	.90	2.50	(12)	2.50	
b	As "a," red "10¢" omitted		9,500.00					
	Perf. 11							
1576	10¢ World Peace Through Law	09/29/75	.20	.20	.85	(4)	1.25	147
a	Tagging omitted		8.00					
	Banking and Commerce Issue							
1577	10¢ Engine Turning, Indian Head							
	Penny and Morgan Silver Dollar	10/06/75	.25	.20			1.00	73
1578	10¢ Seated Liberty Quarter, $20							
	Gold Piece and Engine Turning	10/06/75	.25	.20			1.00	73
a	Attached pair, #1577-78		.50	.40	1.20	(4)	1.75	
b	Brown and blue omitted		2,000.00					
c	As "a," brn., blue and yel. omitted		2,500.00					
	Christmas Issue							
1579	(10¢) Madonna and Child,							
	by Domenico Ghirlandaio	10/14/75	.20	.20	2.50	(12)	1.00	739
a	Imperf., pair		90.00					
	Plate flaw ("d" damaged)		5.00	—				
	Perf. 11.2							
1580	(10¢) Christmas Card,							
	by Louis Prang, 1878	10/14/75	.20	.20	2.50	(12)	1.00	879
a	Imperf., pair		90.00					
c	Perf. 10.9		.25	.20	3.50	(12)		
	Perf. 10.5 x 11.3							
1580B	(10¢) Christmas Card,							
	by Louis Prang, 1878		.65	.20	15.00	(12)		
	Issues of 1977-1981, Americana Issue, Perf. 11 x 10.5 (Designs 18.5 x 22.5mm; #1590-90a, 17.5 x 20mm; see also 1606, 1608, 1610-19, 1622-23, 1625, 1811, 1813, 1816)							
1581	1¢ Inkwell & Quill	12/08/77	.20	.20	.25	(4)	1.00	
a	Untagged (Bureau precanceled)			.20				
d	Tagging omitted		4.50					
1582	2¢ Speaker's Stand	12/08/77	.20	.20	.25	(4)	1.00	
a	Untagged (Bureau precanceled)			.20				
b	Cream paper, dull gum, *1981*		.20	.20	.25	(4)		
c	Tagging omitted		4.50					
1583	Not assigned							
1584	3¢ Early Ballot Box	12/08/77	.20	.20	.30	(4)	1.00	
a	Untagged (Bureau precanceled)			.20				
b	Tagging omitted		7.50					
1585	4¢ Books, Bookmark, Eyeglasses	12/08/77	.20	.20	.40	(4)	1.00	
a	Untagged (Bureau precanceled)			1.25				
1586-89	Not assigned							
	Booklet Stamp							
1590	9¢ Capitol Dome, single (1591)							
	from booklet (1623a)	03/11/77	.45	.20			1.00	
	Booklet Stamp, Perf. 10							
1590A	Single (1591) from booklet (1623c)		22.50	15.00				
	#1590 is on white paper; #1591 is on gray paper.							

1572   1573

1571

1574   1575   1575a

1576

1577   1578   1578a

1581   1582

1579   1580

1584   1585

	Issues of 1975-1981		Un	U	PB/LP	#	FDC
	Coil Stamps, Perf. 10 Vertically						
1613	3.1¢ Six String Guitar	10/25/79	.20	.20	1.25	(2)	1.00
a	Untagged (Bureau precanceled)			.50			
b	Imperf., pair		1,400.00		3,600.00	(2)	
1614	7.7¢ Saxhorns	11/20/76	.20	.20	.90	(2)	1.00
a	Untagged (Bureau precanceled)			.35			
b	As "a," imperf., pair			1,600.00	4,250.00	(2)	
1615	7.9¢ Drum	04/23/76	.20	.20	.75	(2)	1.00
a	Untagged (Bureau precanceled)			.20			
b	Imperf., pair		600.00				
1615C	8.4¢ Steinway Grand Piano	07/13/78	.20	.20	3.25	(2)	1.00
d	Untagged (Bureau precanceled)		.30	.30			
e	As "d," pair, imperf. between			60.00	125.00	(2)	
f	As "d," imperf., pair			17.50	35.00	(2)	
	Americana Issue, Perf. 10 Vertically (See also #1581-82, 1584-85, 1590-99, 1603-05, 1811, 1813, 1816)						
1616	9¢ slate green Capitol Dome (1591)	03/05/76	.20	.20	.90	(2)	1.00
a	Imperf., pair		160.00		375.00	(2)	
b	Untagged (Bureau precanceled)			.35			
c	As "b," imperf., pair			700.00	—	(2)	
1617	10¢ purple Contemplation of Justice (1592)	11/04/77	.20	.20	1.00	(2)	1.00
	Dull finish gum		.30		2.50	(2)	
a	Untagged (Bureau precanceled)			.25			
b	Imperf., pair		60.00		125.00	(2)	
1618	13¢ brown Liberty Bell (1595)	11/25/75	.25	.20	.75	(2)	1.00
a	Untagged (Bureau precanceled)			.45			
b	Imperf., pair		25.00		65.00	(2)	
g	Pair, imperf. between		—				
1618C	15¢ Ft. McHenry Flag (1597)	06/30/78	.40	.20			1.00
d	Imperf., pair		25.00				
e	Pair, imperf. between		150.00				
f	Gray omitted		40.00				
i	Tagging omitted		20.00				
1619	16¢ blue Head of Liberty (1599)	03/31/78	.35	.20	1.50	(2)	1.00
a	Huck Press printing (white background with a bluish tinge, fraction of a millimeter smaller)		.50	.20			
1620-21	Not assigned						
	Perf. 11 x 10.75						
1622	13¢ Flag over Independence Hall	11/15/75	.25	.20	5.75	(20)	1.00
a	Horizontal pair, imperf. between		50.00				
b	Imperf., pair		1,100.00				
e	Horizontal pair, imperf. vertically		—				
f	Tagging omitted		4.00				
	Perf. 11.25						
1622C	13¢ Star Flag over Independence Hall		1.00	.25	20.00	(6)	
d	Vertical pair, imperf.		150.00				
	Booklet Stamps, Perf. 11						
1623	13¢ Flag over Capitol, single from booklet (1623a)		.25	.20			1.50
a	Booklet pane of 8, (1 #1590 and 7 #1623)	03/11/77	2.25	1.25			25.00
d	Attached pair, #1590 and 1623		.70	1.00			

| 1613 | 1614 | 1615 | 1615C |

1622

1623a

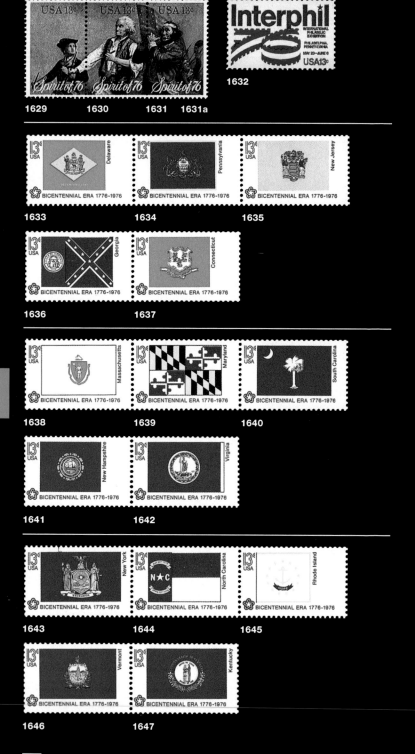

1629 1630 1631 1631a

1632

1633   1634   1635

1636   1637

1638   1639   1640

1641   1642

1643   1644   1645

1646   1647

Issues of 1975-1977		Un	U	PB	#	FDC	Q(M)
Booklet Stamps, Perf. 10 x 9.75							
1623B	13¢ Single from booklet	.80	.80				
c	Booklet pane of 8,						
	(1 #1590a and 7 #1623b)	29.00	—			12.50	
e	Attached pair, #1590a and 1623b	24.00	22.50				
	#1623, 1623b issued only in booklets. All stamps are imperf. at one side or imperf. at one side and bottom.						
1624	Not assigned						
Coil Stamp, Perf. 10 Vertically							
1625	13¢ Flag over Independence Hall (1622)	11/15/75	.25	.20			1.00	
a	Imperf. pair	25.00					
American Bicentennial Issue, Perf. 11							
1629	13¢ Drummer Boy	01/01/76	.25	.20			1.25	73
1630	13¢ Old Drummer	01/01/76	.25	.20			1.25	73
1631	13¢ Fifer	01/01/76	.25	.20			1.25	73
a	Strip of 3, #1629-31	.75	.75	3.50	(12)	2.00	
b	As "a," imperf.	1,050.00					
c	Imperf., pair, #1631	800.00					
1632	13¢ *Interphil* 76	01/17/76	.20	.20	1.00	(4)	1.00	158
State Flags							
1633	13¢ Delaware	02/23/76	.25	.20			1.50	9
1634	13¢ Pennsylvania	02/23/76	.25	.20			1.50	9
1635	13¢ New Jersey	02/23/76	.25	.20			1.50	9
1636	13¢ Georgia	02/23/76	.25	.20			1.50	9
1637	13¢ Connecticut	02/23/76	.25	.20			1.50	9
1638	13¢ Massachusetts	02/23/76	.25	.20			1.50	9
1639	13¢ Maryland	02/23/76	.25	.20			1.50	9
1640	13¢ South Carolina	02/23/76	.25	.20			1.50	9
1641	13¢ New Hampshire	02/23/76	.25	.20			1.50	9
1642	13¢ Virginia	02/23/76	.25	.20			1.50	9
1643	13¢ New York	02/23/76	.25	.20			1.50	9
1644	13¢ North Carolina	02/23/76	.25	.20			1.50	9
1645	13¢ Rhode Island	02/23/76	.25	.20			1.50	9
1646	13¢ Vermont	02/23/76	.25	.20			1.50	9
1647	13¢ Kentucky	02/23/76	.25	.20			1.50	9

Samuel Gompers (1850-1924)

Labor leader Samuel Gompers was born in London, England, but immigrated with his family to the United States in 1863. Gompers became a cigarmaker like his father, joining the Cigarmakers Union in 1864 and becoming its president in 13 years later. He became a naturalized citizen in 1872. Gompers helped establish the Federation of Organized Trades and Labor Unions of the United States and Canada, which in 1886 became the American Federation of Labor (AFL). The AFL's first president, he held this office for almost forty years. His mission was to improve the status of workers in practical ways by concentrating on issues such as shorter hours, higher wages, and safe working conditions. He favored economic action and strong labor organization to achieve these goals. During World War I, President Woodrow Wilson appointed him to the Council on National Defense and to the Commission on International Labor Legislation at the Versailles Peace Conference. ■

1976

	Issues of 1976		Un	U	FDC	Q(M)
	American Bicentennial Issue (continued), State Flags					
1648	13¢ Tennessee	02/23/76	.25	.20	1.50	9
1649	13¢ Ohio	02/23/76	.25	.20	1.50	9
1650	13¢ Louisiana	02/23/76	.25	.20	1.50	9
1651	13¢ Indiana	02/23/76	.25	.20	1.50	9
1652	13¢ Mississippi	02/23/76	.25	.20	1.50	9
1653	13¢ Illinois	02/23/76	.25	.20	1.50	9
1654	13¢ Alabama	02/23/76	.25	.20	1.50	9
1655	13¢ Maine	02/23/76	.25	.20	1.50	9
1656	13¢ Missouri	02/23/76	.25	.20	1.50	9
1657	13¢ Arkansas	02/23/76	.25	.20	1.50	9
1658	13¢ Michigan	02/23/76	.25	.20	1.50	9
1659	13¢ Florida	02/23/76	.25	.20	1.50	9
1660	13¢ Texas	02/23/76	.25	.20	1.50	9
1661	13¢ Iowa	02/23/76	.25	.20	1.50	9
1662	13¢ Wisconsin	02/23/76	.25	.20	1.50	9
1663	13¢ California	02/23/76	.25	.20	1.50	9
1664	13¢ Minnesota	02/23/76	.25	.20	1.50	9
1665	13¢ Oregon	02/23/76	.25	.20	1.50	9
1666	13¢ Kansas	02/23/76	.25	.20	1.50	9
1667	13¢ West Virginia	02/23/76	.25	.20	1.50	9

A·M·E·R·I·C·A·N C·O·M·M·E·M·O·R·A·T·I·V·E C·O·L·L·E·C·T·I·B·L·E·S

American Commemorative Panels

Obtain photo or steel engravings, mint condition stamps and subject related text presented on a beautifully designed page. Only $6.00* each, depending on the value of the stamps.

For more information call **1-800-STAMP-24**

Prices subject to change without notice.

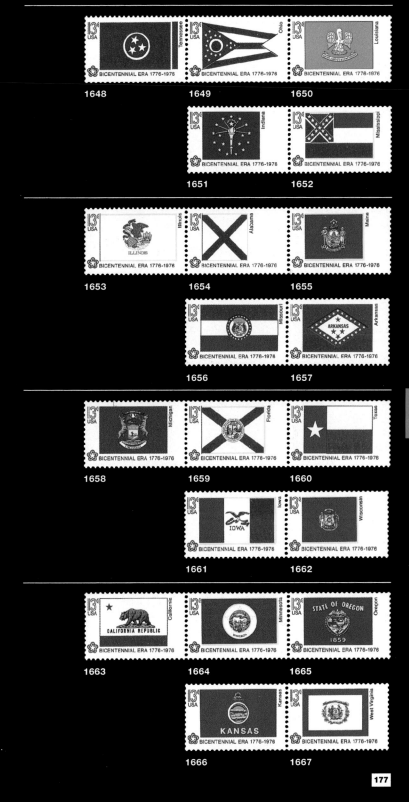

1648

1649

1650

1651

1652

1653

1654

1655

1656

1657

1658

1659

1660

1661

1662

1663

1664

1665

1666

1667

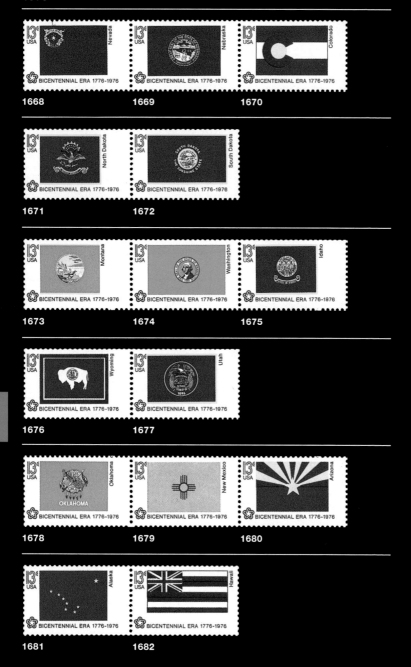

1668   1669   1670

1671   1672

1673   1674   1675

1676   1677

1678   1679   1680

1681   1682

Issues of 1976		Un	U	FDC	Q(M)
American Bicentennial Issue (continued), State Flags					
1668	13¢ Nevada	02/23/76	.25	.20	1.50	9
1669	13¢ Nebraska	02/23/76	.25	.20	1.50	9
1670	13¢ Colorado	02/23/76	.25	.20	1.50	9
1671	13¢ North Dakota	02/23/76	.25	.20	1.50	9
1672	13¢ South Dakota	02/23/76	.25	.20	1.50	9
1673	13¢ Montana	02/23/76	.25	.20	1.50	9
1674	13¢ Washington	02/23/76	.25	.20	1.50	9
1675	13¢ Idaho	02/23/76	.25	.20	1.50	9
1676	13¢ Wyoming	02/23/76	.25	.20	1.50	9
1677	13¢ Utah	02/23/76	.25	.20	1.50	9
1678	13¢ Oklahoma	02/23/76	.25	.20	1.50	9
1679	13¢ New Mexico	02/23/76	.25	.20	1.50	9
1680	13¢ Arizona	02/23/76	.25	.20	1.50	9
1681	13¢ Alaska	02/23/76	.25	.20	1.50	9
1682	13¢ Hawaii	02/23/76	.25	.20	1.50	9
a	Pane of 50, #1633-82		15.00	—	27.50	

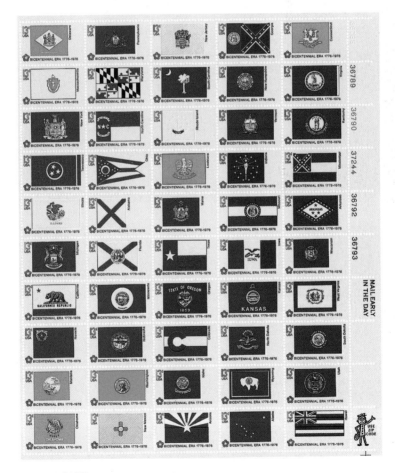

Example of 1682a

1976

	Issues of 1976		Un	U	PB	#	FDC	Q(M)
1683	13¢ Telephone Centennial	03/10/76	.25	.20	1.10	(4)	1.00	158
1684	13¢ Commercial Aviation	03/19/76	.25	.20	2.75	(10)	1.25	156
1685	13¢ Chemistry	04/06/76	.25	.20	3.25	(12)	1.50	158
	Pair with full vertical gutter between		—					
American Bicentennial Issue Souvenir Sheets, 5 stamps each, Perf. 11								
1686	13¢ The Surrender of Lord							
	Cornwallis at Yorktown, by							
	John Trumbull	05/29/76	3.25	—			6.00	2
a	13¢ Two American Officers		.45	.40				2
b	13¢ Gen. Benjamin Lincoln		.45	.40				2
c	13¢ George Washington		.45	.40				2
d	13¢ John Trumbull, Col. David Cobb,							
	General Friedrich von Steuben,							
	Marquis de Lafayette and							
	Thomas Nelson		.45	.40				2
e	13¢ Alexander Hamilton,							
	John Laurens and Walter Stewart		.45	.40				2
f	"USA/13¢" omitted on "b,"							
	"c" and "d," imperf.		—	2,250.00				
g	"USA/13¢" omitted on "a" and "e"		450.00	—				
h	Imperf. (untagged)			2,250.00				
i	"USA/13¢" omitted on "b," "c" and "d"		450.00					
j	"USA/13¢" double on "b"		—					
k	"USA/13¢" omitted on "c" and "d"		750.00					
l	"USA/13¢" omitted on "e"		500.00					
m	"USA/13¢" omitted, imperf.							
	(untagged)		—					
n	As "g", imperf., untagged		—					
1687	18¢ The Declaration of Independence,							
	4 July 1776 at Philadelphia,							
	by John Trumbull	05/29/76	4.25	—			7.50	2
a	18¢ John Adams, Roger Sherman							
	and Robert R. Livingston		.55	.55				2
b	18¢ Thomas Jefferson							
	and Benjamin Franklin		.55	.55				2
c	18¢ Thomas Nelson, Jr., Francis							
	Lewis, John Witherspoon and							
	Samuel Huntington		.55	.55				2
d	18¢ John Hancock and							
	Charles Thomson		.55	.55				2
e	18¢ George Read, John Dickinson							
	and Edward Rutledge		.55	.55				2
f	Design and marginal							
	inscriptions omitted		3,000.00					
g	"USA/18¢" omitted on "a" and "c"		750.00					
h	"USA/18¢" omitted							
	on "b," "d" and "e"		450.00					
i	"USA/18¢" omitted on "d"		500.00	500.00				
j	Black omitted in design		2,000.00					
k	"USA/18¢" omitted,							
	imperf. (untagged)		3,000.00					
m	"USA/18¢" omitted on "b" and "e"		500.00					

1683

1684

1685

The Surrender of Lord Cornwallis at Yorktown
From a Painting by John Trumbull

1686

The Declaration of Independence, 4 July 1776 at Philadelphia
From a Painting by John Trumbull

1687

1976-1977

Issues of 1976		Un	U	PB	#	FDC	Q(M)
American Bicentennial Issue, Perf. 11							
1690 13¢ Bust of Benjamin Franklin, Map of North America, 1776	06/01/76	.25	.20	1.10	(4)	1.00	165
a Light blue omitted		225.00					
b Tagging omitted		7.50					
Declaration of Independence, by John Trumbull							
1691 13¢ Delegates	07/04/76	.30	.20			1.00	41
1692 13¢ Delegates and John Adams	07/04/76	.30	.20			1.00	41
1693 13¢ Roger Sherman, Robert R. Livingston, Thomas Jefferson and Benjamin Franklin	07/04/76	.30	.20			1.00	41
1694 13¢ John Hancock, Charles Thomson, George Read, John Dickinson and Edward Rutledge	07/04/76	.30	.20			1.00	41
a Strip of 4, #1691-94		1.20	1.10	6.00	(20)	2.00	
Olympic Games Issue							
1695 13¢ Diver and Olympic Rings	07/16/76	.25	.20			1.00	46
1696 13¢ Skier and Olympic Rings	07/16/76	.25	.20			1.00	46
1697 13¢ Runner and Olympic Rings	07/16/76	.25	.20			1.00	46
1698 13¢ Skater and Olympic Rings	07/16/76	.25	.20			1.00	46
a Block of 4, #1695-98		1.10	1.40	3.25	(12)	2.00	
b As "a," imperf.		700.00					
1699 13¢ Clara Maass	08/18/76	.25	.20	3.25	(12)	1.25	131
a Horizontal pair, imperf. vertically		450.00					
1700 13¢ Adolph S. Ochs	09/18/76	.25	.20	1.10	(4)	1.00	158
Christmas Issue							
1701 13¢ Nativity, by John Singleton Copley	10/27/76	.25	.20	3.25	(12)	1.00	810
a Imperf., pair		100.00					
1702 13¢ "Winter Pastime," by Nathaniel Currier	10/27/76	.25	.20	2.75	(10)	1.00	482*
a Imperf., pair		100.00					
*Includes #1703 printing							
1703 13¢ as #1702	10/27/76	.25	.20	6.00	(20)	1.00	
a Imperf., pair		110.00					
b Vertical pair, imperf. between		—					
c Tagging omitted		12.50					

#1702 has overall tagging. Lettering at base is black and usually ½mm below design. As a rule, no "snowflaking" in sky or pond. Pane of 50 has margins on 4 sides with slogans. #1703 has block tagging the size of the printed area. Lettering at base is gray-black and usually ¾mm below design. "Snowflaking" generally in sky and pond. Pane of 50 has margin only at right or left and no slogans.

Issues of 1977, American Bicentennial Issue							
1704 13¢ Washington, Nassau Hall, Hessian Prisoners and 13-star Flag, by Charles Willson Peale	01/03/77	.25	.20	2.75	(10)	1.00	150
a Horizontal pair, imperf. vertically		550.00					
1705 13¢ Sound Recording	03/23/77	.25	.20	1.10	(4)	1.25	177

1690

1691   **1692**   **1693**   **1694 1694a**

1695   **1696**

1699   **1700**

1697   **1698 1698a**

1701   **1702**   **1703**

1705

1704

Issues of 1977		Un	U	PB	#	FDC	Q(M)
American Bicentennial Issue, Perf. 11							
1722 13¢ Herkimer at Oriskany,							
by Frederick Yohn	08/06/77	.25	.20	2.75	(10)	1.00	156
Energy Issue							
1723 13¢ Energy Conservation	10/20/77	.25	.20			1.25	79
1724 13¢ Energy Development	10/20/77	.25	.20			1.25	79
a Attached pair, #1723-24		.50	.50	3.25	(12)		
1725 13¢ First Civil Settlement							
Alta, California	09/09/77	.25	.20	1.10	(4)	1.00	154
American Bicentennial Issue							
1726 13¢ Members of Continental							
Congress in Conference	09/30/77	.25	.20	1.10	(4)	1.00	168
1727 13¢ Talking Pictures	10/06/77	.25	.20	1.10	(4)	1.50	157
American Bicentennial Issue							
1728 13¢ Surrender of Burgoyne,							
at Saratoga	10/07/77	.25	.20	2.75	(10)	1.00	154
Christmas Issue							
1729 13¢ Washington at Valley							
Forge, by J.C. Leyendecker	10/21/77	.25	.20	5.75	(20)	1.00	882
a Imperf., pair		75.00					
1730 13¢ Rural Mailbox	10/21/77	.25	.20	2.75	(10)	1.00	922
a Imperf., pair		300.00					
Issues of 1978							
1731 13¢ Carl Sandburg	01/06/78	.25	.20	1.10	(4)	1.00	157
Captain Cook Issue							
1732 13¢ Capt. James Cook							
Alaska, by Nathaniel Dance	01/20/78	.25	.20			1.25	101
1733 13¢ *Resolution* and *Discovery*							
Hawaii, by John Webber	01/20/78	.25	.20			1.25	101
a Vertical pair, imperf. horizontally		—					
b Attached pair, #1732-33		.50	.50	1.10	(4)		
c As " b," imperf. between		4,500.00					
1734 13¢ Indian Head Penny	01/11/78	.25	.20	1.25	(4)	1.00	
Pair with full horizontal gutter between		—					
a Horizontal pair, imperf. vertically		300.00					
1735 (15¢) "A" Stamp	05/22/78	.25	.20	1.25	(4)	1.00	
a Imperf., pair		90.00					
b Vertical pair, imperf. horizontally		700.00					
c Perf. 11.2		.25	.20	1.75	(4)		
Booklet Stamp, Perf. 11 x 10.5							
1736 (15¢) "A" orange Eagle (1735),							
single from booklet	05/22/78	.25	.20			1.00	
a Booklet pane of 8	05/22/78	2.25	1.25			2.50	
Roses Booklet Issue, Perf. 10							
1737 15¢ Roses, single from							
booklet	07/11/78	.25	.20			1.00	
a Booklet pane of 8	07/11/78	2.25	1.25			2.50	
b As "a," imperf.		—					
c As "a," tagging omitted		40.00	—				

#1736-37 issued only in booklets. All stamps are imperf. on one side or on one side and bottom.

1723

1722

1724   1724a

1725

1726   1727

1728

1729   1730

1732

1731

1733   1733b

1734

1735   1737

	Issues of 1978		Un	U	PB	#	FDC	Q(M)
	CAPEX '78 Souvenir Sheet, Perf. 11							
1757	13¢ Souvenir sheet of 8	06/10/78	2.00	2.00	2.25	(8)	2.75	15
a	13¢ Cardinal		.25	.20				15
b	13¢ Mallard		.25	.20				15
c	13¢ Canada Goose		.25	.20				15
d	13¢ Blue Jay		.25	.20				15
e	13¢ Moose		.25	.20				15
f	13¢ Chipmunk		.25	.20				15
g	13¢ Red Fox		.25	.20				15
h	13¢ Raccoon		.25	.20				15
i	Yellow, green, red, brown and black (litho.) omitted		7,000.00					
1758	15¢ Photography	06/26/78	.30	.20	4.00	(12)	1.00	163
1759	15¢ Viking Missions to Mars	07/20/78	.30	.20	1.35	(4)	1.00	159
	Wildlife Conservation: American Owls Issue							
1760	15¢ Great Gray Owl	08/26/78	.30	.20			1.25	47
1761	15¢ Saw-Whet Owl	08/26/78	.30	.20			1.25	47
1762	15¢ Barred Owl	08/26/78	.30	.20			1.25	47
1763	15¢ Great Horned Owl	08/26/78	.30	.20			1.25	47
a	Block of 4, #1760-63		1.25	1.25	1.40	(4)	2.00	
	Wildlife Conservation: American Trees Issue							
1764	15¢ Giant Sequoia	10/09/78	.30	.20			1.25	42
1765	15¢ White Pine	10/09/78	.30	.20			1.25	42
1766	15¢ White Oak	10/09/78	.30	.20			1.25	42
1767	15¢ Gray Birch	10/09/78	.30	.20			1.25	42
a	Block of 4, #1764-67		1.25	1.25	4.00	(12)	2.00	
b	As "a," imperf. horizontally		15,000.00					

Harvey Cushing M.D. (1869-1939)

Harvey Williams Cushing—the leading American neurosurgeon of the early 20th century—developed techniques and procedures that reduced the danger and rate of mortality in brain surgery. A pioneer in the use of x-rays and a proponent of pulse and respiration monitoring during surgery, he also devised a method for using local anesthesia during brain operations. Educated at Yale University and Harvard Medical School, Cushing studied for another four years, first at Johns Hopkins Hospital in Baltimore, Maryland, and then abroad. He returned in 1901—bringing with him a sphygmomanometer (blood pressure measuring device) acquired in Italy—to work as a surgeon at Johns Hopkins. In 1912 he became the Moseley Professor of Surgery at Harvard at the Peter Bent Brigham Hospital in Boston where he worked exclusively as a neuro-surgeon. In 1933 Cushing became the first Sterling professor of neur-ology at Yale. Internationally known for his scientific monographs, particularly *The Pituitary Body and its Disorders*, Cushing spent four years writing *The Life of Sir William Osler*, which won the Pulitzer Prize for biography in 1925. ■

a   b   c   d

1757   e   f   g   h

1758

1759

1760   1761

1762   1763 1763a

1764   1765

1766   1767   1767a

1768

1769

1770

1771

1772

1775   1776

1773   1774

1777   1778   1778a

1779   1780

1781   1782   1782a

1783   1784

1785   1786   1786a

	Issues of 1978		Un	U	PB	#	FDC	Q(M)
	Christmas Issues, Perf. 11							
1768	15¢ Madonna and Child							
	with Cherubim,							
	by Andrea della Robbia	10/18/78	.30	.20	4.00	(12)	1.00	963
a	Imperf., pair		90.00					
1769	15¢ Child on Hobby Horse							
	and Christmas Trees	10/18/78	.30	.20	4.00	(12)	1.00	917
	Pair with full horizontal gutter between		—					
a	Imperf., pair		100.00					
b	Vertical pair, imperf. horizontally		2,000.00					
	Issues of 1979, Perf. 11							
1770	15¢ Robert F. Kennedy	01/12/79	.35	.20	1.75	(4)	1.50	159
	Black Heritage Issue							
1771	15¢ Martin Luther King, Jr.,							
	and Civil Rights Marchers	01/13/79	.30	.20	4.00	(12)	2.00	166
a	Imperf., pair		—					
1772	15¢ International Year							
	of the Child	02/15/79	.30	.20	1.40	(4)	1.00	163
	Literary Arts Issue, Perf. 10.5 x 11							
1773	15¢ John Steinbeck,							
	by Philippe Halsman	02/27/79	.30	.20	1.40	(4)	1.00	155
1774	15¢ Albert Einstein	03/04/79	.35	.20	1.75	(4)	3.00	157
	Pair with full horizontal gutter between		—					
	American Folk Art: Pennsylvania Toleware Issue, Perf. 11							
1775	15¢ Straight-Spout Coffeepot	04/19/79	.30	.20			1.00	44
1776	15¢ Tea Caddy	04/19/79	.30	.20			1.00	44
1777	15¢ Sugar Bowl	04/19/79	.30	.20			1.00	44
1778	15¢ Curved-Spout Coffeepot	04/19/79	.30	.20			1.00	44
a	Block of 4, #1775-78		1.25	1.25	3.25	(10)	2.00	
b	As "a," imperf. horizontally		4,250.00					
	American Architecture Issue							
1779	15¢ Virginia Rotunda,							
	by Thomas Jefferson	06/04/79	.30	.20			1.00	41
1780	15¢ Baltimore Cathedral,							
	by Benjamin Latrobe	06/04/79	.30	.20			1.00	41
1781	15¢ Boston State House,							
	by Charles Bulfinch	06/04/79	.30	.20			1.00	41
1782	15¢ Philadelphia Exchange,							
	by William Strickland	06/04/79	.30	.20			1.00	41
a	Block of 4, #1779-82		1.25	1.50	1.45	(4)	2.00	
	Endangered Flora Issue							
1783	15¢ Persistent Trillium	06/07/79	.30	.20			1.00	41
1784	15¢ Hawaiian Wild							
	Broadbean	06/07/79	.30	.20			1.00	41
1785	15¢ Contra Costa Wallflower	06/07/79	.30	.20			1.00	41
1786	15¢ Antioch Dunes							
	Evening Primrose	06/07/79	.30	.20			1.00	41
a	Block of 4, #1783-86		1.25	1.25	4.00	(12)	2.00	
	As "a," full vertical gutter between		—					
b	As "a," imperf.		600.00					

Issues of 1979			Un	UPB	PB	#	FDC	Q(M)
1787	15¢ Seeing Eye Dogs	06/15/79	.30	.20	6.50	(20)	1.25	162
a	Imperf., pair		425.00					
b	Tagging omitted		10.00					
1788	15¢ Special Olympics	08/09/79	.30	.20	3.25	(10)	1.25	166
	American Bicentennial Issue, Perf. 11 x 12							
1789	15¢ John Paul Jones,							
	by Charles Willson Peale	09/23/79	.30	.20	3.25	(10)	1.50	160
c	Vertical pair, imperf. horizontally		175.00					
1789A	Perf. 11		.55	.20	4.00	(10)		
d	Vertical pair,							
	imperf. horizontally		150.00					
1789B	Perf. 12		2,500.00	1,000.00	27,500.00	(10)		
	Numerous varieties of printer's waste of #1789 exist							
	Olympic Summer Games Issue, Perf. 11 (See also #C97)							
1790	10¢ Javelin Thrower	09/05/79	.20	.20	3.00	(12)	1.00	67
1791	15¢ Runner	09/28/79	.30	.20			1.25	47
1792	15¢ Swimmer	09/28/79	.30	.20			1.25	47
1793	15¢ Rowers	09/28/79	.30	.20			1.25	47
1794	15¢ Equestrian Contestant	09/28/79	.30	.20			1.25	47
a	Block of 4, #1791-94		1.25	1.50	4.00	(12)	2.00	
b	As "a," imperf.		1,500.00					
	Issues of 1980, Olympic Winter Games Issue, Perf. 11 x 10.5							
1795	15¢ Speed Skater	02/01/80	.35	.20			1.25	52
1796	15¢ Downhill Skier	02/01/80	.35	.20			1.25	52
1797	15¢ Ski Jumper	02/01/80	.35	.20			1.25	52
1798	15¢ Ice Hockey	02/01/80	.35	.20			1.25	52
a	Perf. 11, #1795-98		1.05	.60				
b	Block of 4, #1795-98		1.50	1.40	4.50	(12)	2.00	
c	Block of 4, #1795a-98a		4.25	3.50	14.00	(12)		
	Issues of 1979, Christmas Issue, Perf. 11							
1799	15¢ Virgin and Child with							
	Cherubim, by Gerard David	10/18/79	.30	.20	4.00	(12)	1.25	874
a	Imperf., pair		90.00					
b	Vertical pair, imperf. horizontally		700.00					
c	pair, imperf. between		2,250.00					
1800	15¢ Santa Claus, Christmas							
	Tree Ornament	10/18/79	.30	.20	4.00	(12)	1.25	932
a	Green and yellow omitted		625.00					
b	Green, yellow and tan omitted		700.00					
	Performing Arts Issue							
1801	15¢ Will Rogers and Rogers as a							
	Cowboy Humorist	11/04/79	.30	.20	4.00	(12)	1.25	161
a	Imperf., pair		225.00					
1802	15¢ Vietnam Veterans	11/11/79	.30	.20	3.25	(10)	3.00	173
	Issues of 1980 (continued), Performing Arts Issue							
1803	15¢ W.C. Fields and							
	Fields as a Juggler	01/29/80	.30	.20	4.00	(12)	1.75	169
	Black Heritage Issue							
1804	15¢ Benjamin Banneker							
	and Banneker as Surveyor	02/15/80	.35	.20	4.50	(12)	2.00	160
a	Horizontal pair, imperf. vertically		800.00					

1787

1788

1789

1790

1791

1792

1793

1794

1794a

1795

1796

1797

1798

1798b

1799

1800

1801

1802

1803

1804

1980

	Issues of 1980		Un	U	PB	#	FDC	Q(M)
1831	15¢ Organized Labor	09/01/80	.30	.20	3.50	(12)	1.00	167
a	Imperf., pair		375.00					
	Literary Arts Issue, Edith Wharton, Perf. 10.5 x 11							
1832	15¢ Edith Wharton Reading							
	Letter	09/05/80	.30	.20	1.30	(4)	1.00	163
	Perf. 11							
1833	15¢ Education	09/12/80	.30	.20	1.90	(6)	1.50	160
a	Horizontal pair, imperf. vertically		240.00					
	American Folk Art Issue, Pacific Northwest Indian Masks							
1834	15¢ Heiltsuk, Bella Bella Tribe	09/25/80	.30	.20			1.00	39
1835	15¢ Chilkat Tlingit Tribe	09/25/80	.30	.20			1.00	39
1836	15¢ Tlingit Tribe	09/25/80	.30	.20			1.00	39
1837	15¢ Bella Coola Tribe	09/25/80	.30	.20			1.00	39
a	Block of 4, #1834-37		1.25	1.25	4.00	(10)	2.00	
	American Architecture Issue							
1838	15¢ Smithsonian Institution,							
	by James Renwick	10/09/80	.30	.20			1.00	39
1839	15¢ Trinity Church, by Henry							
	Hobson Richardson	10/09/80	.30	.20			1.00	39
1840	15¢ Pennsylvania Academy							
	of Fine Arts, by Frank Furness	10/09/80	.30	.20			1.00	39
1841	15¢ Lyndhurst, by Alexander							
	Jefferson Davis	10/09/80	.30	.20			1.00	39
a	Block of 4, #1838-41		1.25	1.50	1.50	(4)	1.75	
b	As "a", red omitted on #1838,1839		400.00					
	Christmas Issue							
1842	15¢ Madonna and Child							
	from Epiphany Window,							
	Washington Cathedral	10/31/80	.30	.20	4.00	(12)	1.25	693
a	Imperf., pair		70.00					
	Pair with full vertical gutter between		—					
1843	15¢ Wreath and Toys	10/31/80	.30	.20	6.50	(20)	1.25	719
a	Imperf., pair		70.00					
b	Buff omitted		25.00					
c	Vertical pair, imperf. horizontally		—					
d	Horizontal pair, imperf. between		4,000.00					

Organized Labor
Proud and Free
USA 15c

1831

Edith Wharton
USA 15c

1832

1834 **1835**

Heiltsuk, Bella Bella
Indian Art USA 15c

Chilkat Tlingit
Indian Art USA 15c

Tlingit
Indian Art USA 15c

Bella Coola
Indian Art USA 15c

1836 **1837** **1837a**

Olen by Josef Albers USA 15c
Learning
never ends

1833

1838 **1839**

Renwick 1818-1895 Smithsonian Washington
Architecture USA 15c

Richardson 1838-1886 Trinity Church Boston
Architecture USA 15c

Furness 1839-1912 Penn Academy Philadelphia
Architecture USA 15c

AJ Davis 1803-1892 Lyndhurst Tarrytown NY
Architecture USA 15c

1840 **1841** **1841a**

Christmas USA 15c

1842

USA 15c
Season's Greetings

1843

Issues of 1981-1985		Un	U	PB/PNC	#	FDC	Q(M)
Great Americans Issue (continued), Perf. 11							
1864	30¢ Frank C. Laubach 09/02/84	.60	.20	3.50	(6)	1.00	
a	Perf. 11.2, large block tagging	.55	.20	3.25	(4)		
b	Perf. 11.2, overall tagging	1.75	.20	22.50	(4)		
Perf. 11 x 10.5							
1865	35¢ Charles R. Drew, MD 06/03/81	.75	.20	4.25	(4)	1.75	
1866	37¢ Robert Millikan 01/26/82	.80	.20	3.75	(4)	1.25	
a	Tagging omitted	10.00					
Perf. 11							
1867	39¢ Grenville Clark 03/20/85	.90	.20	5.75	(6)	1.25	
a	Vertical pair, imperf. horizontally	600.00					
b	Vertical pair, imperf. between	2,000.00					
c	Perf. 10.9, large block tagging	.90	.20	5.75	(6)		
d	Perf. 11.2, large block tagging	.90	.20	5.75	(4)		
1868	40¢ Lillian M. Gilbreth 02/24/84	.90	.20	6.50	(6)	1.50	
a	Perf. 11.2, large block tagging	.90	.20	6.50	(4)		
1869	50¢ Chester W. Nimitz 02/22/85	.95	.20	7.50	(4)	2.00	
a	Perf. 11.2, large block tagging, dull gum	.95	.20	6.25	(4)		
b	Tagging omitted	11.00					
c	Perf. 11.2, tagging omitted, dull gum	8.00					
d	Perf. 11.2, overall tagging, dull gum	1.50	.20	8.50	(4)		
e	Perf. 11.2, prephosphored uncoated paper, shiny gum	.90	.20	5.00	(4)		
1870-73	Not assigned						
1874	15¢ Everett Dirksen 01/04/81	.30	.20	1.40	(4)	1.00	160
Black Heritage Issue							
1875	15¢ Whitney Moore Young at Desk 01/30/81	.35	.20	1.75	(4)	1.75	160
Flower Issue							
1876	18¢ Rose 04/23/81	.35	.20			1.00	53
1877	18¢ Camellia 04/23/81	.35	.20			1.00	53
1878	18¢ Dahlia 04/23/81	.35	.20			1.00	53
1879	18¢ Lily 04/23/81	.35	.20			1.00	53
a	Block of 4, #1876-79	1.40	1.25	1.75	(4)	2.50	
Wildlife Booklet Issue							
1880	18¢ Bighorn Sheep 05/14/81	.55	.20			1.00	
1881	18¢ Puma 05/14/81	.55	.20			1.00	
1882	18¢ Harbor Seal 05/14/81	.55	.20			1.00	
1883	18¢ Buffalo 05/14/81	.55	.20			1.00	
1884	18¢ Brown Bear 05/14/81	.55	.20			1.00	
1885	18¢ Polar Bear 05/14/81	.55	.20			1.00	
1886	18¢ Elk (Wapiti) 05/14/81	.55	.20			1.00	
1887	18¢ Moose 05/14/81	.55	.20			1.00	
1888	18¢ White-Tailed Deer 05/14/81	.55	.20			1.00	
1889	18¢ Pronghorn Antelope 05/14/81	.55	.20			1.00	
a	Booklet pane of 10, #1880-89	8.50	7.00			5.00	
#1880-89 issued only in booklets. All stamps are imperf. at one side or imperf. at one side and bottom.							
Flag and Anthem Issue							
1890	18¢ "... for amber waves of grain" 04/24/81	.35	.20	2.25	(6)	1.00	
a	Imperf., pair	110.00					
b	Vertical pair, imperf. horizontally	850.00					
Coil Stamp, Perf. 10 Vertically							
1891	18¢ "...from sea to shining sea" 04/24/81	.35	.20	4.00	(3)	1.50	
a	Imperf., pair	30.00	—				

Beginning with #1891, all coil stamps except 1947 feature a small plate number at the bottom of the design at varying intervals in a roll, depending on the press used. The basic "plate number coil" (PNC) collecting unit is a strip of three stamps, with the plate number appearing on the middle stamp. PNC values are for the most common plate number.

1864

1865

1866

1867

1868

1869

1876

1877

USA 15c
Everett Dirksen

1874

Whitney Moore Young
Black Heritage USA 15c

1875

Rose USA 18c

Camellia USA 18c

Dahlia USA 18c

Lily USA 18c

1878

1879

1879a

1880

1881

1882

1883

1884

1885

1886

1887

1888

1889

1889a

...for amber waves of grain

1890

...from sea to shining sea

1891

1981-1984

Issues of 1981-1984			Un	U	PB	#	FDC	Q(M)
Transportation Issue (continued)								
1905	11¢ RR Caboose 1890s	02/03/84	.30	.20	3.50	(3)	1.50	
a	Untagged (Bureau precanceled)		.25	.20	3.00	(3)		
1906	17¢ Electric Auto 1917	06/25/81	.35	.20	2.00	(3)	1.00	
a	Untagged (Bureau precanceled)		.35	.35	3.50	(3)		
b	Imperf., pair		165.00		—	(2)		
c	As "a," imperf., pair		650.00		—	(2)		
1907	18¢ Surrey 1890s	05/18/81	.35	.20	2.75	(3)	1.00	
a	Imperf., pair		140.00		—	(2)		
1908	20¢ Fire Pumper 1860s	12/10/81	.35	.20	2.00	(3)	2.00	
a	Imperf., pair		110.00		300.00	(2)		

Values for plate # coil strips of 3 stamps for #1897-1908 are for the most common plate numbers. Other plate #s and strips of 5 stamps may have higher values.

Issue of 1983, Express Mail Booklet Issue, Perf. 10 Vertically								
1909	$9.35 Eagle and Moon, single from booklet	08/12/83	21.00	15.00			45.00	
a	Booklet pane of 3		65.00	—			125.00	

#1909 issued only in booklets. All stamps are imperf. at top and bottom or imperf. at top, bottom and right side.

Issues of 1981, Perf. 10.5 x 11								
1910	18¢ American Red Cross	05/01/81	.35	.20	1.50	(4)	1.25	165
Perf. 11								
1911	18¢ Savings and Loans	05/08/81	.35	.20	1.50	(4)	1.00	107
Space Achievement Issue, Perf. 11								
1912	18¢ Exploring the Moon — Moon Walk	05/21/81	.40	.20			1.00	42
1913	18¢ Benefiting Mankind (upper left) Columbia Space Shuttle	05/21/81	.40	.20			1.00	42
1914	18¢ Benefiting Mankind— Space Shuttle Deploying Satellite	05/21/81	.40	.20			1.00	42
1915	18¢ Understanding the Sun— Skylab	05/21/81	.40	.20			1.00	42
1916	18¢ Probing the Planets— Pioneer 11	05/21/81	.40	.20			1.00	42
1917	18¢ Benefiting Mankind— Columbia Space Shuttle Lifting Off	05/21/81	.40	.20			1.00	42
1918	18¢ Benefiting Mankind—Space Shuttle Preparing to Land	05/21/81	.40	.20			1.00	42
1919	18¢ Comprehending the Universe — Telescope	05/21/81	.40	.20			1.00	42
a	Block of 8, #1912-19		3.25	3.00	3.75	(8)	3.00	
b	As "a," imperf.		8,000.00					
1920	18¢ Professional Management	06/18/81	.35	.20	1.50	(4)	1.00	99
Preservation of Wildlife Habitats Issue								
1921	18¢ Save Wetland Habitats— Great Blue Heron	06/26/81	.35	.20			1.00	45
1922	18¢ Save Grassland Habitats— Badger	06/26/81	.35	.20			1.00	45
1923	18¢ Save Mountain Habitats— Grizzly Bear	06/26/81	.35	.20			1.00	45
1924	18¢ Save Woodland Habitats— Ruffled Grouse	06/26/81	.35	.20			1.00	45
a	Block of 4, #1921-24		1.50	1.25	2.00	(4)	2.50	

1905   1906   1907   1908

1909   1910   1911

1912   1913   1914   1915

1916   1917   1918   1919   1919a

1920   1921   1922   1923   1924   1924a

1925

1926

1927

1928 **1929**

1930 **1931**

1931a

1932

1933

1934

1935

1936

1937

1938 **1938a**

Issues of 1981		Un	U	PB	#	FDC	Q(M)
Perf. 11							
1925	18¢ International Year of the Disabled 06/29/81	.35	.20	1.50	(4)	1.00	100
a	Vertical pair, imperf. horizontally	2,600.00					
1926	18¢ Edna St. Vincent Millay 07/10/81	.35	.20	1.50	(4)	1.00	100
a	Black omitted	300.00	—				
1927	18¢ Alcoholism 08/19/81	.40	.20	10.00	(6)	2.00	98
a	Imperf., pair	400.00					
b	Vertical pair, imperf. horizontally	2,500.00					
American Architecture Issue							
1928	18¢ NYU Library, by Sanford White 08/28/81	.40	.20			1.00	42
1929	18¢ Biltmore House, by Richard Morris Hunt 08/28/81	.40	.20			1.00	42
1930	18¢ Palace of the Arts, by Bernard Maybeck 08/28/81	.40	.20			1.00	42
1931	18¢ National Farmer's Bank, by Louis Sullivan 08/28/81	.40	.20			1.00	42
a	Block of 4, #1928-31	1.65	1.75	2.10	(4)	2.50	
American Sports Issue, Perf. 10.5 x 11							
1932	18¢ Babe Zaharias Holding Trophy 09/22/81	.40	.20	3.00	(4)	7.00	102
1933	18¢ Bobby Jones Teeing off 09/22/81	.40	.20	3.00	(4)	10.00	99
Perf. 11							
1934	18¢ Frederic Remington 10/09/81	.35	.20	1.60	(4)	1.25	101
a	Vertical pair, imperf. between	275.00					
b	Brown omitted	450.00					
1935	18¢ James Hoban 10/13/81	.35	.20	1.60	(4)	1.00	101
1936	20¢ James Hoban 10/13/81	.35	.20	1.65	(4)	1.00	167
American Bicentennial Issue							
1937	18¢ Battle of Yorktown 1781 10/16/81	.35	.20			1.00	81
1938	18¢ Battle of the Virginia Capes 1781 10/16/81	.35	.20			1.00	81
a	Attached pair, #1937-38	.90	.75	2.00	(4)	1.50	
b	As "a," black omitted	400.00					

Sinclair Lewis (1885 to 1951)

The prolific writer of 22 novels and three plays, Sinclair Lewis, in 1930, became the first American to receive the Nobel Prize for Literature. Born in the midwestern town of Sauk Centre, Minnesota, he drew on his hometown experiences in crafting his novels. *Babbitt* and *Main Street,* two of his most famous works, both nominated for the Pulitzer Prize, portray the provinciality of small-town America. Despite his extensive foreign travel, Lewis claimed, "My real travelling has been sitting in Pullman smoking cars, in a Minnesota village, on a Vermont farm, in a hotel in Kansas City or Savannah, listening to the normal daily drone of what are to me the most fascinating and exotic people in the world—the Average Citizens of the United States, with their friendliness to strangers and their rough teasing, their passion for material advancement and their shy idealism, their interest in all the world and their boastful provincialism...." Addressing issues about race, women, and the powerless in American society, Lewis's works continue to be pertinent today. ■

Issues of 1982		Un	U	FDC	Q(M)
State Birds & Flowers Issue, Perf. 10.5 x 11					
1953 20¢ Alabama: Yellowhammer and Camellia	04/14/82	.50	.25	1.25	13
1954 20¢ Alaska: Willow Ptarmigan and Forget-Me-Not	04/14/82	.50	.25	1.25	13
1955 20¢ Arizona: Cactus Wren and Saguaro Cactus Blossom	04/14/82	.50	.25	1.25	13
1956 20¢ Arkansas: Mockingbird and Apple Blossom	04/14/82	.50	.25	1.25	13
1957 20¢ California: California Quail and California Poppy	04/14/82	.50	.25	1.25	13
1958 20¢ Colorado: Lark Bunting and Rocky Mountain Columbine	04/14/82	.50	.25	1.25	13
1959 20¢ Connecticut: Robin and Mountain Laurel	04/14/82	.50	.25	1.25	13
1960 20¢ Delaware: Blue Hen Chicken and Peach Blossom	04/14/82	.50	.25	1.25	13
1961 20¢ Florida: Mockingbird and Orange Blossom	04/14/82	.50	.25	1.25	13
1962 20¢ Georgia: Brown Thrasher and Cherokee Rose	04/14/82	.50	.25	1.25	13
1963 20¢ Hawaii: Hawaiian Goose and Hibiscus	04/14/82	.50	.25	1.25	13
1964 20¢ Idaho: Mountain Bluebird and Syringa	04/14/82	.50	.25	1.25	13
1965 20¢ Illinois: Cardinal and Violet	04/14/82	.50	.25	1.25	13
1966 20¢ Indiana: Cardinal and Peony	04/14/82	.50	.25	1.25	13
1967 20¢ Iowa: Eastern Goldfinch and Wild Rose	04/14/82	.50	.25	1.25	13
1968 20¢ Kansas: Western Meadowlark and Sunflower	04/14/82	.50	.25	1.25	13
1969 20¢ Kentucky: Cardinal and Goldenrod	04/14/82	.50	.25	1.25	13
1970 20¢ Louisiana: Brown Pelican and Magnolia	04/14/82	.50	.25	1.25	13
1971 20¢ Maine: Chickadee and White Pine Cone and Tassel	04/14/82	.50	.25	1.25	13
1972 20¢ Maryland: Baltimore Oriole and Black-Eyed Susan	04/14/82	.50	.25	1.25	13
1973 20¢ Massachusetts: Black-Capped Chickadee and Mayflower	04/14/82	.50	.25	1.25	13
1974 20¢ Michigan: Robin and Apple Blossom	04/14/82	.50	.25	1.25	13
1975 20¢ Minnesota: Common Loon and Showy Lady Slipper	04/14/82	.50	.25	1.25	13
1976 20¢ Mississippi: Mockingbird and Magnolia	04/14/82	.50	.25	1.25	13
1977 20¢ Missouri: Eastern Bluebird and Red Hawthorn	04/14/82	.50	.25	1.25	13

1982

2003

2004

2005

2006 2007

2010 2012

2008 2009 2009a

2011

2013

2014

2015 2016

2017

2019 2020

2018 2021 2022 2022a

Issues of 1982		Un	U	PB/PNC/LP	#	FDC	Q(M)
	Perf. 11						
2003	20¢ USA/The Netherlands	04/20/82	.40	.20	3.50	(6)	1.00	109
a	Imperf., pair		325.00					
2004	20¢ Library of Congress	04/21/82	.40	.20	1.75	(4)	1.00	113
	Coil Stamp, Perf. 10 Vertically							
2005	20¢ Consumer Education	04/27/82	.55	.20	25.00	(3)	1.00	
a	Imperf., pair		100.00		400.00	(2)		
b	Tagging omitted		7.50					

Value for plate no. coil strip of 3 stamps is for most common plate nos. Other plate nos. and strips of 5 stamps may have higher values.

	Knoxville World's Fair Issue, Perf. 11							
2006	20¢ Solar Energy	04/29/82	.40	.20			1.00	31
2007	20¢ Synthetic Fuels	04/29/82	.40	.20			1.00	31
2008	20¢ Breeder Reactor	04/29/82	.40	.20			1.00	31
2009	20¢ Fossil Fuels	04/29/82	.40	.20			1.00	31
a	Block of 4, #2006-09		1.65	1.50	2.25	(4)	2.50	
2010	20¢ Horatio Alger	04/30/82	.40	.20	1.75	(4)	1.00	108
2011	20¢ Aging Together	05/21/82	.40	.20	1.75	(4)	1.00	173
	Performing Arts Issue							
2012	20¢ John, Ethel and Lionel Barrymore	06/08/82	.40	.20	1.75	(4)	1.00	107
2013	20¢ Dr. Mary Walker	06/10/82	.40	.20	1.75	(4)	1.00	109
2014	20¢ International Peace Garden	06/30/82	.40	.20	1.75	(4)	1.00	183
a	Black and green omitted		260.00					
2015	20¢ America's Libraries	07/13/82	.40	.20	1.75	(4)	1.00	169
a	Vertical pair, imperf. horizontally		300.00					
b	Tagging omitted		7.50					
	Black Heritage Issue, Perf. 10.5 x 11							
2016	20¢ Jackie Robinson and Robinson Stealing Home Plate	08/02/82	1.10	.20	5.50	(4)	6.00	164
	Perf. 11							
2017	20¢ Touro Synagogue	08/22/82	.40	.20	11.00	(20)	1.50	110
a	Imperf., pair		2,500.00					
2018	20¢ Wolf Trap Farm Park	09/01/82	.40	.20	1.75	(4)	1.00	111
	American Architecture Issue							
2019	20¢ Fallingwater, by Frank Lloyd Wright	09/30/82	.45	.20			1.00	41
2020	20¢ Illinois Institute of Technology, by Ludwig Mies van der Rohe	09/30/82	.45	.20			1.00	41
2021	20¢ Gropius House, by Walter Gropius	09/30/82	.45	.20			1.00	41
2022	20¢ Dulles Airport by Eero Saarinen	09/30/82	.45	.20			1.00	41
a	Block of 4, #2019-22		2.00	1.75	2.50	(4)	2.50	

	Issues of 1982		Un	U	PB	#	FDC	Q(M)
2023	20¢ St. Francis of Assisi	10/07/82	.40	.20	1.75	(4)	1.00	174
2024	20¢ Ponce de Leon	10/12/82	.40	.20	3.25	(6)	1.00	110
a	Imperf., pair		500.00					
	Christmas Issue							
2025	13¢ Puppy and Kitten	11/03/82	.25	.20	1.40	(4)	1.25	234
a	Imperf., pair		650.00					
2026	20¢ Madonna and Child,							
	by Tiepolo	10/28/82	.40	.20	11.00	(20)	1.00	703
a	Imperf., pair		150.00					
b	Horizontal pair, imperf. vertically		—					
c	Vertical pair, imperf. horizontally		—					
	Seasons Greetings Issue							
2027	20¢ Children Sledding	10/28/82	.50	.20			1.00	197
2028	20¢ Children Building							
	a Snowman	10/28/82	.50	.20			1.00	197
2029	20¢ Children Skating	10/28/82	.50	.20			1.00	197
2030	20¢ Children Trimming a Tree	10/28/82	.50	.20			1.00	197
a	Block of 4, #2027-30		2.10	1.50	2.50	(4)	2.50	
b	As "a," imperf.		2,750.00					
c	As "a," imperf. horizontally		—					
	Issues of 1983							
2031	20¢ Science & Industry	01/19/83	.40	.20	1.75	(4)	1.00	119
a	Black omitted		1,400.00					
	Balloons Issue							
2032	20¢ Intrepid, 1861	03/31/83	.40	.20			1.00	57
2033	20¢ Hot Air Ballooning							
	(wording lower right)	03/31/83	.40	.20			1.00	57
2034	20¢ Hot Air Ballooning							
	(wording upper left)	03/31/83	.40	.20			1.00	57
2035	20¢ Explorer II, 1935	03/31/83	.40	.20			1.00	57
a	Block of 4, #2032-35		1.65	1.50	1.75	(4)	2.50	
b	As "a," imperf.		4,250.00					
c	As "a," right stamp perf.,							
	otherwise imperf.		4,500.00					
2036	20¢ U.S./Sweden Treaty	03/24/83	.40	.20	1.75	(4)	1.00	118
2037	20¢ Civilian Conservation							
	Corps	04/05/83	.40	.20	1.75	(4)	1.00	114
a	Imperf., pair		2,900.00					
2038	20¢ Joseph Priestley	04/13/83	.40	.20	1.75	(4)	1.00	165
2039	20¢ Voluntarism	04/20/83	.40	.20	3.00	(6)	1.00	120
a	Imperf., pair		750.00					
2040	20¢ Concord-German							
	Immigration, Apr. 29	04/29/83	.40	.20	1.75	(4)	1.00	117

2023

2024

2025

2027

2028

2026

2029

2030

2030a

2032

2033

2031

2034

2035

2035a

2036

2037

2038

2039

2040

Issues of 1983		Un	U	PB	#	FDC	Q(M)
Streetcars Issue, Perf. 11							
2059	20¢ First American Streetcar 10/08/83	.45	.20			1.00	52
2060	20¢ Early Electric Streetcar 10/08/83	.45	.20			1.00	52
2061	20¢ "Bobtail" Horsecar 10/08/83	.45	.20			1.00	52
2062	20¢ St. Charles Streetcar 10/08/83	.45	.20			1.00	52
a	Block of 4, #2059-62	1.80	1.40	2.50	(4)	2.50	
b	As "a," black omitted	425.00					
c	As "a," black omitted on #2059, 2061	—					
Christmas Issue							
2063	20¢ Niccolini-Cowper						
	Madonna, by Raphael 10/28/83	.40	.20	1.75	(4)	1.00	716
2064	20¢ Santa Claus 10/28/83	.40	.20	3.00	(6)	1.00	849
a	Imperf., pair	175.00					
2065	20¢ Martin Luther 11/11/83	.40	.20	1.75	(4)	1.50	165
Issues of 1984							
2066	20¢ 25th Anniversary						
	of Alaska Statehood 01/03/84	.40	.20	1.75	(4)	1.00	120
Winter Olympic Games Issue, Perf. 10.5 x 11							
2067	20¢ Ice Dancing 01/06/84	.50	.20			1.00	80
2068	20¢ Downhill Skiing 01/06/84	.50	.20			1.00	80
2069	20¢ Cross-country Skiing 01/06/84	.50	.20			1.00	80
2070	20¢ Hockey 01/06/84	.50	.20			1.00	80
a	Block of 4, #2067-70	2.10	1.50	3.00	(4)	2.50	
Perf. 11							
2071	20¢ Federal Deposit						
	Insurance Corporation 01/12/84	.40	.20	1.75	(4)	1.00	103

Sequoyah (1770s-1843)

Sequoyah spent 12 years developing a syllabary—
a system of written characters—for his native
Cherokee language. Although he never learned to
read, write, or speak English, he was fascinated
by the ability of whites to communicate through
written marks. In analyzing his own language,
Sequoyah determined that it was comprised of
particular sound clusters and combinations of consonants and vowels.
He developed an 85-character syllabary that led to a written means of
communication for his people as well as a history of the Cherokee people
that he himself would write. Decried by his friends and family as either
mad or dabbling in witchcraft, Sequoyah eventually unveiled his syllabary
in a demonstration to the tribe in 1812. Within months many members
of the Cherokee Nation had mastered reading and writing their own
language. Sixteen years later, the *Cherokee Phoenix*, printed in side-by-
side columns of Cherokee and English, became the first Native American
newspaper published in the United States. Commemorating his remarkable
accomplishment, the U.S. Postal Service in 1980 paid homage to Sequoyah
with a stamp in the Great Americans series. ■

2059

2060

First American streetcar, New York City, 1832

Early electric streetcar, Montgomery, Ala., 1886

"Bobtail" horsecar, Sulphur Rock, Ark., 1926

St. Charles streetcar, New Orleans, La., 1923

2061

2062

2062a

Christmas USA 20c

Raphael, 1483-1983, National Gallery

2063

Season's Greetings USA 20c

2064

Martin Luther

1483-1983 USA 20c

2065

USA 20c

1959-1984
Alaska Statehood

2066

2067

2068

2069

2070

2070a

FEDERAL DEPOSIT
INSURANCE
CORPORATION

50TH ANNIVERSARY

2071

1984

2072

2073

2074

2075

2076   2077

2078   2079   2079a

2080

2081

2082   2083

2084   2085   2085a

2086

2087

Issues of 1984		Un	U	PB	#	FDC	Q(M)
Perf. 11 x 10.5							
2072	20¢ Love 01/31/84	.40	.20	11.50	(20)	1.00	555
a	Horizontal pair, imperf. vertically	175.00					
b	Tagging omitted	5.00					
Black Heritage Issue, Carter G. Woodson, Perf. 11							
2073	20¢ Carter G. Woodson						
	Holding History Book 02/01/84	.40	.20	1.75	(4)	1.75	120
a	Horizontal pair, imperf. vertically	1,600.00					
2074	20¢ Soil and Water						
	Conservation 02/06/84	.40	.20	1.75	(4)	1.00	107
2075	20¢ 50th Anniversary						
	of Credit Union Act 02/10/84	.40	.20	1.75	(4)	1.00	107
Orchids Issue							
2076	20¢ Wild Pink 03/05/84	.50	.20			1.00	77
2077	20¢ Yellow Lady's-Slipper 03/05/84	.50	.20			1.00	77
2078	20¢ Spreading Pogonia 03/05/84	.50	.20			1.00	77
2079	20¢ Pacific Calypso 03/05/84	.50	.20			1.00	77
a	Block of 4, #2076-79	2.00	1.50	2.50	(4)	2.50	
2080	20¢ 25th Anniversary						
	of Hawaii Statehood 03/12/84	.40	.20	1.70	(4)	1.00	120
2081	20¢ National Archives 04/16/84	.40	.20	1.70	(4)	1.00	108
Olympic Summer Games Issue (See also #2048-52, C101-12)							
2082	20¢ Diving 05/04/84	.55	.20			1.25	78
2083	20¢ Long Jump 05/04/84	.55	.20			1.25	78
2084	20¢ Wrestling 05/04/84	.55	.20			1.25	78
2085	20¢ Kayak 05/04/84	.55	.20			1.25	78
a	Block of 4, #2082-85	2.40	1.90	3.50	(4)	2.50	
2086	20¢ Louisiana World						
	Exposition 05/11/84	.40	.20	1.75	(4)	1.00	130
2087	20¢ Health Research 05/17/84	.40	.20	1.75	(4)	1.00	120

Booker T. Washington

(1856-1915)

Born into slavery on a Virginia plantation, educator Booker T. Washington became a leader in the African-American community. As a child, his keen intellect kept him immersed in books when he wasn't working in the coal mines and salt furnaces of Malden, West Virginia, where his family had moved when he was nine. He went on to attend Virginia's Hampton Normal and Agricultural Institute, graduating with honors in 1876. At age 25, Washington was tapped for a job as the first head of the new Tuskegee Normal and Industrial Institute in Alabama, a tuition-free school that would teach skills to blacks, providing them with a livelihood. In 1900, Washington founded the National Negro Business League to encourage blacks to become business owners and to promote and protect their business interests, believing, as he theorized in his 1901 autobiography *Up from Slavery,* that blacks would gain civil and political rights once they had achieved economic strength. Washington's portrait appeared on a stamp in 1940 as part of the Famous Americans series. ■

	Issues of 1985		Un	U	PNC	#	FDC
	Seashells Booklet Issue, Perf. 10						
2117	22¢ Frilled Dogwinkle	04/04/85	.40	.20			1.00
2118	22¢ Reticulated Helmet	04/04/85	.40	.20			1.00
2119	22¢ New England Neptune	04/04/85	.40	.20			1.00
2120	22¢ Calico Scallop	04/04/85	.40	.20			1.00
2121	22¢ Lightning Whelk	04/04/85	.40	.20			1.00
a	Booklet pane of 10		4.00	3.00			7.50
b	As "a," violet omitted		800.00				
c	As "a," imperf. between vertically		600.00				
e	Strip of 5, #2117-21		2.00	—			
	Express Mail Booklet Issue, Perf. 10 Vertically						
2122	$10.75 Eagle and Moon,						
	booklet single	04/29/85	19.00	7.50			40.00
a	Booklet pane of 3		60.00	—			95.00
b	Type II		22.50	10.00			
c	As "b," booklet pane of 3		70.00	—			
	#2122 issued only in booklets. All stamps are imperf. at top and bottom or at top, bottom and one side.						
	Issues of 1985-1989, Coil Stamps, Transportation Issue (See also #1897-1908, 2225-31, 2252-66, 2451-68)						
2123	3.4¢ School Bus 1920s	06/08/85	.20	.20	.90	(5)	1.00
a	Untagged (Bureau precanceled)		.20	.20	4.25	(5)	
2124	4.9¢ Buckboard 1880s	06/21/85	.20	.20	.85	(5)	1.00
a	Untagged (Bureau precanceled)		.20	.20	1.40	(5)	
2125	5.5¢ Star Route Truck 1910s	11/01/86	.20	.20	1.50	(5)	1.00
a	Untagged (Bureau precanceled)		.20	.20	1.75	(5)	
2126	6¢ Tricycle 1880s	05/06/85	.20	.20	1.50	(5)	1.00
a	Untagged (Bureau precanceled)		.20	.20	1.75	(5)	
b	As "a," imperf., pair		200.00				
2127	7.1¢ Tractor 1920s	02/06/87	.20	.20	2.10	(5)	1.00
a	Untagged (Bureau precanceled "Nonprofit org.")		.20	.20	3.00	(5)	5.00
b	Untagged (Bureau precanceled "Nonprofit 5-Digit ZIP + 4")	05/26/89	.20	.20	1.75	(5)	
2128	8.3¢ Ambulance 1860s	06/21/85	.20	.20	1.50	(5)	1.00
a	Untagged (Bureau precanceled)		.20	.20	1.50	(5)	
2129	8.5¢ Tow Truck 1920s	01/24/87	.20	.20	3.00	(5)	1.25
a	Untagged (Bureau precanceled)		.20	.20	2.75	(5)	
2130	10.1¢ Oil Wagon 1890s	04/18/85	.25	.20	2.50	(5)	1.25
a	Untagged (Bureau precanceled, red)		.25	.25	2.25	(5)	1.25
	Untagged (Bureau precanceled, black)		.25	.25	2.50	(5)	
b	As "a," red precancel, imperf., pair		15.00		100.00	(6)	
	As "a," black precancel, imperf., pair		95.00				
2131	11¢ Stutz Bearcat 1933	06/11/85	.25	.20	1.40	(5)	1.25
2132	12¢ Stanley Steamer 1909	04/02/85	.25	.20	2.25	(5)	1.25
a	Untagged (Bureau precanceled)		.25	.25	2.40	(5)	
b	As "a," type II		.40	.30	19.00	(5)	
	Type II has "Stanley Steamer 1909" .5 mm shorter (17.5 mm) than #2132 (18mm).						
2133	12.5¢ Pushcart 1880s	04/18/85	.25	.20	3.00	(5)	1.25
a	Untagged (Bureau precanceled)		.25	.25	3.00	(5)	
b	As "a," imperf., pair		50.00				
2134	14¢ Iceboat 1880s	03/23/85	.30	.20	2.25	(5)	1.25
a	Imperf., pair		100.00				
b	Type II		.30	.20	3.25	(5)	
2135	17¢ Dog Sled 1920s	08/20/86	.30	.20	3.25	(5)	1.25
a	Imperf., pair		450.00				
2136	25¢ Bread Wagon 1880s	11/22/86	.45	.20	3.50	(5)	1.25
a	Imperf., pair		10.00				
b	Pair, imperf. between		750.00				
c	Tagging omitted		25.00				

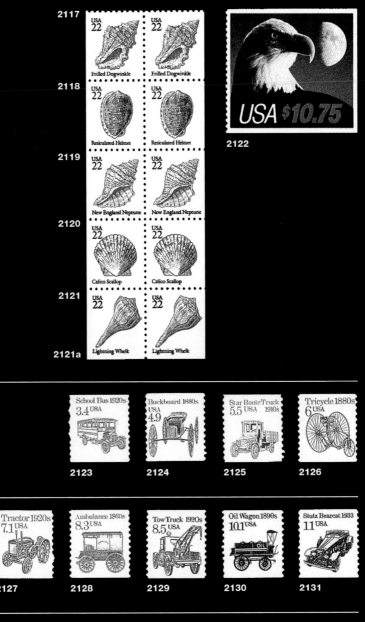

2117
2118
2119
2120
2121
2121a

2122

2123   2124   2125   2126

2127   2128   2129   2130   2131

2132   2133   2134   2135   2136

2138 2139

Broadbill Decoy

Mallard Decoy

Folk Art USA 22 Folk Art USA 22

Mary McLeod Bethune

Canvasback Decoy

Redhead Decoy

Black Heritage USA 22

Folk Art USA 22 Folk Art USA 22

2137

2140 2141 2141a

22 USA
Winter Special Olympics

LOVE
USA 22

22 USA
Rural
Electrification
Administration 1935 1985

2142

2143

2144

AMERIPEX 86
International Stamp Show, Chicago
May 22 to June 1, 1986

Abigail Adams

USA

USA 22

USA 22

F.A. Bartholdi, Statue of Liberty Sculptor

2145

USA 22

2147

2146

18
USA

USA
21.1

2149

2150

Veterans Korea

Social Security Act 1935-1985 USA 22

USA 22

2152

2153

	Issues of 1985		Un	U	PB/PNC	#	FDC	Q(M)
	Black Heritage Issue, Perf. 11							
2137	22¢ Mary McLeod Bethune	03/05/85	.40	.20	2.60	(4)	1.50	120
	American Folk Art: Duck Decoys Issue							
2138	22¢ Broadbill Decoy	03/22/85	.65	.20			1.00	75
2139	22¢ Mallard Decoy	03/22/85	.65	.20			1.00	75
2140	22¢ Canvasback Decoy	03/22/85	.65	.20			1.00	75
2141	22¢ Redhead Decoy	03/22/85	.65	.20			1.00	75
a	Block of 4, #2138-41		4.00	2.75	5.00	(4)	2.50	
2142	22¢ Winter Special Olympics	03/25/85	.40	.20	1.75	(4)	1.00	121
a	Vertical pair, imperf. horizontally		550.00					
2143	22¢ Love	04/17/85	.40	.20	1.70	(4)	1.00	730
a	Imperf., pair		1,500.00					
2144	22¢ Rural Electrification							
	Administration	05/11/85	.45	.20	17.50	(20)	1.00	125
2145	22¢ AMERIPEX '86	05/25/85	.40	.20	1.75	(4)	1.00	203
a	Red, black and blue omitted		200.00					
b	Red and black omitted		1,250.00					
2146	22¢ Abigail Adams	06/14/85	.40	.20	2.00	(4)	1.00	126
a	Imperf., pair		275.00					
2147	22¢ Frederic A. Bartholdi	07/18/85	.40	.20	1.90	(4)	1.00	130
2148	Not assigned							
	Coil Stamps, Perf. 10 Vertically							
2149	18¢ George Washington,							
	Washington Monument	11/06/85	.35	.20	3.00	(5)	1.00	
a	Untagged (Bureau precanceled)		.35	.35	6.00	(5)		
b	Imperf., pair		950.00					
c	As "a," imperf. pair		800.00					
d	Tagging omitted		—	—				
e	As "a," tagged (error), dull gum		2.00	1.75	—			
2150	21.1¢ Sealed Envelopes	10/22/85	.40	.20	3.25	(5)	1.00	
a	Untagged (Bureau precanceled)		.40	.40	40.00	(5)		
b	As "a," tagged (error)		.40	.40	3.25	(5)		
2151	Not assigned							
	Perf. 11							
2152	22¢ Korean War Veterans	07/26/85	.40	.20	2.50	(4)	1.75	120
2153	22¢ Social Security Act,							
	50th Anniversary	08/14/85	.40	.20	1.90	(4)	1.00	120

Visit us online at The Postal Store at www.usps.com

or call 1-800-STAMP-24

2167

2168

2169

2170

2171

2172

2173

2175

2176

2177

2178

2179

2180

2181

2182

2183

2184

2185

2186

2187

2188

2189

2190

2191

	Issues of 1986		Un	U	PB	#	FDC	Q(M)
2167	22¢ Arkansas Statehood	01/03/86	.40	.20	2.00	(4)	1.00	130
a	Vertical pair, imperf. horizontally		—					
	Issues of 1986-1991, Great Americans Issue (See also #1844-69)							
2168	1¢ Margaret Mitchell	06/30/86	.20	.20	.25	(4)	2.00	
a	Tagging omitted		5.00					
2169	2¢ Mary Lyon	02/28/87	.20	.20	.30	(4)	1.00	
a	Untagged		.20	.20	.35	(4)		
2170	3¢ Paul Dudley White, MD	09/15/86	.20	.20	.50	(4)	1.00	
a	Untagged, dull gum		.20	.20	.50	(4)		
2171	4¢ Father Flanagan	07/14/86	.20	.20	.60	(4)	1.00	
a	Grayish violet, untagged		.20	.20	.40	(4)		
b	Deep grayish blue, untagged		.20	.20	.50	(4)		
2172	5¢ Hugo L. Black	02/27/86	.20	.20	.65	(4)	1.00	
a	Tagging omitted		10.00					
2173	5¢ Luis Munoz Marin	02/18/90	.20	.20	.75	(4)	1.00	
a	Untagged		.20	.20	.60	(4)		
2174	Not assigned							
2175	10¢ Red Cloud	08/15/87	.20	.20	.85	(4)	1.50	
a	Overall tagging	1990	.30	.20	10.00	(4)		
b	Tagging omitted		12.50					
c	Prephosphored coated paper (solid tagging)		.30	.20	1.40	(4)		
d	Prephosphored uncoated paper (mottled tagging)		.20	.20	1.25	(4)		
e	Carmine, prephosphored uncoated paper (mottled tagging)		.25	.20	1.25	(4)		
2176	14¢ Julia Ward Howe	02/12/87	.25	.20	1.50	(4)	1.00	
2177	15¢ Buffalo Bill Cody	06/06/88	.35	.20	10.00	(4)	1.00	
a	Overall tagging	1990	.30	—	3.25	(4)		
b	Prephosphored coated paper (solid tagging)		.40	—	3.25	(4)		
c	Tagging omitted		15.00	—				
2178	17¢ Belva Ann Lockwood	06/18/86	.35	.20	2.00	(4)	1.00	
a	Tagging omitted		10.00					
	Perf. 11 x 11.1							
2179	20¢ Virginia Apgar	10/24/94	.40	.20	2.00	(4)	1.00	
a	Orange brown		.40	.20	2.25	(4)		
	Perf. 11							
2180	21¢ Chester Carlson	10/21/88	.40	.20	2.50	(4)	1.00	
2181	23¢ Mary Cassatt	11/04/88	.45	.20	2.50	(4)	1.00	
a	Overall tagging, dull gum		.45	—	5.00	(4)		
b	Prephosphored coated paper (solid tagging)		.60	—	3.25	(4)		
c	Prephosphored uncoated paper (mottled tagging)		.50	.20	3.25	(4)		
d	Tagging omitted		7.50					
2182	25¢ Jack London	01/11/86	.45	.20	2.75	(4)	1.25	
a	Booklet pane of 10	05/03/88	4.50	3.75			6.00	
b	Tagging omitted	1990	—					
2183	28¢ Sitting Bull	09/28/89	.50	.20	2.50	(4)	1.50	
2184	29¢ Earl Warren	03/09/92	.55	.20	2.50	(4)	1.25	
	Perf. 11.5 x 11							
2185	29¢ Thomas Jefferson	04/13/93	.50	.20	2.50	(4)	1.25	
2186	35¢ Dennis Chavez	04/03/91	.65	.20	3.25	(4)	1.25	
2187	40¢ Claire Lee Chennault	09/06/90	.70	.20	3.75	(4)	2.00	
a	Prephosphored coated paper (solid tagging)		.75	.35	4.25	(4)		
b	Prephosphored uncoated paper (mottled tagging)		.75	.20	7.50	(4)		
2188	45¢ Harvey Cushing, MD	06/17/88	.85	.20	3.75	(4)	1.25	
a	Overall tagging	1990	1.65	.20	11.00	(4)		
b	Tagging omitted		15.00					
2189	52¢ Hubert H. Humphrey	06/03/91	1.10	.20	7.50	(4)	1.40	
a	Prephosphored uncoated paper (mottled tagging)		1.10	—	5.50	(4)		
2190	56¢ John Harvard	09/03/86	1.10	.20	6.00	(4)	2.50	
2191	65¢ H.H. 'Hap' Arnold	11/05/88	1.20	.20	5.00	(4)	2.50	

Issues of 1986-1992			Un	U	PB	#	FDC	Q(M)
Perf. 11								
2192	75¢ Wendell Willkie	02/16/92	1.30	.20	5.50	(4)	2.50	
a	Prephosphored uncoated paper (mottled tagging)		1.30	—	5.50	(4)		
2193	$1 Bernard Revel	09/23/86	2.50	.50	14.00	(4)	3.50	
2194	$1 Johns Hopkins	06/07/89	1.75	.50	7.00	(4)	3.00	
b	Overall tagging	1990	1.75	.50	7.00	(4)		
c	Tagging omitted		10.00					
d	Dark blue, prephosphored coated paper (solid tagging)		1.75	.50	7.00	(4)		
e	Blue, prephosphored uncoated paper (mottled tagging)		2.00	.60	8.00	(4)		
f	Blue, prephosphored coated paper (grainy solid tagging)		1.75	.50	7.00	(4)		
2195	$2 William Jennings Bryan	03/19/86	4.00	.50	19.00	(4)	5.50	
a	Tagging omitted		45.00					
2196	$5 Bret Harte	08/25/87	8.50	1.00	35.00	(4)	15.00	
a	Tagging omitted		—					
b	Prephosphored paper (solid tagging)		8.50	—	35.00	(4)		
Booklet Stamp, Perf. 10								
2197	25¢ Jack London (2182), single from booklet.		.45	.20			1.00	
a	Booklet pane of 6	05/03/88	3.00	2.25			4.00	
b	Tagging omitted		4.50					
c	As "b," booklet pane of 6		60.00					
United States — Sweden Stamp Collecting Booklet Issue, Perf. 10 Vertically								
2198	22¢ Handstamped Cover	01/23/86	.45	.20			1.00	17
2199	22¢ Boy Examining Stamp Collection	01/23/86	.45	.20			1.00	17
2200	22¢ #836 Under Magnifying Glass	01/23/86	.45	.20			1.00	17
2201	22¢ 1986 Presidents Miniature Sheet	01/23/86	.45	.20			1.00	17
a	Booklet pane of 4, #2198-2201		2.00	1.75			4.00	17
b	As "a," black omitted on #2198, 2201		50.00	—				
c	As "a," blue omitted on #2198-2200		2,500.00					
d	As "a," buff omitted		—					
#2198-2201 issued only in booklets. All stamps are imperf. at top and bottom or imperf. at top, bottom and right side.								
Perf. 11								
2202	22¢ Love	01/30/86	.40	.20	1.75	(4)	1.00	949
Black Heritage Issue								
2203	22¢ Sojourner Truth and Truth Lecturing	02/04/86	.40	.20	1.75	(4)	1.75	130
2204	22¢ Republic of Texas, 150th Anniversary	03/02/86	.40	.20	1.90	(4)	1.75	137
a	Horizontal pair, imperf. vertically		1,100.00					
b	Dark red omitted		2,750.00					
c	Dark blue omitted		8,500.00					
Fish Booklet Issue, Perf. 10 Horizontally								
2205	22¢ Muskellunge	03/21/86	.60	.20			1.25	44
2206	22¢ Atlantic Cod	03/21/86	.60	.20			1.25	44
2207	22¢ Largemouth Bass	03/21/86	.60	.20			1.25	44
2208	22¢ Bluefin Tuna	03/21/86	.60	.20			1.25	44
2209	22¢ Catfish	03/21/86	.60	.20			1.25	44
a	Booklet pane of 5, #2205-09		5.50	2.75			3.50	44
#2205-09 issued only in booklets. All stamps are imperf. at sides or imperf. at sides and bottom.								

2192   2193   2194   2195   2196

2198   2199   2200   2201   2201a

2205

2206

2207

2208

2209

2202   2203

2204   2209

2209a

1986

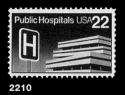

2210

2211

2216a **2216b** **2216c** **2216d** **2216e**

2216f **2216g** **2216h** **2216i**

2217a **2217b** **2217c** **2217d** **2217e**

2217f **2217g** **2217h** **2217i**

Issues of 1986		Un	U	PB	#	FDC	Q(M)
Perf. 11							
2210 22¢ Public Hospitals	04/11/86	.40	.20	1.75	(4)	1.00	130
a Vertical pair, imperf. horizontally		325.00					
b Horizontal pair, imperf. vertically		1,350.00					
Performing Arts Issue							
2211 22¢ Duke Ellington							
and Piano Keys	04/29/86	.40	.20	1.90	(4)	2.25	130
a Vertical pair, imperf. horizontally		1,000.00					
2212-15 Not assigned							
AMERIPEX '86 Issue, Presidents Miniature Sheets							
2216 Sheet of 9	05/22/86	4.25	—			4.00	6
a 22¢ George Washington		.45	.25			1.50	
b 22¢ John Adams		.45	.25			1.50	
c 22¢ Thomas Jefferson		.45	.25			1.50	
d 22¢ James Madison		.45	.25			1.50	
e 22¢ James Monroe		.45	.25			1.50	
f 22¢ John Quincy Adams		.45	.25			1.50	
g 22¢ Andrew Jackson		.45	.25			1.50	
h 22¢ Martin Van Buren		.45	.25			1.50	
i 22¢ William H. Harrison		.45	.25			1.50	
j Blue omitted		3,250.00					
k Black inscription omitted		2,000.00					
l Imperf.		10,500.00					
2217 Sheet of 9	05/22/86	4.25	—			4.00	6
a 22¢ John Tyler		.45	.25			1.50	
b 22¢ James Polk		.45	.25			1.50	
c 22¢ Zachary Taylor		.45	.25			1.50	
d 22¢ Millard Fillmore		.45	.25			1.50	
e 22¢ Franklin Pierce		.45	.25			1.50	
f 22¢ James Buchanan		.45	.25			1.50	
g 22¢ Abraham Lincoln		.45	.25			1.50	
h 22¢ Andrew Johnson		.45	.25			1.50	
i 22¢ Ulysses S. Grant		.45	.25			1.50	

#2216

#2217

2220 2221

USA22 Elisha Kent Kane
USA22 Adolphus W. Greely
USA22 Vilhjalmur Stefansson
USA22 Robert E. Peary, Matthew Henson

2222 2223 2223a

Liberty 1886-1986
USA 22

2224

Omnibus 1880s 1 USA

2225

Locomotive 1870s 2 USA

2226

2235 2236

Navajo Art USA 22
Navajo Art USA 22
Navajo Art USA 22
Navajo Art USA 22

2237 2238 2238a

T.S.Eliot
22 USA

2239

2240 2241

Wood Carving: Highlander Figure Folk Art USA 22
Wood Carving: Ship Figurehead Folk Art USA 22
Wood Carving: Nautical Figure Folk Art USA 22
Wood Carving: Cigar-Store Figure Folk Art USA 22

2242 2243 2243a

CHRISTMAS 22 USA
Perugino, National Gallery

2244

USA 22 GREETINGS

2245

USA 22
1837-1987 Michigan Statehood

2246

22 USA
Pan American Games Indianapolis 1987

2247

LOVE USA 22

2248

Jean Baptiste Pointe Du Sable 22
Black Heritage USA

2249

	Issues of 1986		Un	U	PB/PNC	#	FDC	Q(M)
	Arctic Explorers Issue, Perf. 11							
2220	22¢ Elisha Kent Kane	05/28/86	.65	.20			1.25	33
2221	22¢ Adolphus W. Greely	05/28/86	.65	.20			1.25	33
2222	22¢ Vilhjalmur Stefansson	05/28/86	.65	.20			1.25	33
2223	22¢ Robt. Peary, Matt. Henson	05/28/86	.65	.20			1.25	33
a	Block of 4, #2220-23		2.75	2.25	4.50	(4)	3.75	
b	As "a," black omitted		8,500.00					
2224	22¢ Statue of Liberty	07/04/86	.40	.20	2.25	(4)	1.25	221
	Issues of 1986-1987, Reengraved Transportation Issue, Coil Stamps, Perf. 10 Vertically							
	(See also #1897-1908, 2123-36, 2252-66, 2452-53A, 2457, 2464, 2468)							
2225	1¢ Omnibus	11/26/86	.20	.20	.60	(5)	1.00	
a	Prephosphored uncoated paper							
	(mottled tagging)		.20	.20	13.50	(5)		
b	Untagged, dull gum		.20	.20	.65	(5)		
c	Imperf., pair		2,000.00					
2226	2¢ Locomotive	03/06/87	.20	.20	.70	(5)	1.50	
a	Untagged, dull gum		.20	.20	.70	(5)		
2227, 2229-30, 2232-34 Not assigned								
2228	4¢ Stagecoach (1898A)	08/86	.20	.20	1.25	(5)		
a	Overall tagging		.70	.20	11.00	(5)		
b	Imperf., pair		300.00					
2231	8.3¢ Ambulance (2128)							
	(Bureau precanceled)	08/29/86	.20	.20	5.25	(5)		
	On #2228, "Stagecoach 1890s" is 17mm long; on #1898A, it is 19.5mm long. On #2231,							
	"Ambulance 1860s" is 18mm long; on #2128, it is 18.5mm long.							
	American Folk Art: Navajo Art Issue, Perf. 11							
2235	22¢ Navajo Art, four "+" marks							
	horizontally through middle	09/04/86	.50	.20			1.00	60
2236	22¢ Navajo Art, vertical							
	diamond pattern	09/04/86	.50	.20			1.00	60
2237	22¢ Navajo Art, horizontal							
	diamond pattern	09/04/86	.50	.20			1.00	60
2238	22¢ Navajo Art, jagged line							
	horizontally through middle	09/04/86	.50	.20			1.00	60
a	Block of 4, #2235-38		2.50	2.25	4.00	(4)	2.00	
b	As "a," black omitted		350.00					
	Literary Arts Issue							
2239	22¢ T.S. Eliot	09/26/86	.40	.20	1.90	(4)	1.00	132
	American Folk Art: Wood Carved Figurines Issue							
2240	22¢ Highlander Figure	10/01/86	.40	.20			1.00	60
2241	22¢ Ship Figurehead	10/01/86	.40	.20			1.00	60
2242	22¢ Nautical Figure	10/01/86	.40	.20			1.00	60
2243	22¢ Cigar Store Figure	10/01/86	.40	.20			1.00	60
a	Block of 4, #2240-43		1.75	2.00	3.00	(4)	2.00	
b	As "a," imperf. vertically		1,500.00					
	Christmas Issue							
2244	22¢ Madonna and Child	10/24/86	.40	.20	2.00	(4)	1.00	690
2245	22¢ Village Scene	10/24/86	.40	.20	1.90	(4)	1.00	882
	Issues of 1987							
2246	22¢ Michigan Statehood	01/26/87	.40	.20	1.90	(4)	1.00	167
	Pair with full vertical gutter between							
2247	22¢ Pan American Games	01/29/87	.40	.20	1.90	(4)	1.00	167
a	Silver omitted		1,500.00					
	Perf. 11.5 x 11							
2248	22¢ Love	01/30/87	.40	.20	1.90	(4)	1.00	842
	Black Heritage Issue, Perf. 11							
2249	22¢ Jean Baptiste Point Du Sable							
	and Chicago Settlement	02/20/87	.40	.20	1.90	(4)	1.50	143
a	Tagging omitted		10.00					

2275

2276

2277

2278

2279

2280

2281

2282a

2283

2283c

2284   2285

2285b

	Issues of 1987		Un	U	PB/PNC	#	FDC	Q(M)
2275	22¢ United Way	04/28/87	.40	.20	1.90	(4)	1.00	157
2276	22¢ Flag with Fireworks	05/09/87	.40	.20	1.90	(4)	1.00	
a	Booklet pane of 20	11/30/87	8.50	—			8.00	
	Issues of 1988-1989 (All issued in 1988 except #2280 on prephosphored paper)							
2277	(25¢) "E" Stamp	03/22/88	.45	.20	2.00	(4)	1.25	
2278	25¢ Flag with Clouds	05/06/88	.45	.20	1.90	(4)	1.25	
	Pair with full vertical gutter between		—					
	Coil Stamps, Perf. 10 Vertically							
2279	(25¢) "E" Earth	03/22/88	.45	.20	2.75	(5)	1.25	
a	Imperf., pair		85.00	—				
2280	25¢ Flag over Yosemite	05/20/88	.45	.20	3.50	(5)	1.25	
a	Prephosphored paper	02/14/89	.45	.20	3.50	(5)	1.25	
b	Imperf., pair, large block tagging		32.50					
c	Imperf., pair, prephosphored paper		14.00					
d	Tagging omitted		5.00					
e	Black trees		100.00	—				
f	Pair, imperf. between		800.00					
2281	25¢ Honeybee	09/02/88	.45	.20	3.75	(3)	1.25	
a	Imperf., pair		50.00					
b	Black (engr.) omitted		60.00					
c	Black (litho) omitted		450.00					
d	Pair, imperf. between		1,000.00					
e	Yellow (litho) omitted		1,200.00					
	Booklet Stamp, Perf. 10							
2282	(25¢) "E" Earth (#2277), single from booklet		.50	.20			1.25	
a	Booklet pane of 10	03/22/88	6.50	3.50			6.00	
	Pheasant Booklet Issue, Perf. 11							
2283	25¢ Pheasant, single from booklet		.50	.20			1.25	
a	Booklet pane of 10	04/29/88	6.00	3.50			6.00	
b	Single, red removed from sky		6.25	.20				
c	As "b," booklet pane of 10		67.50	—				
d	As "a," imperf. horizontally between		2,250.00					
	#2283 issued only in booklets. All stamps have one or two imperf. edges. Imperf. and part perf. pairs and panes exist from printer's waste.							
	Owl and Grosbeak Booklet Issue, Perf. 10							
2284	25¢ Grosbeak, single from booklet		.50	.20			1.25	
2285	25¢ Owl, single from booklet		.50	.20			1.25	
b	Booklet pane of 10, 5 each of #2284, 2285	05/28/88	5.00	3.50			6.00	
d	Pair, #2284, 2285		1.10	.25				
e	As "d," tagging omitted		12.50					
	#2284 and 2285 issued only in booklets. All stamps are imperf. at one side or imperf. at one side and bottom.							
2285A	25¢ Flag with Clouds (#2278), single from booklet		.50	.20			1.00	
c	Booklet pane of 6	07/05/88	3.00	2.00			4.00	

1987

	Issues of 1987		Un	U	FDC	Q(M)
	American Wildlife Issue, Perf. 11					
2286	22¢ Barn Swallow	06/13/87	.85	.20	1.50	13
2287	22¢ Monarch Butterfly	06/13/87	.85	.20	1.50	13
2288	22¢ Bighorn Sheep	06/13/87	.85	.20	1.50	13
2289	22¢ Broad-tailed Hummingbird	06/13/87	.85	.20	1.50	13
2290	22¢ Cottontail	06/13/87	.85	.20	1.50	13
2291	22¢ Osprey	06/13/87	.85	.20	1.50	13
2292	22¢ Mountain Lion	06/13/87	.85	.20	1.50	13
2293	22¢ Luna Moth	06/13/87	.85	.20	1.50	12
2294	22¢ Mule Deer	06/13/87	.85	.20	1.50	13
2295	22¢ Gray Squirrel	06/13/87	.85	.20	1.50	13
2296	22¢ Armadillo	06/13/87	.85	.20	1.50	13
2297	22¢ Eastern Chipmunk	06/13/87	.85	.20	1.50	13
2298	22¢ Moose	06/13/87	.85	.20	1.50	13
2299	22¢ Black Bear	06/13/87	.85	.20	1.50	13
2300	22¢ Tiger Swallowtail	06/13/87	.85	.20	1.50	13
2301	22¢ Bobwhite	06/13/87	.85	.20	1.50	13
2302	22¢ Ringtail	06/13/87	.85	.20	1.50	13
2303	22¢ Red-winged Blackbird	06/13/87	.85	.20	1.50	13
2304	22¢ American Lobster	06/13/87	.85	.20	1.50	13
2305	22¢ Black-tailed Jack Rabbit	06/13/87	.85	.20	1.50	13
2306	22¢ Scarlet Tanager	06/13/87	.85	.20	1.50	13
2307	22¢ Woodchuck	06/13/87	.85	.20	1.50	13
2308	22¢ Roseate Spoonbill	06/13/87	.85	.20	1.50	13
2309	22¢ Bald Eagle	06/13/87	.85	.20	1.50	13
2310	22¢ Alaskan Brown Bear	06/13/87	.85	.20	1.50	13

A·M·E·R·I·C·A·N C·O·M·M·E·M·O·R·A·T·I·V·E C·O·L·L·E·C·T·I·B·L·E·S

American Commemorative Panels

Obtain photo or steel engravings, mint condition stamps and subject related text presented on a beautifully designed page. Only $6.00* each, depending on the value of the stamps.

For more information call
1-800-STAMP-24

Prices subject to change without notice.

2286	2287	2288	2289	2290
2291	2292	2293	2294	2295
2296	2297	2298	2299	2300
2301	2302	2303	2304	2305
2306	2307	2308	2309	2310

22^{USA} Iiwi — 2311
22^{USA} Badger — 2312
22^{USA} Pronghorn — 2313
22^{USA} River Otter — 2314
22^{USA} Ladybug — 2315

22^{USA} Beaver — 2316
22^{USA} White-tailed Deer — 2317
22^{USA} Blue Jay — 2318
22^{USA} Pika — 2319
22^{USA} Bison — 2320

22^{USA} Snowy Egret — 2321
22^{USA} Gray Wolf — 2322
22^{USA} Mountain Goat — 2323
22^{USA} Deer Mouse — 2324
22^{USA} Black-tailed Prairie Dog — 2325

22^{USA} Box Turtle — 2326
22^{USA} Wolverine — 2327
22^{USA} American Elk — 2328
22^{USA} California Sea Lion — 2329
22^{USA} Mockingbird — 2330

22^{USA} Raccoon — 2331
22^{USA} Bobcat — 2332
22^{USA} Black-footed Ferret — 2333
22^{USA} Canada Goose — 2334
22^{USA} Red Fox — 2335

Issues of 1987		Un	U	FDC	Q(M)
American Wildlife Issue (continued), Perf. 11					
2311 22¢ Iiwi	06/13/87	.85	.20	1.50	13
2312 22¢ Badger	06/13/87	.85	.20	1.50	13
2313 22¢ Pronghorn	06/13/87	.85	.20	1.50	13
2314 22¢ River Otter	06/13/87	.85	.20	1.50	13
2315 22¢ Ladybug	06/13/87	.85	.20	1.50	13
2316 22¢ Beaver	06/13/87	.85	.20	1.50	13
2317 22¢ White-tailed Deer	06/13/87	.85	.20	1.50	13
2318 22¢ Blue Jay	06/13/87	.85	.20	1.50	13
2319 22¢ Pika	06/13/87	.85	.20	1.50	13
2320 22¢ Bison	06/13/87	.85	.20	1.50	13
2321 22¢ Snowy Egret	06/13/87	.85	.20	1.50	13
2322 22¢ Gray Wolf	06/13/87	.85	.20	1.50	13
2323 22¢ Mountain Goat	06/13/87	.85	.20	1.50	13
2324 22¢ Deer Mouse	06/13/87	.85	.20	1.50	13
2325 22¢ Black-tailed Prairie Dog	06/13/87	.85	.20	1.50	13
2326 22¢ Box Turtle	06/13/87	.85	.20	1.50	13
2327 22¢ Wolverine	06/13/87	.85	.20	1.50	13
2328 22¢ American Elk	06/13/87	.85	.20	1.50	13
2329 22¢ California Sea Lion	06/13/87	.85	.20	1.50	13
2330 22¢ Mockingbird	06/13/87	.85	.20	1.50	13
2331 22¢ Raccoon	06/13/87	.85	.20	1.50	13
2332 22¢ Bobcat	06/13/87	.85	.20	1.50	13
2333 22¢ Black-footed Ferret	06/13/87	.85	.20	1.50	13
2334 22¢ Canada Goose	06/13/87	.85	.20	1.50	13
2335 22¢ Red Fox	06/13/87	.85	.20	1.50	13
a Pane of 50, #2286-2335		*47.50*		50.00	

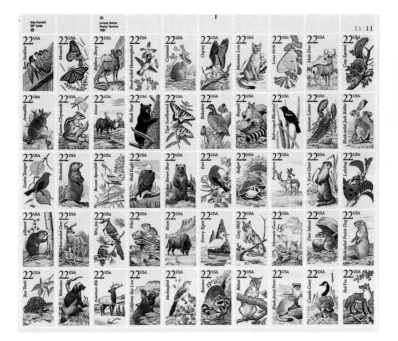

Example of 2335a

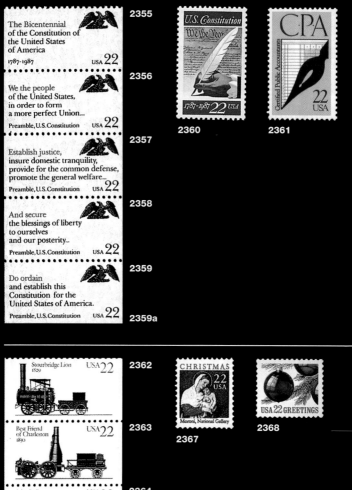

2355

The Bicentennial of the Constitution of the United States of America
1787-1987 USA 22

2356

We the people of the United States, in order to form a more perfect Union...
Preamble, U.S. Constitution USA 22

2357

Establish justice, insure domestic tranquility, provide for the common defense, promote the general welfare...
Preamble, U.S. Constitution USA 22

2358

And secure the blessings of liberty to ourselves and our posterity...
Preamble, U.S. Constitution USA 22

2359

Do ordain and establish this Constitution for the United States of America.
Preamble, U.S. Constitution USA 22

2359a

2360

2361

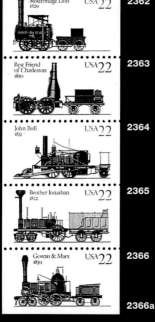

2362

Stourbridge Lion 1829 USA 22

2363

Best Friend of Charleston 1830 USA 22

2364

John Bull 1831 USA 22

2365

Brother Jonathan 1832 USA 22

2366

Gowan & Marx 1839 USA 22

2366a

2367

CHRISTMAS 22 USA
Moroni, National Gallery

2368

USA 22 GREETINGS

Issues of 1987		Un	U	PB	#	FDC	Q(M)
Drafting of the Constitution Booklet Issue, Perf. 10 Horizontally							
2355	22¢ "The Bicentennial..." 08/28/87	.55	.20			1.25	122
2356	22¢ "We the people..." 08/28/87	.55	.20			1.25	122
2357	22¢ "Establish justice..." 08/28/87	.55	.20			1.25	122
2358	22¢ "And secure..." 08/28/87	.55	.20			1.25	122
2359	22¢ "Do ordain..." 08/28/87	.55	.20			1.25	122
a	Booklet pane of 5, #2355-59	2.75	2.25			4.00	122
	#2355-59 issued only in booklets. All stamps are imperf. at sides or imperf. at sides and bottom.						
Signing of the Constitution Issue, Perf. 11							
2360	22¢ Constitution and Signer's Hand-Holding Quill Pen 09/17/87	.45	.20	2.25	(4)	1.25	169
2361	22¢ Certified Public Accountants 09/21/87	*1.50*	.20	*7.00*	(4)	7.50	163
a	Black omitted	*725.00*					
Locomotives Booklet Issue, Perf. 10 Horizontally							
2362	22¢ Stourbridge Lion, 1829 10/01/87	.55	.20			1.25	143
2363	22¢ Best Friend of Charleston, 1830 10/01/87	.55	.20			1.25	143
2364	22¢ John Bull, 1831 10/01/87	.55	.20			1.25	143
2365	22¢ Brother Jonathan, 1832 10/01/87	.55	.20			1.25	143
a	Red omitted	—					
2366	22¢ Gowan & Marx, 1839 10/01/87	.55	.20			1.25	143
a	Booklet pane of 5, #2362-66	2.75	2.50			3.00	143
	#2362-66 issued only in booklets. All stamps are imperf. at sides or imperf. at sides and bottom.						
Christmas Issue, Perf. 11							
2367	22¢ Madonna and Child, by Moroni 10/23/87	.40	.20	2.00	(4)	1.25	529
2368	22¢ Christmas Ornaments 10/23/87	.40	.20	1.75	(4)	1.25	978
	Pair with full vertical gutter between	—					

Horace Mann (1796-1859)

Horace Mann—a pioneer in the field of public education—advocated free and nonsectarian schools for all children. Largely self-taught, he graduated in 1819 from Brown University. A distinguished lawyer in Boston, he was elected to the Massachusetts legislature where he voted in 1837 to create the nation's first state board of education. He was selected as its first secretary. During his 12-year tenure, he transformed the state's schools by establishing standards for teachers and a school to train them; increasing the number of schools; and successfully establishing free libraries. The annual reports he issued are today still considered masterpieces of educational thought. After serving briefly in the U.S. Congress, Mann became president of Antioch College in Ohio in 1853. It was at this new nonsectarian institution committed to coeducation and equal opportunity that Mann worked for the balance of his life. Just weeks before he died, he told the graduating class, "Be ashamed to die until you have won some victory for humanity." ▪

1988

Issues of 1988		Un	U	PB	#	FDC	Q(M)
Winter Olympic Games Issue, Perf. 11							
2369	22¢ Skier and Olympic Rings 01/10/88	.40	.20	1.75	(4)	1.00	159
2370	22¢ Australia Bicentennial 01/10/88	.40	.20	1.75	(4)	1.75	146
Black Heritage Issue							
2371	22¢ James Weldon Johnson and Music from "Lift Ev'ry Voice and Sing" 02/02/88	.40	.20	1.75	(4)	1.75	97
American Cats Issue							
2372	22¢ Siamese and Exotic Shorthair 02/05/88	.45	.20			2.00	40
2373	22¢ Abyssinian and Himalayan 02/05/88	.45	.20			2.00	40
2374	22¢ Maine Coon and Burmese 02/05/88	.45	.20			2.00	40
2375	22¢ American Shorthair and Persian 02/05/88	.45	.20			2.00	40
a	Block of 4, #2372-75	1.90	1.90	4.00	(4)	4.50	
American Sports Issue							
2376	22¢ Knute Rockne Holding Football on Field 03/09/88	.40	.20	2.25	(4)	3.50	97
2377	25¢ Francis Ouimet and Ouimet Hitting Fairway Shot 06/13/88	.45	.20	2.50	(4)	4.50	153
2378	25¢ Love 07/04/88	.45	.20	1.90	(4)	1.00	841
a	Imperf., pair	3,250.00					
2379	45¢ Love 08/08/88	.65	.20	3.25	(4)	1.25	180
Summer Olympic Games Issue							
2380	25¢ Gymnast on Rings 08/19/88	.45	.20	1.90	(4)	1.25	157

Louisa May Alcott (1832-1888)

Author Louisa May Alcott grew up in the company of such luminaries as Ralph Waldo Emerson and Henry David Thoreau, acquaintances of her father, Amos Bronson Alcott, a noted teacher and abolitionist. She was educated at home and as a young woman began to work as a teacher and domestic. She then began to write, first turning out potboilers under an assumed name. During the Civil War, she served as a nurse in the Union Hospital in Washington's Georgetown. Her letters from this period were revised and published in *Hospital Sketches*, establishing her literary reputation. She briefly worked as editor of a children's magazine, *Merry's Museum*, before publishing her autobiographical classic, *Little Women*, in two installments, in 1868 and 1869. Both volumes were great successes; the book has been translated into many languages and is still considered a definitive portrait of family life in middle-class American households of the period. Through her writing, Louisa was able to support her family and pay off the debt that hounded her father. Living mostly in Boston, she also spent time on reform efforts on behalf of temperance and women's rights. ■

2369

2370

2371

2372   **2373**

2374   **2375**   **2375a**

2376   **2377**

2378

2379

2380

	Issues of 1988		Un	U	PB	#	FDC	Q(M)
2394	$8.75 Express Mail	10/04/88	13.50	8.00	54.00	(4)	27.50	
	Special Occasions Booklet Issue							
2395	25¢ Happy Birthday	10/22/88	.50	.20			1.25	120
2396	25¢ Best Wishes	10/22/88	.50	.20			1.25	120
a	Booklet pane of 6, 3 #2395 and							
	3 #2396 with gutter between		3.50	3.25			4.00	
2397	25¢ Thinking of You	10/22/88	.50	.20			1.25	120
2398	25¢ Love You	10/22/88	.50	.20			1.25	120
a	Booklet pane of 6, 3 #2397 and							
	3 #2398 with gutter between		3.50	3.25			4.00	
b	As "a," imperf. horizontally		—					
	#2395-98a issued only in booklets. All stamps are imperf. on one side or on one side and top or bottom.							
	Christmas Issue							
2399	25¢ Madonna and Child,							
	by Botticelli	10/20/88	.45	.20	1.90	(4)	1.25	844
a	Gold omitted		30.00					
2400	25¢ One-Horse Open							
	Sleigh and Village Scene	10/20/88	.45	.20	1.90	(4)	1.25	1,038
	Pair with full vertical gutter between		—					

Dorothea Dix (1802-1887)

Born into a troubled New England family, social reformer and political activist Dorothea Dix drew on her indomitable spirit in facing life's adversities. Resisting conventional expectations for women, Dix rejected marriage and devoted her life to the causes that mattered to her. A champion of the mentally ill—her mother reportedly suffered from mental illness, her father from alcoholism—Dix brought about significant improvements in treatment, helping to establish specialized hospitals throughout the country. As part of her campaign, Dix documented her field observations and reported before major legislative bodies about the wretched conditions in which mentally ill people were locked away in prisons and poorhouses. During the Civil War, she became the first Superintendent of United States Army Nurses, along the way improving conditions for the wounded as well as recruiting and protecting the welfare of a legion of female nurses. Ever resourceful, Dix managed to secure needed supplies and medicines from private sources when the government failed to provide them. After the war, Dix returned to her crusade to help the mentally ill. ■

2394

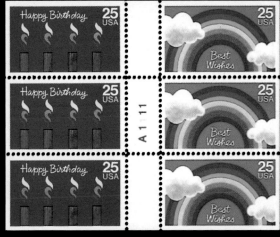

2395   2396   2396a

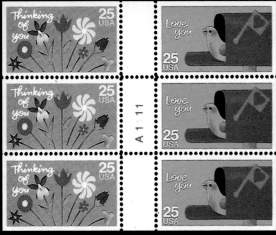

2397   2398   2398a

2399

2400

	Issues of 1989		Un	U	PB	#	FDC	Q(M)
	Priority Mail Issue, Perf. 11 x 11.5							
2419	$2.40 Moon Landing	07/20/89	4.00	2.00	17.50	(4)	7.50	
a	Black (engr.) omitted		2,500.00					
b	Imperf., pair		750.00					
c	Black (litho.) omitted		3,250.00					
	Perf. 11							
2420	25¢ Letter Carriers	08/30/89	.45	.20	1.90	(4)	1.25	188
	Constitution Bicentennial Issue							
2421	25¢ Bill of Rights	09/25/89	.45	.20	3.00	(4)	1.00	192
a	Black omitted		325.00					
	Prehistoric Animals Issue							
2422	25¢ Tyrannosaurus	10/01/89	.65	.20			1.50	102
2423	25¢ Pteranodon	10/01/89	.65	.20			1.50	102
2424	25¢ Stegosaurus	10/01/89	.65	.20			1.50	102
2425	25¢ Brontosaurus	10/01/89	.65	.20			1.50	102
a	Block of 4, #2422-25		3.00	2.00	3.50	(4)	3.00	
b	As "a," black omitted		750.00					
	America/PUAS Issue (See also #C121)							
2426	25¢ Southwest Carved Figure							
	(A.D. 1150-1350), Emblem of the							
	Postal Union of the Americas	10/12/89	.45	.20	2.00	(4)	1.00	137
	Christmas Issue, Perf. 11.5							
2427	25¢ Madonna and							
	Child, by Caracci	10/19/89	.45	.20	2.00	(4)	1.00	913
a	Booklet pane of 10		4.75	3.50			6.00	
b	Red (litho.) omitted		850.00					
	Perf. 11							
2428	25¢ Sleigh Full of Presents	10/19/89	.45	.20	1.90	(4)	1.00	900
a	Vertical pair, imperf.							
	horizontally		2,000.00					
	Booklet Stamp Issue, Perf. 11.5 on 2 or 3 sides							
2429	25¢ Single from booklet							
	pane (#2428)	10/19/89	.45	.20			1.00	399
a	Booklet pane of 10		4.75	3.50			6.00	40
b	As "a," imperf. horiz. between		—					
c	Vertical pair, imperf. horizontally		—					
d	As "a," red omitted		—					
e	Imperf., pair		—					
	In #2429, runners on sleigh are twice as thick as in 2428; bow on package at rear of sleigh							
	is same color as package; board running underneath sleigh is pink.							
2430	Not assigned							
	Self-Adhesive, Die-Cut							
2431	25¢ Eagle and Shield	11/10/89	.50	.20			1.25	75
a	Booklet pane of 18		11.00					
b	Vertical pair, no							
	die-cutting between		850.00					
2432	Not assigned							

2419

2420

2421

2422   2423

2424   2425

2425a

2426

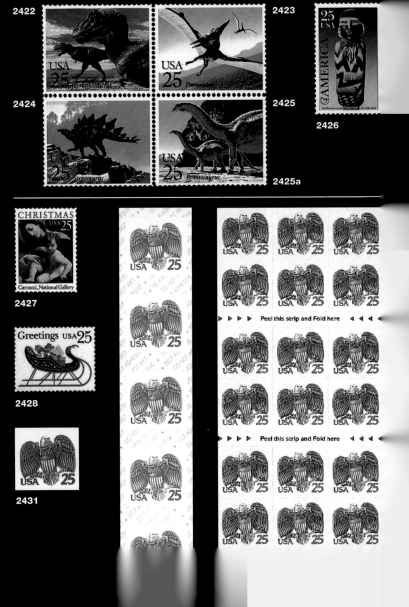

2427

2428

2431

1990-1995

	Issues of 1990		Un	U	PB	#	FDC	Q(M)
	Perf 11							
2444	25¢ Wyoming Statehood	02/23/90	.45	.20	2.00	(4)	1.00	169
a	Black (engr.) omitted		2,100.00	—				
	Classic Films Issue							
2445	25¢ The Wizard of Oz	03/23/90	1.00	.20			2.50	44
2446	25¢ Gone With the Wind	03/23/90	1.00	.20			2.50	44
2447	25¢ Beau Geste	03/23/90	1.00	.20			2.50	44
2448	25¢ Stagecoach	03/23/90	1.00	.20			2.50	44
a	Block of 4, #2445-48		4.50	3.50	6.00	(4)	5.00	
	Literary Arts Issue							
2449	25¢ Marianne Moore	04/18/90	.45	.20	2.00	(4)	1.25	150
2450	Not assigned							
	Issues of 1990-1995, Transportation Issue, Coil Stamps, Perf. 9.8 Vertically							
2451	4¢ Steam Carriage 1866	01/25/91	.20	.20	1.10	(5)	1.25	
a	Imperf., pair		700.00					
b	Untagged		.20	.20	1.10	(5)		
2452	5¢ Circus Wagon 1900s,							
	intaglio printing	08/31/91	.20	.20	1.25	(5)	1.50	
a	Untagged, dull gum		.20	.20	1.25	(5)		
c	Imperf., pair		900.00					
2452B	5¢ Circus Wagon							
	(2452), gravure printing	12/08/92	.20	.20	1.50	(5)	1.50	
f	Printed with luminescent ink		.20	.20	2.10	(5)		
2452D	5¢ Circus Wagon							
	(2452), gravure printing	03/20/95	.20	.20	1.60	(5)	2.00	
e	Imperf., pair		—					
g	Printed with luminescent ink		.20	.20	1.90	(5)		
2453	5¢ Canoe 1800s, precanceled,							
	intaglio printing	05/25/91	.20	.20	1.50	(5)	1.25	
a	Imperf., pair		300.00					
2454	5¢ Canoe 1800s,							
	precanceled, gravure printing	10/22/91	.20	.20	1.40	(5)	1.25	
2455-56	Not assigned							
2457	10¢ Tractor Trailer, Bureau							
	precanceled, intaglio printing	05/25/91	.20	.20	2.10	(5)	1.25	
a	Imperf., pair		250.00					
2458	10¢ Tractor Trailer, Bureau							
	precanceled, gravure printing	05/25/94	.20	.20	2.10	(5)	1.25	
2459-62	Not assigned							
2463	20¢ Cog Railway Car 1870s	06/09/95	.40	.20	4.00	(5)	1.25	
a	Imperf., pair		125.00					
2464	23¢ Lunch Wagon 1890s	04/12/91	.45	.20	3.75	(5)	1.25	
a	Prephosphored uncoated paper		.45	.20	4.50	(5)		
b	Imperf., pair		150.00					
2465	Not assigned							
2466	32¢ Ferryboat 1900s	06/02/95	.60	.20	5.50	(5)	1.25	
a	Imperf., pair		—					
b	Bright blue, prephosphored							
	uncoated paper		6.00	4.50	125.00	(5)		
2467	Not assigned							
2468	$1 Seaplane 1914	04/20/90	1.75	.50	9.25	(5)	2.50	
a	Imperf., pair		2,750.00	—				
b	Prephosphored uncoated paper		1.75	.50	9.25	(5)		
c	Prephosphored coated paper		1.75	.50	9.00	(5)		
2469	Not assigned							

2445

2446

2444

The WIZARD OF OZ USA 25

USA 25 **GONE WITH THE WIND**

2447

BEAU GESTE USA 25

STAGECOACH USA 25

2448

2448a

Marianne Moore 25 USA

American Poet 1887-1972

2449

Steam Carriage 04 USA 1866

2451

Circus Wagon 1900s 05 USA

2452

Circus Wagon 1900's USA 5¢

2452D

Canoe 1800s Additional Nonprofit Postage Paid USA 05

2453

Canoe 1800s Additional Nonprofit Postage Paid USA 05

2454

Tractor Trailer Additional Presort 1930s Postage Paid USA 10

2457

Cog Railway 1870s 20 USA

2463

Lunch Wagon 1890s 23 USA

2464

Ferryboat 1900s 32 USA

2466

$1 USA Seaplane 1914

2468

1990-1995

	Issues of 1993-1995		Un	U	PB	#	FDC	Q(M)
	Perf. 10 x 11 on 2 or 3 sides							
2486	29¢ African Violet	10/08/93	.50	.20			1.00	
a	Booklet pane of 10		5.50	*4.00*			4.00	
2487	32¢ Peach	07/08/95	.60	.20			1.50	
2488	32¢ Pear	07/08/95	.60	.20			1.50	
a	Booklet pane, 5 each #2487-88		6.00	*4.25*			7.50	
b	Pair, #2487-88		1.25	.30				
	Issues of 1993, Self-Adhesive, Die-Cut							
2489	29¢ Red Squirrel	06/25/93	.50	.20			1.25	
a	Booklet pane of 18		10.00					
2490	29¢ Red Rose	08/19/93	.50	.20			1.25	
a	Booklet pane of 18		10.00					
2491	29¢ Pine Cone	11/05/93	.50	.20			1.25	
a	Booklet pane of 18		11.00					
b	Horizontal pair, no die cutting between		—					
c	Coil with plate #B1		—	5.00	6.75	(5)		
	Serpentine Die-Cut 11.3 x 11.7 on 2, 3 or 4 sides							
2492	32¢ Pink Rose	06/02/95	.60	.20			1.25	
a	Booklet pane of 20 plus label		12.00					
b	Booklet pane of 15 plus label		8.75					
c	Horizontal pair, no die cutting between		—					
d	As "a," 2 stamps and parts of 7 others printed on backing liner		—					
e	Booklet pane of 14		21.00					
f	Booklet pane of 16		21.00					
g	Coil with plate #S111		—	3.00	6.00	(5)		
h	Vertical pair, no die cutting between		—					
2493	32¢ Peach	07/08/95	.60	.20			1.25	
2494	32¢ Pear	07/08/95	.60	.20			1.25	
a	Booklet pane, 10 each #2493-2494		12.50					
b	Pair, #2493-2494		1.20					
	Coil Stamps, Serpentine Die Cut Vert.							
2495	32¢ Peach	07/08/95	.60	.20			1.25	
2495A	32¢ Pear	07/08/95	.60	.20			1.25	
b	Pair #2495-2495A		1.20		6.25	(5)		
	Issues of 1990, Olympians Issue, Perf. 11							
2496	25¢ Jesse Owens	07/06/90	.60	.20			1.25	36
2497	25¢ Ray Ewry	07/06/90	.60	.20			1.25	36
2498	25¢ Hazel Wightman	07/06/90	.60	.20			1.25	36
2499	25¢ Eddie Eagan	07/06/90	.60	.20			1.25	36
2500	25¢ Helene Madison	07/06/90	.60	.20			1.25	36
a	Strip of 5, #2496-2500		3.25	2.50	8.00	(10)	4.00	7
	Indian Headdresses Booklet Issue, Perf. 11 on 2 or 3 sides							
2501	25¢ Assiniboine Headdress	08/17/90	.80	.20			1.25	124
2502	25¢ Cheyenne Headdress	08/17/90	.80	.20			1.25	124
2503	25¢ Comanche Headdress	08/17/90	.80	.20			1.25	124
2504	25¢ Flathead Headdress	08/17/90	.80	.20			1.25	124
2505	25¢ Shoshone Headdress	08/17/90	.80	.20			1.25	124
a	Booklet pane of 10, 2 each of #2501-05		8.50	*3.50*			6.00	62
b	As "a," black omitted		*3,250.00*					
c	Strip of 5		2.75	1.00				
d	As "a," horizontal imperf. between		—					
	#2501-05 issued only in booklets. All stamps imperf. top or bottom, or top or bottom and right edge.							

2486

2487   **2488**

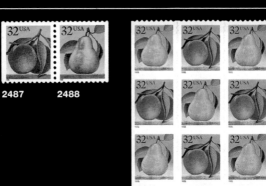

2487-2488a

2489   **2490**   **2491**   **2492**

2496   **2497**   **2498**   **2499**   **2500** **2500a**

2501   **2502**   **2503**   **2504**   **2505** **2505a**

	Issues of 1991		Un	U	PB	#	FDC	Q(M)
	Perf. 11							
2524	29¢ Tulip	04/05/91	.50	.20	2.25	(4)	1.00	
2524A	Perf. 13		.75	.20	4.50	(4)		
	Coil Stamps, Roulette 10 Vertically							
2525	29¢ Tulip	08/16/91	.50	.20	4.50	(5)	1.00	
	Issues of 1992, Perf. 10 Vertically							
2526	29¢ Tulip	03/03/92	.50	.20	4.50	(5)	1.00	
	Issues of 1991, Booklet Stamp, Perf. 11 on 2 or 3 sides							
2527	29¢ Tulip (2524), single from bklt.		.50	.20			1.00	
a	Booklet pane of 10	04/05/91	5.50	3.50			4.00	
b	As "a," vertically imperf. between		1,500.00					
c	Horizontal pair, imperf. vertically		250.00					
d	As "a," imperf. horizontally		2,750.00					
	Flag With Olympic Rings Booklet Issue, Perf. 11							
2528	29¢ U.S. Flag, Olympic Rings,							
	single from booklet	04/21/91	.50	.20			1.25	
a	Booklet pane of 10	04/21/91	5.25	3.50			5.00	
	Issues of 1991-94, Perf. 10 Vertically							
2529	19¢ Fishing Boat	08/08/91	.35	.20	3.25	(5)	1.50	
a	New printing, Type II	1993	.35	.20	3.75	(5)		
b	As "a," untagged		1.00	.40	7.50	(5)		
	Perf. 9.8							
2529C	19¢ Fishing Boat	06/25/94	.50	.20	5.25	(5)	1.50	
	Type II stamps have finer dot pattern, smoother edges along type. #2529C has only one loop of rope tying up the boat.							
	Issue of 1991, Ballooning Booklet Issue, Perf. 10							
2530	19¢ Overhead View of Balloon,							
	single from booklet	05/17/91	.35	.20			1.25	
a	Booklet pane of 10	05/17/91	3.50	2.75			5.00	
	#2530 was issued only in booklets. All stamps are imperf. on one side or on one side and bottom.							
	Perf. 11							
2531	29¢ Flags on Parade	05/30/91	.50	.20	2.40	(4)	1.00	
	Self-Adhesive, Die-Cut, Imperf.							
2531A	29¢ Liberty Torch, single							
	stamp from pane	06/25/91	.55	.25			1.25	
b	Pane of 18	06/25/91	10.50					
	Perf. 11							
2532	50¢ Founding of Switzerland	02/22/91	1.00	.25	5.00	(4)	1.40	100
a	Vertical pair, imperf. horizontally		2,250.00					
2533	29¢ Vermont Statehood	03/01/91	.55	.20	3.00	(4)	1.50	0.1
2534	29¢ Savings Bonds	04/30/91	.50	.20	2.50	(4)	1.25	151
	Perf. 12.5 x 13							
2535	29¢ Love	05/09/91	.50	.20	2.50	(4)	1.25	631
2535A	Perf. 11		.75	.20	4.00	(4)		
	Booklet Stamp, Perf. 11 on 2 or 3 sides							
2536	29¢ (2535), single from booklet		.50	.20			1.25	
a	Booklet pane of 10	05/09/91	5.25	3.50			5.00	
	Perf. 11							
2537	52¢ Love	05/09/91	.90	.20	4.50	(4)	1.25	200

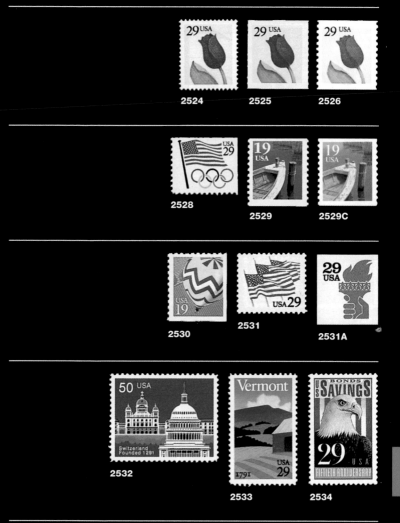

2524   2525   2526

2528   2529   2529C

2530   2531   2531A

2532   2533   2534

2535

2537

	Issues of 1991		Un	U	PB	#	FDC	Q(M)
	Performing Arts Issue, Perf. 11							
2550	29¢ Cole Porter at Piano,							
	Sheet Music	06/08/91	.50	.20	2.50	(4)	1.25	150
a	Vertical pair, imperf. horizontally		650.00					
2551	29¢ Operations Desert Shield/							
	Desert Storm	07/02/91	.50	.20	2.50	(4)	2.50	200
a	Vertical pair, imperf. horizontally		1,500.00					
	Booklet Stamp, Perf. 11 on 1 or 2 sides							
2552	29¢ Operations Desert Shield/Desert							
	Storm (2551), single from booklet	07/02/91	.50	.20			2.50	200
a	Booklet pane of 5	07/02/91	2.75	2.25			4.75	40
	Summer Olympic Games Issue, Perf. 11							
2553	29¢ Pole Vaulter	07/12/91	.50	.20			1.25	34
2554	29¢ Discus Thrower	07/12/91	.50	.20			1.25	34
2555	29¢ Women Sprinters	07/12/91	.50	.20			1.25	34
2556	29¢ Javelin Thrower	07/12/91	.50	.20			1.25	34
2557	29¢ Women Hurdlers	07/12/91	.50	.20			1.25	34
a	Strip of 5, #2553-57		2.75	2.25	7.50	(10)	3.00	34
2558	29¢ Numismatics	08/13/91	.50	.20	2.50	(4)	1.25	150
	World War II Issue, 1941: A World at War, Miniature Sheet							
2559	Sheet of 10 and central label	09/03/91	5.25	5.00			7.00	15
a	29¢ Burma Road		.50	.30			1.50	15
b	29¢ America's First Peacetime Draft		.50	.30			1.50	15
c	29¢ Lend-Lease Act		.50	.30			1.50	15
d	29¢ Atlantic Charter		.50	.30			1.50	15
e	29¢ Arsenal of Democracy		.50	.30			1.50	15
f	29¢ Destroyer *Reuben James*		.50	.30			1.50	15
g	29¢ Civil Defense		.50	.30			1.50	15
h	29¢ Liberty Ship		.50	.30			1.50	15
i	29¢ Pearl Harbor		.50	.30			1.50	15
j	29¢ U.S. Declaration of War		.50	.30			1.50	15
k	29¢ Black omitted		10,000.00					

Jesse Owens (1913-1980)

Born to an Alabama sharecropper in the days of segregation, Jesse Owens overcame tremendous odds to become the first American in Olympic track and field history to win four gold medals in a single Olympics. Held in Berlin, Germany, the 1936 Olympics proved to be a colossal disappointment for Adolf Hitler, who witnessed Owens's athletic triumphs over the so-called "superior" German competitors. From the moment Jesse Owens burst on the track and field scene as a college student at Ohio State University, records began to fall. In 1935 he tied one and set three world records, including shattering the record for the broad jump. Overcoming the humiliations of segregation and bigotry, Owens's strength of spirit and natural ability made him one of the finest athletes of all time. His accomplishments affirmed that individual excellence, not race or national origin, distinguishes one person from another. Awarded the Medal of Freedom in 1976, Owens died an American icon four years later at the age of 66. ■

2550

2551

2553

2554

2555

2556

2557

2557a

NUMISMATICS

2558

a
29
USA
Burma Road, 717-mile lifeline to China

b
29
USA
America's first peacetime draft, 1940

c
29
USA
U.S. supports allies with Lend Lease Act

d
29
USA
Atlantic Charter sets war aims of allies

e
29
USA
America becomes "arsenal of democracy"

1941: A World at War

f
29
USA
Destroyer Reuben James sunk October 31

g
29
USA
Civil Defense mobilizes Americans at home

h
29
USA
First Liberty ship delivered December 30

i
29
USA
Japanese bomb Pearl Harbor, December 7

j
29
USA
U.S. declares war on Japan, December 8

2559

	Issues of 1991-1995		Un	U	PB	#	FDC	Q(M)
	Christmas Issue, Perf. 11							
2578	29¢ Madonna and Child,							
	by Antoniazzo Romano	10/17/91	.50	.20	2.50	(4)	1.25	401
a	Booklet pane of 10		5.50	3.25				30
b	As "a," single, red and black omitted		3,500.00					
2579	29¢ Santa Claus in Chimney	10/17/91	.50	.20	2.50	(4)	1.25	900
a	Horizontal pair, imperf. vertically		300.00					
b	Vertical pair, imperf. horizontally		500.00					
	Booklet Stamps, Perf. 11 on 2 or 3 sides							
2580	29¢ Santa Claus (2579),							
	Type I, single from booklet	10/17/91	1.75	.20			1.25	
2581	29¢ Santa Claus (2579),							
	Type II, single from booklet	10/17/91	1.75	.20			1.25	
a	Pair, #2580, 2581	10/17/91	3.50	.25				28
b	Booklet pane, 2 each		7.50	1.25			2.50	
	The extreme left brick in top row of chimney is missing from Type II, #2581.							
2582	29¢ Santa Claus Checking							
	List, single from booklet	10/17/91	.50	.20			1.25	
a	Booklet pane of 4	10/17/91	2.00	1.25			2.50	28
2583	29¢ Santa Claus with Present							
	Under Tree, single from booklet	10/17/91	.50	.20			1.25	
a	Booklet pane of 4	10/17/91	2.00	1.25			2.50	28
2584	29¢ Santa Claus at Fireplace,							
	single from booklet	10/17/91	.50	.20			1.25	
a	Booklet pane of 4	10/17/91	2.00	1.25			2.50	28
2585	29¢ Santa Claus and Sleigh,							
	single from booklet	10/17/91	.50	.20			1.25	
a	Booklet pane of 4	10/17/91	2.00	1.25			2.50	28
	#2582-85 issued only in booklets. All stamps are imperf. at top or bottom, or at top or bottom and right side.							
	Perf. 11.2							
2587	32¢ James K. Polk	11/02/95	.60	.20	3.00	(4)	1.25	
	Issues of 1994, Perf. 11.5							
2590	$1 Victory at Saratoga	05/05/94	1.90	.50	7.60	(4)	2.50	
2592	$5 Washington and Jackson	08/19/94	8.00	2.50	40.00	(4)	10.00	

Visit us online at The Postal Store at www.usps.com

or call 1-800-STAMP-24

2578

2579

2580   **2581**   **2581a**

2582   **2583**

2584   **2585**

2587

2590   **2592**

	Issues of 1992		Un	U	PB	#	FDC	Q(M)
	Winter Olympic Games Issue							
2611	29¢ Hockey	01/11/92	.50	.20			1.25	32
2612	29¢ Figure Skating	01/11/92	.50	.20			1.25	32
2613	29¢ Speed Skating	01/11/92	.50	.20			1.25	32
2614	29¢ Skiing	01/11/92	.50	.20			1.25	32
2615	29¢ Bobsledding	01/11/92	.50	.20			1.25	32
a	Strip of 5, #2611-15		2.75	2.50	6.50	(10)	3.50	
2616	29¢ World Columbian							
	Stamp Expo	01/24/92	.50	.20	2.50	(4)	1.25	149
a	Tagging omitted		8.50					
	Black Heritage Issue							
2617	29¢ W.E.B. DuBois	01/31/92	.50	.20	2.50	(4)	1.75	150
2618	29¢ Love	02/06/92	.50	.20	2.50	(4)	1.25	835
a	Horizontal pair, imperf. vertically		750.00					
2619	29¢ Olympic Baseball	04/03/92	.50	.20	2.75	(4)	2.00	160
	First Voyage of Christopher Columbus Issue, Perf. 11 x 10.5							
2620	29¢ Seeking Queen Isabella's							
	Support	04/24/92	.50	.20			1.25	40
2621	29¢ Crossing The Atlantic	04/24/92	.50	.20			1.25	40
2622	29¢ Approaching Land	04/24/92	.50	.20			1.25	40
2623	29¢ Coming Ashore	04/24/92	.50	.20			1.25	40
a	Block of 4, #2620-23		2.00	2.00	2.50	(4)	2.75	

Virginia Dare

On August 18, 1587, when Virginia Dare was born on Roanoke Island, Virginia (now North Carolina), she became the first child born to English parents in America. Dare's parents had sailed from England on May 8, 1587, with a group of approximately 120 settlers. The expedition was sponsored by Sir Walter Raleigh, who intended for the group to settle in the Chesapeake Bay area; instead, the ship landed on Roanoke Island. On August 27, 1587, John White, governor of the colony and Virginia Dare's grandfather, sailed for England to obtain supplies. The war between England and Spain delayed his return to the colony. When he arrived with a relief expedition in August 1590, there was no sign of the colonists except for the word "CROATOAN" carved into a post and the letters "CRO" on a tree. No one has ever explained the mystery of the vanished "Lost Colony."

2611 2612 2613 2614 2615 2615a

2616

2617

2618

2619

2620 2621

2622 2623 2623a

1992

2624

2625

2626

2627

2628

2629

Issues of 1992		Un	U	PB	#	FDC	Q(M)
The Voyages of Columbus Souvenir Sheets, Perf. 10.5							
2624	First Sighting of Land,						
	sheet of 3 05/22/92	1.75	—			2.10	2
a	1¢ deep blue	.20	.20			1.50	
b	4¢ ultramarine	.20	.20			1.50	
c	$1 salmon	1.65	1.00			2.00	
2625	Claiming a New World,						
	sheet of 3 05/22/92	6.75	—			8.00	2
a	2¢ brown violet	.20	.20			1.50	
b	3¢ green	.20	.20			1.50	
c	$4 crimson lake	6.50	4.00			8.00	
2626	Seeking Royal Support,						
	sheet of 3 05/22/92	1.40	—			1.75	2
a	5¢ chocolate	.20	.20			1.50	
b	30¢ orange brown	.50	.30			1.50	
c	50¢ slate blue	.80	.50			1.50	
2627	Royal Favor Restored,						
	sheet of 3 05/22/92	5.25	—			6.25	2
a	6¢ purple	.20	.20			1.50	
b	8¢ magenta	.20	.20			1.50	
c	$3 yellow green	4.75	3.00			6.00	
2628	Reporting Discoveries,						
	sheet of 3 05/22/92	3.75	—			4.50	2
a	10¢ black brown	.20	.20			1.50	
b	15¢ dark green	.25	.20			1.50	
c	$2 brown red	3.25	2.00			4.00	
2629	$5 Christopher Columbus,						
	sheet of 1 05/22/92	8.50	—			10.00	2
a	$5 black	8.00	5.00				

John Muir (1838-1914)

The American conservation movement owes its beginnings to the extraordinary vision and energy of Scottish-born naturalist John Muir, who has been dubbed "the Father of our National Parks." Muir's love of nature and abiding appreciation for its beauty were transformed into activism after he spent time in California's Yosemite Valley and in Alaska during the second half of the 19th century. Muir believed nature was being sacrificed to one-sided economic interests. To counteract the menace and enlist others in his struggle to protect America's natural bounty, he wrote extensively and eventually founded the Sierra Club, an environmental organization named for the Sierra Nevada mountains, which Muir called the "Range of Light." In 1890, he achieved his greatest victory when Yosemite was established as a national park. In 1964, fifty years after Muir's death, the U.S. Postal Service issued a stamp commemorating the man who had done so much to preserve America's natural legacy. ■

1992

	Issues of 1992		Un	U	FDC	Q(M)
	Wildflowers Issue (continued)					
2672	29¢ Fringed Gentian	07/24/92	.50	.20	1.25	11
2673	29¢ Yellow Lady's Slipper	07/24/92	.50	.20	1.25	11
2674	29¢ Passionflower	07/24/92	.50	.20	1.25	11
2675	29¢ Bunchberry	07/24/92	.50	.20	1.25	11
2676	29¢ Pasqueflower	07/24/92	.50	.20	1.25	11
2677	29¢ Round-Lobed Hepatica	07/24/92	.50	.20	1.25	11
2678	29¢ Wild Columbine	07/24/92	.50	.20	1.25	11
2679	29¢ Fireweed	07/24/92	.50	.20	1.25	11
2680	29¢ Indian Pond Lily	07/24/92	.50	.20	1.25	11
2681	29¢ Turk's Cap Lily	07/24/92	.50	.20	1.25	11
2682	29¢ Dutchman's Breeches	07/24/92	.50	.20	1.25	11
2683	29¢ Trumpet Honeysuckle	07/24/92	.50	.20	1.25	11
2684	29¢ Jacob's Ladder	07/24/92	.50	.20	1.25	11
2685	29¢ Plains Prickly Pear	07/24/92	.50	.20	1.25	11
2686	29¢ Moss Campion	07/24/92	.50	.20	1.25	11
2687	29¢ Bearberry	07/24/92	.50	.20	1.25	11
2688	29¢ Mexican Hat	07/24/92	.50	.20	1.25	11
2689	29¢ Harebell	07/24/92	.50	.20	1.25	11
2690	29¢ Desert Five Spot	07/24/92	.50	.20	1.25	11
2691	29¢ Smooth Solomon's Seal	07/24/92	.50	.20	1.25	11
2692	29¢ Red Maids	07/24/92	.50	.20	1.25	11
2693	29¢ Yellow Skunk Cabbage	07/24/92	.50	.20	1.25	11
2694	29¢ Rue Anemone	07/24/92	.50	.20	1.25	11
2695	29¢ Standing Cypress	07/24/92	.50	.20	1.25	11
2696	29¢ Wild Flax	07/24/92	.50	.20	1.25	11
a	Pane of 50, #2647-96		25.00	—	30.00	11

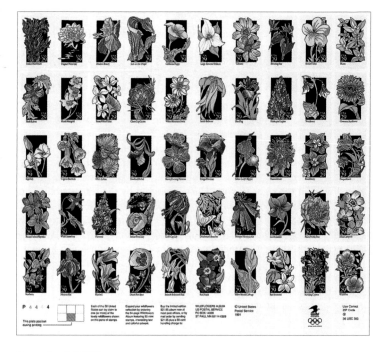

Example of #2696a

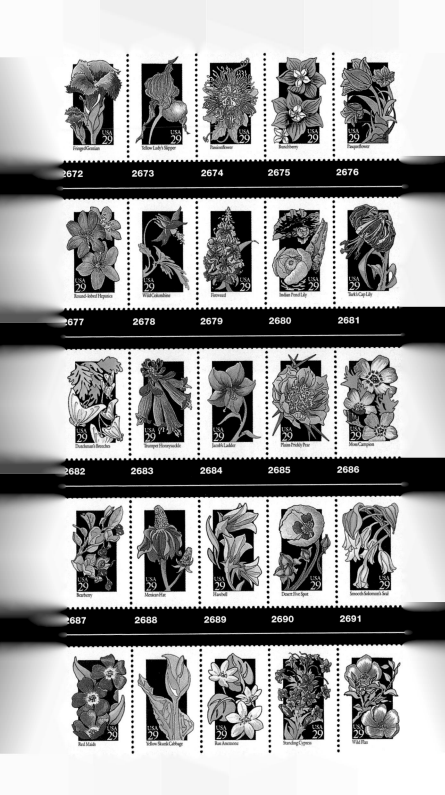

Fringed Gentian
Yellow Lady's Slipper
Passionflower
Bunchberry
Pasqueflower

2672 | 2673 | 2674 | 2675 | 2676

Round-lobed Hepatica
Wild Columbine
Fireweed
Indian Pond Lily
Turk's Cap Lily

2677 | 2678 | 2679 | 2680 | 2681

Dutchman's Breeches
Trumpet Honeysuckle
Jacob's Ladder
Plains Prickly Pear
Moss Campion

2682 | 2683 | 2684 | 2685 | 2686

Bearberry
Mexican Hat
Harebell
Desert Five Spot
Smooth Solomon's Seal

2687 | 2688 | 2689 | 2690 | 2691

Red Maids
Yellow Skunk Cabbage
Rue Anemone
Standing Cypress
Wild Flax

	Issues of 1992		Un	U	PB	#	FDC	Q(M)
	Wild Animals Issue, Perf. 11 Horizontally							
2705	29¢ Giraffe	10/01/92	.50	.20			1.25	80
2706	29¢ Giant Panda	10/01/92	.50	.20			1.25	80
2707	29¢ Flamingo	10/01/92	.50	.20			1.25	80
2708	29¢ King Penguins	10/01/92	.50	.20			1.25	80
2709	29¢ White Bengal Tiger	10/01/92	.50	.20			1.25	80
a	Booklet pane of 5, #2705-09		2.50	2.00			3.25	
b	As "a," imperf.		3,000.00					
	Christmas Issue, Perf. 11.5 x 11							
2710	29¢ Madonna and Child							
	by Giovanni Bellini	10/22/92	.50	.20	2.50	(4)	1.25	300
a	Booklet pane of 10		5.25	3.50			7.25	349
2711	29¢ Horse and Rider	10/22/92	.50	.20			1.25	125
2712	29¢ Toy Train	10/22/92	.50	.20			1.25	125
2713	29¢ Toy Steamer	10/22/92	.50	.20			1.25	125
2714	29¢ Toy Ship	10/22/92	.50	.20			1.25	125
a	Block of 4, #2711-14		2.00	1.10	2.75	(4)	2.75	
	Perf. 11							
2715	29¢ Horse and Rider	10/22/92	.85	.20			1.25	102
2716	29¢ Toy Train	10/22/92	.85	.20			1.25	102
2717	29¢ Toy Steamer	10/22/92	.85	.20			1.25	102
2718	29¢ Toy Ship	10/22/92	.85	.20			1.25	102
a	Booklet pane of 4, #2715-18		3.50	1.25			2.75	
2719	29¢ Toy Train (self-adhesive)	10/22/92	.60	.20			1.25	22
a	Booklet pane of 18		11.00					
	Lunar New Year Issue							
2720	29¢ Year of the Rooster	12/30/92	.50	.20	2.00	(4)	2.25	

Jackie Robinson (1919-1972)

In 1947, when black baseball players were confined to the Negro Leagues, 28-year-old Jackie Robinson signed on with the Brooklyn Dodgers. The landmark event broke the color barrier in Major League Baseball, and brought to an eventual end the practice of excluding black athletes from major league sports. Despite the hardships and insults he had to endure, the talented and stouthearted Robinson excelled, winning the respect and gratitude of blacks and whites alike. A string of honors marked his baseball career; he won the National League's batting title in 1949 and was named its most valuable player that same year. In 1962 he was inducted into the National Baseball Hall of Fame, having spent his entire Major League Baseball career with the Brooklyn Dodgers, where he led the team to a World Series victory and six National League pennants. In time, Robinson would speak out publicly for civil rights, and earn the posthumous honor from the U.S. Postal Service of no less than three stamps bearing his likeness. ▪

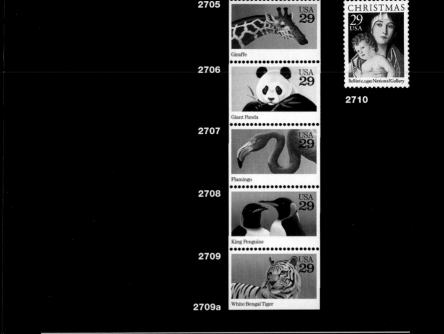

2705

2706

2707

2708

2709

2709a

Giraffe

Giant Panda

Flamingo

King Penguins

White Bengal Tiger

2710

2711 2712

2713 2714 2714a

2715 2716

2717 2718 2718a

2719

2720

2721 2722 2723

2724 2725 2726 2727 2728

2729 2730

2731
2732
2733
2734
2735
2736
2737
2731

2737b 2737a

Issues of 1993		Un	U	PB	#	FDC	Q(M)
Legends of American Music Series, Perf. 11							
2721	29¢ Elvis Presley	01/08/93	.50	.20	2.50	(4)	1.75	517
	Perf. 10							
2722	29¢ *Oklahoma!*	03/30/93	.50	.20	2.50	(4)	1.25	150
2723	29¢ Hank Williams	06/09/93	.50	.20	2.50	(4)	1.25	152
	Perf. 11.2 x 11.5							
2723A	29¢ Hank Williams		22.50	9.00	140.00	(4)	—	
Legends of American Music Series, Rock & Roll/Rhythm & Blues Issue, Perf. 10							
2724	29¢ Elvis Presley	06/16/93	.60	.20			1.25	14
2725	29¢ Bill Haley	06/16/93	.60	.20			1.25	14
2726	29¢ Clyde McPhatter	06/16/93	.60	.20			1.25	14
2727	29¢ Ritchie Valens	06/16/93	.60	.20			1.25	14
2728	29¢ Otis Redding	06/16/93	.60	.20			1.25	14
2729	29¢ Buddy Holly	06/16/93	.60	.20			1.25	14
2730	29¢ Dinah Washington	06/16/93	.60	.20			1.25	14
a	Vertical strip of 7, #2724-30		4.25		8.00	(10)	5.00	
	Perf. 11 Horizontally							
2731	29¢ Elvis Presley	06/16/93	.55	.20			1.25	99
2732	29¢ Bill Haley (2725)	06/16/93	.55	.20			1.25	33
2733	29¢ Clyde McPhatter (2726)	06/16/93	.55	.20			1.25	33
2734	29¢ Ritchie Valens (2727)	06/16/93	.55	.20			1.25	33
2735	29¢ Otis Redding	06/16/93	.55	.20			1.25	66
2736	29¢ Buddy Holly	06/16/93	.55	.20			1.25	66
2737	29¢ Dinah Washington	06/16/93	.55	.20			1.25	66
a	Booklet pane, 2 #2731, 1 each #2732-37		5.00	2.25			5.25	
b	Booklet pane of 4, #2731, 2735-37		2.25	1.50			2.75	
2738-40	Not assigned							

Elizabeth Blackwell (1821-1910)

Elizabeth Blackwell was the first woman to receive a medical degree in the United States. She was born in England and educated at home by her progressive father, who gave his daughters a better education than was customary for girls at that time. In 1832 the family moved to America. Six years later, after the death of her father, Blackwell worked as a teacher to help support her family. Determined to become a doctor, she applied to several medical schools but was rejected by all but one, Geneva College in upstate New York. She later learned that the male medical students, not the faculty, had voted to accept her application. After graduating, Blackwell—now a naturalized citizen of the United States—faced further discouragement when she was barred from practice at many institutions and snubbed by male colleagues. In 1853 she opened her own clinic in New York City, which grew into a busy hospital for women and children. She organized the Women's Medical College of the New York Infirmary in 1868, closing it 30 years later when Cornell University Medical College began accepting women. A devoted medical professional, she stressed and wrote about the importance of hygiene in preventing illness. ▪

2760 2761 2762 2763 2764 2764a

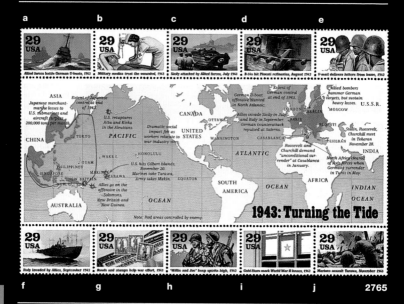

a b c d e

1943: Turning the Tide

f g h i j 2765

2766

2767

2768

2769

2770

2770a

Issues of 1993			Un	U	PB	#	FDC	Q(M)
Garden Flowers Issue, Perf. 11 Vertically								
2760	29¢ Hyacinth	05/15/93	.50	.20			1.50	200
2761	29¢ Daffodil	05/15/93	.50	.20			1.50	200
2762	29¢ Tulip	05/15/93	.50	.20			1.50	200
2763	29¢ Iris	05/15/93	.50	.20			1.50	200
2764	29¢ Lilac	05/15/93	.50	.20			1.50	200
a	Booklet pane of 5, #2760-64		2.50	*2.00*			3.00	
b	As "a," black omitted		*240.00*					
c	As "a," imperf.		*2,500.00*					
World War II Issue, 1943: Turning The Tide, Miniature Sheet, Perf. 11								
2765	Sheet of 10 and central label	05/31/93	5.25	5.00			7.00	
a	29¢ Allied Forces Battle German U-boats		.50	.30			1.50	12
b	29¢ Military Medics Treat the Wounded.		.50	.30			1.50	12
c	29¢ Sicily Attacked by Allied Forces		.50	.30			1.50	12
d	29¢ B-24s Hit Ploesti Refineries		.50	.30			1.50	12
e	29¢ V-Mail Delivers Letters from Home.		50	.30			1.50	12
f	29¢ Italy Invaded by Allies		.50	.30			1.50	12
g	29¢ Bonds and Stamps Help War Effort		.50	.30			1.50	12
h	29¢ "Willie and Joe" Keep Spirits High .		50	.30			1.50	12
i	29¢ Gold Stars Mark World War II Losses		.50	.30			1.50	12
j	29¢ Marines Assault Tarawa		.50	.30			1.50	12
2766	29¢ Joe Louis	06/22/93	.50	.20	2.50	(4)	2.00	160
Legends of American Music Series, Broadway Musicals Issue, Perf. 11 Horizontally								
2767	29¢ *Show Boat*	07/14/93	.50	.20			1.25	129
2768	29¢ *Porgy & Bess*	07/14/93	.50	.20			1.25	129
2769	29¢ *Oklahoma!*	07/14/93	.50	.20			1.25	129
2770	29¢ *My Fair Lady*	07/14/93	.50	.20			1.25	129
a	Booklet pane of 4, #2767-70		2.50	*2.00*			3.50	

Dr. Mary Walker (1832-1919)

Mary Edwards Walker was born into an abolitionist family in upstate New York. Passionate about women's rights and wanting to be a doctor, she entered Syracuse Medical College in 1853. When the Civil War broke out, Walker attempted to secure an appointment as an army surgeon. Denied a commission, she worked as an unpaid volunteer in a military hospital in Washington, D.C., and at tent hospitals in the Virginia battle zone. She finally was appointed an assistant surgeon in the Union Army. Believed to be a spy due to her frequent ventures into Confederate territory, Walker was imprisoned for four months. In 1865, she was awarded the Medal of Honor by President Andrew Johnson. The award was withdrawn in 1917 when Congress revised the criteria to require actual combat with the enemy. Walker never relinquished her medal and wore it for the rest of her life. In 1977 President Jimmy Carter restored her medal, making her the first woman to receive a Congressional Medal of Honor. ▪

1993

Issues of 1993		Un	U	PB	#	FDC	Q(M)
Legends of American Music Series, Country & Western Issue, Perf. 10							
2771	29¢ Hank Williams (2775)	09/25/93	.55	.20			1.25	25
2772	29¢ Patsy Cline (2777)	09/25/93	.55	.20			1.25	25
2773	29¢ The Carter Family (2776)	09/25/93	.55	.20			1.25	25
2774	29¢ Bob Wills (2778)	09/25/93	.55	.20			1.25	25
a	Block or horiz. strip of 4, #2771-74		2.20	1.75	3.00	(4)	3.00	
Booklet Stamps, Perf. 11 Horizontally							
2775	29¢ Hank Williams	09/25/93	.50	.20			1.25	170
2776	29¢ The Carter Family	09/25/93	.50	.20			1.25	170
2777	29¢ Patsy Cline	09/25/93	.50	.20			1.25	170
2778	29¢ Bob Wills	09/25/93	.50	.20			1.25	170
a	Booklet pane of 4, #2775-78		2.50	2.00			3.00	
National Postal Museum Issue, Perf. 11							
2779	Independence Hall, Benjamin Franklin, Printing Press, Colonial Post Rider	07/30/93	.50	.20			1.25	38
2780	Pony Express Rider, Civil War Soldier, Concord Stagecoach	07/30/93	.50	.20			1.25	38
2781	Biplane, Charles Lindbergh, Railway Mail Car, 1931 Model A Ford Mail Truck	07/30/93	.50	.20			1.25	38
2782	California Gold Rush Miner's Letter, Barcode and Circular Date Stamp	07/30/93	.50	.20			1.25	38
a	Block or strip of 4, #2779-82		2.00	1.75	2.00	(4)	2.75	
c	As "a," imperf.	3,500.00					
American Sign Language Issue, Perf. 11.5							
2783	29¢ Recognizing Deafness	09/20/93	.50	.20			1.25	42
2784	29¢ American Sign Language	09/20/93	.50	.20			1.25	42
a	Pair, #2783-84		1.00	.65	2.00	(4)	2.25	
Classic Books Issues, Perf. 11							
2785	29¢ *Rebecca of Sunnybrook Farm*	10/23/93	.50	.20			1.25	38
2786	29¢ *Little House on the Prairie*	10/23/93	.50	.20			1.25	38
2787	29¢ *The Adventures of Huckleberry Finn*	10/23/93	.50	.20			1.25	38
2788	29¢ *Little Women*	10/23/93	.50	.20			1.25	38
a	Block or horiz. strip of 4, #2785-88		2.00	2.00	5.00	(4)	2.75	
b	As "a," imperf.	3,000.00					

2771   **2772**

2775

2776

2777

2778

2773   **2774**   **2774a**

2778a

2779   **2780**

2781   **2782**   **2782a**

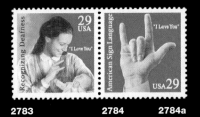

2783   **2784**   **2784a**

2785   **2786**

2787   **2788**   **2788a**

2791 **2792** **2795** **2796**

2789

2790

2793 **2794** **2794a**

2797 **2798** **2798c**

2799 **2800**

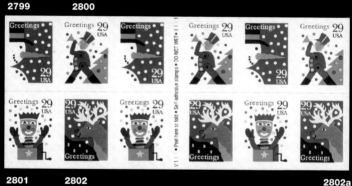

2801 **2802** **2802a**

2803 **2804** **2805**

2806 **2806a**

	Issues of 1993		Un	U	PB	#	FDC	Q(M)
	Christmas Issue, Perf. 11							
2789	29¢ Madonna and Child	10/21/93	.50	.20	2.50	(4)	1.25	500
	Booklet Stamps, Perf. 11.5 x 11 on 2 or 3 sides							
2790	29¢ Madonna and Child (2789)	10/21/93	.50	.20			1.25	500
a	Booklet pane of 4		2.25	*1.75*			2.50	
	Perf. 11.5							
2791	29¢ Jack-in-the-Box	10/21/93	.50	.20			1.25	250
2792	29¢ Red-Nosed Reindeer	10/21/93	.50	.20			1.25	250
2793	29¢ Snowman	10/21/93	.50	.20			1.25	250
2794	29¢ Toy Soldier	10/21/93	.50	.20			1.25	250
a	Block or strip of 4, #2791-94		2.00	2.00	3.75	(4)	2.75	
	Booklet Stamps, Perf. 11 x 10 on 2 or 3 sides							
2795	29¢ Toy Soldier (2794)	10/21/93	.85	.20			1.25	200
2796	29¢ Snowman (2793)	10/21/93	.85	.20			1.25	200
2797	29¢ Red-Nosed Reindeer (2792)	10/21/93	.85	.20			1.25	200
2798	29¢ Jack-in-the-Box (2791)	10/21/93	.85	.20			1.25	200
a	Booklet pane, 3 each #2795-96, 2 each #2797-98		8.50	*4.00*			6.50	
b	Booklet pane, 3 each #2797-98, 2 each #2795-96		8.50	*4.00*			6.50	
c	Block of 4		3.40	1.75				
	Self-Adhesive, Die-Cut							
2799	29¢ Snowman	10/28/93	.50	.20			1.25	120
a	Coil with plate		—	3.50	6.00	(5)		
2800	29¢ Toy Soldier	10/28/93	.50	.20			1.25	120
2801	29¢ Jack-in-the-Box	10/28/93	.50	.20			1.25	120
2802	29¢ Red-Nosed Reindeer	10/28/93	.50	.20			1.25	120
a	Booklet pane, 3 each #2799-2802		7.00					
b	Block of 4		2.00					
2803	29¢ Snowman	10/28/93	.50	.20			1.25	18
a	Booklet pane of 18		10.00					
	Perf. 11							
2804	29¢ Northern Mariana Islands	11/04/93	.50	.20	2.00	(4)	1.25	88
2805	29¢ Columbus Landing in Puerto Rico	11/19/93	.50	.20	2.50	(4)	1.25	105
2806	29¢ AIDS Awareness	12/01/93	.50	.20	2.50	(4)	1.75	100
a	Booklet version		.50	.20			1.75	250
b	Booklet pane of 5		2.50	*2.00*			3.75	

*Visit us online at The Postal Store at www.usps.com
or call 1-800-STAMP-24*

1994

	Issues of 1994		Un	U	PB	#	FDC	Q(M)
	Norman Rockwell Issue, Perf. 10.9 x 11.1							
2839	29¢ Rockwell Self-Portrait	07/01/94	.50	.20	2.50	(4)	1.25	209
2840	Four Freedoms souvenir sheet	07/01/94	4.00	2.75			3.50	20
a	50¢ Freedom from Want		1.00	.65			1.50	20
b	50¢ Freedom from Fear		1.00	.65			1.50	20
c	50¢ Freedom of Speech		1.00	.65			1.50	20
d	50¢ Freedom of Worship		1.00	.65			1.50	20
	First Moon Landing Issue, Perf. 11.2 x 11.1							
2841	29¢ sheet of 12	07/20/94	7.50	—			6.50	13
a	Single stamp		.60	.60			1.50	155
	Perf. 10.7 x 11.1							
2842	$9.95 Moon Landing	07/20/94	17.50	7.50	70.00	(4)	15.00	101
	Locomotives Issue, Perf. 11 Horizontally							
2843	29¢ Hudson's General	07/28/94	.55	.20			1.50	159
2844	29¢ McQueen's Jupiter	07/28/94	.55	.20			1.50	159
2845	29¢ Eddy's No. 242	07/28/94	.55	.20			1.50	159
2846	29¢ Ely's No. 10	07/28/94	.55	.20			1.50	159
2847	29¢ Buchanan's No. 999	07/28/94	.55	.20			1.50	159
a	Booklet pane of 5, #2843-2847		2.75	2.00			3.25	159
	Perf. 11.1 x 11							
2848	29¢ George Meany	08/16/94	.50	.20	2.50	(4)	1.25	151
	Legends of American Music Series, Popular Singers Issue, Perf. 10.1 x 10.2							
2849	29¢ Al Jolson	09/01/94	.60	.20			1.50	35
2850	29¢ Bing Crosby	09/01/94	.60	.20			1.50	35
2851	29¢ Ethel Waters	09/01/94	.60	.20			1.50	35
2852	29¢ Nat "King" Cole	09/01/94	.60	.20			1.50	35
2853	29¢ Ethel Merman	09/01/94	.60	.20			1.50	35
a	Vert. strip of 5, #2849-2853		3.00	2.00			4.50	

a   b

2839

Norman Rockwell

From our doughboys in WWI to our astronauts striding across the moon, Norman Rockwell's artwork has captured America's traditional values along with the characteristic optimism of its people. Rockwell loved people, and people loved him. He was an enormously skilled technician and, according to several new reassessments, a true artist. He had a genius for capturing the emotional content of the commonplace.

1894 1994

© USPS 1993

c   d   2840

2841a

2842

2843

2844

2845

2846

2847

2847a

George Meany
Labor Leader USA 29

2848

29 AL JOLSON USA   2849

29 BING CROSBY USA   2850

29 ETHEL WATERS USA   2851

29 NAT 'KING' COLE USA   2852

29 ETHEL MERMAN USA   2853

2853a

Issues of 1994		Un	U	PB	#	FDC	Q(M)
Legends of the West Issue, Perf. 10.1 x 10							
2869	Sheet of 20 10/18/94	12.00	—			14.00	20
a	29¢ Home on the Range	.60	.20			1.75	20
b	29¢ Buffalo Bill Cody	.60	.20			1.75	20
c	29¢ Jim Bridger	.60	.20			1.75	20
d	29¢ Annie Oakley	.60	.20			1.75	20
e	29¢ Native American Culture	.60	.20			1.75	20
f	29¢ Chief Joseph	.60	.20			1.75	20
g	29¢ Bill Pickett	.60	.20			1.75	20
h	29¢ Bat Masterson	.60	.20			1.75	20
i	29¢ John C. Fremont	.60	.20			1.75	20
j	29¢ Wyatt Earp	.60	.20			1.75	20
k	29¢ Nellie Cashman	.60	.20			1.75	20
l	29¢ Charles Goodnight	.60	.20			1.75	20
m	29¢ Geronimo	.60	.20			1.75	20
n	29¢ Kit Carson	.60	.20			1.75	20
o	29¢ Wild Bill Hickok	.60	.20			1.75	20
p	29¢ Western Wildlife	.60	.20			1.75	20
q	29¢ Jim Beckwourth	.60	.20			1.75	20
r	29¢ Bill Tilghman	.60	.20			1.75	20
s	29¢ Sacagawea	.60	.20			1.75	20
t	29¢ Overland Mail	.60	.20			1.75	20
2870	29¢ Sheet of 20 (recalled) 10/18/94	190.00	—				0.1

Bessie Smith (1898-1937)

Elizabeth "Bessie" Smith, who was known as the "Empress of the Blues," was born in Chattanooga, Tennessee, where she sang for tips on the city's street corners, accompanied by her brother, Andrew, on guitar. Her initial attempts to win a recording contract failed because executives thought her powerful and affecting voice "too rough." After the phenomenal success of her recording of "Down Hearted Blues"—it sold more than 750,000 copies—Smith went on to record with some of her era's greatest musicians, including Louis Armstrong and James P. Johnson. One of the few black performers of her time to perform for white audiences, she was reportedly the first black woman to be broadcast live in concert on local radio stations in Memphis and Atlanta. She became a cultural leader by singing the music of the people, addressing themes of love and pain, poverty, injustice, and work. A song she wrote, "Poor Man's Blues," is considered a classic of social protest. Smith's fortunes fell during the Depression, when the record industry suffered due to declining sales and the rise of radio, but she continued to perform until her death in an auto accident in 1937. ■

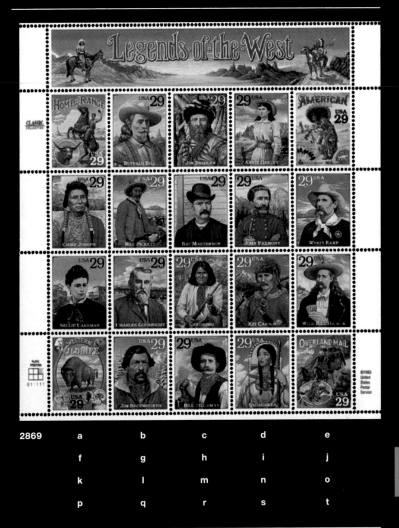

2869 a   b   c   d   e

f   g   h   i   j

k   l   m   n   o

p   q   r   s   t

2870g

	Issues of 1994-1997		Un	U	PB	#	FDC	Q(M)
	Tagged, Perf. 11.2 x 11.1							
2879	(20¢) Old Glory Postcard Rate	12/13/94	.40	.20	5.00	(4)	1.25	
	Perf. 11 x 10.9							
2880	(20¢) Old Glory Postcard Rate	12/13/94	.50	.20	9.00	(4)	1.25	
	Perf. 11.2 x 11.1							
2881	(32¢) "G" Old Glory	12/13/94	.75	.20	70.00	(4)	1.25	
a	Booklet pane of 10		6.00	3.75			7.50	
	Perf. 11 x 10.9							
2882	(32¢) "G" Old Glory	12/13/94	.60	.20	3.00	(4)	1.25	
	Booklet Stamps, Perf. 10 x 9.9 on 2 or 3 sides							
2883	(32¢) "G" Old Glory	12/13/94	.60	.20			1.25	
a	Booklet pane of 10		6.25	3.75			7.50	
	Perf. 10.9							
2884	(32¢) "G" Old Glory	12/13/94	.60	.20			1.25	
a	Booklet pane of 10		6.00	3.75			7.50	
	Perf. 11 x 10.9							
2885	(32¢) "G" Old Glory	12/13/94	.65	.20			1.25	
a	Booklet pane of 10		6.50	3.75			7.50	
	Self-Adhesive, Die-Cut							
2886	(32¢) "G" Old Glory	12/13/94	.60	.20	5.50	(5)	1.25	
a	Booklet pane of 18		11.50					
b	Coil with plate		—	3.25				
2887	(32¢) "G" Old Glory	12/13/94	.60	.20			1.25	
a	Booklet pane of 18		11.50					
	Coil Stamps, Perf. 9.8 Vertically							
2888	(25¢) Old Glory First-Class Presort	12/13/94	.50	.50	4.50	(5)	1.25	
2889	(32¢) Black "G"	12/13/94	.60	.20	11.50	(5)	1.25	
a	Imperf., pair		325.00					
2890	(32¢) Blue "G"	12/13/94	.60	.20	5.00	(5)	1.25	
2891	(32¢) Red "G"	12/13/94	.60	.20	5.00	(5)	1.25	
	Rouletted							
2892	(32¢) Red "G"	12/13/94	.60	.20	6.00	(5)	1.25	
	Issue of 1995, Perf. 9.8 Vertically							
2893	(5¢) Green	01/12/95	.20	.20	1.90	(5)		
	Perf. 10.4							
2897	32¢ Flag Over Porch	05/19/95	.60	.20	3.00	(4)	1.25	
	Coil Stamps, Perf. 9.8 Vertically							
2902	(5¢) Butte	03/10/95	.20	.20	1.50	(5)	1.25	
a	Imperf., pair		750.00					
	Self-Adhesive, Serpentine Die-Cut 11.5 Vertically							
2902B	(5¢) Butte	06/15/96	.20	.20	1.50	(5)	1.25	550
	Perf. 9.8 Vertically							
2903	(5¢) Mountain, purple and multi	03/16/96	.20	.20	1.50	(5)	1.25	150
a	Tagged (error)		4.00	3.50	85.00	(5)		
2904	(5¢) Mountain, blue and multi	03/16/96	.20	.20	1.50	(5)	1.25	150
c	Imperf., pair		500.00					
	Self-Adhesive, Serpentine Die-Cut 11.2							
2904A	(5¢) Mountain, purple and multi	06/15/96	.20	.20	1.75	(5)	1.25	
	Self-Adhesive, Serpentine Die-Cut 9.8 Vertically							
2904B	(5¢) Mountain, purple and multi	01/24/97	.20	.20	1.50	(5)	1.25	148
c	Tagged (error)		4.00	3.50	85.00	(5)		
	Perf. 9.8 Vertically							
2905	(10¢) Automobile	03/10/95	.20	.20	2.40	(5)	1.25	
	Self-Adhesive, Serpentine Die-Cut 11.5 Vertically							
2906	(10¢) Automobile	06/15/96	.20	.20	2.50	(5)	1.25	450
2907	(10¢) Eagle and Shield	05/21/96	.20	.20	2.75	(5)	1.25	450

2879 2880 2881 2882 2883

2884 2885 2886 2887 2888

2889 2890 2891 2892 2893

2897 2902 2903 2904 2905

2906 2907

For details and illustrations of the new 2003 issues, see page 14.

	Issues of 1995-1998		Un	U	PB	#	FDC
	Self-Adhesive, Serpentine Die-Cut 11.7 x 11.5						
2942	77¢ Mary Breckinridge	11/09/98	1.50	.20	6.00	(4)	1.75
	Perf. 11.2						
2943	78¢ Alice Paul	08/18/95	1.60	.20	7.50	(4)	1.75
a	78¢ dull violet		1.60	.20	7.50	(4)	
b	78¢ pale violet		1.75	.30	12.00	(4)	
	Love Issue, Perf. 11.2						
2948	(32¢) Love, Cherub from Sistine Madonna, by Raphael	02/01/95	.60	.20	3.00	(4)	1.50
	Self-Adhesive, Die-Cut						
2949	(32¢) Love, Cherub from Sistine Madonna, by Raphael	02/01/95	.60	.20			1.50
a	Booklet pane of 20 + label		12.00				
b	Red (engr.) omitted		450.00				
c	As "a," red (engr.) omitted		9,000.00				
	Perf. 11.1						
2950	32¢ Florida Statehood, 150th Anniversary	03/03/95	.60	.20	2.40	(4)	1.25
	Kids Care Earth Day Issue, Perf. 11.1 x 11						
2951	32¢ Earth Clean-Up	04/20/95	.60	.20			1.25
2952	32¢ Solar Energy	04/20/95	.60	.20			1.25
2953	32¢ Tree Planting	04/20/95	.60	.20			1.25
2954	32¢ Beach Clean-Up	04/20/95	.60	.20			1.25
a	Block of 4, #2951-54		2.40	1.75	2.40	(4)	2.75
	Perf. 11.2						
2955	32¢ Richard Nixon	04/26/95	.60	.20	3.00	(4)	1.25
a	Red (engr.) omitted		1,400.00				
	Black Heritage Issue						
2956	32¢ Bessie Coleman	04/27/95	.60	.20	3.00	(4)	1.50
	Love Issue						
2957	32¢ Love, Cherub from Sistine Madonna, by Raphael	05/12/95	.60	.20	3.00	(4)	1.25
2958	55¢ Love, Cherub from Sistine Madonna, by Raphael	05/12/95	1.10	.20	5.50	(4)	1.25
	Booklet Stamps, Perf. 9.8 x 10.8						
2959	32¢ Love, Cherub from Sistine Madonna, by Raphael	05/12/95	.60	.20			1.25
a	Booklet pane of 10		6.00	3.25			7.50
	Self-Adhesive, Die-Cut						
2960	55¢ Love, Cherub from Sistine Madonna, by Raphael	05/12/95	1.10	.20			1.40
a	Booklet pane of 20 + label		22.50				
	Recreational Sports Issue, Perf. 11.2						
2961	32¢ Volleyball	05/20/95	.60	.20			1.50
2962	32¢ Softball	05/20/95	.60	.20			1.50
2963	32¢ Bowling	05/20/95	.60	.20			1.50
2964	32¢ Tennis	05/20/95	.60	.20			1.50
2965	32¢ Golf	05/20/95	.60	.20			1.50
a	Vertical strip of 5, #2961-65		3.00	2.00	6.00	(10)	3.25
b	As "a," imperf.						
c	As "a," yellow omitted		2,500.00				
d	As "a," yellow, blue and magenta omitted		2,500.00				
2966	32¢ Prisoners of War and Missing in Action	05/29/95	.60	.20	2.40	(4)	1.75
	Pane of 20		12.00	—			

2942

2943

2948

2950

2951 2952

2953 2954

2955

2954a

2956

2958

2961

2962

2963

2965

2964

2966

2965a

	Issues of 1995		Un	U	PB	#	FDC
2974	32¢ United Nations,						
	50th Anniversary	06/26/95	.60	.20	2.40	(4)	1.50
	Civil War Issue, Perf. 10.1						
2975	Sheet of 20	06/29/95	12.00	—			16.00
a	32¢ *Monitor and Virginia*		.60	.20			1.50
b	32¢ Robert E. Lee		.60	.20			1.50
c	32¢ Clara Barton		.60	.20			1.50
d	32¢ Ulysses S. Grant		.60	.20			1.50
e	32¢ Battle of Shiloh		.60	.20			1.50
f	32¢ Jefferson Davis		.60	.20			1.50
g	32¢ David Farragut		.60	.20			1.50
h	32¢ Frederick Douglass		.60	.20			1.50
i	32¢ Raphael Semmes		.60	.20			1.50
j	32¢ Abraham Lincoln		.60	.20			1.50
k	32¢ Harriet Tubman		.60	.20			1.50
l	32¢ Stand Watie		.60	.20			1.50
m	32¢ Joseph E. Johnston		.60	.20			1.50
n	32¢ Winfield Hancock		.60	.20			1.50
o	32¢ Mary Chesnut		.60	.20			1.50
p	32¢ Battle of Chancellorsville		.60	.20			1.50
q	32¢ William T. Sherman		.60	.20			1.50
r	32¢ Phoebe Pember		.60	.20			1.50
s	32¢ "Stonewall" Jackson		.60	.20			1.50
t	32¢ Battle of Gettysburg		.60	.20			1.50

A·M·E·R·I·C·A·N C·O·M·M·E·M·O·R·A·T·I·V·E C·O·L·L·E·C·T·I·B·L·E·S

American Commemorative Panels

Obtain photo or steel engravings, mint condition stamps and subject related text presented on a beautifully designed page. Only $6.00* each, depending on the value of the stamps.

For more information call **1-800-STAMP-24**

Prices subject to change without notice.

2974

2975   a   b   c   d   e

          f   g   h   i   j

          k   l   m   n   o

          p   q   r   s   t

2976   2977

2980

2978   2979   2979a

a   b   c   d   e

f   g   h   i   j

2981

Visit us online at The Postal Store @ www.usps.com

or call 1-800-STAMP-24

Issues of 1995		Un	U	PB	#	FDC
Carousel Horse Issue, Perf. 11						
2976	32¢ Golden Horse with Roses 07/21/95	.60	.20			1.25
2977	32¢ Black Horse with Gold Bridle 07/21/95	.60	.20			1.25
2978	32¢ Horse with Armor 07/21/95	.60	.20			1.25
2979	32¢ Brown Horse with					
	Green Bridle 07/21/95	.60	.20			1.25
a	Block of 4, #2976-79	2.40	2.00	2.40	(4)	3.25
	Perf. 11.1 x 11					
2980	32¢ Women's Suffrage 08/26/95	.60	.20	3.00	(4)	1.25
a	Black (engr.) omitted	425.00				
	World War II Issue, 1945: Victory at Last, Miniature Sheet, Perf. 11.1					
2981	Block of 10 and central label 09/02/95	6.00	5.50			7.00
a	32¢ Marines Raise					
	Flag on Iwo Jima	.60	.30			1.50
b	32¢ Fierce Fighting Frees Manila					
	by March 3, 1945	.60	.30			1.50
c	32¢ Soldiers Advancing: Okinawa,					
	the Last Big Battle	.60	.30			1.50
d	32¢ Destroyed Bridge: U.S. and					
	Soviets Link Up at Elbe River	.60	.30			1.50
e	32¢ Allies Liberate Holocaust					
	Survivors	.60	.30			1.50
f	32¢ Germany Surrenders at Reims	.60	.30			1.50
g	32¢ Refugees: By 1945, World War II					
	Has Uprooted Millions	.60	.30			1.50
h	32¢ Truman Announces Japan's					
	Surrender	.60	.30			1.50
i	32¢ Sailor Kissing Nurse: News of					
	Victory Hits Home	.60	.30			1.50
j	32¢ Hometowns Honor Their					
	Returning Veterans	.60	.30			1.50

Paul Dudley White, M.D. (1886-1973)

Paul Dudley White, a founder of the American Heart Association, was a world leader in the diagnosis and treatment of heart disease. An early advocate of disease prevention, White believed in the value of frequent exercise, a proper diet, and weight control. He earned a medical degree at Harvard in 1911. His internship at Massachusetts General Hospital in Boston marked the beginning of an enduring professional relationship. In 1919, after serving in World War I, White returned to Massachusetts General where he established an internationally known cardiac unit. He was one of the first doctors to use the electrocardiograph in the United States, and his 1931 monograph, *Heart Disease*, was an important reference work for many years. He taught at Harvard Medical School from 1914 to 1956. When President Eisenhower suffered a heart attack in 1955, White was the chief medical consultant. A cycling enthusiast, he rode a bicycle as part of his daily fitness regimen. A 17-mile bike path along Boston's Charles River is named for him. ◼

3000
a   b   c   d

e   f   g   h

i   j   k   l

m   n   o   p

q   r   s   t

3001

3002

Issues of 1995		Un	U	PB	#	FDC
Comic Strip Classics Issue, Perf. 10						
3000 Pane of 20	10/01/95	12.00	—			13.00
a	32¢ The Yellow Kid	.60	.20			1.75
b	32¢ Katzenjammer Kids	.60	.20			1.75
c	32¢ Little Nemo in Slumberland	.60	.20			1.75
d	32¢ Bringing Up Father	.60	.20			1.75
e	32¢ Krazy Kat	.60	.20			1.75
f	32¢ Rube Goldberg's Inventions	.60	.20			1.75
g	32¢ Toonerville Folks	.60	.20			1.75
h	32¢ Gasoline Alley	.60	.20			1.75
i	32¢ Barney Google	.60	.20			1.75
j	32¢ Little Orphan Annie	.60	.20			1.75
k	32¢ Popeye	.60	.20			1.75
l	32¢ Blondie	.60	.20			1.75
m	32¢ Dick Tracy	.60	.20			1.75
n	32¢ Alley Oop	.60	.20			1.75
o	32¢ Nancy	.60	.20			1.75
p	32¢ Flash Gordon	.60	.20			1.75
q	32¢ Li'l Abner	.60	.20			1.75
r	32¢ Terry and the Pirates	.60	.20			1.75
s	32¢ Prince Valiant	.60	.20			1.75
t	32¢ Brenda Starr, Reporter	.60	.20			1.75
Perf 10.9						
3001 32¢ U.S. Naval Academy, 150th Anniversary	10/10/95	.60	.20	2.40	(4)	1.75
Literary Arts Issue, Perf 11.1						
3002 32¢ Tennessee Williams	10/13/95	.60	.20	2.40	(4)	1.25

Jane Addams (1860-1935)

During her lifetime, Jane Addams became internationally famous as a result of her pioneering social work. With a companion, Ellen Gates Starr, she acquired the run-down Hull mansion in Chicago, Illinois, and transformed it into a multipurpose center for the neighborhood. Hull-House offered child care, a gymnasium, and many other services, including courses in cooking and sewing. For decades, Hull-House gave meeting space to trade unions and other groups and provided young social workers with superb training. Addams saw the relation between art and social justice, and provided opportunities for cultural expression through a music school, art gallery, and theater. She was the author of several books, including *Twenty Years at Hull-House* (1910), now considered a classic of American autobiography. She worked on behalf of women's suffrage and was a committed pacifist who sometimes took controversial stands. She helped found the American Civil Liberties Union and other influential institutions. A co-winner of the 1931 Nobel Peace Prize, she was the first American woman to be so honored. Jane Addams believed that the greatest benefit from doing good works went to the people who did them. In 1967 Hull-House became a National Historic Landmark. ■

3019

3020

3021

3022

3023

3024

3023a

3025   3026   3027   3028   3029   3029a

3030   3032   3033   3036   3044

3048   3049   3050   3052

Issues of 1995-1999		Un	U	PB	#	FDC	Q(M)
Antique Automobiles Issue							
3019	32¢ 1893 Duryea	11/03/95	.60	.20			1.25	
3020	32¢ 1894 Haynes	11/03/95	.60	.20			1.25	
3021	32¢ 1898 Columbia	11/03/95	.60	.20			1.25	
3022	32¢ 1899 Winton	11/03/95	.60	.20			1.25	
3023	32¢ 1901 White	11/03/95	.60	.20			1.25	
a	Vertical or horizontal strip of 5, #3019-23		3.00	2.00			3.00	
3024	32¢ Utah Statehood	01/04/96	.60	.20	3.00	(4)	1.25	
Issues of 1996, Garden Flowers Issue, Perf 10.9 Vertically							
3025	32¢ Crocus	01/19/96	.60	.20			1.25	
3026	32¢ Winter Aconite	01/19/96	.60	.20			1.25	
3027	32¢ Pansy	01/19/96	.60	.20			1.25	
3028	32¢ Snowdrop	01/19/96	.60	.20			1.25	
3029	32¢ Anemone	01/19/96	.60	.20			1.25	
a	Booklet pane of 5, #3025-3029		3.00	2.50			3.50	
Love Issue, Serpentine Die-Cut Perf. 11.3							
3030	32¢ Love Cherub from Sistine Madonna, by Raphael	01/20/96	.60	.20			1.25	
a	Booklet pane of 20 + label		12.00					
b	Booklet pane of 15 + label		9.00					
Flora and Fauna Issue, Self-Adhesive, Serpentine Die-Cut 10.5							
3031	1¢ American Kestrel	11/19/99	.20	.20	.25		1.50	120
Perf. 11							
3032	2¢ Red-Headed Woodpecker	02/02/96	.20	.20	.25	(4)	1.25	311
3033	3¢ Eastern Bluebird	04/03/96	.20	.20	.25	(4)	1.25	317
Self-Adhesive, Serpentine Die-Cut 11.5 x 11.25							
3036	$1 Red Fox	08/14/98	2.00	.50	8.00	(4)	3.50	
Coil Stamps, Perf. 9.75 Vertically							
3044	1¢ American Kestrel	01/20/96	.20	.20	.60	(5)	1.25	
a	Large date		.20	.20	.85	(5)		
3045	2¢ Red-Headed Woodpecker	06/22/99	.20	.20	.80	(5)	1.25	100
Booklet Stamps, Self-Adhesive, Serpentine Die-Cut 10.5 x 10.75 on 3 sides							
3048	20¢ Blue Jay	08/02/96	.40	.20			1.25	491
a	Booklet pane of 10		4.00					
b	Booklet pane of 4		1.60					
c	Booklet pane of 6		2.40					
Serpentine Die-Cut 11.25 x 11.75 on 2, 3 or 4 sides							
3049	32¢ Yellow Rose	10/24/96	.60	.20			1.25	2,900
a	Booklet pane of 20 and label		12.00					
b	Booklet pane of 4	12/96	2.75					
c	Booklet pane of 5	12/96	3.20					
d	Booklet pane of 6	12/96	3.60					
Serpentine Die-Cut 11.25 on 2 or 3 sides							
3050	20¢ Ring-neck Pheasant	07/31/98	.40	.20			1.25	
a	Booklet pane of 10		4.00					
Serpentine Die-Cut 10.5 x 11 on 3 sides							
3051	20¢ Ring-neck Pheasant	07/99	.60	.20				634
a	Serpentine Die-Cut 10.5 on 3 Sides		3.75	.50				
b	Booklet pane of 5, 4 #3051, 1 #3051a turned sideways at top		6.00					
c	Booklet pane of 5, 4 #3051, 1 #3051a turned sideways at bottom		6.00					
Serpentine Die-Cut 11.5 x 11.25 on 2, 3 or 4 sides							
3052	33¢ Coral Pink Rose	08/13/99	.80	.20			1.25	1,000
a	Booklet pane of 4		3.20					
b	Booklet pane of 5 + label		4.00					
c	Booklet pane of 6		4.80					
d	Booklet pane of 20		13.00					

	Issues of 1996-2000		Un	U	PB	#	FDC	Q(M)
	Serpentine Die Cut 10.75 x 10.5 on 2 or 3 Sides							
3052E	33¢ Coral Pink Rose	04/07/00	.65	.20			1.25	
f	Booklet pane of 20		13.00					
	Coil Stamps, Serpentine Die-Cut 11.5 Vertically							
3053	20¢ Blue Jay	08/02/96	.40	.20	3.25	(5)	1.25	330
	Coil Stamps, Self-Adhesive, Serpentine Die-Cut 9.75 Vertically							
3054	32¢ Yellow Rose	08/01/97	.60	.20	5.25	(5)	1.25	
a	Imperf., pair		90.00					
3055	20¢ Ring-necked Pheasant	07/31/98	.40	.20	3.50	(5)	1.25	
a	Imperf., pair		200.00					
	Black Heritage Issue, Perf. 11.1							
3058	32¢ Ernest E. Just	02/01/96	.60	.20	2.40	(4)	1.75	92
3059	32¢ Smithsonian Institution	02/07/96	.60	.20	2.40	(4)	1.25	115
	Lunar New Year Issue							
3060	32¢ Year of the Rat	02/08/96	.60	.20	3.00	(4)	1.50	93
	Pioneers of Communication Issue, Perf. 11.1 x 11							
3061	32¢ Eadweard Muybridge	02/22/96	.60	.20			1.25	96
3062	32¢ Ottmar Mergenthaler	02/22/96	.60	.20			1.25	96
3063	32¢ Frederic E. Ives	02/22/96	.60	.20			1.25	96
3064	32¢ William Dickson	02/22/96	.60	.20			1.25	96
a	Block or strip of 4, #3061-3064		2.40	2.00	2.40	(4)	2.50	
	Perf. 11.1							
3065	32¢ Fulbright Scholarships	02/28/96	.60	.20	3.00	(4)	1.25	130
	Pioneers of Aviation Issue							
3066	50¢ Jacqueline Cochran	03/09/96	1.00	.20	5.00	(4)	1.40	314
a	Black omitted		60.00					
3067	32¢ Marathon	04/11/96	.60	.20	2.40	(4)	1.75	209

Franklin Delano Roosevelt

(1882-1945)

Elected to the American Presidency during the Great Depression, Franklin Delano Roosevelt went on to guide the nation through the wrenching years of World War II. While Roosevelt is well-known for the social programs he instituted during his 12-year presidency, and the indelible mark they left on American lives, few realize that he was an avid philatelist who delighted in collecting and designing stamps. He submitted a number of original design ideas, such as a 1938 eagle-emblazoned airmail stamp, and was outspoken in his critique of stamp designs. Working in tandem with his first Postmaster General, James A. Farley, Roosevelt introduced practices that are used to this day, including press releases for new stamps and First Day of Issue ceremonies. Portrait artist Elizabeth Shoumatoff reported that Roosevelt's lifelong love of stamps was evident just moments before he suffered the brain hemorrhage that killed him: In response to her comments about the recently released Florida statehood stamp, he had acknowledged his part in its creation. From 1945 to 1998, the U.S. Postal Service issued no less than ten stamps bearing his likeness, commemorating the man who not only inspired stamps, but collected and designed them as well. ■

3058

3059

3060

3063

3064

3061

3062

3064a

3065

3066

3067

1996

Issues of 1996			Un	U	PB	#	FDC	Q(M)
Prehistoric Animals Issue, Perf. 11.1 x 11								
3077	32¢ Eohippus	06/08/96	.60	.20			1.50	150
3078	32¢ Woolly Mammoth	06/08/96	.60	.20			1.50	150
3079	32¢ Mastodon	06/08/96	.60	.20			1.50	150
3080	32¢ Saber-tooth Cat	06/08/96	.60	.20			1.50	150
a	Block or strip of 4, #3077-3080		2.40	1.50	2.40	(4)	2.75	150
	Pane of 20		12.00	—				
Perf. 11.1								
3081	32¢ Breast Cancer Awareness	06/15/96	.60	.20	2.40	(4)	1.25	96
	Pane of 20		12.00	—				
Legends of Hollywood Issue, Perf. 11.1								
3082	32¢ James Dean	06/24/96	.60	.20	2.75	(4)	1.75	300
	Pane of 20		14.00	—				
a	Imperf., pair		325.00					
Folks Heroes Issue, Perf. 11.1 x 11								
3083	32¢ Mighty Casey	07/11/96	.60	.20			1.25	113
3084	32¢ Paul Bunyan	07/11/96	.60	.20			1.25	113
3085	32¢ John Henry	07/11/96	.60	.20			1.25	113
3086	32¢ Pecos Bill	07/11/96	.60	.20			1.25	113
a	Block or strip of 4, #3083-3086		2.40	2.00	2.40	(4)	2.75	
	Pane of 20		12.00	—				
Centennial Olympic Games Issue, Perf. 11.1								
3087	32¢ Centennial Olympic Games	07/11/96	.65	.20	3.75	(4)	1.25	134
	Pane of 20		17.50	—				
3088	32¢ Iowa Statehood	08/01/96	.60	.20	3.00	(4)	1.25	103
Booklet Stamp, Self-Adhesive, Serpentine Die-Cut 11.6 x 11.4								
3089	32¢ Iowa Statehood	08/01/96	.60	.30			1.25	60
a	Booklet pane of 20		12.00					
Perf. 11.2 x 11								
3090	32¢ Rural Free Delivery	08/07/96	.60	.20	2.40	(4)	1.25	134

George Eastman (1854-1932)

The first Kodak cameras went on sale in 1888, stirring widespread interest in amateur photography. Marketed with the slogan "You press the button, we do the rest," the early Kodak was a simple, hand-held box camera containing a strip of film with 100 exposures. After the film was used, the entire camera was sent back to the manufacturer for developing, printing, and reloading. In 1900, Eastman Kodak introduced the first Brownie; priced at one dollar, this simple box camera was intended for children. These and other products represented a revolution in photography spearheaded by George Eastman, an inventor and industrialist born in Waterville, New York. Before Eastman developed his simple and portable cameras, photography was a cumbersome pursuit requiring photographers to carry lots of equipment and to coat each photographic plate with chemicals. Eastman began the development, production, and sale of photographic goods while in his twenties; by the end of his life, he had given away more than $75,000,000 to beneficiaries such as the Massachusetts Institute of Technology and the University of Rochester, home of the Eastman School of Music, which he founded. Eastman's Rochester, New York, residence today houses the International Museum of Photography and Film. ∎

3077 Eohippus 32 USA

3078 Woolly mammoth 32 USA

3079 Mastodon 32 USA

3080 Saber-tooth cat 32 USA

3080a

3081 Breast Cancer Awareness 32 USA

3082 JAMES DEAN

3083 MIGHTY CASEY 32 USA

3086 PECOS BILL 32 USA

3085 JOHN HENRY 32 USA

3084 PAUL BUNYAN 32 USA

3086a

3087 Centennial Olympic Games 1896 1996 32 USA

3088 USA 32 1846 IOWA

3090 USA 32 RURAL FREE DELIVERY RFD

Visit us online at The Postal Store at www.usps.com

or call 1-800-STAMP-24

1996

	Issues of 1996		Un	U	PB	#	FDC	Q(M)
	Endangered Species Issue, Perf. 11.1 x 11							
3105	Pane of 15	10/02/96	9.00	—			7.50	224
a	32¢ Black-footed ferret		.60	.20			1.25	
b	32¢ Thick-billed parrot		.60	.20			1.25	
c	32¢ Hawaiian monk seal		.60	.20			1.25	
d	32¢ American crocodile		.60	.20			1.25	
e	32¢ Ocelot		.60	.20			1.25	
f	32¢ Schaus swallowtail butterfly		.60	.20			1.25	
g	32¢ Wyoming toad		.60	.20			1.25	
h	32¢ Brown pelican		.60	.20			1.25	
i	32¢ California condor		.60	.20			1.25	
j	32¢ Gilatrout		.60	.20			1.25	
k	32¢ San Francisco garter snake		.60	.20			1.25	
l	32¢ Woodland caribou		.60	.20			1.25	
m	32¢ Florida panther		.60	.20			1.25	
n	32¢ Piping plover		.60	.20			1.25	
o	32¢ Florida manatee		.60	.20			1.25	
	Perf. 10.9 x 11.1							
3106	32¢ Computer Technology	10/08/96	.60	.20	3.00	(4)	1.75	94
	Christmas Issue, Perf. 11.1 x 11.2							
3107	32¢ Madonna and Child							
	by Paolo de Matteis	10/08/96	.60	.20	3.00	(4)	1.25	848
	Perf. 11.3							
3108	32¢ Family at Fireplace	10/08/96	.60	.20			1.25	226
3109	32¢ Decorating Tree	10/08/96	.60	.20			1.25	226
3110	32¢ Dreaming of Santa Claus	10/08/96	.60	.20			1.25	226
3111	32¢ Holiday Shopping	10/08/96	.60	.20			1.25	226
a	Block or strip of 4, #3108-3111		2.40	1.75	3.00	(4)	2.75	
	Self-Adhesive Booklet Stamps, Serpentine Die-Cut 10 on 2, 3 or 4 sides							
3112	32¢ Madonna and Child							
	by Paolo de Matteis	10/08/96	.60	.20			1.25	244
a	Booklet pane of 20 + label		12.00					
b	No die-cutting, pair		75.00					
3113	32¢ Family at Fireplace	10/08/96	.60	.20			1.25	1,805
3114	32¢ Decorating Tree	10/08/96	.60	.20			1.25	1,805
3115	32¢ Dreaming of Santa Claus	10/08/96	.60	.20			1.25	1,805
3116	32¢ Holiday Shopping	10/08/96	.60	.20			1.25	1,805
a	Booklet pane, 5 ea #3113-3116		12.00				3.25	
	Die-Cut							
3117	32¢ Skaters	10/08/96	.60	.20			1.25	495
a	Booklet pane of 18		11.00					
	Self-Adhesive, Serpentine Die-Cut 11.1							
3118	32¢ Hanukkah	10/22/96	.60	.20	2.40	(4)	1.75	104
	Cycling Issue, Perf. 11 x 11.1							
3119	32¢ Souvenier sheet of 2	11/01/96	2.00	2.00			3.25	
a	50¢ orange		1.00	1.00			1.75	
b	50¢ blue and green		1.00	1.00			1.75	

Endangered Species

3105

National Stamp Collecting Month 1996 highlights these 15 species to promote awareness of endangered wildlife. Each generation must work to protect the delicate balance of nature, so that future generations may share a sound and healthy planet.

a b c

d e f

g h i

j k l

m n o

3106

3107

3108   3111

3111a

3109   3110

3117   3118

3119a   3119b

3120

3121

3122

3123

3124

3125

3126

3127

3130

3131

3132

3133

3134

3135

Issues of 1997		Un	U	PB	#	FDC	Q(M)
Lunar New Year Issue, Perf. 11.2							
3120 32¢ Year of the Ox	01/05/97	.60	.20	2.40	(4)	1.50	106
Black Heritage Issue, Serpentine Die-Cut 11.4							
3121 32¢ Brig. Gen. Benjamin O. Davis Sr.	01/28/97	.60	.20	2.40	(4)	1.75	112
Self-Adhesive Booklet Stamps, Serpentine Die-Cut 11 on 2, 3 or 4 sides							
3122 32¢ Statue of Liberty, Type of 1994	02/01/97	.60	.20			1.25	2,855
a Booklet panel of 20 + label		12.00					
b Booklet pane of 4		2.50					
c Booklet pane of 5 + label		3.20					
d Booklet pane of 6		3.60					
Self-Adhesive, Serpentine Die-Cut 11.5 x 11.8 on 2, 3 or 4 sides							
3122E 32¢ Statue of Liberty		1.10	.20				
f Booklet pane of 20 + label		35.00					
g Booklet pane of 6		7.00					
Self-Adhesive, Serpentine Die-Cut 11.8 x 11.6 on 2, 3 or 4 sides							
3123 32¢ Love Swans	02/04/97	.60	.20			1.25	1,660
a Booklet pane of 20 + label		12.00					
b No die-cutting, pair		250.00					
Serpentine Die-Cut 11.6 x 11.8 on 2, 3 or 4 sides							
3124 55¢ Love Swans	02/04/97	1.00	.20			1.50	814
a Booklet pane of 20 + label		21.00					
Self-Adhesive, Serpentine Die-Cut 11.6 x 11.7							
3125 32¢ Helping Children Learn	02/18/97	.60	.20	2.40	(4)	1.25	122
Merian Botanical Print Issues, Self-Adhesive, Serpentine Die-Cut 10.9 x 10.2 on 2, 3 or 4 sides							
3126 32¢ Citron, Roth, Larvae, Pupa, Beetle	03/03/97	.60	.20			1.25	2,048
3127 32¢ Flowering Pineapple, Cockroaches	03/03/97	.60	.20			1.25	2,048
a Booklet pane, 10 each #3126-3127 + label		12.00					
b Pair, #3126-3127		1.20					
Serpentine Die-Cut 11.2 x 10.8 on 2 or 3 sides							
3128 32¢ Citron, Roth, Larvae, Pupa, Beetle	03/03/97	.75	.20			1.25	30
b Booklet pane, 2 each #3128-3129		4.00					
3129 32¢ Flowering Pineapple, Cockroaches	03/03/97	.75	.20			1.25	30
b Booklet pane of 5, 2 each #3128-29, 1 #3129a		4.00					
c Pair, #3128-3129		1.50					
Pacific 97 Issues, Perf. 11.2							
3130 32¢ Sailing Ship	03/13/97	.60	.20			1.25	130
3131 32¢ Stagecoach	03/13/97	.60	.20			1.25	130
a Pair #3130-31		1.25	.60	2.50	(4)	1.75	
Coil Stamps, Self-Adhesive, Imperf.							
3132 25¢ Juke Box	03/14/97	.50	.50	4.75	(5)	1.25	24
Coil Stamps, Serpentine Die-Cut 9.9 Vertically							
3133 32¢ Flag Over Porch	03/14/97	.60	.20	6.50	(5)	1.25	1
Literary Arts Issue, Perf. 11.1							
3134 32¢ Thornton Wilder	04/17/97	.60	.20	2.40	(4)	1.25	98
3135 32¢ Raoul Wallenberg	04/24/97	.60	.20	2.40	(4)	2.00	96

Issues of 1997		Un	U	FDC	Q(M)
The World of Dinosaurs Issue, Perf. 11 x 11.1					
3136 Sheet of 15	05/01/97	9.00	—	7.50	219
a	32¢ Ceratosaurus	.60	.20	1.25	
b	32¢ Camptosaurus	.60	.20	1.25	
c	32¢ Camarasaurus	.60	.20	1.25	
d	32¢ Brachiosaurus	.60	.20	1.25	
e	32¢ Goniopholis	.60	.20	1.25	
f	32¢ Stegosaurus	.60	.20	1.25	
g	32¢ Allosaurus	.60	.20	1.25	
h	32¢ Opisthias	.60	.20	1.25	
i	32¢ Edmontonia	.60	.20	1.25	
j	32¢ Einiosaurus	.60	.20	1.25	
k	32¢ Daspletosaurus	.60	.20	1.25	
l	32¢ Palaeosaniwa	.60	.20	1.25	
m	32¢ Corythosaurus	.60	.20	1.25	
n	32¢ Ornithominus	.60	.20	1.25	
o	32¢ Parasaurolophus	.60	.20	1.25	
Looney Tunes Issue, Self-Adhesive, Serpentine Die-Cut 11					
3137 Bugs Bunny Pane of 10	05/22/97	6.00			265
a	32¢ single	.60	.20	1.75	
b	Booklet pane of 9	5.40			
c	Booklet pane of 1	.60			
Die-cutting on #3137b does not extend through the backing paper.					
3138 Pane of 10	05/22/97	*125.00*			
a	32¢ single	*2.00*			
b	Booklet pane of 9	—			
c	Booklet pane of 1, imperf.	—			
Die-cutting on #3138b extends through the backing paper.					

Moina Michael (1869-1944)

"If ye break faith with us who die, we shall not sleep, though poppies grow in Flanders Fields." This line from a poem by Colonel John McCrae inspired Moina Michael, a Georgia schoolteacher, to begin a personal campaign to remember the soldiers of World War I. Michael was working in New York City for the Overseas YMCA War Workers when the armistice was announced. Believing that Americans should show their support for those who had fought and died in the war, she bought 25 red silk poppies as remembrance symbols and distributed them to her enthusiastic colleagues. It took Michael two years to find an organization that would adopt the Memorial Poppy as its national emblem. On September 29, 1920, the American Legion voted to make the poppy its emblem and to sell them every November on Armistice Day (now Veterans Day) with proceeds used to assist soldiers and their dependents. When the war ended, Michael, who would be known as the "Poppy Lady" for the rest of her life, returned to teaching at the University of Georgia in Athens. ∎

A scene in Colorado, 150 million years ago

A scene in Montana, 75 million years ago

i   j   k   m   n   o

l

	Issues of 1997		Un	U	PB	#	FDC	Q(M)
	Classic American Aircraft Issue, Perf. 10.1							
3142	Pane of 20	07/19/97	12.00	—			10.00	161
a	32¢ Mustang		.60	.20			1.25	
b	32¢ Model B		.60	.20			1.25	
c	32¢ Cub		.60	.20			1.25	
d	32¢ Vega		.60	.20			1.25	
e	32¢ Alpha		.60	.20			1.25	
f	32¢ B-10		.60	.20			1.25	
g	32¢ Corsair		.60	.20			1.25	
h	32¢ Stratojet		.60	.20			1.25	
i	32¢ Gee Bee		.60	.20			1.25	
j	32¢ Staggerwing		.60	.20			1.25	
k	32¢ Flying Fortress		.60	.20			1.25	
l	32¢ Stearman		.60	.20			1.25	
m	32¢ Constellation		.60	.20			1.25	
n	32¢ Lightning		.60	.20			1.25	
o	32¢ Peashooter		.60	.20			1.25	
p	32¢ Tri-Motor		.60	.20			1.25	
q	32¢ DC-3		.60	.20			1.25	
r	32¢ 314 Clipper		.60	.20			1.25	
s	32¢ Jenny		.60	.20			1.25	
t	32¢ Wildcat		.60	.20			1.25	
	Legendary Football Coaches Issue, Perf. 11.2							
3143	32¢ Bear Bryant	07/25/97	.60	.20			1.50	90
3144	32¢ Pop Warner	07/25/97	.60	.20			1.50	90
3145	32¢ Vince Lombardi	07/25/97	.60	.20			1.50	90
3146	32¢ George Halas	07/25/97	.60	.20			1.50	90
a	Block or strip of 4, #3143-3146		2.40	—	2.40	(4)	2.50	

James Madison (1751-1836)

Drawing on his extensive study of ancient republics, fourth President of the United States James Madison became known as the "father of the U.S. Constitution" after contributing significantly to the drafting and ratification of the world-renowned document. Later, as a member of the House of Representatives, Madison led the creation, and adoption in 1791, of the Bill of Rights, which comprised the first ten amendments to the Constitution. Madison was committed to the concept of a strong central government, subject to a system of checks and balances that would prevent any one branch of government from gaining excessive power. He wrote in *The Federalist* in January 1788: "The accumulation of all powers, legislative, executive, and judiciary, in the same hands, whether of one, a few, or many, and whether hereditary, self-appointed, or elective, may justly be pronounced the very definition of tyranny." The first stamp honoring Madison was issued in 1894. Since then, he has been pictured on numerous stamps, most recently in 2001 on the 250th anniversary of his birth. ▨

3142

a   b   c   d

e   f   g   h

i   j   k   l

m   n   o   p

q   r   s   t

Issues of 1997		Un	U	PB	#	FDC	Q(M)
Legends of Hollywood Issue, Perf. 11.1							
3152 32¢ Humphrey Bogart	07/31/97	.60	.20	2.50	(4)	1.50	195
3153 32¢ "The Stars and Stripes Forever"	08/21/97	.60	.20	3.00	(4)	1.25	323
Legends of American Music Series, Opera Singers Issue, Perf. 11							
3154 32¢ Lily Pons	09/10/97	.65	.20			1.25	86
3155 32¢ Richard Tucker	09/10/97	.65	.20			1.25	86
3156 32¢ Lawrence Tibbett	09/10/97	.65	.20			1.25	86
3157 32¢ Rosa Ponselle	09/10/97	.65	.20			1.25	86
a Block or strip of 4, #3154-3157		2.60	1.75	2.60	(4)	2.75	

Antique Automobiles

Drivers today who think that cars powered by electricity are a recent innovation might be surprised to learn of the 1898 *Columbia.* The Pope Manufacturing Company of Hartford, Connecticut, makers of the Columbia bicycle, began production in May 1897 of their electric "horseless carriage." Two of the remaining four antique vehicles commemorated in this issue—the 1893 *Duryea* and the 1894 *Haynes*—were prototypes that never reached production. The Duryea brothers built a factory in Springfield, Massachusetts, where they became the first manufacturers in America to produce more than one car at a time. Inventor Elwood Haynes, of Kokomo, Indiana, designed one of the earliest cars powered by gasoline. In October 1896, Alexander Winton, of Cleveland, Ohio, announced his own first automobile. The 1899 *Winton* had an 8-horse-power, one-cylinder 117-cubic-inch engine, and sold for $1,000. The steam-propelled 1901 *White* was manufactured by the White Sewing Machine Company, also in Cleveland, after Thomas White decided to diversify his company's operations. Designer Ken Dallison re-created these five turn-of-the-century automobiles in a tribute to America's spirit of invention. ■

LEGENDS OF HOLLYWOOD

Over the course of a career spanning
a quarter of a century and 75 films,
Humphrey Bogart rose to legendary status
as one of America's most beloved 'tough guys'.
Renowned for his roles in *The Maltese Falcon* (1941)
and *Casablanca* (1943), he won the Academy Award
for Best Actor in *The African Queen* (1951).
"Bogie" became an international
cult figure in the 1960s.

3152

3153

3154   3155
3156   3157

3157a

3158   3159   3160   3161

32 USA — LEOPOLD STOKOWSKI

32 USA — ARTHUR FIEDLER

32 USA — GEORGE SZELL

32 USA — EUGENE ORMANDY

32 USA — SAMUEL BARBER

32 USA — FERDE GROFÉ

32 USA — CHARLES IVES

32 USA — LOUIS MOREAU GOTTSCHALK

3162   3163   3164   3165   3165a

USA 32 Social Reformer

Padre Félix Varela

3166

USA 32

US Department
of the Air Force
1947–1997

3167

Classic Movie Monsters

3169   3170   3171   3172   3168

Issues of 1997			Un	U	PB	#	FDC	Q(M)
Legends of American Music Series, Classical Composers & Conductors Issue, Perf. 11								
3158	32¢ Leopold Stokowski	09/12/97	.65	.20			1.25	86
3159	32¢ Arthur Fiedler	09/12/97	.65	.20			1.25	86
3160	32¢ George Szell	09/12/97	.65	.20			1.25	86
3161	32¢ Eugene Ormandy	09/12/97	.65	.20			1.25	86
3162	32¢ Samuel Barber	09/12/97	.65	.20			1.25	86
3163	32¢ Ferde Grofé	09/12/97	.65	.20			1.25	86
3164	32¢ Charles Ives	09/12/97	.65	.20			1.25	86
3165	32¢ Louis Moreau Gottschalk	09/12/97	.65	.20			1.25	86
a	Block of 8, #3158-3165		5.25	4.00	8.00	(8)	5.25	
	Perf. 11.2							
3166	32¢ Padre Félix Varela	09/15/97	.60	.20	2.40	(4)	1.25	2,855
Department of the Air Force, 50th Anniversary Issue, Perf. 11.2 x 11.1								
3167	32¢ Thunderbirds Aerial Demonstration Squadron	09/18/97	.60	.20	2.40	(4)	1.50	45
Classic Movie Monsters Issue, Perf. 10.2								
3168	32¢ Lon Chaney as the Phantom of the Opera	09/30/97	.60	.20			1.50	145
3169	32¢ Bela Lugosi as Dracula	09/30/97	.60	.20			1.50	145
3170	32¢ Boris Karloff as Frankenstein's Monster	09/30/97	.60	.20			1.50	145
3171	32¢ Boris Karloff as the Mummy	09/30/97	.60	.20			1.50	145
3172	32¢ Lon Chaney, Jr. as the Wolf Man	09/30/97	.60	.20			1.50	145
a	Strip of 5, #3168-3172		3.00	2.25	6.00	(10)	3.75	

Beginning with No. 3167, a hidden 3-D design can be seen on some stamps when they are viewed with a special viewer sold by the post office.

Martha Washington (1731-1802)

Martha Dandridge Custis Washington—the nation's first "First Lady"—was a young widow with two children when she married George Washington in 1759 and moved to Mount Vernon. Educated in the traditional social and household skills of Tidewater Virginia, she enjoyed ordinary domestic life. This life ended when her husband was called to lead the Continental Army in the Revolutionary War. For eight years, she followed him to his winter headquarters, where her presence comforted him and encouraged the troops. When the war ended, the couple resumed life at Mount Vernon. But in 1789 after George Washington's inauguration as President, Martha Washington moved to New York and later to Philadelphia to serve the new nation as First Lady. Although required to entertain at formal receptions several times a week, Martha Washington added her gracious and warm style to these events, thus beginning a tradition for her successors. In 1797, at the conclusion of George Washington's second term as president, the Washingtons finally and happily returned to Mount Vernon. The first stamp honoring Martha Washington was issued in 1902; it was the first United States postage stamp to honor an American woman. ■

Issues of 1998			Un	U	PB	#	FDC	Q(M)
Celebrate The Century® Issue, Perf. 11.5								
3182	Pane of 15, 1900-1909	2/3/98	9.00	—			8.50	188
a	32¢ Model T Ford		.60	.30			1.25	
b	32¢ Theodore Roosevelt		.60	.30			1.25	
c	32¢ Motion picture,							
	"The Great Train Robbery"		.60	.30			1.25	
d	32¢ Crayola Crayons introduced,							
	1903		.60	.30			1.25	
e	32¢ St. Louis World's Fair, 1904		.60	.30			1.25	
f	32¢ Design used on Hunt's							
	Remedy stamp (#RS56), Pure							
	Food & Drug Act, 1906		.60	.30			1.25	
g	32¢ Wright Brothers first flight,							
	Kitty Hawk, 1903		.60	.30			1.25	
h	32¢ Boxing match shown in painting							
	"Stag at Sharkey's," by George							
	Bellows of the Ash Can School		.60	.30			1.25	
i	32¢ Immigrants arrive		.60	.30			1.25	
j	32¢ John Muir, preservationist		.60	.30			1.25	
k	32¢ "Teddy" Bear created		.60	.30			1.25	
l	32¢ W.E.B. Du Bois, social activist		.60	.30			1.25	
m	32¢ Gibson Girl		.60	.30			1.25	
n	32¢ First baseball World Series, 1903		.60	.30			1.25	
o	32¢ Robie House, Chicago,							
	designed by Frank Lloyd Wright		.60	.30			1.25	
Celebrate The Century® Issue, Perf. 11.5								
3183	Pane of 15, 1910-1919	02/03/98	9.00	—			8.50	188
a	32¢ Charlie Chaplin as the							
	Little Tramp		.60	.30	1.25			
b	32¢ Federal Reserve System							
	created, 1913		.60	.30	1.25			
c	32¢ George Washington Carver		.60	.30	1.25			
d	32¢ Avant-garde art introduced							
	at Armory Show, 1913		.60	.30	1.25			
e	32¢ First transcontinental							
	telephone line, 1914		.60	.30	1.25			
f	32¢ Panama Canal opens, 1914		.60	.30	1.25			
g	32¢ Jim Thorpe wins decathlon							
	at Stockholm Olympics, 1912		.60	.30	1.25			
h	32¢ Grand Canyon National Park,							
	1919		.60	.30	1.25			
i	32¢ U.S. enters World War I		.60	.30	1.25			
j	32¢ Boy Scouts started in 1910,							
	Girl Scouts formed in 1912		.60	.30	1.25			
k	32¢ Woodrow Wilson		.60	.30	1.25			
l	32¢ First crossword puzzle							
	published, 1913		.60	.30	1.25			
m	32¢ Jack Dempsey wins							
	heavyweight title, 1919		.60	.30	1.25			
n	32¢ Construction toys		.60	.30	1.25			
o	32¢ Child labor reform		.60	.30	1.25			

Issues of 1999		Un	U	FDC	Q(M)
Celebrate The Century®, Perf. 11.5					
3186	Pane of 15, 1940–1949 02/18/99	9.75	—	8.50	12.5
a	33¢ World War II	.65	.30	1.25	
b	33¢ Antibiotics save lives	.65	.30	1.25	
c	33¢ Jackie Robinson	.65	.30	1.25	
d	33¢ Harry S. Truman	.65	.30	1.25	
e	33¢ Women support war effort	.65	.30	1.25	
f	33¢ TV entertains America	.65	.30	1.25	
g	33¢ Jitterbug sweeps nation	.65	.30	1.25	
h	33¢ Jackson Pollock, Abstract Expressionism	.65	.30	1.25	
i	33¢ GI Bill, 1944	.65	.30	1.25	
j	33¢ The Big Band Sound	.65	.30	1.25	
k	33¢ International style of architecture	.65	.30	1.25	
l	33¢ Postwar baby boom	.65	.30	1.25	
m	33¢ Slinky, 1945	.65	.30	1.25	
n	33¢ "A Streetcar Named Desire", 1947	.65	.30	1.25	
o	33¢ Orson Welles' "Citizen Kane"	.65	.30	1.25	
Celebrate The Century®, Perf. 11.5					
3187	Pane of 15, 1950–1959 05/26/99	9.75	—	8.50	12.5
a	33¢ Polio vaccine developed	.65	.30	1.25	
b	33¢ Teen fashions	.65	.30	1.25	
c	33¢ The "Shot Heard 'Round the World"	.65	.30	1.25	
d	33¢ U.S. launches satellites	.65	.30	1.25	
e	33¢ Korean War	.65	.30	1.25	
f	33¢ Desegregating public schools	.65	.30	1.25	
g	33¢ Tail fins, chrome	.65	.30	1.25	
h	33¢ Dr. Seuss' "The Cat in the Hat"	.65	.30	1.25	
i	33¢ Drive-in movies	.65	.30	1.25	
j	33¢ World Series rivals	.65	.30	1.25	
k	33¢ Rocky Marciano, undefeated boxer	.65	.30	1.25	
l	33¢ "I Love Lucy"	.65	.30	1.25	
m	33¢ Rock 'n Roll	.65	.30	1.25	
n	33¢ Stock car racing	.65	.30	1.25	
o	33¢ Movies go 3-D	.65	.30	1.25	

First Man on the Moon

On July 20, 1969, millions watched on television as astronaut Neil Armstrong climbed down a ladder and stepped onto the moon's surface. The first man on the moon said for all to hear, "That's one small step for man; one giant leap for mankind." Four days earlier, Apollo 11 had been launched into space for its journey to the moon. Three astronauts—Flight Commander Neil Armstrong, command module pilot Michael Collins, and lunar module pilot Edwin E. Aldrin, Jr.—were aboard for the 8-day mission. Two of them—Armstrong and Aldrin—would walk, and jump, on the moon's surface, collect rocks to bring back to Earth, and leave an American flag as proof of their achievement. On September 9, 1969, the U.S. Postal Service issued a commemorative airmail stamp designed by Paul Calle as a tribute to the "first man on the moon." ■

CTC Issues of 2000			Un	U	FDC	Q(M)
Celebrate The Century®, Perf. 11.6						
3191	Pane of 15, 1990-1999	05/02/00	9.75	—	8.50	5.5
a	33¢	New Baseball Records	.65	.30	1.25	
b	33¢	Gulf War	.65	.30	1.25	
c	33¢	"Seinfeld", television series	.65	.30	1.25	
d	33¢	Extreme Sports	.65	.30	1.25	
e	33¢	Improving Education	.65	.30	1.25	
f	33¢	Computer Art and Graphics	.65	.30	1.25	
g	33¢	Recovering Species	.65	.30	1.25	
h	33¢	Return to Space	.65	.30	1.25	
i	33¢	Special Olympics	.65	.30	1.25	
j	33¢	Virtual Reality	.65	.30	1.25	
k	33¢	"Jurassic Park"	.65	.30	1.25	
l	33¢	"Titanic"	.65	.30	1.25	
m	33¢	Sports Utility Vehicle	.65	.30	1.25	
n	33¢	World Wide Web	.65	.30	1.25	
o	33¢	Cellular Phones	.65	.30	1.25	

Gift Collection for Kids

Give a youngster the thrill of stamp collecting with this fun, educational **Gift Collection for Kids**! This gift provides a child with colorful collectibles specially chosen to bring joy to all young collectors.

In your collection you will receive:

❏ interesting and exciting stamps and stamp products

❏ exclusive commemorative binder and acetate pages to keep your collection safe for years to come

❏ official personalized membership certicate

❏ stamp decoder to reveal hidden images on certain stamp

And throughout the year, kids have the excitement of receiving something in the mail just for them.

Your young friend will receive four shipments, each with stamps and stamp products in a variety of formats and the Cool-lecting newsletter.

Item #20122A–Gift Collection for Kids: Annual subscribtion $49.95

To order, call **1-800-STAMP-24**

*Prices subject to change without notice.

3191

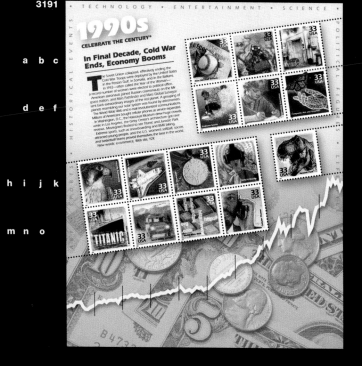

a b c

d e f

h i j k

m n o

To order these new stamps and other related philatelic products
call **1-800-STAMP-24** or visit us online at **www.usps.com**

Purple Heart

First Flight

Southeastern Lighthouses

3192

3193   **3194**   **3195**   **3196**   **3197**   **3197a**

3198   **3199**   **3200**   **3201**   **3202**   **3202a**

3203

3204b

Issues of 1998		Un	U	PB	#	FDC	Q(M)
Perf. 11.2 x 11							
3192	32¢ "Remember the Maine"						
	Spanish-American War	02/15/98	.60	.20	2.40	(4)	1.75	30
Flowering Trees Issue, Die-Cut, Perf. 11.3							
3193	32¢ Southern Magnolia	03/19/98	.60	.20			1.50
3194	32¢ Blue Paloverde	03/19/98	.60	.20			1.50
3195	32¢ Yellow Poplar	03/19/98	.60	.20			1.50
3196	32¢ Prairie Crab Apple	03/19/98	.60	.20			1.50
3197	32¢ Pacific Dogwood	03/19/98	.60	.20			1.50
a	Strip of 5, #3193-3197	03/19/98	3.00		6.00	(10)	3.75	250
Alexander Calder Issue, Perf. 10.2							
3198	32¢ Black Cascade	03/25/98	.60	.20			1.50
3199	32¢ Untitled	03/25/98	.60	.20			1.50
3200	32¢ Rearing Stallion	03/25/98	.60	.20			1.50
3201	32¢ Portrait of a Young Man	03/25/98	.60	.20			1.50
3202	32¢ Un Effet du Japonais	03/25/98	.60	.20			1.50
a	Strip of 5, #3198-3202	03/25/98	3.00	2.25	6.00	(10)	3.75	80
Holiday Celebrations Issue, Self-Adhesive, Serpentine Die-Cut 11.7 x 10.9							
3203	32¢ Cinco de Mayo	04/16/98	.60	.20	2.40	(4)	1.25	85
Looney Tunes Issue, Self-Adhesive, Serpentine Die-Cut 11.1							
3204	Sylvester & Tweety Pane of 10	04/27/98	6.00					300
a	32¢ single		.60	.20			1.25
b	Booklet pane of 9, #3204a		5.40				
c	Booklet pane of 1, #3204a		.60				

Amelia Earhart (1897-1937)

At the age of ten, Amelia Earhart was unimpressed by the first airplane she saw and described it as "not at all interesting." In 1920, however, after her first flight, she knew that she wanted to fly. Earhart took flying lessons and bought a plane; she soon set a women's altitude record of 14,000 feet. In the early 1920s, Earhart moved to Boston where she continued to fly and actively promote flying events, especially for women. In 1928 she was the first woman to fly across the Atlantic, albeit as a passenger; when the plane landed in Wales, she, and not the pilots, became the public's darling. Four years later, piloting a monoplane, she became the first woman to fly the Atlantic alone—an achievement that won her the Distinguished Flying Cross. She was also the first woman to fly solo across the United States (1932) and across the Pacific from Hawaii to California (1935). It was not long before Earhart was contemplating "one more long flight." This one would take her around the world. On June 1, 1937, she and her navigator, Frederick Noonan, took off from Miami, Florida, heading east. On July 2, with only 7000 miles to go—all over the Pacific—Earhart left New Guinea for tiny Howland Island. She never arrived. Despite massive searches by the government and privately financed expeditions, no trace of Earhart, Noonan, or the plane was ever found. ■

3212   3213

3214   3215   3215a

3219   3218

3216   3217   3219a

3220   3221

3222   3223

3224   3225   3225a

Issues of 1998		Un	U	PB	#	FDC	Q(M)
Legends of American Music Series, Folk Musicians, Perf. 10.1 x 10.2							
3212 32¢ Huddle "Leadbelly" Ledbetter	06/26/98	.60	.20			1.25	
3213 32¢ Woody Guthrie	06/26/98	.60	.20			1.25	
3214 32¢ Sonny Terry	06/26/98	.60	.20			1.25	
3215 32¢ Josh White	6/26/98	.60	.20			1.25	
a Block or strip of 4, #3212-3215	06/26/98	2.50	2.00	2.50	(4)	3.25	45
Legends of American Music Series, Gospel Singers Issue, Perf. 10.1 x 10.3							
3216 32¢ Mahalia Jackson	07/15/98	.60	.20			1.25	
3217 32¢ Roberta Martin	07/15/98	.60	.20			1.25	
3218 32¢ Clara Ward	07/15/98	.60	.20			1.25	
3219 32¢ Sister Rosetta Tharpe	07/15/98	.60	.20			1.25	
a Block or strip of 4, #3216-3219	07/15/98	2.40	2.00	2.40	(4)	3.25	45
Perf. 11.2							
3220 32¢ Spanish Settlement of the Southwest	07/11/98	.60	.20	2.40	(4)	1.25	46
Literary Arts Series							
3221 32¢ Stephen Vincent Benét	07/22/98	.60	.20	2.40	(4)	1.25	
Tropical Birds Issue							
3222 32¢ Antillean Euphonia	07/29/98	.60	.20			1.25	
3223 32¢ Green-throated Carib	07/29/98	.60	.20			1.25	
3224 32¢ Crested Honeycreeper	07/29/98	.60	.20			1.25	
3225 32¢ Cardinal Honeyeater	07/29/98	.60	.20			1.25	
a Block of 4, #3222-3225		2.40	2.00	2.40	(4)	3.00	70

Thomas A. Edison (1847-1931)

At the age of 10, Thomas Alva Edison, who later would invent the incandescent light bulb, the phonograph, and the motion picture camera, already had set up his first laboratory—in the basement of his home. While still a teenager, he became a roving telegrapher, but turned to inventing and business in his early twenties. His first invention—an electric vote recorder—was a commercial failure and Edison vowed that in the future he would invent only what the public wanted. The phonograph, his first major invention, brought him international fame; he toured the country demonstrating it. Determined to develop a practical light bulb, Edison not only invented incandescent electric light—his first bulb burned for more than 13 hours—but also a system to make the light practical, safe, and economical. He demonstrated the system at his own laboratory—lighted electrically—in December 1879. The success of his electric light brought him fame and wealth. His many electric companies were merged to form Edison General Electric but his name was dropped in 1892, and the company became General Electric. He lived to see the nation celebrate the golden jubilee of the incandescent light in 1929. ∎

1998

	Issues of 1998		Un	U	PB	#	FDC	Q(M)
	Space Discovery Issue, Perf. 11.1							
3238	32¢ Multicolored	10/01/98	.60	.20			1.25	
3239	32¢ Multicolored	10/01/98	.60	.20			1.25	
3240	32¢ Multicolored	10/01/98	.60	.20			1.25	
3241	32¢ Multicolored	10/01/98	.60	.20			1.25	
3242	32¢ Multicolored	10/01/98	.60	.20			1.25	
a	Strip of 5, #3238-3242		3.00	2.25			3.75	
	Self-Adhesive, Serpentine Die-Cut 11.1							
3243	32¢ Philanthropy, Giving and Sharing	10/07/98	.60	.20			1.25	50
	Holiday Traditional, Booklet Stamps, Self-Adhesive, Serpentine Die-Cut 10.1 x 9.9 on 2, 3 or 4 sides							
3244	32¢ The Madonna and Child by Hans Memling	10/15/98	.60	.20			1.25	925.2
a	Booklet pane of 20 + label		12.00					
	Holiday Contemporary, Booklet Stamps, Self-Adhesive, Serpentine Die-Cut 11.3 x 11.6 on 2 or 3 sides							
3245	32¢ Evergreen Wreath	10/15/98	1.50	.20			1.25	
3246	32¢ Victorian Wreath	10/15/98	1.50	.20			1.25	
3247	32¢ Chili Pepper Wreath	10/15/98	1.50	.20			1.25	
3248	32¢ Tropical Wreath	10/15/98	1.50	.20			1.25	
a	Booklet pane of 4, #3245-3248		12.50				3.25	
b	Booklet pane of 5, #3245, #3246, 3248, 2 #3247 and label		15.00					
c	Booklet pane of 6, #3247-3248, 2 each #3245-3246		17.50					
	Serpentine Die-Cut 11.4 x 11.6 on 2, 3 or 4 sides							
3249	32¢ Evergreen Wreath	10/15/98	.60	.20			1.25	
3250	32¢ Victorian Wreath	10/15/98	.60	.20			1.25	
3251	32¢ Chili Pepper Wreath	10/15/98	.60	.20			1.25	
3252	32¢ Tropical Wreath	10/15/98	.60	.20			1.25	
a	Block of 4, #3249-3252		2.40		2.40	(4)	3.00	
b	Booklet pane, 5 each #3249-3252		12.00					
	Perf. 11.2							
3257	(1¢) Make-Up Rate Weathervane	11/09/98	.20	.20	.25	(4)	1.25	
3258	(1¢) Make-Up Rate Weathervane	11/09/98	.20	.20	.25	(4)	1.25	
	#3257 is 18mm high, has thin letters, white USA, and black 1998.							
	#3258 is 17mm high, has thick letters, pale blue USA, and blue 1998.							
	Self-Adhesive, Serpentine Die-Cut 10.8							
3259	22¢ Uncle Sam	11/09/98	.45	.20	2.25	(4)	1.25	
	Perf. 11.2							
3260	(33¢) H-Series	11/09/98	.65	.20	2.60	(4)	1.25	

Visit us online at The Postal Store at www.usps.com

or call 1-800-STAMP-24

3238   3239   3240   3241   3242 3242a

3243

3245

3246

3244

3247

3248

3248a

CHRISTMAS

3258   3259   3260

Visit us online at The Postal Store at www.usps.com

or call 1-800-STAMP-24

3261

3262

B1

Visit us online at The Postal Store at www.usps.com

or call 1-800-STAMP-24

	Issues of 1998		Un	U	PB	#	FDC	Q(M)
	Self-Adhesive, Serpentine Die-Cut 11.5							
3261	$3.20 Space Shuttle Landing	11/09/98	6.00	3.00	24.00	(4)	5.00	245
	Self-Adhesive, Serpentine Die-Cut 11.5							
3262	$11.75 Express Mail	11/19/98	22.50	11.50	90.00	(4)	25.00	21
	Coil Stamps, Self-Adhesive, Serpentine Die-Cut 9.9 Vertically							
3263	22¢ Uncle Sam	11/09/98	.45	.20	3.50	(5)	1.25	
	Perf. 9.8 Vertically							
3264	33¢ Unce Sam's Hat	11/09/98	.65	.20	5.00	(5)	1.25	
	Self-Adhesive, Serpentine Die-Cut 9.9 Vertically							
3265	33¢ H-Series	11/09/98	.65	.20	5.50	(5)	1.25	
	Serpentine Die-Cut 9.9 Vertically							
3266	33¢ Uncle Sam's Hat	11/09/98	.65	.20	5.00	(5)	1.50	
	Booklet Stamps, Self-Adhesive, Serpentine Die-Cut 9.9 on 2 or 3 sides							
3267	33¢ H-Series	11/09/98	.65	.20			1.25	
a	Booklet pane of 10		6.50					
	Serpentine Die-Cut 11.2 x 11.1 on 2, 3 or 4 sides							
3268	33¢ Uncle Sam's Hat	11/09/98	.65	.20			1.25	
a	Booklet pane of 10		6.50					
b	Serpentine die-cut II		.65	.20				
c	As "b", booklet pane of 20 + label		13.00					
	Die-Cut 8 on 2, 3 or 4 sides							
3269	33¢ Uncle Sam's Hat	11/09/98	.65	.20			1.25	
a	Booklet pane of 18		12.00					
	Coil Stamps, Perf. 9.8 Vertically							
3270	10¢ Eagle with Shield	12/14/98	.20	.20	2.75	(5)	1.25	
	Self-Adhesive, Serpentine Die-Cut 9.9 Vertically							
3271	10¢ Eagle with Shield	12/14/98	.20	.20	2.75	(5)	1.25	
a	Large date		.20	.20	3.25	(5)		
b	Tagged (error)		1.25	1.10				
	Semi-postal Stamp, Self-Adhesive, Serpentine Die-Cut 11							
B1	32¢ + 8¢ Breast Cancer							
	Research	07/29/98	.80	.60	3.25	(4)		200

Hattie W. Caraway (1878-1950)

Hattie Wyatt Caraway was the first woman elected to the U.S. Senate. She was appointed to the Senate on November 13, 1931, a few days after the death of her husband, Senator Thaddeus Caraway. On January 12, 1932, she won a special election to fill the remaining months of his term. Subsequently elected to two six-year terms, she served in the Senate until January 1945. In 1933, Senator Caraway—a Democrat from Arkansas—became the first woman to chair a Senate committee. On October 19, 1943—in the absence that day of the Vice President and the president *pro tempore* (the Senate's presiding officer)—Senator Caraway was appointed acting president *pro tempore*, the first woman to preside formally over the Senate. A strong supporter of New Deal legislation, Senator Caraway was known for her dedication and diligence. On December 19, 1944, her last day at work in the Senate chamber, Senator Caraway was honored by her colleagues with a standing ovation. The stamp honoring her is the third issuance in the Distinguished Americans series. ■

1999

	Issues of 1999		Un	U	PB	#	FDC	Q(M)
	Lunar New Year Issue, Perf. 11.2							
3272	33¢ Year of the Rabbit	01/05/99	.65	.20	2.60	(4)	1.50	51
	Black Heritage Issue, Self-Adhesive, Serpentine Die-Cut 11.4							
3273	33¢ Malcolm X	01/20/99	.65	.20	2.60	(4)	1.75	100
	Booklet Stamp, Self-Adhesive, Die-Cut							
3274	33¢ Love	01/28/99	.65	.20			1.25	1,500
a	Booklet pane of 20		13.00					
3275	55¢ Love	01/20/99	1.10	.20	4.40	(4)	1.50	300
	Serpentine Die-Cut 11.4							
3276	33¢ Hospice Care	02/09/99	.65	.20	2.80	(4)	1.25	100
	Perf. 11.2							
3277	33¢ City Flag	02/25/99	.65	.20	12.50	(4)	1.25	200
	Self-Adhesive, Serpentine Die-Cut 11.1 on 2, 3 or 4 sides							
3278	33¢ City Flag	02/25/99	.65	.20	2.60	(4)	1.25	
a	Booklet pane of 4		2.60					
b	Booklet pane of 5 + label		3.25					
c	Booklet pane of 6		3.90					
d	Booklet pane of 10		6.50					
e	Booklet pane of 20 + label		13.00					
	Booklet Stamps, Serpentine Die-Cut 11.5 x 11.75 on 2, 3 or 4 sides							
3278F	33¢ City Flag		.65	.20				
g	Booklet pane of 20 + label		13.00					
	Self-Adhesive, Serpentine Die-Cut 9.8 on 2 or 3 sides							
3279	33¢ City Flag	02/25/99	.65	.20			1.25	
a	Booklet pane of 10		6.50					
	Coil Stamps, Perf. 9.9 Vertically							
3280	33¢ City Flag	02/25/99	.65	.20	5.00	(5)	1.25	
	Self-Adhesive, Serpentine Die-Cut 9.8 Vertically							
3281	33¢ City Flag	02/25/99	.65	.20	5.00	(5)	1.25	
3282	33¢ City Flag	02/25/99	.65	.20	5.00	(5)	1.25	
	Rounded corners.							
	Booklet Stamp, Self-Adhesive, Serpentine Die-Cut 7.9 on 2, 3 or 4 sides							
3283	33¢ Flag and Chalkboard	03/13/99	.65	.20			1.25	306
a	Booklet pane of 18		12.00					
	Perf. 11.2							
3286	33¢ Irish Immigration	02/26/99	.65	.20	2.60	(4)	1.50	40.4
3287	33¢ Alfred Lunt & Lynn Fontanne	03/02/99	.65	.20	2.60	(4)	1.25	42.5

Visit us online at The Postal Store at www.usps.com

or call 1-800-STAMP-24

3272

3273

3274

3275

3276

3277   3278   3279   3280

3286   3287

3288   3289   3290   3291   3292 3292a

Issues of 1999		Un	U	PB	#	FDC	Q(M)
Arctic Animals Issue, Perf. 11							
3288	33¢ Arctic Hare	03/12/99	.65	.20			1.25	15.3
3289	33¢ Arctic Fox	03/12/99	.65	.20			1.25	15.3
3290	33¢ Snowy Owl	03/12/99	.65	.20			1.25	15.3
3291	33¢ Polar Bear	03/12/99	.65	.20			1.25	15.3
3292	33¢ Gray Wolf	03/12/99	.65	.20			1.25	15.3
a	Strip of 5, #3288-3292		3.25				3.25	

Gift Collection for Kids

Give a youngster the thrill of stamp collecting with this fun, educational **Gift Collection for Kids!** This gift provides a child with colorful collectibles specially chosen to bring joy to all young collectors.

In your collection you will receive:

❏ interesting and exciting stamps and stamp products

❏ exclusive commemorative binder and acetate pages to keep your collection safe for years to come

❏ official personalized membership certicate

❏ stamp decoder to reveal hidden images on certain stamp

And throughout the year, kids have the excitement of receiving something in the mail just for them.

Your young friend will receive four shipments, each with stamps and stamp products in a variety of formats and the Cool-lecting newsletter.

Item #20122A–Gift Collection for Kids: Annual subscribtion $49.95

To order, call **1-800-STAMP-24**

*Prices subject to change without notice.

1999-2000

	Issues of 1999-2000		Un	U	PB	#	FDC	Q(M
	Sonoran Desert Issue, Self-Adhesive, Serpentine Die-Cut Perf. 11.2							
3293	Pane of 10	04/06/99	6.50				6.75	10.3
a	33¢ Cactus Wren, brittlebush,							
	teddy bear cholla		.65	.20			1.25	
b	33¢ Desert tortoise		.65	.20			1.25	
c	33¢ White-winged dove		.65	.20			1.25	
d	33¢ Gambel quail		.65	.20			1.25	
e	33¢ Saguaro cactus		.65	.20			1.25	
f	33¢ Desert mule deer		.65	.20			1.25	
g	33¢ Desert cottontail, hedgehog cactus		.65	.20			1.25	
h	33¢ Gila monster		.65	.20			1.25	
i	33¢ Western diamondback rattlesnake,							
	cactus mouse		.65	.20			1.25	
j	33¢ Gila woodpecker		.65	.20			1.25	
	Fruit Berries Issue, Self-Adhesive, Serpentine Die-Cut 11.25 x 11.75 on 2,3 or 4 sides,							
	Serpentine Die-Cut 11.5 x 11.75 on 2 or 3 sides (3294a-3297a)							
3294	33¢ Blueberries	04/10/99	.65	.20			1.25	
a	Dated "2000"	03/15/00	.65	.20			1.25	
3295	33¢ Raspberries	04/10/99	.65	.20			1.25	
a	Dated "2000"	03/15/00	.65	.20			1.25	
3296	33¢ Strawberries	04/10/99	.65	.20			1.25	
a	Dated "2000"	03/15/00	.65	.20			1.25	
3297	33¢ Blackberries	04/10/99	.65	.20			1.25	
a	Dated "2000"	03/15/00	.65	.20			1.25	
b	Booklet pane, 5 each #3294-3297 + label		13.00	—			3.25	
c	Block of 4, #3294-3297		2.60					
d	Booklet pane, 5 #3297e		13.00					
e	Block of 4, #3294a-3297a		2.60					
	Serpentine Die-Cut 9.5 x 10 on 2 or 3 sides							
3298	33¢ Blueberries	04/10/99	.65	.20			1.25	
3299	33¢ Raspberries	04/10/99	.65	.20			1.25	
3300	33¢ Strawberries	04/10/99	.65	.20			1.25	
3301	33¢ Blackberries	04/10/99	.65	.20			1.25	
a	Booklet pane of 4							
	#3298-#3301		2.60				3.25	
b	Booklet pane of 5							
	#3298, #3299, #3301							
	2 #3300 + label		3.25					
c	Booklet pane of 6							
	#3300, #3301,							
	2 #3298, #3299		4.00					
d	Block of 4, #3298-#3301		2.60					
	Coil Stamps, Serpentine Die-Cut 8.5 Vertically							
3302	33¢ Blueberries	04/10/99	.65	.20			1.25	
3303	33¢ Raspberries	04/10/99	.65	.20			1.25	
3304	33¢ Strawberries	04/10/99	.65	.20			1.25	
3305	33¢ Blackberries	04/10/99	.65	.20			1.25	
a	Strip of 4		2.60				3.25	

SONORAN DESERT

N A T U R E   O F   A M E R I C A

3293

e

c   f   j

a   b   d   g   h

i

3294   **3296**

3295   **3297**

3297c

3305a

1999

3306a

3308

3309

3310   3311

3312   3313   3313a

3314

3315

3316

3317   3318   3319   3320   3320a

Issues of 1999		Un	U	PB	#	FDC	Q(M)
Looney Tunes Issue, Self-Adhesive, Serpentine Die-Cut 11.1							
3306	Pane of 10	04/16/99	6.50				
a	33¢ Daffy Duck		.65	.20			1.50	427
b	Booklet pane of 9 #3306a		5.85				
c	Booklet pane of 1 #3306a		.65				
3307	Pane of 10		6.50				
a	33¢ Single		.65				
Literary Arts Issue, Perf. 11.2							
3308	33¢ Ayn Rand	04/22/99	.65	.20	2.60	(4)	1.25	42.5
Self-Adhesive, Serpentine Die-Cut 11.6 x 11.3							
3309	33¢ Cinco De Mayo	04/27/99	.65	.20	2.60	(4)	1.25	113
Tropical Flowers Issue, Self-Adhesive, Serpentine Die-Cut 10.9 on 2 or 3 sides							
3310	33¢ Bird of Paradise	05/01/99	.65	.20			1.25
3311	33¢ Royal Poinciana	05/01/99	.65	.20			1.25
3312	33¢ Gloriosa Lily	05/01/99	.65	.20			1.25
3313	33¢ Chinese Hibiscus	05/01/99	.65	.20			1.25
a	Block of 4 #3310-3313		2.60				3.25
b	Booklet pane of 5 #3313a		13.00				
Self-Adhesive, Perf. 11.5							
3314	33¢ John & William Bartram	05/18/99	.65	.20	2.60	(4)	1.25	145
Self-Adhesive, Perf. 11							
3315	33¢ Prostate Cancer Awareness	05/28/99	.65	.20	2.60	(4)	1.25	78
Perf. 11.25							
3316	33¢ California Gold Rush 1849	06/18/99	.65	.20	2.60	(4)	1.25	89
Aquarium Fish Issue, Self-Adhesive, Serpentine Die-Cut 11.5							
3317	33¢ Yellow fish, red fish, cleaner shrimp	06/24/99	.65	.20			1.25	39
3318	33¢ Fish, thermometer	06/24/99	.65	.20			1.25	39
3319	33¢ Red fish, blue & yellow fish	06/24/99	.65	.20			1.25	39
3320	33¢ Fish, heater/aerator	06/24/99	.65	.20			1.25	39
a	Strip of 4, #3317-3320		2.60		5.20	(8)	3.25

Thomas H. Gallaudet (1787-1851)

Philadelphia-born Thomas H. Gallaudet, a pioneer in the instruction of deaf students, grew up in Hartford, Connecticut. He graduated first in his class from Yale, where he later earned a master of arts degree. A graduate as well of Andover Theological Seminary, he planned to enter the ministry but changed his mind when he met Alice Cogswell, the deaf child of a neighbor. Asked by her father to travel to Europe to study methods for teaching deaf students, Gallaudet agreed. While abroad, he learned sign language; he returned to America with Laurent Clerc, a deaf faculty member from a renowned school for the deaf in Paris. Gallaudet and Clerc successfully raised funds to establish in Hartford the first permanent school for the deaf; Alice Cogswell was one of its first students. After more than 15 years as principal of the school, Gallaudet resigned to devote his time to writing children's books and to the ministry. In 1893, more than 40 years after his death, the National Deaf-Mute College in Washington, D.C., changed its name to Gallaudet College in his memory. ∎

3338

3339
3340
3341
3342
3343
3344
3344a

3345
3346
3347
3348
3349
3350
3350a

	Issues of 1999		Un	U	PB	#	FDC	Q(M)
	Perf. 11							
3338	33¢ Frederick Law Olmstead	09/13/99	.65	.20	2.60	(4)	1.25	42.5
	Legends of American Music Series, Hollywood Composers Issue							
3339	33¢ Max Steiner	09/16/99	.65	.20			1.25	
3340	33¢ Dimitri Tiomkin	09/16/99	.65	.20			1.25	
3341	33¢ Bernard Herrmann	09/16/99	.65	.20			1.25	
3342	33¢ Franz Waxman	09/16/99	.65	.20			1.25	
3343	33¢ Alfred Newman	09/16/99	.65	.20			1.25	
3344	33¢ Erich Wolfgang Korngold	09/16/99	.65	.20			1.25	
a	Block of 6, #3339-3344		3.90	—	3.90	(6)	3.75	
	Legends of American Music Series, Broadway Songwriters Issue							
3345	33¢ Ira & George Gershwin	09/21/99	.65	.20			1.25	
3346	33¢ Lerner & Loewe	09/21/99	.65	.20			1.25	
3347	33¢ Lorenz Hart	09/21/99	.65	.20			1.25	
3348	33¢ Rodgers & Hammerstein	09/21/99	.65	.20			1.25	
3349	33¢ Meredith Willson	09/21/99	.65	.20			1.25	
3350	33¢ Frank Loesser	09/21/99	.65	.20			1.25	
a	Block of 6, #3345-3350		3.90	—	3.90	(6)	3.75	

A·M·E·R·I·C·A·N C·O·M·M·E·M·O·R·A·T·I·V·E C·O·L·L·E·C·T·I·B·L·E·S

American Commemorative Panels

Obtain photo or steel engravings, mint condition stamps and subject related text presented on a beautifully designed page. Only $6.00* each, depending on the value of the stamps.

For more information call
1-800-STAMP-24

Prices subject to change without notice.

3352

3353

3354

3355

3356

3357

3359

3358

3359a

3368

	Issues of 1999		Un	U	PB	#	FDC	Q(M)
	Self-Adhesive, Serpentine Die-Cut 11							
3352	33¢ Hanukkah	10/08/99	.65	.20	2.60	(4)	1.50	65
	Coil Stamp, Perf. 9.75							
3353	22¢ Uncle Sam	10/08/99	.45	.20	3.50	(5)	1.25	150
	Perf. 11.25							
3354	33¢ NATO 50th Anniversary	10/13/99	.65	.20	2.60	(4)	1.25	44.6
	Holiday Traditional, Issue, Self-Adhesive Booklet Stamps, Serpentine Die-Cut 11.25 on 2 or 3 sides							
3355	33¢ Madonna and child by Bartolomeo Vivarini	10/20/99	.65	.15			1.25	1,556
a	Booklet pane of 20		13.00					
	Holiday Contemporary Issue, Self-Adhesive, Serpentine Die-Cut 11.25							
3356	33¢ Red Deer	10/20/99	.65	.20			1.25	
3357	33¢ Blue Deer	10/20/99	.65	.20			1.25	
3358	33¢ Purple Deer	10/20/99	.65	.20			1.25	
3359	33¢ Green Deer	10/20/99	.65	.20			1.25	
a	Block or strip, #3356-3359		2.60		2.60	(4)	3.00	
	Booklet Stamps, Serpentine Die-Cut 11.25 on 2, 3 or 4 sides							
3360	33¢ Red Deer	10/20/99	.65	.20			1.25	
3361	33¢ Blue Deer	10/20/99	.65	.20			1.25	
3362	33¢ Purple Deer	10/20/99	.65	.20			1.25	
3363	33¢ Green Deer	10/20/99	.65	.20			1.25	
a	Booklet pane of 20		13.00				3.00	
	Booklet Stamps, Serpentine Die-Cut 11.5 x 11.25 on 2 or 3 sides							
3364	33¢ Red Deer	10/20/99	.65	.20			1.25	
3365	33¢ Blue Deer	10/20/99	.65	.20			1.25	
3366	33¢ Purple Deer	10/20/99	.65	.20			1.25	
3367	33¢ Green Deer	10/20/99	.65	.20			1.25	
a	Booklet pane of 4		2.60				3.00	
b	Block pane of 5, #3364, #3366, #3367 2 #3365 + label		3.25					
c	Block pane of 6, #3365, #3367, 2 #3364, #3366		4.00					
	Self-Adhesive, Serpentine Die-Cut 11							
3368	33¢ Kwanzaa	10/29/99	.65	.20	2.60	(4)	1.75	95

Visit us online at The Postal Store at www.usps.com

or call 1-800-STAMP-24

Issues of 1999-2000		Un	U	PB	#	FDC	Q(M)
Self-Adhesive, Serpentine Die-Cut 11.25							
3369 33¢ Year 2000	12/27/99	.65	.20	2.75	(4)	1.25	124
Lunar New Year Issue, Perf. 11.25							
3370 33¢ Year of the Dragon	01/06/00	.65	.20	2.60	(4)	1.50	106
Black Heritage Issue, Serpentine Die-Cut 11.5 x 11.25							
3371 33¢ Patricia Harris	01/27/00	.65	.20	2.60	(4)	1.75	150
U.S. Navy Submarines Issue, Perf. 11							
3372 33¢ *Los Angeles* Class	03/27/00	.65	.20	2.60	(4)	1.25	65.15
3373 22¢ *S* Class	03/27/00	.45	.20			1.25	3
3374 33¢ *Los Angeles* Class	03/27/00	.65	.30			1.25	3
3375 55¢ *Ohio* Class	03/27/00	1.10	.50			1.50	3
3376 60¢ USS *Holland*	03/27/00	1.25	.55			1.50	3
3377 $3.20 *Gato* Class	03/27/00	6.50	3.00			6.00	3
a Booklet Pane of 5, #3373-3377		10.00					

Alice Hamilton (1869-1970)

Alice Hamilton—considered by many to be the founder of industrial medicine—was the first American doctor whose life was devoted to research in this field. After completing her medical studies, she moved into Jane Addams's Hull-House in Chicago where she opened a well-baby clinic for poor families. Her concerns for the poor, and the occupational diseases they experienced, led her to study the effects of lead, arsenic, mercury, and other toxic substances. Her findings contributed to safer working conditions and to workers' compensation laws. In 1919, Hamilton became the first woman professor at Harvard Medical School (where she was not allowed to use the faculty club, march at commencement, or have access to football tickets) when she was appointed assistant professor of industrial medicine. She retired in 1935 and became a consultant to the U.S. Department of Labor, continuing her studies and interest in social reforms. In 1943, she published her autobiography, *Exploring the Dangerous Trades*. The following year, she was listed in *Men of Science* and in 1947 received the Lasker Award from the U.S. Public Health Association. ▓

3369

3370

3371

3372

3376

3377

3374

3373

3375

3377a

Creating a WORLD   Shaping a LIFE

Adopting a CHILD

Building a HOME

USA 33

3398

3399

USA 33

3400

USA 33

3401

33 USA

3402

33 USA

3402a

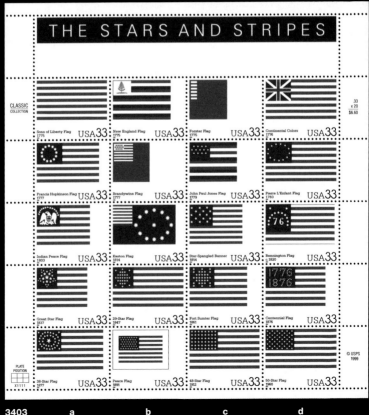

THE STARS AND STRIPES

CLASSIC COLLECTION

.33 x 20 $6.60

Sons of Liberty Flag 1775   USA33

New England Flag 1775   USA33

Forster Flag 1775   USA33

Continental Colors 1776   USA33

Francis Hopkinson Flag 1777   USA33

Brandywine Flag 1777   USA33

John Paul Jones Flag 1779   USA33

Pierre L'Enfant Flag 1783   USA33

Indian Peace Flag 1803   USA33

Easton Flag 1814   USA33

Star-Spangled Banner 1814   USA33

Bennington Flag c. 1820   USA33

Great Star Flag 1837   USA33

29-Star Flag 1847   USA33

Fort Sumter Flag 1861   USA33

Centennial Flag 1876   USA33

PLATE POSITION   X1111

38-Star Flag 1877   USA33

Peace Flag 1891   USA33

48-Star Flag 1912   USA33

50-Star Flag 1960   USA33

© USPS 1999

3403   **a**   **b**   **c**   **d**

2000

Issues of 2000		Un	U	PB	#	FDC	Q(M)
Self-Adhesive, Serpentine Die-Cut 11.5							
3398	33¢ Adoption 05/10/00	.65	.20	2.60	(4)	1.25	200
Youth Team Sports Issue, Self-Adhesive, Serpentine Die-Cut 11.5							
3399	33¢ Basketball 05/27/00	.65	.20	2.60	(4)	1.25	22
3400	33¢ Football 05/27/00	.65	.20	2.60	(4)	1.25	22
3401	33¢ Soccer 05/27/00	.65	.20	2.60	(4)	1.25	22
3402	33¢ Baseball 05/27/00	.65	.20	2.60	(4)	1.25	22
a	Block strip of 4, #3399-3402	2.60				3.25	
The Stars and Stripes Issue, Perf. 10.5 x 11							
3403	Pane of 20 06/14/00	13.00				10.00	
a	33¢ Sons of Liberty Flag, 1775	.65	.30			1.25	80
b	33¢ New England Flag, 1775	.65	.30			1.25	80
c	33¢ Forster Flag, 1775	.65	.30			1.25	80
d	33¢ Continental Colors, 1776	.65	.30			1.25	80
e	33¢ Francis Hopkinson Flag, 1777	.65	.30			1.25	80
f	33¢ Brandywine Flag, 1777	.65	.30			1.25	80
g	33¢ John Paul Jones Flag, 1779	.65	.30			1.25	80
h	33¢ Pierre L'Enfant Flag, 1783	.65	.30			1.25	80
i	33¢ Indian Peace Flag, 1803	.65	.30			1.25	80
j	33¢ Easton Flag, 1814	.65	.30			1.25	80
k	33¢ Star-Spangled Banner, 1814	.65	.30			1.25	80
l	33¢ Bennington Flag, c. 1820	.65	.30			1.25	80
m	33¢ Great Star Flag, 1837	.65	.30			1.25	80
n	33¢ 29-Star Flag, 1847	.65	.30			1.25	80
o	33¢ Fort Sumter Flag, 1861	.65	.30			1.25	80
p	33¢ Centennial Flag, 1876	.65	.30			1.25	80
q	33¢ 38-Star Flag, 1877	.65	.30			1.25	80
r	33¢ Peace Flag, 1891	.65	.30			1.25	80
s	33¢ 48-Star Flag, 1912	.65	.30			1.25	80
t	33¢ 50-Star Flag, 1960	.65	.30			1.25	80

George Gershwin (1898-1937)

Composer George Gershwin has appeared on two U.S. postage stamps, first in 1973, and again in 1999, when he was paired with his brother and songwriting partner, Ira, on a stamp in the Legends of American Music series. Born in Brooklyn, New York, to Russian immigrants, Gershwin entered the music business while still in his teens, working as a "song plugger" for a music publisher (playing and singing the firm's songs to spur sales). He was still a young man when he composed the scores (with lyrics by his brother) for Broadway shows such as *Funny Face* and *Girl Crazy*. Rhythmic innovation and inventive construction distinguished many songs by the Gershwin brothers, who also created music for films, contributing such gems as "The Man I Love" and "They Can't Take That Away From Me" to American popular music. Gershwin also composed orchestral works, becoming world-famous in 1924 when *Rhapsody in Blue* demonstrated that elements of jazz could be at home in the concert hall. In 1934, Gershwin began work on the score for the opera *Porgy and Bess*, which had its premiere the following year. ■

	Issues of 2000		Un	U	PB	#	FDC	Q(M)
	Fruit Berries Issue, Self-Adhesive, Serpentine Die-Cut 8.5 Horizontally							
3404	33¢ Blueberries	06/16/00	.65	.20			1.25	82.5
3405	33¢ Strawberries	06/16/00	.65	.20			1.25	82.5
3406	33¢ Blackberries	06/16/00	.65	.20			1.25	82.5
3407	33¢ Raspberries	06/16/00	.65	.20			1.25	82.5
a	Strip of 4, #3404-3407		2.60				3.25	
	Legends of Baseball Issue, Self-Adhesive, Serpentine Die-Cut 11.25							
3408	Pane of 20	07/06/00	13.00				10.00	
a	33¢ Jackie Robinson		.65	.20			1.50	11.25
b	33¢ Eddie Collins		.65	.20			1.50	11.25
c	33¢ Christy Mathewson		.65	.20			1.50	11.25
d	33¢ Ty Cobb		.65	.20			1.50	11.25
e	33¢ George Sisler		.65	.20			1.50	11.25
f	33¢ Rogers Hornsby		.65	.20			1.50	11.25
g	33¢ Mickey Cochrane		.65	.20			1.50	11.25
h	33¢ Babe Ruth		.65	.20			1.50	11.25
i	33¢ Walter Johnson		.65	.20			1.50	11.25
j	33¢ Roberto Clemente		.65	.20			1.50	11.25
k	33¢ Lefty Grove		.65	.20			1.50	11.25
l	33¢ Tris Speaker		.65	.20			1.50	11.25
m	33¢ Cy Young		.65	.20			1.50	11.25
n	33¢ Jimmie Foxx		.65	.20			1.50	11.25
o	33¢ Pie Traynor		.65	.20			1.50	11.25
p	33¢ Satchel Paige		.65	.20			1.50	11.25
q	33¢ Honus Wagner		.65	.20			1.50	11.25
r	33¢ Josh Gibson		.65	.20			1.50	11.25
s	33¢ Dizzy Dean		.65	.20			1.50	11.25
t	33¢ Lou Gehrig		.65	.20			1.50	11.25

Queen Isabella (1451-1504)

In 1893 the Post Office issued the nation's first commemorative stamps. The Columbian Exposition Issue, as they are known, and the World's Columbian Exposition held in Chicago from May-October 1893, both honored the 400th anniversary of Christopher Columbus's voyage to America. The 15 original stamps—plus one added later by Postmaster General John Wanamaker—featured engravings of existing art that depicted people and events related to Columbus's expedition. A recurring figure in the stamp art, which included titles such as the "Landing of Columbus," "Isabella Pledging Her Jewels," and "Columbus Announcing His Discovery," was Isabella I of Spain. Thus, the monarch who funded Columbus's voyage to America became the first woman to appear on an official U.S. stamp. It would be almost 10 years before another woman appeared on a stamp: Martha Washington was featured on a 1902 issuance. The 500th anniversary of Columbus's voyage was commemorated in 1992 with 4 newly designed stamps and 6 souvenir sheets based on the original commemorative stamps. ■

33USA
33USA
33USA
33USA

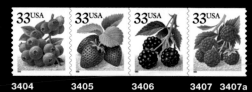

3404 3405 3406 3407 3407a

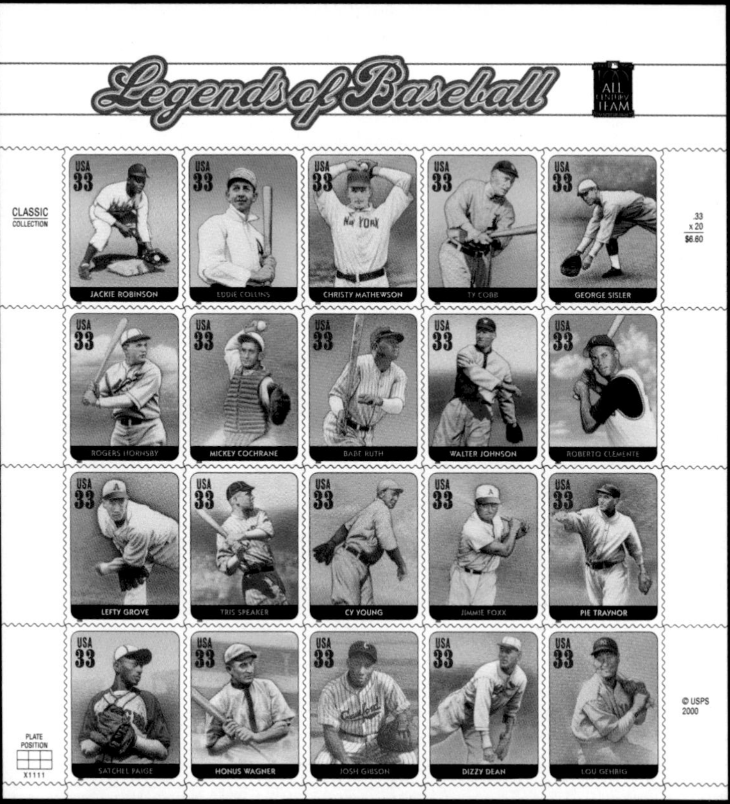

Legends of Baseball
ALL CENTURY TEAM
CLASSIC COLLECTION
.33
x 20
$6.60
USA 33
JACKIE ROBINSON
EDDIE COLLINS
CHRISTY MATHEWSON
TY COBB
GEORGE SISLER
ROGERS HORNSBY
MICKEY COCHRANE
BABE RUTH
WALTER JOHNSON
ROBERTO CLEMENTE
LEFTY GROVE
TRIS SPEAKER
CY YOUNG
JIMMIE FOXX
PIE TRAYNOR
SATCHEL PAIGE
HONUS WAGNER
JOSH GIBSON
DIZZY DEAN
LOU GEHRIG
© USPS
2000
PLATE
POSITION
X1111

3408	a	b	c	d	e
	f	g	h	i	j
	k	l	m	n	o
	p	q	r	s	t

	Issues of 2000-2001		Un	U	PB	#	FDC	Q(M)
	Stampin' The Future™ Issue, Self-Adhesive, Serpentine Die-Cut 11.25							
3414	33¢ By Zachary Canter	07/13/00	.65	.20	5.25	(8)	1.25	25
3415	33¢ By Sarah Lipsey	07/13/00	.65	.20	5.25	(8)	1.25	25
3416	33¢ By Morgan Hill	07/13/00	.65	.20	5.25	(8)	1.25	25
3417	33¢ By Ashley Young	07/13/00	.65	.20	5.25	(8)	1.25	25
a	Horizontal Strip of 4, #3414-3417		2.60		5.25	(8)	3.25	
	Perf. 11							
3420	10¢ Joseph W. Stilwell	08/24/00	.20	.20	.80	(4)	1.50	100
3426	33¢ Claude Pepper	09/07/00	.65	.20	2.60	(4)	1.25	56
	Self-Adhesive, Serpentine Die-Cut 11							
3431	76¢ Hattie Caraway	02/21/01	1.50	.20	6.00	(4)	1.75	108
3438	33¢ California Statehood	09/08/00	.65	.20	2.60	(4)	1.25	53
	Deep Sea Creatures Issue, Perf. 10 x 10.25							
3439	33¢ Fanfin Angelfish	10/02/00	.65	.20			1.25	17
3440	33¢ Sea Cucumber	10/02/00	.65	.20			1.25	17
3441	33¢ Fangtooth	10/02/00	.65	.20			1.25	17
3442	33¢ Amphipod	10/02/00	.65	.20			1.25	17
3443	33¢ Medusa	10/02/00	.65	.20			1.25	17
a	Vertical Strip 5, #3439-3443		3.25	—			3.75	

The S.S. *Savannah*

When the S.S. *Savannah* arrived in Liverpool, England, on June 20, 1819, she became the first steamship to cross the Atlantic Ocean. Twenty-seven days earlier, on May 22, the steam-powered vessel had "put to sea with steam and sails" on the trip to England with stops in Scandinavia and Russia before returning to Savannah in November 1819. The *Savannah* was a revolutionary design for the times—a sailing ship with an auxiliary steam engine that operated paddle wheels for use when the weather was unfavorable for sails. Many who saw the *Savannah* moving through the water with bare masts and heavy black smoke pouring from her stack thought she was on fire. On her voyage to England, at least one British cutter was dispatched to her rescue. Despite the accomplishments of the *Savannah*, she was a financial failure as an oceangoing vessel. Not until 1838 when ships crossed the Atlantic under continuous steam did the public trust themselves or their cargo to transoceanic steamships. ■

3414
3415

3416
3417

3417a

3420
3426

3439

3431

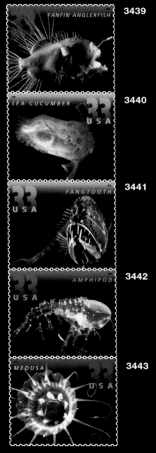

3440

3441

3442

3438

3443

3443a

3444

3445

3446

3447

3448

3451

3454   3455

3456   3457   3457a

Issues of 2000		Un	U	PB	#	FDC	Q(M)
	Literary Arts Issue, Perf. 11						
3444	33¢ Thomas Wolfe	10/03/00	.65	.20	2.60	(4)	1.25	53
	Serpentine Die-Cut 11.25						
3445	33¢ White House	10/18/00	.65	.20	2.60	(4)	1.25	125
	Legends of Hollywood Issue, Perf. 11						
3446	33¢ Edward G. Robinson	10/24/00	.65	.20	2.60	(4)	1.50	52
	Serpentine Die-Cut 11.5 Vertically						
3447	(10¢) The New York Public Library	11/09/00	.20	.20			1.25	100
	Perf. 11.25						
3448	(34¢) Flag Over Farm	12/15/00	.65	.20	2.60	(4)	1.25	25
	Self-Adhesive, Serpentine Die-Cut 11.25						
3449	(34¢) Flag Over Farm	12/15/00	.65	.20	2.60	(4)	1.25	200
	Booklet Stamps, Self-Adhesive, Serpentine Die-Cut 8 on 2, 3 or 4 sides						
3450	(34¢) Flag Over Farm	12/15/00	.65	.20			1.25	
a	Booklet Pane of 18		12.00					300
	Booklet Stamps, Self-Adhesive, Serpentine Die-Cut 11 on 2, 3 or 4 sides						
3451	34¢ Statue of Liberty	12/15/00	.65	.20	2.60	(4)	1.25	1.5
	Coil Stamps, Perf. 9.75 Vertically						
3452	34¢ Statue of Liberty	12/15/00	.65	.20	5.00	(5)	1.25	200
	Serpentine Die-Cut 10 Vertically						
3453	34¢ Statue of Liberty	12/15/00	.65	.20	5.00	(5)	1.25	
	Booklet Stamps, Self-Adhesive, Serpentine Die-Cut 10.25 x 10.75 on 2 or 3 sides						
3454	(34¢) Purple Flower	12/15/00	.65	.20			1.25	375
3455	(34¢) Tan Flower	12/15/00	.65	.20			1.25	375
3456	(34¢) Green Flower	12/15/00	.65	.20			1.25	375
3457	(34¢) Red Flower	12/15/00	.65	.20			1.25	375
a	Block of 4		2.60				3.25	
b	Booklet pane of 4		2.60					
c	Booklet pane of 6		3.90					
d	Booklet pane of 6		3.90					
e	Booklet pane of 20		13.00					
	Booklet Stamps, Self-Adhesive, Serpentine Die-Cut 11.5 x 11.75 on 2 or 3 sides						
3458	34¢ Purple Flower	12/15/00	.65	.20			1.25	125
3459	34¢ Tan Flower	12/15/00	.65	.20			1.25	125
3460	34¢ Green Flower	12/15/00	.65	.20			1.25	125
3461	34¢ Red Flower	12/15/00	.65	.20			1.25	125
a	Block of 4		2.60				3.25	
b	Booklet pane of 20, 2 each #3461a		25.00					
c	Booklet pane of 20, 3 each #3461a		30.00					
	Coil Stamps, Serpentine Die-Cut 8.5 Vertically						
3462	34¢ Green Flower	12/15/00	.65	.20			1.25	125
3463	34¢ Red Flower	12/15/00	.65	.20			1.25	125
3464	34¢ Tan Flower	12/15/00	.65	.20			1.25	125
3465	34¢ Purple Flower	12/15/00	.65	.20			1.25	125
a	Strip of 4		2.60		4.50	(5)	3.25	

Issues of 2001		Un	U	PB	#	FDC	Q(M)
Coil Stamp, Self-Adhesive, Serpentine Die-Cut 9.75							
3466	34¢ Statue of Liberty 01/07/01	.65	.20	5.00	(5)	1.25	240
Tagged, Self-Adhesive, Serpentine Die-Cut 11							
3468	21¢ Buffalo 02/22/01	.40	.20	1.60	(4)	1.25	25
Tagged, Serpentine Die-Cut, Perf. 11.25							
3469	34¢ Flag Over Farm 02/07/01	.65	.20	2.60	(4)	1.25	200
Self-Adhesive, Serpentine Die-Cut 11.25							
3470	34¢ Flag Over Farm 03/06/01	.65	.20	2.60	(4)	1.25	204
Self-Adhesive, Serpentine Die-Cut 10.75							
3471	55¢ Art Deco Eagle 02/22/01	1.10	.20	4.40	(4)	1.50	100
Self-Adhesive, Serpentine Die-Cut 11.25 x 11.5							
3472	$3.50 U. S. Capitol 01/29/01	7.00	3.50	28.00	(4)	6.25	125
Self-Adhesive, Serpentine Die-Cut 11.25 x 11.5							
3473	$12.25 Washington Monument 01/29/01	22.50	10.00	90.00	(4)	15.00	35
Coil Stamp, Self-Adhesive, Serpentine Die-Cut 8.5 Vertically							
3475	21¢ Buffalo 02/22/01	.40	.20	3.50	(5)	1.25	680
Self-Adhesive, Perf. 9.75 Vertically							
3476	34¢ Statue of Liberty 02/07/01	.65	.20	5.00	(5)	1.25	379.8
Self-Adhesive, Serpentine Die-Cut 9.75 Vertically							
3477	34¢ Statue of Liberty 02/07/01	.65	.20	5.00	(5)	1.25	281

Jacqueline Cochran (1910-1980)

In 1953, Jacqueline Cochran became the first woman pilot to break the sound barrier. This pioneering aviator was also the first woman to participate in the prestigious Bendix air race across the U.S. (winning it in 1938), to pilot a bomber—and later a jet plane—across the Atlantic, and to serve as president of the Fédération Aeronautique Internationale. As founder and director of the Women Airforce Service Pilots during World War II, she trained other women aviators. Cochran was also a businesswoman—she had founded a successful cosmetics company before becoming a pilot—and a writer, publishing her autobiography, *The Stars At Noon,* in 1954. In December 1971 she became the first living woman inducted into the Aviation Hall of Fame in Dayton, Ohio. At the time of her death in 1980, Cochran held more records for speed, altitude, and distance than any other male or female pilot in aviation history. ■

3466

3468

3470

3471

3472

3473

Visit us online at The Postal Store at www.usps.com

or call 1-800-STAMP-24

2001

3478 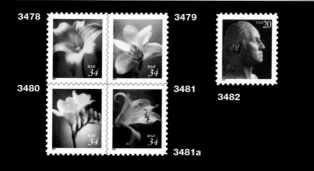 3479

3480 3481

3481a

3482

3492a

3491   3492

3497

3499

3500

3501

	Issues of 2001		Un	U	PB	#	FDC	Q(M)
	Coil Stamps, Self-Adhesive, Serpentine Die-Cut 8.5 Vertically							
3478	34¢ Green Flower	02/07/01	.65	.20			1.25	200
3479	34¢ Red Flower	02/07/01	.65	.20			1.25	200
3480	34¢ Tan Flower	02/07/01	.65	.20			1.25	200
3481	34¢ Purple Flower	02/07/01	.65	.20			1.25	200
a	Strip of 4, #3478-3481		2.60		4.50	(5)	3.25	
	Booklet Stamps, Self-Adhesive, Serpentine Die-Cut 11.25 on 3 sides							
3482	20¢ George Washington	02/22/01	.40	.20			1.25	20.5
a	Booklet pane of 10		4.00					
b	Booklet pane of 4		1.60					
c	Booklet pane of 6		2.40					
	Self-Adhesive, Serpentine Die-Cut 10.5 x 11.25 on 3 sides							
3483	20¢ George Washington	02/22/01	.40	.20			1.25	
a	Booklet pane of 4		5.00					
b	Booklet pane of 6		8.00					
c	Booklet pane of 10		10.00					
d	Booklet pane of 4		5.00					
e	Booklet pane of 6		8.00					
f	Booklet pane of 10		10.00					
	Self-Adhesive, Serpentine Die-Cut 11 on 2, 3 or 4 sides							
3485	34¢ Statue of Liberty	02/07/01	.65	.20			1.25	
a	Booklet pane of 10		6.50					
b	Booklet pane of 20		13.00					
c	Booklet pane of 4		2.60					
d	Booklet pane of 6		3.90					
	Self-Adhesive, Serpentine Die-Cut 10.25 x 10.75 on 2 or 3 sides							
3487	34¢ Purple Flower	02/07/01	.65	.20			1.25	
3488	34¢ Tan Flower	02/07/01	.65	.20			1.25	
3489	34¢ Green Flower	02/07/01	.65	.20			1.25	
3490	34¢ Red Flower	02/07/01	.65	.20			1.25	
	Block of 4, #3487-3490		2.60				3.25	
	Self-Adhesive, Serpentine Die-Cut 11.25 on 2, 3 or 4 sides							
3491	34¢ Apple	03/06/01	.65	.20			1.25	3
3492	34¢ Orange	03/06/01	.65	.20			1.25	3
a	Pair, #3491-3492		1.30				2.25	
b	Booklet pane of 20, #3491-3492		13.00					
	Booklet Stamps, Self-Adhesive, Serpentine Die-Cut 11.5 x 10.75 on 2 or 3 sides							
3493	34¢ Apple	05/01	.65	.20				101
3494	34¢ Orange	05/01	.65	.20				101
a	Pair, #3493-3494		1.30		2.60	(4)		
b	Booklet pane of 2, #3493-3494		2.60					
	Self-Adhesive, Serpentine Die-Cut 11.75, on 2, 3 or 4 sides							
3496	34¢ Rose and Love Letter	01/19/01	.65	.20			1.25	
a	Booklet pane of 20		13.00					
	Self-Adhesive, Serpentine Die-Cut 11.25							
3497	34¢ Rose and Love Letter	02/14/01	.65	.20			1.25	1.50
a	Booklet pane of 20		13.00					
	Self-Adhesive, Serpentine Die-Cut 11.5 x 10.75 on 2 or 3 sides							
3498	34¢ Rose and Love Letter	02/14/01	.65	.20			1.25	81
a	Booklet pane of 4		2.60					
b	Booklet pane of 6		3.90					
3499	55¢ Rose and Love Letter	02/14/01	1.10	.20	4.50	(4)	1.50	
	Lunar New Year Issue, Self-Adhesive, Serpentine Die-Cut, Perf. 11.25							
3500	34¢ Year of the Snake	01/20/01	.65	.20	2.60	(4)	1.50	55
	Black Heritage Issue, Self-Adhesive, Serpentine Die-Cut 11.5 x 11.25							
3501	34¢ Roy Wilkins	01/24/01	.65	.20	2.60	(4)	1.25	200

	Issues of 2001		Un	U	PB	#	FDC	Q(M)
	American Illustrators Issue, Self-Adhesive, Serpentine Die-Cut 11.25							
3502	Pane of 20	02/01/01	13.00				9.50	
a	34¢ James Montgomery Flagg		.65	.30			1.25	144.8
b	34¢ Maxfield Parrish		.65	.30			1.25	144.8
c	34¢ J. C. Leyendecker		.65	.30			1.25	144.8
d	34¢ Robert Fawcett		.65	.30			1.25	144.8
e	34¢ Coles Phillips		.65	.30			1.25	144.8
f	34¢ Al Parker		.65	.30			1.25	144.8
g	34¢ A. B. Frost		.65	.30			1.25	144.8
h	34¢ Howard Pyle		.65	.30			1.25	144.8
i	34¢ Rose O'Neill		.65	.30			1.25	144.8
j	34¢ Dean Cornwell		.65	.30			1.25	144.8
k	34¢ Edwin Austin Abbey		.65	.30			1.25	144.8
l	34¢ Jessie Willcox Smith		.65	.30			1.25	144.8
m	34¢ Neysa McMein		.65	.30			1.25	144.8
n	34¢ Jon Whitcomb		.65	.30			1.25	144.8
o	34¢ Harvey Dunn		.65	.30			1.25	144.8
p	34¢ Frederic Remington		.65	.30			1.25	144.8
q	34¢ Rockwell Kent		.65	.30			1.25	144.8
r	34¢ N. C. Wyeth		.65	.30			1.25	144.8
s	34¢ Norman Rockwell		.65	.30			1.25	144.8
t	34¢ John Held, Jr.		.65	.30			1.25	144.8
	Self-Adhesive, Serpentine Die-Cut 11.25							
3503	34¢ Diabetes Awareness	03/16/01	.65	.20	2.60	(4)	1.25	100
	Tagged, Perf. 11							
3504	34¢ The Nobel Prize	03/22/01	.65	.20	2.60	(4)	1.50	35

Lillian M. Gilbreth (1878-1972)

Lillian M. Gilbreth, a noted pioneer in the fields of industrial engineering and management, worked with her husband and business partner, Frank, to develop theories and practices to increase both labor efficiency and worker satisfaction in industry and at home. One of the first "superwomen," she combined a successful career with domestic life that included being the mother of 12 children. Two of her children became writers and collaborated on *Cheaper By the Dozen* and *Belles on Their Toes,* in which they described life in their busy home—where many of the management techniques developed by their parents were tried out on the family. In 1930, Gilbreth headed the President's Emergency Committee for Unemployment Relief, helping industry and the work-force overcome the effects of the Depression. She was the first woman elected to the National Academy of Engineering and the American Society of Mechanical Engineers. By the time of her death at the age of 92, she had been the recipient of more than a dozen honorary degrees. ■

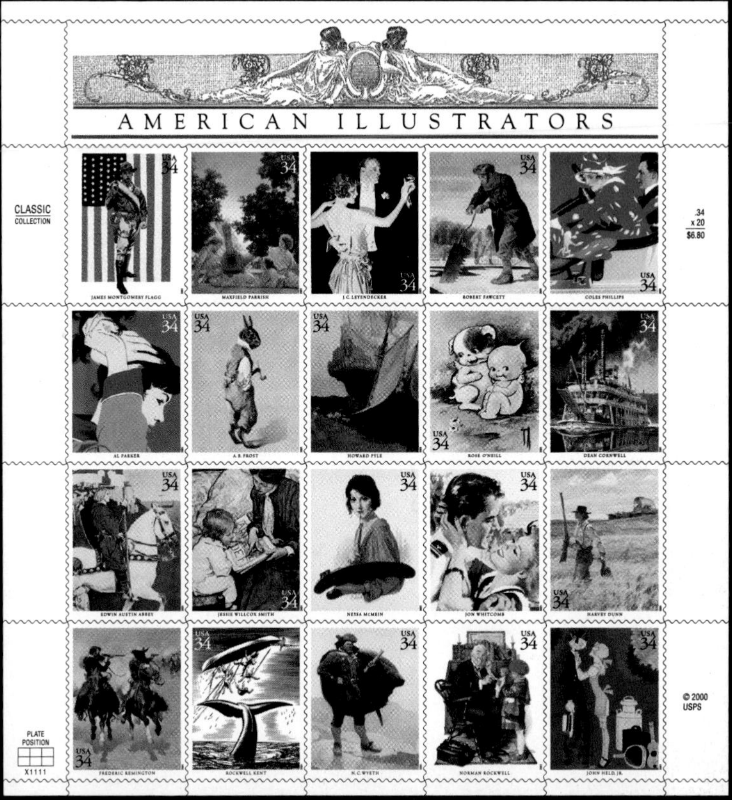

AMERICAN ILLUSTRATORS
CLASSIC COLLECTION
.34 x 20 $6.80
© 2000 USPS
PLATE POSITION
X1111
USA 34
JAMES MONTGOMERY FLAGG
MAXFIELD PARRISH
J.C. LEYENDECKER
ROBERT FAWCETT
COLES PHILLIPS
AL PARKER
A.B. FROST
HOWARD PYLE
ROSE O'NEILL
DEAN CORNWELL
EDWIN AUSTIN ABBEY
JESSIE WILLCOX SMITH
NEYSA McMEIN
JON WHITCOMB
HARVEY DUNN
FREDERIC REMINGTON
ROCKWELL KENT
N.C. WYETH
NORMAN ROCKWELL
JOHN HELD, JR.

3502

a	b	c	d	e
f	g	h	i	j
k	l	m	n	o
p	q	r	s	t

KNOW
MORE
ABOUT
DIABETES
31 USA

3503

The Nobel Prize
1901-2001
USA 34
ALFRED NOBEL

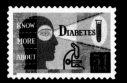

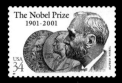

3504

The
Pan-American
Inverts

PAN-AMERICAN EXPOSITION 1901. BUFFALO N.Y. U.S.A.

3505   a   b   c   d

GREAT PLAINS PRAIRIE

THIRD IN A SERIES

N A T U R E   O F   A M E R I C A

3506   a   b   c   d   e   f

         g   h   i   j

	Issues of 2001		Un	U	PB	#	FDC	Q(M)
	The Pan-American Inverts Issue, Tagged, Perf. 12							
3505	34¢ Pane of 7	03/29/01	6.75	—			6.00	11.18
a	1¢ green		.20	.20			1.25	
b	2¢ carmine		.20	.20			1.25	
c	4¢ deep red brown		.20	.20			1.25	
d	80¢ red & blue		1.60	.35			1.75	
	Great Plains Prairie Issue, Self-Adhesive, Serpentine Die-Cut 10							
3506	Pane of 10	04/19/01	7.00				7.00	89.6
a	34¢ Pronghorns, Canada geese		.65	.20				
b	34¢ Burrowing owls, American buffalo		.65	.20				
c	34¢ American buffalo, Black-tailed prairie dogs, wild alfalfa		.65	.20				
d	34¢ Black-tailed prairie dog, American buffalo		.65	.20				
e	34¢ Painted lady butterfly, American buffalo, prairie coneflowers, prairie wild roses		.65	.20				
f	34¢ Western meadowlark, camel cricket, prairie coneflowers, prairie wild roses		.65	.20				
g	34¢ Badger, harvester ants		.65	.20				
h	34¢ Eastern short-horned lizard, plains pocket gopher		.65	.20				
i	34¢ Plains spadefoot, dung beetle, prairie wild roses		.65	.20				
j	34¢ Two-stripped grasshopper, Ord's kangaroo rat		.65	.20				

An American Postal Portrait

The rich history of the U.S. Postal Service from 1860 until the present day comes to life in more than 200 dazzling photographs—from behind-the-scenes stories of individual postal workers, to a visual record of the growth of technology. The book also includes color reproductions of every U.S. stamp that commemorates the Post Office and its employees. Sixty-one stamp images and four stationery selections make this book a fascinating tribute to America's leading communications institution.

To order call **1-800-STAMP-24** or visit us online at **www.usps.com**

Item #989100–2001 Portrait Book: An American Postal Portrait $31.50

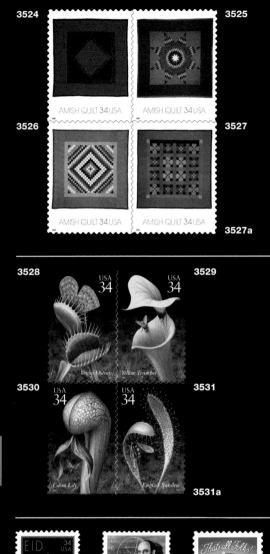

3524

3525

3526

3527

3527a

3528

3529

3530

3531

3531a

3532

3533

3534a

	Issues of 2001		Un	U	PB	#	FDC	Q(M)
	American Treasures Issue: Amish Quilts, Self-Adhesive, Serpentine Die-Cut 11.25 x 11.5							
3524	34¢ Diamond in the Square	08/09/01	.65	.20			1.25	96
3525	34¢ Lone Star	08/09/01	.65	.20			1.25	96
3526	34¢ Sunshine and Shadow	08/09/01	.65	.20			1.25	96
3527	34¢ Double Ninepatch	08/09/01	.65	.20			1.25	96
a	Block or strip of 4 #3524-3527		2.60		2.60	(4)	3.25	
	Carnivorous Plants Issue, Self-Adhesive, Serpentine Die-Cut 11.5							
3528	34¢ Venus Flytrap	08/23/01	.65	.20				98.6
3529	34¢ Yellow Trumpet	08/23/01	.65	.20				98.6
3530	34¢ Cobra Lily	08/23/01	.65	.20				98.6
3531	34¢ English Sundew	08/23/01	.65	.20				98.6
a	Block or strip of 4 #3528-3531		2.60		2.60	(4)		
	Holiday Celebration Issue, Self-Adhesive, Serpentine Die-Cut 11.25							
3532	34¢ EID	09/01/01	.65	.20	2.60	(4)		75
	Self-Adhesive, Serpentine Die-Cut 11.25							
3533	34¢ Enrico Fermi	09/29/01	.65	.20	2.60		1.25	30
	Looney Tunes Issue, Self-Adhesive, Serpentine Die-Cut 11.1							
3534	Pane of 10	10/01/01	6.50					
a	34¢ Porky Pig "That's all Folks!"		.65	.20			1.25	275

A. Philip Randolph (1889-1979)

Asa Philip Randolph spent his long and distinguished career as a labor leader working for racial and economic justice. As a young man, he moved from his native Florida to New York City, where he settled in Harlem. In 1917, with Chandler Owen, he founded and began co-editing *The Messenger*, a progressive magazine. In 1925, Randolph spearheaded a drive to organize thousands of workers in the Brotherhood of Sleeping Car Porters (BSCP). After years of struggle, BSCP succeeded in winning bargaining recognition in 1937. Randolph later persuaded President Roosevelt to sign an executive order banning the exclusion of blacks from employment in defense plants. He was in the forefront of the effort to secure another executive order—signed by President Truman in 1948—integrating the armed forces. In the 1950s, Randolph met with President Eisenhower to push for faster school integration. Randolph was a major force behind the 1963 March on Washington for Jobs and Freedom; he retired as vice president of the AFL-CIO, which had become one of the most conspicuously integrated public institutions in American life. In 1964, President Johnson awarded Randolph the Presidential Medal of Freedom, the nation's highest civilian honor. ■

3552 3553
3554 3555

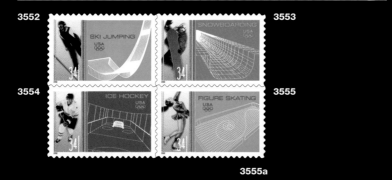

3555a

3556

3557

3558

3559

3560

Issues of 2002		Un	U	PB	#	FDC	Q(M)
Winter Olympics, Tagged, Self-Adhesive, Serpentine Die-Cut 11.5 x 10.75							
3552	34¢ Ski Jumping	01/08/02	.65	.20	2.60	(4)	1.25	
3553	34¢ Snowboarding	01/08/02	.65	.20	2.60	(4)	1.25	
3554	34¢ Ice Hockey	01/08/02	.65	.20	2.60	(4)	1.25	
3555	34¢ Figure Skating	01/08/02	.65	.20	2.60	(4)	1.25	
a	Block or strip of 4, #3552-3555	01/08/02	2.60		2.60	(4)	1.25	
Tagged, Self-Adhesive, Serpentine Die-Cut 11 x 10.75							
3556	34¢ Mentoring a Child	01/10/02	.65	.20	2.60	(4)	1.25	
Black Heritage Series, Tagged, Self-Adhesive, Serpentine Die-Cut 10.25 x 10.5							
3557	34¢ Langston Hughes	02/01/02	.65	.20	2.60	(4)	1.25	
Tagged, Self-Adhesive, Serpentine Die-Cut 11							
3558	34¢ Happy Birthday	02/08/02	.65	.20	2.60	(4)	1.25	
Lunar New Year Issue, Tagged, Self-Adhesive, Serpentine Die-Cut 10.5 x 10.25							
3559	34¢ Year of the Horse	02/11/02	.65	.20	2.60	(4)	1.25	
Tagged, Self-Adhesive, Serpentine Die-Cut 10.5 x 11							
3560	34¢ U.S. Military Academy	03/16/02	.65	.20	2.60	(4)	1.25	

Ready to Mail Stamped Cards

Old Glory 23¢

Twenty Stamped Cards

Five Designs

Item #882066–$9.75

Teddy Bears 23¢

Twenty Stamped Cards

Four Designs

Item #453566–$9.25

Snowman 23¢

Twenty Stamped Cards

Four Designs

Item #562566–$9.75

To order call **1-800-STAMP-24** or visit us online at **www.usps.com**

	Issues of 2002		Un	U	PB	#	FDC	Q(M)
	Greetings From America, Tagged, Self-Adhesive, Serpentine Die-Cut 10.75							
3561	34¢ Alabama	04/04/02	.65	.20			1.25	
3562	34¢ Alaska	04/04/02	.65	.20			1.25	
3563	34¢ Arizona	04/04/02	.65	.20			1.25	
3564	34¢ Arkansas	04/04/02	.65	.20			1.25	
3565	34¢ California	04/04/02	.65	.20			1.25	
3566	34¢ Colorado	04/04/02	.65	.20			1.25	
3567	34¢ Connecticut	04/04/02	.65	.20			1.25	
3568	34¢ Delaware	04/04/02	.65	.20			1.25	
3569	34¢ Florida	04/04/02	.65	.20			1.25	
3570	34¢ Georgia	04/04/02	.65	.20			1.25	
3571	34¢ Hawaii	04/04/02	.65	.20			1.25	
3572	34¢ Idaho	04/04/02	.65	.20			1.25	
3573	34¢ Illinois	04/04/02	.65	.20			1.25	
3574	34¢ Indiana	04/04/02	.65	.20			1.25	
3575	34¢ Iowa	04/04/02	.65	.20			1.25	
3576	34¢ Kansas	04/04/02	.65	.20			1.25	
3577	34¢ Kentucky	04/04/02	.65	.20			1.25	
3578	34¢ Louisiana	04/04/02	.65	.20			1.25	
3579	34¢ Maine	04/04/02	.65	.20			1.25	
3580	34¢ Maryland	04/04/02	.65	.20			1.25	
3581	34¢ Massachusetts	04/04/02	.65	.20			1.25	
3582	34¢ Michigan	04/04/02	.65	.20			1.25	
3583	34¢ Minnesota	04/04/02	.65	.20			1.25	
3584	34¢ Mississippi	04/04/02	.65	.20			1.25	
3585	34¢ Missouri	04/04/02	.65	.20			1.25	
3586	34¢ Montana	04/04/02	.65	.20			1.25	
3587	34¢ Nebraska	04/04/02	.65	.20			1.25	
3588	34¢ Nevada	04/04/02	.65	.20			1.25	
3589	34¢ New Hampshire	04/04/02	.65	.20			1.25	
3590	34¢ New Jersey	04/04/02	.65	.20			1.25	
3591	34¢ New Mexico	04/04/02	.65	.20			1.25	
3592	34¢ New York	04/04/02	.65	.20			1.25	
3593	34¢ North Carolina	04/04/02	.65	.20			1.25	
3594	34¢ North Dakota	04/04/02	.65	.20			1.25	
3595	34¢ Ohio	04/04/02	.65	.20			1.25	
3596	34¢ Oklahoma	04/04/02	.65	.20			1.25	
3597	34¢ Oregon	04/04/02	.65	.20			1.25	
3598	34¢ Vermont	04/04/02	.65	.20			1.25	
3599	34¢ Rhode Island	04/04/02	.65	.20			1.25	
3600	34¢ South Carolina	04/04/02	.65	.20			1.25	
3601	34¢ South Dakota	04/04/02	.65	.20			1.25	
3602	34¢ Tennessee	04/04/02	.65	.20			1.25	
3603	34¢ Texas	04/04/02	.65	.20			1.25	
3604	34¢ Utah	04/04/02	.65	.20			1.25	
3605	34¢ Vermont	04/04/02	.65	.20			1.25	
3606	34¢ Virginia	04/04/02	.65	.20			1.25	
3607	34¢ Washington	04/04/02	.65	.20			1.25	
3608	34¢ West Virginia	04/04/02	.65	.20			1.25	
3609	34¢ Wisconsin	04/04/02	.65	.20			1.25	
3610	34¢ Wyoming	04/04/02	.65	.20			1.25	
a	Pane of 50, #3561-3610		32.50					

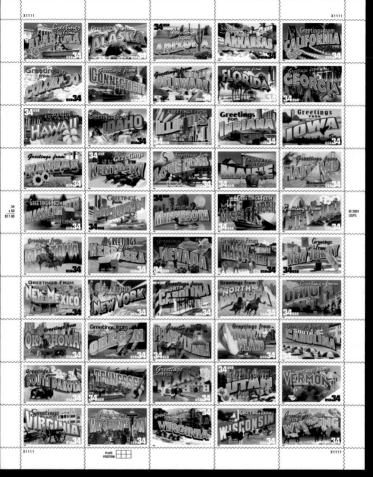

3610a	3561	3562	3563	3564	3565
	3566	3567	3568	3569	3570
	3571	3572	3573	3574	3575
	3576	3577	3578	3579	3580

LONGLEAF PINE FOREST

FOURTH IN A SERIES

USA 34

USA 34

USA 34

USA 34

USA 34

USA 34

USA 34

USA 34

USA 34

USA 34

N A T U R E O F A M E R I C A

3611   a   b   c   d

e   f   g   h

i   j

3612

3613

3616

3620

	Issues of 2002		Un	U	PB	#	FDC	Q(M)
	Longleaf Pine Forest, Tagged, Self-Adhesive, Serpentine Die-Cut 10.5 x 10.75, 10.75 x 10.5							
3611	34¢ Wildlife and Flowers, Pane of 10	04/26/02	7.00				7.00	
a	Bachman's sparrow		.65	.20			1.25	
b	Northern bobwhite,							
	yellow pitcher plants		.65	.20			1.25	
c	Fox squirrel,							
	red-bellied woodpecker		.65	.20			1.25	
d	Brown-headed nuthatch		.65	.20			1.25	
e	Broadhead skink,							
	yellow pitcher plants, pipeworts		.65	.20			1.25	
f	Eastern towhee, yellow pitcher							
	plants, Savannah meadow beauties,							
	toothache grass		.65	.20			1.25	
g	Gray fox, gopher tortoise, horiz.		.65	.20			1.25	
h	Blind click beetle, sweetbay,							
	pine woods treefrog		.65	.20			1.25	
i	Rosebud orchid, pipeworts,							
	southern toad, yellow pitcher plants		.65	.20			1.25	
j	Grass-pink orchid, yellow-sided							
	skimmer, pipeworts, yellow pitcher							
	plants, horiz.		.65	.20			1.25	
	American Design Series, Coil, Perf. 10 Vertically							
3612	5¢ American Toleware	05/31/02	.20	.20	1.60	(5)	1.25	
	Self-Adhesive, Serpentine Die-Cut 11							
3613	3¢ Star (year at lower left)	06/07/02	.20	.20	.25	(4)	1.25	
3614	3¢ Star (year at lower right)	06/07/02	.20	.20	.25	(4)	1.25	
	Tagged, Perf. 11.25							
3616	23¢ George Washington (green)	06/07/02	.45	.20	1.80	(4)	1.00	
	Self-Adhesive, Coil, Serpentine Die-Cut 8.5 Vertically							
3617	23¢ George Washington (gray green)	06/07/02	.45	.20	1.80	(4)	1.00	
	Booklet Stamps, Self-Adhesive Serpentine Die-Cut 11.25 on 3 sides							
3618	23¢ George Washington (green)	06/07/02	.45	.20		1.00		
a	Booklet pane of 4		1.80					
b	Booklet pane of 6		2.70					
	Self-Adhesive, Serpentine Die-Cut 10. 5 x 11.25 on 3 sides							
3619	23¢ George Washington (green)	06/07/02	.45	.20				
a	Booklet pane of 4		5.00					
b	Booklet pane of 6		8.00					
	Tagged, Perf. 11.25 x 11							
3620	(37¢) U.S. Flag (First Class)	06/07/02	.70	.20	2.80	(4)	1.25	
	Self-Adhesive, Serpentine Die-Cut 11.25 x 11							
3621	(37¢) U.S. Flag (First Class)	06/07/02	.70	.20	2.80	(4)	1.25	
	Self-Adhesive, Coil Stamp, Serpentine Die-Cut 10 Vertically							
3622	(37¢) U.S. Flag (First Class)	06/07/02	.70	.20	5.25	(5)	1.25	
	Booklet, Self-Adhesive, Serpentine Die-Cut 11.25 on 2, 3 or 4 sides							
3623	(37¢) U.S. Flag (First Class)	06/07/02	.70	.20			1.25	
a	Booklet pane of 20		14.00					
	Booklet, Self-Adhesive, Serpentine Die-Cut 10.5 x 10.75 on 2 or 3 sides							
3624	(37¢) U.S. Flag (First Class)	06/07/02	.70	.20			1.25	
a	Booklet pane of 4		2.80					
b	Booklet pane of 6		4.20					
	Booklet, Self-Adhesive, Serpentine Die-Cut 8 on 2, 3 or 4 sides							
3625	(37¢) U.S. Flag (First Class)	06/07/02	.70	.20			1.25	
a	Booklet pane of 18		13.00					

2002

	Issues of 2002		Un	U	PB	#	FDC	Q(M)
	Antique Toys, Booklet, Self-Adhesive, Serpentine Die-Cut 11 on 2, 3 or 4 sides							
3626	(37¢) Toy Mail Wagon	06/07/02	.70	.20			1.25	
3627	(37¢) Toy Locomotive	06/07/02	.70	.20			1.25	
3628	(37¢) Toy Taxicab	06/07/02	.70	.20			1.25	
3629	(37¢) Toy Fire Pumper	06/07/02	.70	.20			1.25	
a	Block of 4, 3626-3629		2.80				3.25	
	Self-Adhesive, Serpentine Die-Cut 11.25 x 11							
3630	37¢ U.S. Flag	06/07/02	.70	.20	2.80	(4)	1.25	
	Coil, Perf 10 Vertically							
3631	37¢ U.S. Flag	06/07/02	.70	.20	5.25	(5)	1.25	
	Self Adhesive, Serpentine Die-Cut 10 Vertically							
3632	37¢ U.S. Flag	06/07/02	.70	.20	5.25	(5)	1.25	
	Self-Adhesive, Serpentine Die-Cut 8.25 Vertically							
3633	37¢ U.S. Flag	06/07/02	.70	.20	5.25	(5)	1.25	
	Booklet, Self-Adhesive, Serpentine Die-Cut 11.25 on 2, 3 or 4 sides							
3635	37¢ U.S. Flag	06/07/02	.70	.20			1.25	
a	Booklet pane of 20		14.00					
	Serpentine Die-Cut 10.5 x 10.25 on 2 or 3 sides							
3636	37¢ U.S. Flag	06/07/02	.70	.20			1.25	
c	Booklet pane of 20		14.00					
3646	60¢ Coverlet Eagle	07/12/02						
3647	$3.85 Jefferson Memorial	07/30/02	.					
3648	$13.65 Capitol Dome	07/30/02						
	Masters of American Photography, Tagged, Self-Adhesive Serpentine Die-Cut 10.5 x 10.75							
3649	37¢ Pane of 20	06/13/02	14.00				10.00	
a	Southworth & Hawes		.70	.20			1.25	
b	Timothy H. O'Sullivan		.70	.20			1.25	
c	Carleton E. Watkins		.70	.20			1.25	
d	Gertrude Kasebir		.70	.20			1.25	
e	Lewis W. Hine		.70	.20			1.25	
f	Alvin Langdon Coburn		.70	.20			1.25	
g	Edward Steichen		.70	.20			1.25	
h	Alfred Stieglitz		.70	.20			1.25	
i	Man Ray		.70	.20			1.25	
j	Edward Weston		.70	.20			1.25	
k	James VanDerZee		.70	.20			1.25	
l	Dorothea Lange		.70	.20			1.25	
m	Walker Evans		.70	.20			1.25	
n	W. Eugene Smith		.70	.20			1.25	
o	Paul Strand		.70	.20			1.25	
p	Ansel Adams		.70	.20			1.25	
q	Imogen Cunningham		.70	.20			1.25	
r	Andre' Kertesz		.70	.20			1.25	
s	Garry Winogrand		.70	.20			1.25	
t	Minor White		.70	.20			1.25	
	Sheet of 120		85.00					

3626 3627 3628 3629 3629a 3630 3646

3647 3648

3649 a b c d e f g h i j

2002

	Issues of 2002		Un	U	PB	#	FDC	Q(M)
	Women in Journalism Issue							
3665	37¢ Nellie Bly	09/14/02	.70	.20			1.25	
3666	37¢ Ida M. Tarbell	09/14/02	.70	.20			1.25	
3667	37¢ Ethel L. Payne	09/14/02	.70	.20			1.25	
3668	37¢ Marguerite Higgins	09/14/02	.70	.20			1.25	
a	Block or horizontal strip of 4							
	#3665-3668		2.80					
3669	37¢ Irving Berlin	09/15/02	.70	.20			1.25	
3670	37¢ Neuter & Spay (Kitten)	09/20/02	.70	.20			1.25	
3671	37¢ Neuter & Spay (Puppy)	09/20/02	.70	.20			1.25	
	Self-Adhesive, Serpentine Die-Cut 11.25							
3672	37¢ Hanukkah	10/10/02	.70	.20			1.25	
3673	37¢ Kwanzaa	10/10/02	.70	.20			1.25	
	Holiday Celebration, Self-Adhesive, Serpentine Die-Cut 11.25							
3674	37¢ Eid							
	Holiday Traditional, Booklet, Self-Adhesive, Serpentine Die-Cut 11.25 on 2 or 3 sides							
3675	37¢ Madonna and Child							
	by Gossaert	10/10/02	.70	.20			1.25	
a	Booklet of 20		14.00					
	Holiday Contemporary Issue, Self-Adhesive, Serpentine Die-Cut 11.25							
3676	37¢ Snowman w/red & green							
	plaid scarf	10/28/02	.70	.20				
3677	37¢ Snowman w/blue plaid scarf	10/28/02	.70	.20				
3678	37¢ Snowman w/pipe	10/28/02	.70	.20				
3679	37¢ Snowman w/top hat	10/28/02	.70	.20				
a	Block or vertical strip of 4, #3676-3679							
	Coil Stamp							
3680	37¢ Snowman w/blue plaid scarf	10/28/02	.70	.20				
3681	37¢ Snowman w/pipe	10/28/02	.70	.20				
3682	37¢ Snowman w/top hat	10/28/02	.70	.20				
3683	37¢ Snowman w/red & green							
	plaid scarf	10/28/02	.70	.20				
	Strip of 4, 3680-3683							
	Booklet Stamp							
3684	37¢ Snowman w/red & green							
	plaid scarf	10/28/02	.70	.20				
3685	37¢ Snowman w/blue plaid scarf	10/28/02	.70	.20				
3686	37¢ Snowman w/pipe	10/28/02	.70	.20				
3687	37¢ Snowman w/top hat	10/28/02	.70	.20				
a	Block of 4, #3684-3687			2.80				
	Booklet Stamp							
3688	37¢ Snowman w/red & green							
	plaid scarf	10/28/02	.70	.20				
3689	37¢ Snowman w/blue plaid scarf	10/28/02	.70	.20				
3690	37¢ Snowman w/pipe	10/28/02	.70	.20				
3691	37¢ Snowman w/top hat	10/28/02	.70	.20				
a	Block of 4 #3688-3691							
	Legends of Hollywood, Self Adhesive, Serpentine Die-Cut 11							
3692	37¢ Cary Grant	10/15/02	.70	.20				
	Coil Stamp							
3693	5¢ Sea Coast	10/21/02	.20	.20				

3665 Marguerite Higgins
3666 Ida M. Tarbell
3667 Ethel L. Payne
3668 Nellie Bly
3668a

3669 IRVING BERLIN

3670 Spay Neuter USA
3671 Spay
3672 HAPPY BIRTHDAY

3673 KWANZAA
3674 EID GREETINGS
3675 CHRISTMAS — J. Gossaert Art Institute of Chicago

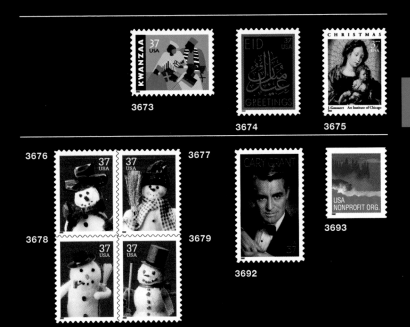

3676
3677
3678
3679
3679a

3692 CARY GRANT

3693 USA NONPROFIT ORG.

The "Hawaiian Missionary" Stamps of 1851-1853

The first official Hawaiian post office was established in December 1850. Postmaster Henry M. Whitney had stamps printed locally in three denominations. Philatelists call these rare stamps "Hawaiian Missionaries" because virtually all were used by Christian missionaries on outbound mail. Only 28 covers with Missionary stamps are known to exist; only the Dawson cover (right) bears the 2¢ stamp. The two 13¢ stamps were unusual as they prepaid postage in two countries–Hawaii and the U.S.

© 2001 USPS

3694

     a   b   c   d

3695

3696

	Issues of 2002		Un	U	PB	#	FDC	Q(M)
3694	37¢ Hawaiian Missionary	10/24/02						
a	37¢ Hawaii Scott (2¢ of 1851)		.70	.20				
b	37¢ Hawaii Scott (5¢ of 1851)		.70	.20				
c	37¢ Hawaii Scott (13¢ of 1851)		.70	.20				
d	37¢ Hawaii Scott (13¢ of 1852)		.70	.20				
	Tagged, Self-Adhesive, Serpentine Die-Cut 11							
3695	37¢ Happy Birthday	10/25/02	.70	.20				
	Greetings From America, Tagged, Self-Adhesive, Serpentine Die-Cut 10.75							
3696	37¢ Alabama	10/25/02	.70	.20				
3697	37¢ Alaska	10/25/02	.70	.20				
3698	37¢ Arizona	10/25/02	.70	.20				
3699	37¢ Arkansas	10/25/02	.70	.20				
3700	37¢ California	10/25/02	.70	.20				
3701	37¢ Colorado	10/25/02	.70	.20				
3702	37¢ Connecticut	10/25/02	.70	.20				
3703	37¢ Delaware	10/25/02	.70	.20				
3704	37¢ Florida	10/25/02	.70	.20				
3705	37¢ Georgia	10/25/02	.70	.20				
3706	37¢ Hawaii	10/25/02	.70	.20				
3707	37¢ Idaho	10/25/02	.70	.20				
3708	37¢ Illinois	10/25/02	.70	.20				
3709	37¢ Indiana	10/25/02	.70	.20				
3710	37¢ Iowa	10/25/02	.70	.20				
3711	37¢ Kansas	10/25/02	.70	.20				
3712	37¢ Kentucky	10/25/02	.70	.20				
3713	37¢ Louisiana	10/25/02	.70	.20				
3714	37¢ Maine	10/25/02	.70	.20				
3715	37¢ Maryland	10/25/02	.70	.20				
3716	37¢ Massachusetts	10/25/02	.70	.20				
3717	37¢ Michigan	10/25/02	.70	.20				
3718	37¢ Minnesota	10/25/02	.70	.20				
3719	37¢ Mississippi	10/25/02	.70	.20				
3720	37¢ Missouri	10/25/02	.70	.20				
3721	37¢ Montana	10/25/02	.70	.20				
3722	37¢ Nebraska	10/25/02	.70	.20				
3723	37¢ Nevada	10/25/02	.70	.20				
3724	37¢ New Hampshire	10/25/02	.70	.20				
3725	37¢ New Jersey	10/25/02	.70	.20				
3726	37¢ New Mexico	10/25/02	.70	.20				
3727	37¢ New York	10/25/02	.70	.20				
3728	37¢ North Carolina	10/25/02	.70	.20				
3729	37¢ North Dakota	10/25/02	.70	.20				
3730	37¢ Ohio	10/25/02	.70	.20				
3731	37¢ Oklahoma	10/25/02	.70	.20				
3732	37¢ Oregon	10/25/02	.70	.20				
3733	37¢ Pennsylvania	10/25/02	.70	.20				
3734	37¢ Rhode Island	10/25/02	.70	.20				
3735	37¢ South Carolina	10/25/02	.70	.20				
3736	37¢ South Dakota	10/25/02	.70	.20				
3737	37¢ Tennessee	10/25/02	.70	.20				
3738	37¢ Texas	10/25/02	.70	.20				
3739	37¢ Utah	10/25/02	.70	.20				
3740	37¢ Vermont	10/25/02	.70	.20				
3741	37¢ Virginia	10/25/02	.70	.20				
3742	37¢ Washington	10/25/02	.70	.20				
3743	37¢ West Virginia	10/25/02	.70	.20				
3744	37¢ Wisconsin	10/25/02	.70	.20				
3745	37¢ Wyoming	10/25/02	.70	.20				
a	Pane of 50, #3696-3745		35.00					

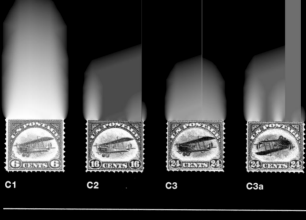

C1   C2   C3   C3a

C4   C5   C6   C7

C10   C11   C12

C13   C14

C15   C18

	Issues of 1918		Un	U	PB	#	FDC	Q(M)
	Perf. 11							
	For prepayment of postage on all mailable matter sent by airmail. All unwatermarked.							
C1	6¢ Curtiss Jenny	12/10/18	65.00	30.00	725.00	(6)	*32,500.00*	3
	Double transfer		90.00	45.00				
C2	16¢ Curtiss Jenny	07/11/18	85.00	35.00	1,050.00	(6)	*32,500.00*	4
C3	24¢ Curtiss Jenny	05/13/18	85.00	35.00	400.00	(4)	*27,500.00*	2
a	Center Inverted		*170,000.00*		*1,200,000.00*	(4)		0.0001
	Issues of 1923							
C4	8¢ Airplane Radiator and							
	Wooden Propeller	08/15/23	22.50	14.00	225.00	(6)	450.00	6
C5	16¢ Air Service Emblem	08/17/23	85.00	30.00	1,600.00	(6)	650.00	5
C6	24¢ De Havilland Biplane	08/21/23	95.00	30.00	2,100.00	(6)	850.00	5
	Issues of 1926-1927							
C7	10¢ Map of U.S. and							
	Two Mail Planes	02/13/26	2.60	.35	35.00	(6)	60.00	42
	Double transfer		5.75	1.10				
C8	15¢ olive brown (C7)	09/18/26	3.00	2.50	35.00	(6)	75.00	16
C9	20¢ yellow green (C7)	01/25/27	8.00	2.00	75.00	(6)	100.00	18
	Issue of 1927-1928							
C10	10¢ Lindbergh's							
	"Spirit of St. Louis"	06/18/27	7.25	2.50	90.00	(6)	25.00	20
a	Booklet pane of 3	05/26/28	80.00	*65.00*			875.00	
	Issue of 1928							
C11	5¢ Beacon on Rocky							
	Mountains	07/25/28	5.00	.75	175.00	(8)	50.00	107
	Recut frame line at left		6.50	1.25				
a	Vertical pair, imperf. between		*5,500.00*					
	Issues of 1930							
C12	5¢ Winged Globe	02/10/30	10.50	.50	140.00	(6)	12.00	98
a	Horizontal pair, imperf. between		*4,500.00*					
	Graf Zeppelin Issue							
C13	65¢ Zeppelin over							
	Atlantic Ocean	04/19/30	250.00	160.00	2,300.00	(6)	1,250.00	0.09
C14	$1.30 Zeppelin							
	Between Continents	04/19/30	475.00	375.00	5,750.00	(6)	1,100.00	0.07
C15	$2.60 Zeppelin							
	Passing Globe	04/19/30	750.00	575.00	8,250.00	(6)	1,250.00	0.06
	Issues of 1931-1932, Perf. 10.5 x 11							
C16	5¢ violet (C12)	08/19/31	5.25	.60	75.00	(4)	175.00	57
C17	8¢ olive bister (C12)	09/26/32	2.25	.40	27.50	(4)	15.00	77
	Issue of 1933, Century of Progress Issue, Perf. 11							
C18	50¢ Zeppelin, Federal Building							
	at Chicago Exposition and							
	Hangar at Friedrichshafen	10/02/33	70.00	65.00	550.00	(6)	200.00	0.3
	Beginning with #C19, unused values are for never-hinged stamps.							
	Issue of 1934, Perf. 10.5 x 11							
C19	6¢ dull orange (C12)	06/30/34	3.50	.25	21.00	(4)	*175.00*	302
	Issues of 1935-1937, Trans-Pacific Issue, Perf. 11							
C20	25¢ "China Clipper"							
	over the Pacific	11/22/35	1.40	1.00	20.00	(6)	40.00	10
C21	20¢ "China Clipper"							
	over the Pacific	02/15/37	11.00	1.75	100.00	(6)	45.00	13
C22	50¢ carmine (C21)	02/15/37	10.00	5.00	100.00	(6)	50.00	9
	Issue of 1938							
C23	6¢ Eagle Holding Shield,							
	Olive Branch and Arrows	05/14/38	.50	.20	7.00	(4)	15.00	350
	6¢ ultramarine and carmine		*150.00*	*300.00*	*1,500.00*	(4)		
a	Vertical pair, imperf. horizontally		*350.00*					
b	Horizontal pair, imperf. vertically		*12,500.00*		*37,500.00*	(4)		

	Issue of 1939		Un	U	PB/LP	#	FDC	Q(M)
	Transatlantic Issue, Perf. 11							
C24	30¢ Winged Globe	05/16/39	10.50	1.50	130.00	(6)	47.50	20
	Issues of 1941-1944, Perf. 11 x 10.5							
C25	6¢ Twin-Motor Transport Plane	06/25/41	.20	.20	.60	(4)	3.75	4,477
a	Booklet pane of 3	03/18/43	5.00	1.50			25.00	
	Singles of #C25a are imperf. at sides or imperf. at sides and bottom.							
b	Horizontal pair, imperf. between		2,250.00					
C26	8¢ olive green (C25)	03/21/44	.20	.20	1.10	(4)	3.75	1,745
C27	10¢ violet (C25)	08/15/41	1.25	.20	5.75	(4)	8.00	67
C28	15¢ brn. carmine (C25)	08/19/41	2.25	.35	10.50	(4)	10.00	78
C29	20¢ bright green (C25)	08/27/41	2.25	.30	10.00	(4)	12.50	42
C30	30¢ blue (C25)	09/25/41	2.25	.35	10.50	(4)	20.00	60
C31	50¢ orange (C25)	10/29/41	11.00	3.25	52.50	(4)	40.00	11
	Issue of 1946							
C32	5¢ DC-4 Skymaster	09/25/46	.20	.20	.45	(4)	2.00	865
	Issues of 1947, Perf. 10.5 x 11							
C33	5¢ DC-4 Skymaster	03/26/47	.20	.20	.55	(4)	2.00	972
	Perf. 11 x 10.5							
C34	10¢ Pan American Union Bldg., Washington, D.C. and Martin 2-0-2	08/30/47	.25	.20	1.10	(4)	2.00	208
a	Dry printing		.40	.20	1.75	(4)		
C35	15¢ Statue of Liberty, N.Y. Skyline and Lockheed Constellation	08/20/47	.35	.20	1.50	(4)	1.75	756
a	Horizontal pair, imperf. between		2,250.00					
b	Dry printing		.55	.20	2.50	(4)		
C36	25¢ San Francisco-Oakland Bay Bridge and Boeing Stratocruiser	07/30/47	.85	.20	3.50	(4)	2.25	133
a	Dry printing		1.00	.20	4.25	(4)		
	Issues of 1948, Coil Stamp, Perf. 10 Horizontally							
C37	5¢ carmine (C33)	01/15/48	1.00	.80	10.00	(2)	1.75	33
	Perf. 11 x 10.5							
C38	5¢ New York City	07/31/48	.20	.20	3.50	(4)	1.75	38
	Issues of 1949, Perf. 10.5 x 11							
C39	6¢ carmine (C33)	01/18/49	.20	.20	.50	(4)	1.50	5,070
a	Booklet pane of 6	11/18/49	10.00	5.00				
b	Dry printing		.50	.20	2.25	(4)		
c	As "a," dry printing		22.50	—				
	Perf. 11 x 10.5							
C40	6¢ Alexandria, Virginia	05/11/49	.20	.20	.50	(4)	1.50	75
	Coil Stamp, Perf. 10 Horizontally							
C41	6¢ carmine (C33)	08/25/49	3.00	.20	14.00	(2)	1.25	260
	Universal Postal Union Issue, Perf. 11 x 10.5							
C42	10¢ Post Office Dept. Bldg.	11/18/49	.20	.20	1.40	(4)	1.75	21
C43	15¢ Globe and Doves Carrying Messages	10/07/49	.30	.25	1.25	(4)	2.75	37
C44	25¢ Boeing Stratocruiser and Globe	11/30/49	.50	.40	5.25	(4)	3.75	16
C45	6¢ Wright Brothers	12/17/49	.20	.20	.65	(4)	2.75	80
	Issue of 1952							
C46	80¢ Diamond Head, Honolulu, Hawaii	03/26/52	5.00	1.25	22.50	(4)	17.50	19
	Issue of 1953							
C47	6¢ Powered Flight	05/29/53	.20	.20	.55	(4)	1.50	78
	Issue of 1954							
C48	4¢ Eagle in Flight	09/03/54	.20	.20	1.25	(4)	1.00	50

C24

C25

C32

C33

C34

C35

C36

C38

C40

C42

C43

C44

C45

C46

C47

C48

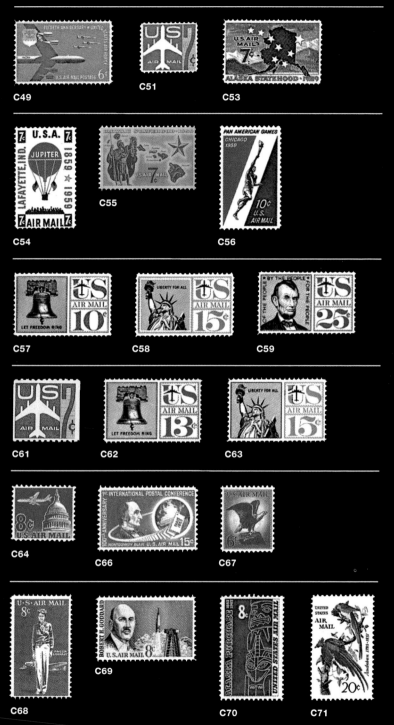

C49

C51

C53

C54

C55

C56

C57

C58

C59

C61

C62

C63

C64

C66

C67

C68

C69

C70

C71

Issue of 1957		Un	U	PB/LP	#	FDC	Q(M)
Perf. 11 x 10.5							
C49 6¢ Air Force	08/01/57	.20	.20	.65	(4)	1.25	63
Issues of 1958							
C50 5¢ rose red (C48)	07/31/58	.20	.20	1.25	(4)	1.00	72
Perf. 10.5 x 11							
C51 7¢ Jet Airliner	07/31/58	.20	.20	.60	(4)	1.00	1,327
a Booklet pane of 6		13.00	7.00			9.00	221
Coil Stamp, Perf. 10 Horizontally							
C52 7¢ blue (C51)	07/31/58	2.00	.20	14.00	(2)	1.00	157
Issues of 1959, Perf. 11 x 10.5							
C53 7¢ Alaska Statehood	01/03/59	.20	.20	.60	(4)	1.25	90
Perf. 11							
C54 7¢ Balloon Jupiter	08/17/59	.20	.20	.60	(4)	1.75	79
Perf. 11 x 10.5							
C55 7¢ Hawaii Statehood	08/21/59	.20	.20	.60	(4)	1.00	85
Perf. 11							
C56 10¢ Pan American Games	08/27/59	.25	.25	1.25	(4)	1.00	39
Issues of 1959-1966							
C57 10¢ Liberty Bell	06/10/60	1.10	.70	4.75	(4)	1.25	40
C58 15¢ Statue of Liberty	11/20/59	.35	.20	1.50	(4)	1.25	98
C59 25¢ Abraham Lincoln	04/22/60	.50	.20	2.00	(4)	1.25	
a Tagged	12/29/66	.60	.30	2.50	(4)	15.00	
Issues of 1960, Perf. 10.5 x 11							
C60 7¢ carmine (C61)	08/12/60	.20	.20	.60	(4)	1.00	1,289
Pair with full horizontal gutter between							
a Booklet pane of 6	08/19/60	16.00	8.00			8.00	
b Vertical pair, imperf. between		5,500.00					
Coil Stamp, Perf. 10 Horizontally							
C61 7¢ Jet Airliner	10//22/60	4.00	.25	35.00	(2)	1.00	87
Issues of 1961-1967, Perf. 11							
C62 13¢ Liberty Bell	06/28/61	.40	.20	1.65	(4)	1.00	
a Tagged	02/15/67	.75	.50	5.00	(4)	10.00	
C63 15¢ Statue of Liberty	01/13/61	.30	.20	1.25	(4)	1.00	
a Tagged	01/11/67	.35	.20	1.50	(4)	15.00	
b As "a," horiz. pair, imperf. vertically		15,000.00					
#C63 has a gutter between the two parts of the design; C58 does not.							
Issues of 1962-1965, Perf. 10.5 x 11							
C64 8¢ Jetliner over Capitol	12/05/62	.20	.20	.65	(4)	1.00	
a Tagged	08/01/63	.20	.20	.65	(4)	1.25	
b Bklt. pane of 5 + label		7.00	3.00			3.50	
c As "b," tagged	1964	2.00	.75				
Coil Stamp, Perf. 10 Horizontally							
C65 8¢ carmine (C64)	12/05/62	.40	.20	3.75	(2)	1.00	
a Tagged	01/14/65	.35	.20	1.50	(2)	—	
Issue of 1963, Perf. 11							
C66 15¢ Montgomery Blair	05/03/63	.60	.55	2.60	(4)	1.10	42
Issues of 1963-1967, Perf. 11 x 10.5							
C67 6¢ Bald Eagle	07/12/63	.20	.20	1.60	(4)	1.00	
a Tagged	02/15/67	4.00	3.00	55.00	(4)	15.00	
Issue of 1963, Perf. 11							
C68 8¢ Amelia Earhart	07/24/63	.20	.20	1.00	(4)	3.00	64
Issue of 1964							
C69 8¢ Robert H. Goddard	10/05/64	.40	.20	1.75	(4)	2.75	62
Issues of 1967							
C70 8¢ Alaska Purchase	03/30/67	.25	.20	1.25	(4)	1.25	56
C71 20¢ "Columbia Jays," by Audubon, (See also #1241)	04/26/67	.80	.20	3.50	(4)	2.00	165
a Tagging omitted		10.00					

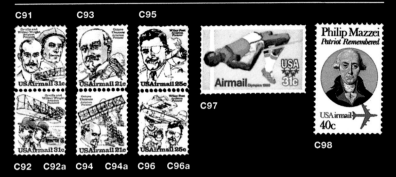

C91   C93   C95

C97

C98

C92 C92a C94 C94a C96 C96a

C99

C100

C101   C102   C105   C106

C103   C104 C104a   C107   C108   C108b

C109   C110

C111   C112   C112a

	Issues of 1978		Un	U	PB	#	FDC	Q(M)
	Aviation Pioneers Issue, Perf. 11 (See also #C93-96)							
C91	31¢ Wright Brothers, Flyer A	09/23/78	.65	.30			3.00	157
C92	31¢ Wright Brothers, Flyer A							
	and Shed	09/23/78	.65	.30			3.00	157
a	Vert. pair, #C91-92		1.30	1.20	3.00	(4)	4.00	
b	As "a," ultramarine and black omitted		*750.00*					
c	As "a," black omitted		—					
d	As "a," black, yellow, magenta,							
	blue and brown omitted		*2,250.00*					
	Issues of 1979, Aviation Pioneers Issue							
C93	21¢ Octave Chanute and Biplane							
	Hang-Glider	03/29/79	.70	.35			3.00	29
C94	21¢ Biplane Hang-Glider							
	and Chanute	03/29/79	.70	.35			3.00	29
a	Attached pair, #C93-94		1.40	1.20	3.25	(4)	4.00	
b	As "a," ultramarine and black omitted		*4,500.00*					
	Aviation Pioneers Issue (See also #C99-100)							
C95	25¢ Wiley Post and							
	"Winnie Mae"	11/20/79	1.10	.45			3.00	32
C96	25¢ NR-105-W, Post in							
	Pressurized Suit and Portrait	11/20/79	1.10	.45			3.00	32
a	Vert. pair, #C95-96		2.25	1.50	5.50	(4)	4.00	
	Olympic Summer Games Issue (See also #1790-94)							
C97	31¢ High Jumper	11/01/79	.70	.30	9.50	(12)	1.50	47
	Issues of 1980-1982							
C98	40¢ Philip Mazzei	10/13/80	.80	.20	10.00	(12)	1.50	81
b	Imperf., pair		*2,750.00*					
d	Tagging omitted		*10.00*					
	Perf. 10.5 x 11.25							
C98A	40¢ Philip Mazzei	1982	7.50	1.50	125.00	(12)		
	Issues of 1980, Aviation Pioneers Issue, Perf. 11							
C99	28¢ Blanche Stuart Scott							
	and Biplane	12/30/80	.60	.20	8.50	(12)	1.50	20
C100	35¢ Glen Curtiss							
	and "Pusher" Biplane	12/30/80	.65	.20	9.00	(12)	1.50	23
	Issues of 1983, Olympic Summer Games Issue (See also #2048-51 and 2082-85)							
C101	28¢ Gymnast	06/17/83	1.00	.30			1.75	43
C102	28¢ Hurdler	06/17/83	1.00	.30			1.75	43
C103	28¢ Basketball Player	06/17/83	1.00	.30			1.75	43
C104	28¢ Soccer Player	06/17/83	1.00	.30			1.75	43
a	Block of 4, #C101-04		4.50	2.50	6.00	(4)	3.75	
	Olympic Summer Games Issue, Perf. 11.2 Bullseye (See also #2048-51 and 2082-85)							
C105	40¢ Shotputter	04/08/83	.90	.40			1.75	67
a	Perf. 11 line		1.00	.45				
C106	40¢ Gymnast	04/08/83	.90	.40			1.75	67
a	Perf. 11 line		1.00	.45				
C107	40¢ Swimmer	04/08/83	.90	.40			1.75	67
a	Perf. 11 line		1.00	.45				
C108	40¢ Weightlifter	04/08/83	.90	.40			1.75	67
a	Perf. 11 line		1.00	.45			5.00	
b	Block of 4, #C105-#C108		4.25	3.00	5.00	(4)		
c	Block of 4, #C105a-#C108a		5.00	4.00	7.50	(4)		
d	Block of 4, imperf.		*1,250.00*					
	Olympic Summer Games Issue, Perf. 11 (See also #2048-51 and 2082-85)							
C109	35¢ Fencer	11/04/83	.90	.55			1.75	43
C110	35¢ Bicyclist	11/04/83	.90	.55			1.75	43
C111	35¢ Volleyball Players	11/04/83	.90	.55			1.75	43
C112	35¢ Pole Vaulter	11/04/83	.90	.55			1.75	43
a	Block of 4, #C109-12		4.00	3.25	7.00	(4)	4.50	

1873-1879

Issues of 1873	Un	U
Dept. of State Issue: Green, Perf. 12		
O57 1¢ Franklin	120.00	57.50
O58 2¢ Jackson	225.00	80.00
O59 3¢ Washington	90.00	18.00
Double paper	—	—
O60 6¢ Lincoln	85.00	24.00
O61 7¢ Stanton	170.00	55.00
Ribbed paper	190.00	60.00
O62 10¢ Jefferson	130.00	42.50
Short transfer	175.00	55.00
O63 12¢ Clay	210.00	100.00
O64 15¢ Webster	220.00	70.00
O65 24¢ Scott	450.00	190.00
O66 30¢ Hamilton	425.00	150.00
O67 90¢ Perry	800.00	300.00
O68 $2 Seward	1,000.00	800.00
O69 $5 Seward	6,000.00	3,750.00
O70 $10 Seward	4,500.00	2,600.00
O71 $20 Seward	3,500.00	1,900.00
Treasury Dept. Issue: Brown		
O72 1¢ Franklin	40.00	5.50
Double transfer	47.50	6.75
O73 2¢ Jackson	50.00	5.50
Double transfer	—	9.00
Cracked plate	67.50	—
O74 3¢ Washington	35.00	1.40
Shaded circle outside right frame line	—	—
O75 6¢ Lincoln	45.00	2.60
Dirty plate	45.00	4.00
O76 7¢ Stanton	95.00	26.00
O77 10¢ Jefferson	95.00	8.25
O78 12¢ Clay	95.00	6.50
O79 15¢ Webster	90.00	8.25
O80 24¢ Scott	450.00	75.00
O81 30¢ Hamilton	150.00	9.50
Short transfer top right	190.00	20.00
O82 90¢ Perry	160.00	10.50
War Dept. Issue: Rose		
O83 1¢ Franklin	145.00	9.00
O84 2¢ Jackson	130.00	10.00
Ribbed paper	140.00	12.00
O85 3¢ Washington	135.00	3.00
O86 6¢ Lincoln	450.00	6.50
O87 7¢ Stanton	130.00	77.50
O88 10¢ Jefferson	45.00	16.00

Issues of 1873	Un	U
War Dept. Issue (continued): Rose		
O89 12¢ Clay	170.00	10.50
Ribbed paper	185.00	11.00
O90 15¢ Webster	40.00	12.00
Ribbed paper	45.00	15.00
O91 24¢ Scott	40.00	7.25
O92 30¢ Hamilton	42.50	7.25
O93 90¢ Perry	95.00	42.50
Issues of 1879, Soft, Porous Paper		
Dept. of Agriculture: Yellow		
O94 1¢ Franklin, issued without gum	3,750.00	
O95 3¢ Washington	375.00	70.00
Dept. of the Interior Issue: Vermilion		
O96 1¢ Franklin	250.00	230.00
O97 2¢ Jackson	6.00	1.40
O98 3¢ Washington	5.50	1.10
O99 6¢ Lincoln	8.00	6.00
O100 10¢ Jefferson	85.00	65.00
O101 12¢ Clay	160.00	100.00
O102 15¢ Webster	325.00	240.00
Double transfer	375.00	—
O103 24¢ Scott	3,500.00	—
O104-05 Not assigned		
Dept. of Justice Issue: Bluish Purple		
O106 3¢ Washington	100.00	70.00
O107 6¢ Lincoln	250.00	190.00
Post Office Dept. Issue: Black		
O108 3¢ Figure of Value	20.00	5.50
Treasury Dept. Issue: Brown		
O109 3¢ Washington	60.00	7.25
O110 6¢ Lincoln	100.00	37.50
O111 10¢ Jefferson	175.00	55.00
O112 30¢ Hamilton	1,500.00	300.00
O113 90¢ Perry	2,400.00	300.00
War Dept. Issue: Rose Red		
O114 1¢ Franklin	3.75	3.00
O115 2¢ Jackson	7.00	3.50
O116 3¢ Washington	7.00	1.30
b Double impression	750.00	
Double transfer	11.00	4.75
O117 6¢ Lincoln	7.00	1.10
O118 10¢ Jefferson	40.00	37.50
O119 12¢ Clay	35.00	11.00
O120 30¢ Hamilton	110.00	75.00

Issues of 1910-1985	Un	U
Perf. 12		

Official Postal Savings Mail

These stamps were used to prepay postage on official correspondence of the Postal Savings Division of the Post Office Department. Discontinued Sept. 23, 1914.

		Un	U
O121	2¢ Postal Savings	15.00	1.50
	Double transfer	20.00	2.50
O122	50¢ dark green	145.00	40.00
O123	$1 ultramarine	135.00	11.00
	Wmkd. (190)		
O124	1¢ dark violet	8.00	1.50
O125	2¢ Postal Savings (O121)	47.50	5.50
O126	10¢ carmine	18.00	1.60

Penalty Mail Stamps

Stamps for use by government departments were reinstituted in 1983. Now known as Penalty Mail stamps, they help provide a better accounting of actual mail costs for official departments and agencies, etc.

Beginning with #O127, unused values are for never-hinged stamps.

Issues of 1983-1985, Unwmkd.,			
Perf. 11 x 10.5, O129A is Perf. 11			
O127	1¢, Jan. 12, 1983	.20	.20
O128	4¢, Jan. 12, 1983	.20	.25
O129	13¢, Jan. 12, 1983	.45	.75
O129A	14¢, May 15, 1985	.45	.50
O130	17¢, Jan. 12, 1983	.60	.40

Issues of 1983-2002	Un	U
Perf. 11 x 10.5		

		Un	U
O131, O134, O137, O142 Not assigned			
O132	$1, Jan. 12, 1983	2.00	1.00
O133	$5, Jan. 12, 1983	9.00	9.00
	Coil Stamps, Perf. 10 Vertically		
O135	20¢, Jan. 12, 1983	1.75	2.00
a	Imperf. pair	2,000.00	
O136	22¢, May 15, 1985	.80	2.00
	Perf. 11		
O138	"D" postcard rate (14¢) Feb. 04, 1985	5.25	5.00
	Coil Stamps, Perf. 10 Vertically		
O138A	15¢, June 11, 1988	.45	.50
O138B	20¢, May 19, 1988	.45	.30
O139	"D" (22¢), Feb. 04, 1985	5.25	3.00
O140	"E" (25¢), Mar. 22, 1988	.75	2.00
O141	25¢, June 11, 1988	.65	.50
	Perf. 11		
O143	1¢, July 05, 1989	.20	.20
	Perf. 10		
O144	"F" (29¢), Jan. 22, 1991	.75	.50
O145	29¢, May 24, 1991	.65	.30
	Perf. 11		
O146	4¢, Apr. 06, 1991	.20	.30
O146A	10¢, Oct. 19, 1993	.25	.30
O147	19¢, May 24, 1991	.40	.50
O148	23¢, May 24, 1991	.45	.30
O151	$1, Sept., 1993	2.00	.75
O152	(32¢), Dec. 13, 1994	.65	—
O153	32¢, May 09, 1995	.65	.30
O154	1¢, May 09, 1995	.20	.20
O155	20¢, May 09, 1995	.45	.30
O156	23¢, May 09, 1995	.50	.30
O157	33¢, Oct. 08, 1999	.65	—
O158	34¢, Feb. 27, 2001	.65	.30
O159	37¢, Aug. 02, 2002	.65	.30

Variable Rate Coil Stamps

These are coil postage stamps printed without denominations. The denomination is imprinted by the dispensing equipment called a Postage and Mailing Center (PMC). Denominations can be set between 1¢ and $99.99. In 1993, the minimum denomination was adjusted to 19¢ (the postcard rate at the time).

Date of Issue: August 20, 1992
Printing: Intaglio

Date of Issue: February 19, 1994
Printing: Gravure

Date of Issue: January 26, 1996
Printing: Gravure

Stamped Envelopes

1853-1886

U9 **U14** **U19** **U36**

U45 **U46** **U62** **U64**

U84 **U85** **U97**

U103 **U113** **U142**

Issues of 1853-1865 — Un / U

Represented below is only a partial listing of stamped envelopes. At least one example is listed for most die types; most die types exist on several colors of envelope paper. Values are for cut squares; prices for entire envelopes are higher. Color in italic is the color of the envelope paper; when no color is specified, envelope paper is white. "W" with catalog number indicates wrapper instead of envelope.

		Un	U
U1	3¢ red Washington (top label 13mm wide), *buff*	325.00	30.00
U4	3¢ red Washington (top label 15mm wide) *buff*	310.00	25.00
U5	3¢ red (label has octagonal ends)	6,000.00	450.00
U7	3¢ red (label 20mm wide)	1,500.00	90.00
U9	3¢ red (label 14½mm)	35.00	3.50
U12	6¢ red Washington, *buff*	150.00	65.00
U14	6¢ green Washington, *buff*	200.00	85.00
U15	10¢ green Washington (label 15½mm wide)	475.00	85.00
U17	10¢ green (label 20mm)	350.00	125.00
a	10¢ pale green	350.00	100.00
U19	1¢ blue Franklin (period after "POSTAGE"), *buff*	37.50	15.00
U23	1¢ blue (bust touches inner frame line), *orange*	750.00	350.00
U24	1¢ blue (no period after "POSTAGE"), *buff*	375.00	125.00
U27	3¢ red, no label, *buff*	26.00	13.00
U28	3¢ + 1¢ (U12 and U9)	375.00	240.00
U30	6¢ red Wash., no label	2,750.00	1,250.00
U33	10¢ green, no label, *buff*	1,500.00	250.00
U34	3¢ pink Washington (outline lettering)	27.00	5.75
U36	3¢ pink, blue (letter sheet)	80.00	50.00
U39	6¢ pink Washington, *buff*	70.00	62.50
U40	10¢ yellow green Wash.	37.50	30.00
U42	12¢ red, brn. Wash., *buff*	210.00	160.00
U44	24¢ Washington, *buff*	240.00	200.00
U45	40¢ blk., red Wash., *buff*	375.00	350.00
U46	2¢ black Jackson ("U.S. POSTAGE" downstroke, tail of "2" unite near point)	45.00	20.00
U49	2¢ black ("POSTAGE" downstroke and tail of "2" touch but do not merge), *orange*	1,400.00	
U50	2¢ blk. Jack. ("U.S. POST." stamp 24-25mm wide), *buff*	17.00	9.00
W51	2¢ blk. Jack. ("U.S. POST." stamp 24-25mm wide), *buff*	325.00	160.00
U54	2¢ blk. Jack. ("U.S. POST." stp. 25½-26½mm), *buff*	16.00	9.00
W55	2¢ blk. Jack. ("U.S. POST." stp. 25½-26½mm), *buff*	90.00	57.50
U58	3¢ pink Washington (solid lettering)	8.50	1.60
U60	3¢ brown Washington	50.00	30.00
U62	6¢ pink Washington	77.50	29.00

Issues of 1863-1886 — Un / U

		Un	U
U64	6¢ purple Washington	55.00	26.00
U66	9¢ lemon Washington, *buff*	425.00	250.00
U67	9¢ orange Washington, *buff*	125.00	90.00
U68	12¢ brn. Wash., *buff*	325.00	250.00
U69	12¢ red brown Wash., *buff*	125.00	55.00
U70	18¢ red Washington, *buff*	95.00	95.00
U71	24¢ bl. Washington, *buff*	100.00	95.00
U72	30¢ green Washington, *buff*	125.00	75.00
U73	40¢ rose Washington, *buff*	125.00	250.00
U75	1¢ blue Franklin (bust points to end of "N" of "ONE"), *amber*	32.50	27.50
U78	2¢ brown Jackson (bust narrow at back; small, thick numerals)	40.00	16.00
U84	3¢ grn. Washington ("ponytail" projects below bust), *cream*	10.00	4.25
U85	6¢ dark red Lincoln (neck very long at back)	25.00	16.00
a	6¢ vermilion	25.00	16.00
U88	7¢ verm. Stanton (figures 7 normal), *amber*	50.00	*190.00*
U89	10¢ olive blk. Jefferson	850.00	750.00
U92	10¢ brown Jefferson, *amber*	87.50	50.00
U93	12¢ plum Clay (chin prominent)	100.00	82.50
U97	15¢ red orange Webster (has side whiskers), *amber*	210.00	300.00
U99	24¢ purple Scott (locks of hair project, top of head)	140.00	140.00
U103	30¢ black Hamilton (back of bust very narrow), *amber*	250.00	500.00
U105	90¢ carmine Perry (front of bust very narrow, pointed)	150.00	350.00
U113	1¢ lt. blue Frank. (lower part of bust points to end of "E" in "ONE")	1.75	1.00
a	1¢ dark blue	8.50	7.50
U114	1¢ lt. blue (lower part of bust points to end of "E" in "Postage"), *amber*	4.25	4.00
U122	2¢ brown Jackson (bust narrow at back; numerals thin)	110.00	40.00
U128	2¢ brown Jackson (numerals in long ovals)	47.50	32.50
U132	2¢ brown, die 3 (left numeral touches oval)	72.50	27.50
U134	2¢ brown Jackson (similar to U128-31 but "O" of "TWO" has center netted instead of plain)	1,250.00	150.00
U139	2¢ brown (bust broad; numerals short, thick)	52.50	35.00
U142	2¢ verm. Jackson (U139)	7.00	3.00

1916-1978

	Issues of 1916-1962	Un	U
U525	2¢ carmine Mount Vernon	.40	.20
a	2¢, die 2 "S" of		
	"POSTAGE" raised	70.00	16.00
U526	3¢ violet Mount Vernon	2.00	.35
U527	4¢ black Mount Vernon	18.00	16.00
U528	5¢ dark blue Mount Vernon	4.00	3.50
U529	6¢ orange Washington	5.50	4.00
U530	6¢ orange Wash., *amber*	11.00	8.00
U531	6¢ or. Washington, *blue*	11.00	10.00
U532	1¢ green Franklin	5.00	1.75
U533	2¢ carmine Wash. (oval)	.75	.25
U534	3¢ dk. violet Washington, die 4		
	(short N in UNITED,thin		
	crossbar in A of STATES)	.40	.20
U535	1½¢ brown Washington	5.00	3.50
U536	4¢ red violet Franklin	.80	.20
U537	2¢ + 2¢ Wash. (U429)	3.25	1.50
U538	2¢ + 2¢ Washington (U533)	.75	.20
U539	3¢ + 1¢ purple, die 1		
	(4½mm tall, thick "3")	15.00	11.00
U540	3¢ + 1¢ purple, die 3		
	(4mm tall, thin "3")	.50	.20
a	Die 2 (4½mm tall,		
	thin "3" in medium		
	circle), entire	—	—
U541	1¼¢ turquoise Franklin	.75	.50
a	Die 2 ("4" 3½mm		
	high), precanceled		1.50
U542	2½¢ dull blue Washington	.85	.50
U543	4¢ brn. Pony Express Rider	.60	.30
U544	5¢ dark blue Lincoln	.85	.20
c	With albino impression		
	of 4¢ U536)	65.00	—
U545	4¢ + 1¢, type 1 (U536)	1.40	.50
U546	5¢ New York World's Fair	.60	.40
U547	1¼¢ brown Liberty Bell		.20
U548	1⁹⁄₁₀¢ brown Liberty Bell		.20
U548A	1⁹⁄₁₀¢ orange Liberty Bell		.20
U549	4¢ blue Old Ironsides	.75	.20
U550	5¢ purple Eagle	.75	.20
a	Tagged	2.00	.50
U551	6¢ green Statue of Liberty	.70	.20
U552	4¢ + 2¢ brt. bl. (U549)	3.75	2.00
U553	5¢ + 1¢ brt. pur. (U550)	3.50	2.50
U554	6¢ lt. blue Herman Melville	.50	.20
U555	6¢ Youth Conference	.75	.20
U556	1⁷⁄₁₀¢ lilac Liberty Bell		.20
U557	8¢ ultramarine Eagle	.40	.20
U561	6¢ + (2¢) lt. grn.	1.00	.30
U562	6¢ + (2¢) lt. blue	2.00	1.60
U563	8¢ rose red Bowling	.70	.20
U564	8¢ Aging Conference	.50	.20
U565	8¢ Transpo '72	.50	.20
U566	8¢ + 2¢ brt. ultra.	.40	.20
U567	10¢ emerald Liberty Bell	.40	.20
U568	1⁹⁄₁₀¢ Volunteer Yourself		.20

	Issues of 1962-1978	Un	U
U569	10¢ Tennis Centenary	.65	.20
U571	10¢ Compass Rose	.30	.20
a	Brown "10¢/USA"		
	omitted, entire	150.00	
U572	13¢ Quilt Pattern	.35	.20
U573	13¢ Sheaf of Wheat	.35	.20
U574	13¢ Mortar and Pestle	.35	.20
U575	13¢ Tools	.35	.20
U576	13¢ Liberty Tree	.30	.20
U577	2¢ red Nonprofit		.20
U578	2.1¢ yel. green Nonprofit		.20
U579	2.7¢ green Nonprofit		.20
U580	15¢ orange Eagle, A	.40	.20
U581	15¢ red Uncle Sam	.40	.20
U582	13¢ emerald Centennial	.35	.20
U583	13¢ Golf	.65	.20
U584	13¢ Energy Conservation	.40	.20
d	Blk. red omitted, ent.	425.00	
U585	13¢ Energy Development	.40	.20
U586	15¢ on 16¢ blue USA	.35	.20
U587	15¢ Auto Racing	.35	.20
a	Black omitted, entire	120.00	
U588	15¢ on 13¢ (U576)	.35	.20
U589	3.1¢ ultramarine nonprofit		.20
U590	3.5¢ purple Violins		.20
U591	5.9¢ Auth Nonprofit Org		.20
U592	18¢ violet Eagle, B	.45	.20
U593	18¢ dark blue Star	.45	.20
U594	20¢ brown Eagle, C	.45	.20
U595	15¢ Veterinary Medicine	.50	.20
U596	15¢ Summer Oly. Games	.60	.20
a	Red, grn. omitted, ent.	225.00	
U597	15¢ Highwheeler Bicycle	.40	.20
a	Blue "15¢ USA"		
	omitted, entire	100.00	
U598	15¢ America's Cup	.40	.20
U599	Brown 15¢ Honeybee	.35	.20
a	Brown "15¢ USA"		
	omitted, entire	125.00	
U600	18¢ Blind Veterans	.45	.20
U601	20¢ Capitol Dome	.45	.20
U602	20¢ Great Seal of U.S.	.45	.20
U603	20¢ Purple Heart	.65	.20
U604	5.2¢ Auth Nonprofit Org		.20
U605	20¢ Paralyzed Veterans	.45	.20
U606	20¢ Small Business	.50	.20
U607	22¢ Eagle, D	.55	.20
U608	22¢ Bison	.55	.20
U609	6¢ *USS Constitution*		.20
U610	8.5¢ *Mayflower*		.20
U611	25¢ Stars	.60	.20
U612	8.4¢ *US Frigate Constellation*		.20
U613	25¢ Snowflake	.60	.25
U614	25¢ USA, Stars (Philatelic Mail)	.50	.25

U530

U531

U541

U542

U543

U569

U576

U581

U587

U601

U609

U610

U611

U614

U616

U617

U631

U632

U634

U635

U636

U637

Issues of 1989-1992	Un	U
U615 25¢ Stars (lined paper)	.50	.25
U616 25¢ Love	.50	.25
U617 25¢ Space hologram	.60	.30
U618 25¢ Football hologram	.60	.25
U619 29¢ Star	.60	.30
U620 11.1¢ Birds		.20
U621 29¢ Love	.60	.30
U622 29¢ Magazine Industry	.60	.30
U623 29¢ Star and Bars	.60	.30
U624 29¢ Country Geese	.60	.60
U625 29¢ Space Shuttle	.60	.25
U626 29¢ Western Americana	.60	.30
U627 29¢ Protect the Environment	.60	.30
U628 19.8¢ Bulk Rate precanceled		.40

Issues of 1992-1995	Un	U
U629 29¢ Disabled Americans	.60	.30
U630 29¢ Kitten	.60	.30
U631 29¢ Football	.60	.30
U632 32¢ Liberty Bell	.65	.30
U633 32¢ Old Glory	.65	.30
U634 32¢ Old Glory	.65	.30
U635 5¢ Nonprofit		.20
U636 10¢ Graphic Eagle		.20
U637 32¢ Spiral Heart	.65	.30

Marguerite Higgins (1920-1966)

Journalist Marguerite Higgins, who covered World War II, Korea, and Vietnam, was the first woman to win a Pulitzer Prize for international reporting. Born in Hong Kong to a French mother and an American father, Higgins grew up in California. After earning a master's degree in journalism from Columbia University, she went to work for the *New York Herald Tribune*. Eager to become a war correspondent, Higgins persuaded the paper to send her to Europe in 1944. By the time war broke out in Korea, she was chief of the *Herald Tribune*'s Tokyo bureau. One of the first reporters on the spot, she was ordered to leave by a U.S. military commander who argued that women did not belong at the front. When General Douglas MacArthur reversed the order, it was a major breakthrough for all female war correspondents. Her accounts from Korea won her the 1951 Pulitzer Prize for international reporting. Higgins continued to cover foreign affairs—interviewing world leaders such as Francisco Franco, Nikita Khrushchev, and Jawaharlal Nehru—and served as chief of the *Herald Tribune*'s Moscow bureau and as its diplomatic correspondent in Washington, D.C. ■

Issues of 1995-1999		Un	U
U639	32¢ Space Shuttle	.65	.35
U640	32¢ Save Our Environment	.60	.30
U641	32¢ 1996 Paralympic Games	.60	.30
U642	33¢ Flag (yellow, red, blue)	.65	.30

Issues of 1999-2002			Un	U
U643	33¢ Flag (blue & red)		.65	.30
U644	33¢ Victorian Love		.65	.30
U645	33¢ Lincoln		.65	.30
U646	34¢ Federal Eagle	01/07/01	.65	.30
U647	34¢ Lovebirds	01/14/01	.65	.30
U648	34¢ Federal Eagle	02/20/01	.65	.30
U649	37¢ Ribbon Star	06/07/02	.75	.35
U650	(10¢) Presorted Standard Eagle	08/08/02		

A·M·E·R·I·C·A·N C·O·M·M·E·M·O·R·A·T·I·V·E C·O·L·L·E·C·T·I·B·L·E·S

An easy and affordable way to acquire all of your stamp collectibles!

Choose any or all of the official U.S. Postal Service American Commemorative Collectibles to enhance your collection.

American Commemorative Panels

Obtain photo or steel engravings, mint condition stamps and subject related text presented on a beautifully designed page. Only $6.00* each, depending on the value of the stamps.

American Commemorative Collection

An easy and uniform way to collect and learn about commemorative issues. Just mount the stamps on the specially designed sheet and place them in a three ring binder. Just $3.25* each, depending on the value of the stamps.

American Commemorative Cancellations

Get first day cancellations and stamp(s) that have been affixed to colorful, specially tinted sheets to enhance your display. About $2.00* each, depending on the value of the stamps.

First Day of Issue Ceremony Programs

Receive detailed information about each first day of issue ceremony held for all new stamps and stationery issuances. Collect these valuable programs for only $4.95 each.

For information call **1-800-STAMP-24**

*Prices subject to change without notice.

U639

U640

U641

U642

U643

U644

U645

U646

U647

U648

U649

U650

Airmail Envelopes and Aerogrammes

1929-1973

UC1   UC3   UC7

UC8

UC14

UC21   UC25

UC26   UC30

UC39   UC46

Issues of 1929-1945	Un	U
UC1 5¢ blue Airplane, die 1		
(vertical rudder is not		
semicircular)	3.50	2.00
1933 wmk., entire	750.00	750.00
1937 wmk., entire	—	2,500.00
Bicolored border		
omitted, entire	1,300.00	
UC2 5¢ blue, die 2 (vertical		
rudder is semicircular)	11.00	5.00
1929 wmk., entire	—	1,500.00
1933 wmk., entire	650.00	—
UC3 6¢ orange Airplane, die 2a		
("6" is 6½mm wide)	1.50	.40
a With #U436a added		
impression	4,000.00	
UC4 6¢ orange, die 2b		
("6" is 6mm wide)	2.75	2.00
UC5 6¢ orange, die 2c		
("6" is 5mm wide)	.75	.30
UC6 6¢ orange, die 3 (vertical≤		
rudder leans forward)	1.00	.35
a 6¢ orange, *blue*,		
entire	3,500.00	2,400.00
UC7 8¢ olive green Airplane	13.00	3.50
UC8 6¢ on 2¢ carm.		
Washington (U429)	1.25	.65
d 6¢ on 1¢ green		
(U420)	1,750.00	
f 6¢ on 3¢ purple		
(U437a)	3,000.00	
UC9 6¢ on 2¢ Wash. (U525)	75.00	40.00
Issues of 1946-1956		
UC10 5¢ on 6¢ orange (UC3)	2.75	1.50
a Double surcharge	60.00	
UC11 5¢ on 6¢ orange (UC4)	9.00	5.50
UC13 5¢ on 6¢ orange (UC6)	.80	.60
a Double surcharge	60.00	
UC14 5¢ carm. DC-4, die 1		
(end of wing on right		
is smooth curve)	.75	.20
UC16 10¢ red, DC-4		
2-line back inscription,		
entire, *pale blue*	7.50	6.00
a "Air Letter" on face,		
4-line back inscription	16.00	14.00
Die-cutting reversed	275.00	
b 10¢ chocolate	450.00	
c "Air Letter" and		
"Aerogramme" on face	45.00	12.50
d 3-line back inscription	8.00	8.00

Issues of 1946-1956	Un	U
UC17 5¢ Postage Centenary	.40	.25
UC18 6¢ carm. Airplane (UC14),		
type I (6's lean right)	.35	.20
a Type II (6's upright)	.75	.25
UC20 6¢ on 5¢ (UC15)	.80	.50
a 6¢ on 6¢ carmine,		
entire	1,500.00	
b Double surcharge	500.00	—
UC21 6¢ on 5¢ (UC14)	27.50	17.50
UC22 6¢ on 5¢ (UC14)	3.50	2.50
a Double surcharge	200.00	
UC23 6¢ on 5¢ (UC17)	1,250.00	
UC25 6¢ red Eagle	.75	.50
Issues of 1958-1973		
UC26 7¢ blue (UC14)	.65	.50
UC27 6¢ + 1¢ orange (UC3)	325.00	225.00
UC28 6¢ + 1¢ orange (UC4)	75.00	75.00
UC29 6¢ + 1¢ orange (UC5)	45.00	50.00
UC30 6¢ + 1¢ (UC5)	1.00	.50
UC32 10¢ Jet Airliner, back		
inscription in 2 lines	6.00	5.00
a Type 1, entire	10.00	5.00
UC33 7¢ blue Jet Silhouette	.60	.25
UC34 7¢ carmine (UC33)	.60	.25
UC35 11¢ Jet, Globe, entire	2.75	2.25
a Red omitted	1,000.00	
Die-cutting reversed	35.00	
UC36 8¢ red Jet Airliner	.55	.20
UC37 8¢ red Jet in Triangle	.35	.20
a Tagged	3.50	.30
UC39 13¢ John Kennedy, entire	3.00	2.75
a Red omitted	900.00	
UC40 10¢ Jet in Triangle	.50	.20
UC41 8¢ + 2¢ (UC37)	.65	.20
UC42 13¢ Human Rights, entire	8.00	4.00
Die-cutting reversed	75.00	
UC43 11¢ Jet in Circle	.50	.20
UC44 15¢ gray, red, white		
and blue Birds in Flight	1.50	1.10
UC45 10¢ + (1¢) (UC40)	1.50	.20
UC46 15¢ red, white, bl.	.75	.40

	Issues of 1973-1983	Un	U
UC47	13¢ red Bird in Flight	.30	.20
UC48	18¢ USA, entire	.90	.30
UC50	22¢ red and bl. USA, entire	.90	.40
UC51	22¢ blue USA, entire	.70	.25
	Die-cutting reversed	25.00	
UC52	22¢ Summer Olympic		
	Games	1.50	.25
UC53	30¢ blue, red, brn. Tour		
	the United States, entire	.65	1.00
a	Red "30" omitted	*70.00*	
UC54	30¢ *yellow, magenta, blue*		
	and *black* (UC53), entire	.65	1.00
	Die-cutting reversed	20.00	
UC55	30¢ Made in USA, entire	.65	1.00
UC56	30¢ World Communications		
	Year, entire	.65	1.00
	Die-cutting reversed	25.00	

	Issues of 1983-1999	Un	U
UC57	30¢ Olympic Games, entire	.65	1.50
UC58	36¢ Landsat, entire	.70	1.00
UC59	36¢ Tourism Week, entire	.70	1.00
UC60	36¢ Mark Twain/		
	Halley's Comet, entire	1.00	1.50
UC61	39¢ Envelope	.80	1.00
UC62	39¢ Montgomery Blair	.80	1.00
UC63	45¢ Eagle, entire, *blue*	.90	1.00
a	White paper	.90	.45
UC64	50¢ Thaddeus Lowe,		
	Balloonist	1.00	1.00
UC65	60¢ Voyageurs Nat'l Park,		
	Minnesota	1.25	1.00

Bessie Coleman (1892-1926)

When flight schools in the United States denied admission to Elizabeth "Bessie" Coleman, she went to France for her training. In 1921 she became the first African American to receive an international pilot's license from the Fédération Aeronautique Internationale. A parachuting and stunt-flying specialist, Coleman returned to the U.S. and quickly established a reputation as an exceptional performer while touring as a barnstormer. She wanted to promote aviation among African Americans and women, and establish a flight school to train them. She embarked on a fundraising campaign and began to schedule performances at circuses, carnivals, and county fairs where the audience would be primarily African American. An early civil rights activist, she steadfastly refused to appear before segregated audiences. She was rehearsing for an appearance in 1926 at the Negro Welfare League's First of May Field Day in Jacksonville, Florida, when she fell from her plane and was killed. Although she did not realize her dream to found a school, she paved the way for many men and women to follow in her footsteps. ■

UC48

UC52

UC53

UC56

UC57

UC59

UC63

UC64

UC65

UO1

UO16

UO20

UO73

UO84

UO88

UO89

UO90

Visit us online at The Postal Store at www.usps.com

or call 1-800-STAMP-24

Issues of 1873-1875	Un	U
Official Envelopes		
Post Office Department		
Numeral 9½mm high		
UO1 2¢ black, *lemon*	20.00	9.00
Numeral 10½mm high		
UO5 2¢ black, *lemon*	8.50	4.00
UO9 3¢ black, *amber*	85.00	35.00
Postal Service		
UO16 blue, *amber*	150.00	30.00
War Department		
UO20 3¢ dk. red Washington	62.50	40.00
UO26 12¢ dark red Clay	150.00	50.00
UO39 10¢ vermilion Jefferson	300.00	
UO48 2¢ red Jackson, *amber*	30.00	14.00
UO55 3¢ red Washington, *fawn*	4.50	2.75

Issues of 1983-2002	Un	U
Penalty Mail Envelopes		
UO73 20¢ blue Great Seal	1.25	30.00
UO74 22¢ (seal embossed)	.90	10.00
UO75 22¢ (seal typographed)	1.00	20.00
UO76 "E" (25¢) Great Seal	1.10	20.00
UO77 25¢ black, blue Great Seal (seal embossed)	.80	15.00
UO78 25¢ (seal typographed)	.90	25.00
UO79 45¢ (stars illegible)	1.25	85.00
UO80 65¢ (stars illegible)	1.75	150.00
UO81 45¢ (stars clear)	1.25	75.00
UO82 65¢ (stars clear)	1.60	125.00
UO83 "F" (29¢) Great Seal	1.10	20.00
UO84 29¢ black, blue, entire	.75	10.00
UO88 32¢ Official Mail	.80	10.00
UO89 33¢ Official Mail	.70	10.00
UO90 34¢ Official Mail	.85	—
UO91 37¢ Official Mail	—	—

BLACK HERITAGE
USA 23
Patricia Roberts Harris

Patricia Roberts Harris (1924-1985)

In 1965 Patricia Roberts Harris became the first African-American woman to serve as a U.S. ambassador when President Lyndon B. Johnson named her ambassador to Luxembourg. The daughter of a Pullman car waiter, Harris was born May 31, 1924, in Mattoon, Illinois. In 1945 she graduated *summa cum laude* from Howard University. Fifteen years later, she earned a law degree—graduating first in her class—from George Washington University National Law Center. In 1969 she became the first woman to serve as dean of Howard University School of Law. Appointed Secretary of Housing and Urban Development in 1977 by President Jimmy Carter, Harris was the first African-American woman to serve as a member of a presidential Cabinet. Two years later, President Carter named Harris to her second Cabinet post, Secretary of Health, Education and Welfare. Throughout her multifaceted career, Harris gave special attention to the needs of the disadvantaged, and distinguished herself as an advocate of fairness and equity for all Americans. ■

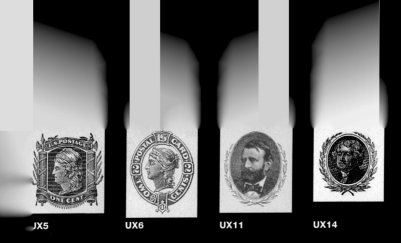

JX5 **UX6** **UX11** **UX14**

UX25 **UX27**

JX16 **UX18**

JX28 **UX37** **UX43**

UX45 **UX46** **UX48**

JX44

Issues of 1873-1917 | Un | U

Represented below is only a partial listing of postal cards. Values are for entire cards. Color in italic is color of card. Cards preprinted with written address or message usually sell for much less.

		Un	U
UX1	1¢ brown Liberty, wmkd. (90 x 60mm)	350.00	19.00
UX3	1¢ brown Liberty, wmkd. (53 x 36mm)	75.00	2.50
UX4	1¢ blk. Liberty, wmkd., USPOD in monogram	2,400.00	325.00
UX5	1¢ blk. Liberty, unwmkd.	70.00	.45
UX6	2¢ blue Liberty, *buff*	30.00	21.00
a	2¢ dark blue, *buff*	30.00	21.00
UX7	1¢ (UX5), inscribed "Nothing But The Address"	60.00	.40
a	23 teeth below "One Cent"	950.00	30.00
b	Printed on both sides	800.00	400.00
UX8	1¢ brown Jefferson, large "one-cent" wreath	47.50	1.25
c	1¢ chocolate	175.00	40.00
UX9	1¢ blk. Jefferson, *buff*	20.00	.55
a	1¢ blk., *dark buff*	40.00	3.00
UX10	1¢ black Grant	37.50	1.50
UX11	1¢ blue Grant	17.50	3.00
UX12	1¢ black Jefferson, wreath smaller than UX14	37.50	.65
UX13	2¢ blue Liberty, *cream*	175.00	85.00
UX14	1¢ Jefferson	30.00	.45
UX15	1¢ black John Adams	42.50	15.00
UX16	2¢ black Liberty	12.50	15.00
UX17	1¢ black McKinley	7,000.00	
UX18	1¢ black McKinley, facing left	12.50	.35
UX19	1¢ black McKinley, triangles in top corners	40.00	.50
UX20	1¢ (UX19), correspondence space at left	52.50	4.25
UX21	1¢ blue McKinley, shaded background	95.00	10.00
a	1¢ bronze blue, *bluish*	200.00	17.50
UX22	1¢ blue McKinley, white background	15.00	.35
UX23	1¢ red Lincoln, solid background	9.00	5.50
UX24	1¢ red McKinley	10.00	.35
UX25	2¢ red Grant	1.50	16.00
UX26	1¢ green Lincoln, solid background	12.00	6.50
UX27	1¢ Jefferson, *buff*	.25	.25
a	1¢ green, *cream*	3.50	.65
UX27C	1¢ green Jefferson, *gray,* die I	4,000.00	175.00
UX28	1¢ green Lincoln, *cream*	.60	.30
a	1¢ green, *buff*	1.50	.60
UX29	2¢ red Jefferson, *buff*	42.50	2.10
a	2¢ lake, *cream*	47.50	2.50
c	2¢ vermilion, *buff*	925.00	75.00

Issues of 1918-1968 | Un | U

		Un	U
UX30	2¢ red Jefferson, *cream*	29.00	1.60
	Surcharged in one line by canceling machine.		
UX31	1¢ on 2¢ red Jefferson	5,000.00	4,500.00
	Surcharged in two lines by canceling machine.		
UX32	1¢ on 2¢ red Jeff., *buff*	52.50	12.50
a	1¢ on 2¢ vermilion	150.00	60.00
b	Double surcharge	150.00	100.00
UX33	1¢ on 2¢ red Jefferson, *cream*	12.00	1.90
a	Inverted surcharge	55.00	100.00
b	Double surcharge	55.00	35.00
d	Triple surcharge	350.00	
	Surcharged in two lines by press printing.		
UX34	1¢ on 2¢ red (UX29)	500.00	47.50
UX35	1¢ on 2¢ red Jefferson, *cream*	200.00	32.50
UX36	1¢ on 2¢ red (UX25)		50,000.00
UX37	3¢ red McKinley, *buff*	4.50	15.00
UX38	2¢ carmine rose Franklin	.35	.25
a	Double impression	500.00	
	Surcharged by canceling machine in light green.		
UX39	2¢ on 1¢ green Jefferson, *buff*	.50	.35
b	Double surcharge	19.00	21.00
UX40	2¢ on 1¢ green (UX28)	.65	.45
	Surcharged typographically in dark green.		
UX41	2¢ on 1¢ green Jefferson, *buff*	4.50	2.00
a	Inverted surcharge lower left	77.50	125.00
UX42	2¢ on 1¢ green (UX29)	5.00	2.50
b	Surcharged on back	160.00	
UX43	2¢ carmine Lincoln	.30	1.00
UX44	2¢ FIPEX	.25	1.00
b	Dk. vio. blue omitted	625.00	350.00
UX45	4¢ Statue of Liberty	1.50	75.00
UX46	3¢ purple Statue of Liberty	.50	.20
a	"N GOD WE TRUST"	13.50	22.50
UX47	2¢ + 1¢ carmine rose Franklin	200.00	500.00
UX48	4¢ red violet Lincoln	.50	.20
UX49	7¢ World Vacationland	4.00	42.50
UX50	4¢ U.S. Customs	.50	1.00
a	Blue omitted	625.00	
UX51	4¢ Social Security	.40	1.00
b	Blue omitted	700.00	650.00
UX52	4¢ blue & red Coast Guard	.30	1.00
UX53	4¢ Bureau of the Census	.30	1.00
UX54	8¢ blue & red (UX49)	4.00	42.50
UX55	5¢ emerald Lincoln	.30	.60
UX56	5¢ Women Marines	.35	1.00

1970-1990

Issues of 1970-1983		Un	U
UX57	5¢ Weather Services	.30	1.00
a	Yellow, black omitted	1,400.00	850.00
b	Blue omitted	1,400.00	
c	Black omitted	1,400.00	850.00
UX58	6¢ brown Paul Revere	.30	1.00
a	Double impression	300.00	
UX59	10¢ blue & red (UX49)	4.50	42.50
UX60	6¢ America's Hospitals	.30	1.00
a	Blue, yellow omitted	1,150.00	
UX61	6¢ USF *Constellation*	.85	6.00
a	Address side blank	300.00	
UX62	6¢ black Monument Valley	.40	6.00
UX63	6¢ Gloucester, MA	.40	6.00
UX64	6¢ blue John Hanson	.25	1.00
UX65	6¢ magenta Liberty	.25	1.00
UX66	8¢ orange Samuel Adams	.25	1.00
UX67	12¢ Visit USA/		
	Ship's Figurehead	.35	37.50
UX68	7¢ Charles Thomson	.30	8.50
UX69	9¢ John Witherspoon	.25	1.00
UX70	9¢ blue Caesar Rodney	.25	1.00
UX71	9¢ Federal Court House	.25	1.00
UX72	9¢ green Nathan Hale	.25	1.00
UX73	10¢ Cincinnati Music Hall	.30	1.00
UX74	10¢ John Hancock	.30	1.00
UX75	10¢ John Hancock	.30	1.00
UX76	14¢ Coast Guard Eagle	.40	21.00
UX77	10¢ Molly Pitcher	.30	1.50
UX78	10¢ George Rogers Clark	.30	1.50
UX79	10¢ Casimir Pulaski	.30	1.50
UX80	10¢ Olympic Sprinter	.60	1.50
UX81	10¢ Iolani Palace	.30	1.50
UX82	14¢ Olympic Games	.60	15.00
UX83	10¢ Salt Lake Temple	.25	1.50
UX84	10¢ Landing of Rochambeau	.25	1.50
UX85	10¢ Battle of Kings Mtn.	.25	1.50
UX86	19¢ Drake's Golden Hinde	.70	25.00
UX87	10¢ Battle of Cowpens	.25	15.00
UX88	12¢ violet Eagle,		
	nondenominated	.30	.65
UX89	12¢ lt. bl. Isaiah Thomas	.30	.60
UX90	12¢ Nathanael Greene	.30	10.00
UX91	12¢ Lewis and Clark	.30	20.00
UX92	13¢ buff Robert Morris	.30	.60
UX93	13¢ buff Robert Morris	.30	.60
UX94	13¢ "Swamp Fox"		
	Francis Marion	.30	1.00
UX95	13¢ LaSalle Claims		
	Louisiana	.30	1.00
UX96	13¢ Academy of Music	.30	1.00
UX97	13¢ Old Post Office,		
	St. Louis, Missouri	.30	1.00
UX100	13¢ Olympic Yachting	.30	1.00

Issues of 1984-1990		Un	U
UX101	13¢ *Ark* and *Dove*, Maryland	.30	1.00
UX102	13¢ Olympic Torch	.30	1.00
UX103	13¢ Frederic Baraga	.30	1.00
UX104	13¢ Dominguez Adobe	.30	1.00
UX105	14¢ Charles Carroll	.30	.50
UX106	14¢ green Charles Carroll	.45	.25
UX107	25¢ Clipper *Flying Cloud*	.70	12.50
UX108	14¢ brt. grn. George Wythe	.30	.75
UX109	14¢ Settlement of		
	Connecticut	.30	1.25
UX110	14¢ Stamp Collecting	.30	1.25
UX111	14¢ Francis Vigo	.30	1.25
UX112	14¢ Settling of Rhode Island	.30	1.25
UX113	14¢ Wisconsin Territory	.30	.85
UX114	14¢ National Guard	.30	1.25
UX115	14¢ Self-Scouring Plow	.30	1.25
UX116	14¢ Constitutional		
	Convention	.30	.60
UX117	14¢ Stars and Stripes	.30	.60
UX118	14¢ Take Pride in		
	America	.30	1.25
UX119	14¢ Timberline Lodge	.30	1.25
UX120	15¢ Bison and Prairie	.30	.60
UX121	15¢ Blair House	.30	.75
UX122	28¢ *Yorkshire*	.60	8.50
UX123	15¢ Iowa Territory	.30	.75
UX124	15¢ Ohio, Northwest Terr.	.30	.75
UX125	15¢ Hearst Castle	.30	.60
UX126	15¢ The Federalist Papers	.30	.75
UX127	15¢ Hawk and Desert	.30	.75
UX128	15¢ Healy Hall	.40	.75
UX129	15¢ Blue Heron and Marsh	.30	.75
UX130	15¢ Settling of Oklahoma	.30	.75
UX131	21¢ Geese and Mountains	.40	6.00
UX132	15¢ Seagull and Seashore	.30	.75
UX133	15¢ Deer and Waterfall	.30	.75
UX134	15¢ Hull House, Chicago	.30	.75
UX135	15¢ Ind. Hall, Philadelphia	.30	.75
UX136	15¢ Inner Harbor, Baltimore	.30	.75
UX137	15¢ Bridge, New York	.30	.75
UX138	15¢ Capitol, Washington	.30	.75
	#UX139-42 issued in sheets of 4 plus 2		
	inscribed labels, rouletted 9½ on 2 or		
	3 sides.		
UX139	15¢ (UX135)	3.25	3.50
UX140	15¢ The White House	3.25	3.50
UX141	15¢ (UX137)	3.25	3.50
UX142	15¢ (UX138)	3.25	3.50
a	Sheet of 4,		
	#UX139-42	13.00	
UX143	15¢ The White House	1.00	2.00
UX144	15¢ Jefferson Memorial	1.00	2.00
UX145	15¢ Papermaking	.30	.40
UX146	15¢ World Literacy Year	.30	.75

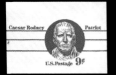

Caesar Rodney
Patriot
U.S. Postage 9¢
UX70

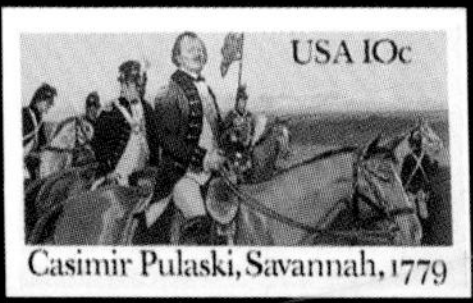

USA 10c
Casimir Pulaski, Savannah, 1779
UX79

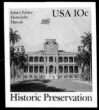

Iolani Palace
Honolulu
Hawaii
USA 10c
Historic Preservation
UX81

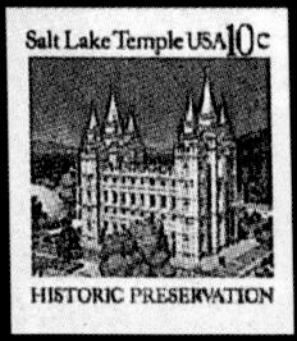

Salt Lake Temple USA 10c
HISTORIC PRESERVATION
UX83

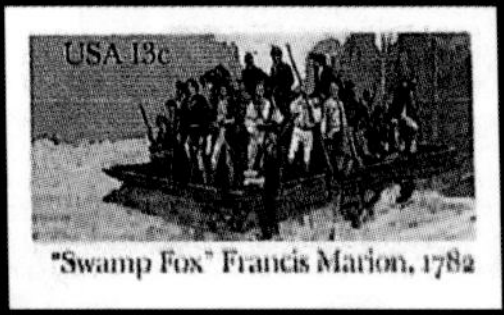

USA 13c
"Swamp Fox" Francis Marion, 1782
UX94

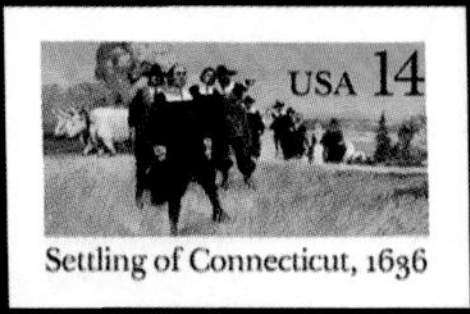

USA 14
Settling of Connecticut, 1636
UX109

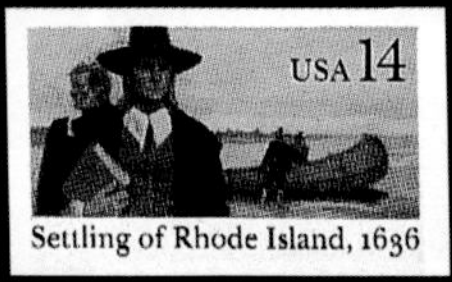

USA 14
Settling of Rhode Island, 1636
UX112

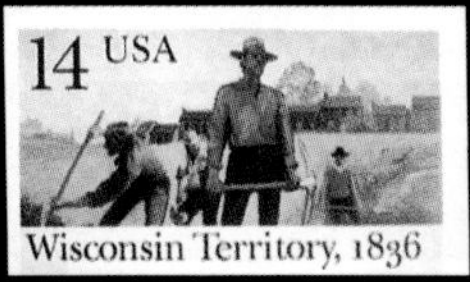

14 USA
Wisconsin Territory, 1836
UX113

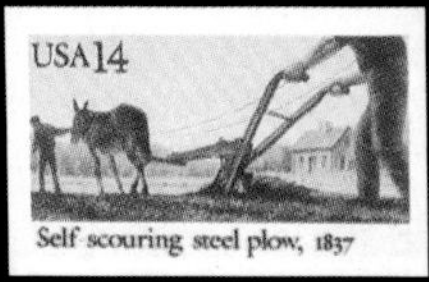

USA 14
Self scouring steel plow, 1837
UX115

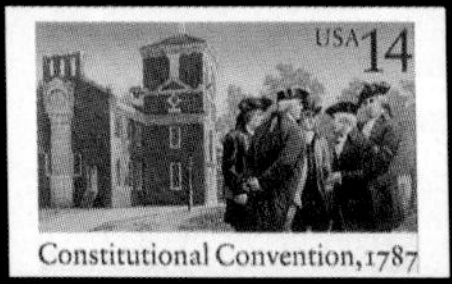

USA 14
Constitutional Convention, 1787
UX116

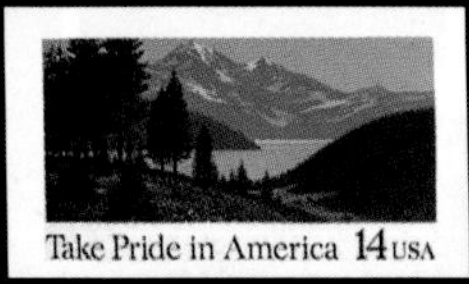

Take Pride in America 14 USA
UX118

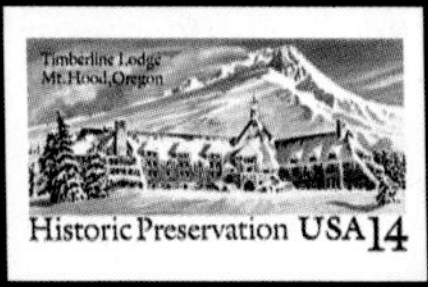

Timberline Lodge
Mt. Hood, Oregon
Historic Preservation USA 14
UX119

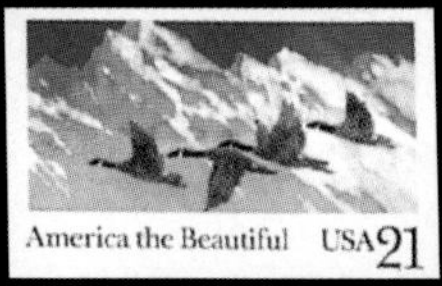

America the Beautiful USA 21
UX131

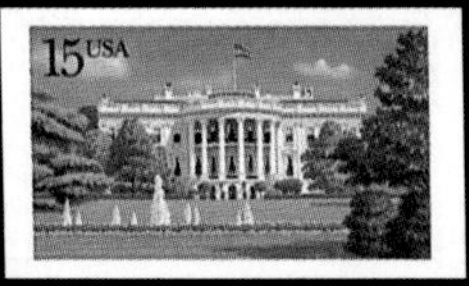

15 USA
UX143

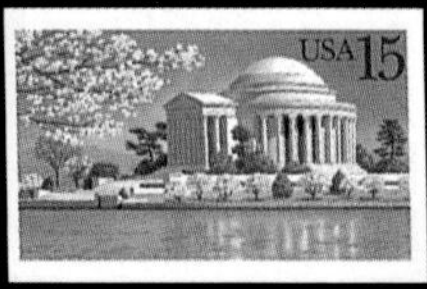

USA 15
UX144

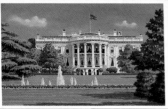

UX143 (picture side)

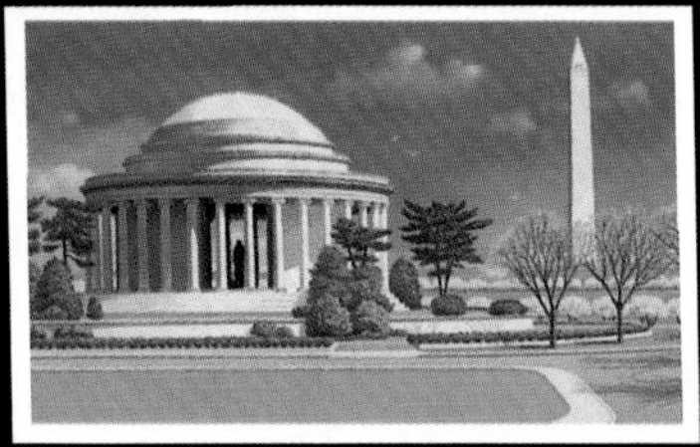

UX144 (picture side)

	Issues of 1998-2002	Un	U
UX301	20¢ University of Wisconsin-Madison	.50	.50
UX302	20¢ Washington and Lee University	.50	.50
UX303	20¢ Redwood Library & Athenæum	.50	.50
UX305	20¢ Mount Vernon	.40	.40
UX306	20¢ Block Island Lighthouse	.40	.45
UX312	20¢ University of Utah	.40	.45
UX313	20¢ Ryman Auditorium	.40	.45
UX316	20¢ Middlebury College	.40	.45
UX361	20¢ Yale University Stamped Card	.40	.50
UX362	20¢ University of South Carolina Stamped Card	.40	.50
UX363	20¢ Northwestern University Stamped Card	.40	.50
UX364	20¢ University of Portland Stamped Card	.40	.50
UX375	21¢ White Barn Stamped Card	.45	.45
UX381	23¢ Carlsbad Caverns National Park Stamped Card	.50	.50
UX386	23¢ Snowman w/red & green plaid scarf	.50	.50
UX387	23¢ Snowman w/blue plaid scarf	.50	.50
UX388	23¢ Snowman w/pipe	.50	.50
UX389	23¢ Snowman w/top hat	.50	.50

	Issues of 1949-1966	Un	U
	Airmail Postal Cards		
UXC1	4¢ orange Eagle	.50	.75
UXC2	5¢ red Eagle (C48)	1.75	.75
UXC3	5¢ UXC2 redrawn "Air Mail-Postal Card" omitted	6.50	2.00
UXC4	6¢ red Eagle	1.10	2.50
UXC5	11¢ Visit The USA	.60	20.00

Rachel Carson (1907-1964)

Rachel Carson, writer and biologist, was born in rural Pennsylvania, the youngest of three children. As an adult she remembered herself as a solitary child who loved writing and nature. She combined these interests professionally as a scientist and editor at the U.S. Fish and Wildlife Service and in four celebrated books on the environment. The first, *Under the Sea Wind* (1941), grew out of an article she had published earlier in the *Atlantic Monthly*. Her second book, *The Sea Around Us* (1951), won a National Book Award. In 1952, she resigned from the government to devote more time to her writing. In *The Edge of the Sea* (1955), Carson described life along the shore of the eastern United States. In 1962, after years of research, she published *Silent Spring*, a critical look at the use of the pesticide DDT and other toxic chemicals in agriculture. The book inspired widespread concern for ecology and heightened awareness of environmental hazards. In 1963, Carson testified before Congress about her findings, calling for policies to protect the environment and human health. After her death in 1964, Congress passed federal regulations restricting the use of certain chemicals and requiring identification of ingredients on product labels. ■

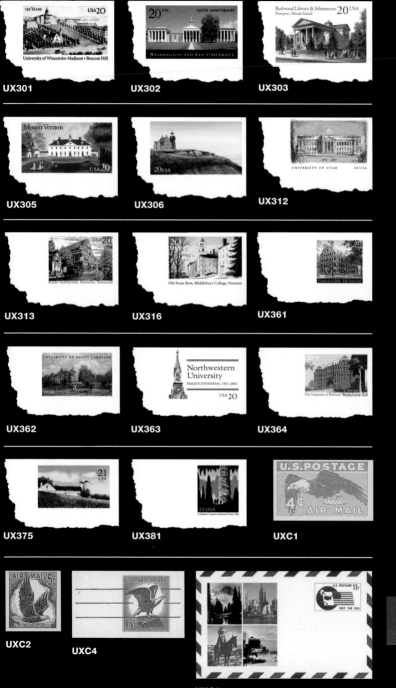

UX301

UX302

UX303

UX305

UX306

UX312

UX313

UX316

UX361

UX362

UX363

UX364

UX375

UX381

UXC1

UXC2

UXC4

UXC5

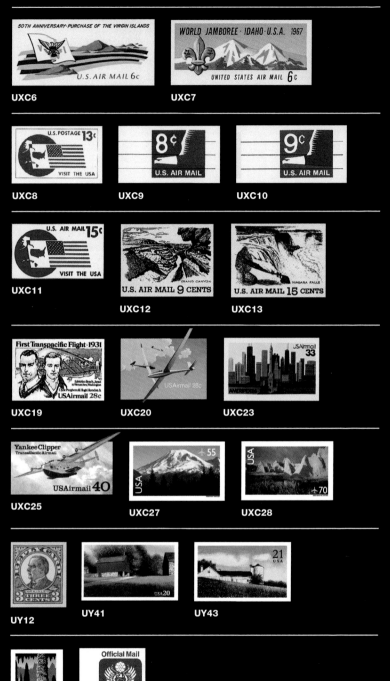

UXC6

UXC7

UXC8

UXC9

UXC10

UXC11

UXC12

UXC13

UXC19

UXC20

UXC23

UXC25

UXC27

UXC28

UY12

UY41

UY43

UY44

UZ6

Issues of 1967-2001		Un	U
UXC6	6¢ Virgin Islands	.75	7.50
a	Red, yellow omitted	1,700.00	
UXC7	6¢ Boy Scout		
	World Jamboree	.75	8.00
UXC8	13¢ blue & red (UXC5)	1.50	20.00
UXC9	8¢ Stylized Eagle	.75	2.50
UXC10	9¢ red & blue (UXC5)	.50	1.25
UXC11	15¢ Travel Service	1.75	35.00
UXC12	9¢ black Grand Canyon	.75	—
UXC13	15¢ black Niagara Falls	.75	75.00
UXC14	11¢ Stylized Eagle	1.00	15.00
UXC15	18¢ Eagle Weather Vane	1.10	15.00
UXC16	21¢ Angel Weather Vane	.85	15.00
UXC17	21¢ Curtiss Jenny	1.00	10.00
UXC18	21¢ Olympic Gymnast	1.25	15.00
UXC19	28¢ First Transpacific Flight	1.00	10.00
UXC20	28¢ Gliders	1.00	10.00
UXC21	28¢ Olympic Speed Skater	1.00	10.00
UXC22	33¢ China Clipper	1.00	10.00
UXC23	33¢ AMERIPEX '86	1.00	10.00
UXC24	36¢ DC-3	.85	10.00
UXC25	40¢ Yankee Clipper	.90	10.00
UXC27	55¢ Mt. Rainier	1.25	10.00
UXC28	70¢ Badlands	1.40	1.50

Issues of 1892-2002		Un	U
Paid Reply Postal Cards			
Prices are: Un=unsevered,			
U=severed card.			
UY1	1¢ + 1¢ black Grant	37.50	9.00
UY6	1¢ + 1¢ green G. and M.		
	Washington, double		
	frame line around		
	instructions	160.00	25.00
UY7	1¢ + 1¢ green G. and M.		
	Washington, single		
	frame line	1.25	.50
UY12	3¢ + 3¢ red McKinley	10.00	25.00
UY18	4¢ + 4¢ Lincoln	3.00	2.50
UY23	6¢ + 6¢ John Adams	1.00	2.00
UY31	"A" (12¢ + 12¢) Eagle	1.00	2.00
UY39	15¢ + 15¢ Bison and Prairie	.75	1.00
UY40	19¢ + 19¢ Flag	.80	1.00
UY41	20¢ Red Barn	.80	1.25
UY43	21¢ White Barn	.90	1.25
UY44	23¢ Carlsbad Caverns	1.00	1.25
Issues of 1913-95			
Official Mail Postal Cards			
UZ1	1¢ black Numeral	500.00	300.00
UZ2	13¢ blue Great Seal	.75	65.00
UZ3	14¢ blue Great Seal	.75	65.00
UZ4	15¢ blue Great Seal	.75	65.00
UZ5	19¢ blue Great Seal	.70	65.00
UZ6	20¢ Official Mail	.60	65.00

Babe Zaharias (1911-1956)

Mildred Ella Didrickson, the daughter of Norwegian immigrants, earned her nickname "Babe"—she reminded everyone of Babe Ruth—on a sandlot baseball diamond. A high school basketball star, she played semiprofessional basketball while working for the team's sponsor. A three-time All-American, Didrickson led the team to a national championship. In 1932 she single-handedly won the team title at the Amateur Athletic Union games and at the Olympic Games that same year, she broke 3 world records, winning 2 gold medals and 1 silver medal. The Associated Press voted her Woman Athlete of the Year. In 1933 she started her golfing career. She won every major golf tournament at least once and was the first American to win the British Women's Amateur Championship. No one has ever matched her record of 17 consecutive wins. In 1938 she married professional wrestler George Zaharias and began to compete as Babe Zaharias. A founder of the Ladies Professional Golf Association, she was also its top money-winner for several years. In 1950 the Associated Press voted her Woman Athlete of the Half-Century. ■

American Commemorative Cancellations

The Postal Service offers American Commemorative Cancellations (formerly known as Souvenir Pages) for new stamps. The series began with a page for the Yellowstone Park Centennial stamp issued March 1, 1972. The pages feature one or more stamps tied by the first day cancel, along with technical data and information on the subject of the issue. More than just collectors' items, American Commemorative Cancellations make wonderful show and conversation pieces. These pages are issued in limited editions. Number in parentheses ( ) indicates the number of stamps on page if there are more than one.

The identifying numbers used below are based on the Postal Service's numbering system for American Commemorative Cancellations; therefore, they do not follow the Scott numbering system.

1972

72-00	Family Planning	400.00
72-01	Yellowstone Park	80.00
72-01a	Yellowstone Park with DC cancel	—
72-02	2¢ Cape Hatteras	65.00
72-03	14¢ Fiorello LaGuardia	65.00
72-04	11¢ City of Refuge Park	70.00
72-05	6¢ Wolf Trap Farm Park	22.50
72-06	Colonial Craftsmen (4)	12.50
72-07	15¢ Mount McKinley	17.50
72-08	6¢-15¢ Olympic Games (4)	9.00
72-08E	Olympic Games with broken red circle on 6¢ stamp	—
72-09	PTA	4.50
72-10	Wildlife Conservation (4)	6.00
72-11	Mail Order	4.50
72-12	Osteopathic Medicine	4.50
72-13	Tom Sawyer	6.00
72-14	7¢ Benjamin Franklin	4.75
72-15	Christmas (2)	5.50
72-16	Pharmacy	6.00
72-17	Stamp Collecting	4.50

1973

73-01	$1 Eugene O'Neill	10.00
73-01E	$1 Eugene O'Neill picture perf. error	—
73-02	Love	5.50
73-03	Pamphleteer Printing	3.50
73-04	George Gershwin	4.50
73-05	Broadside	4.50
73-06	Copernicus	4.25
73-07	Postal Employees	4.75
73-08	Harry S. Truman	3.75
73-09	Post Rider	4.50
73-10	21¢ Amadeo Gianninni	3.50
73-11	Boston Tea Party (4)	4.75
73-12	6¢-15¢ Electronics (4)	5.75
73-13	Robinson Jeffers	3.50
73-14	Lyndon B. Johnson	2.75
73-15	Henry O. Tanner	4.00
73-16	Willa Cather	3.25
73-17	Colonial Drummer	3.25
73-18	Angus Cattle	2.75
73-19	Christmas (2)	5.50
73-20	13¢ Winged Envelope airmail	2.00
73-21	10¢ Crossed Flags	2.25
73-22	10¢ Jefferson Memorial	3.50
73-23	13¢ Winged Envelope airmail coil (2)	2.00

1974

74-01	26¢ Mount Rushmore airmail	4.00
74-02	ZIP Code	3.25
74-02E	ZIP Code with date error 4/4/74	—
74-03	18¢ Statue of Liberty airmail	4.50
74-04	18¢ Elizabeth Blackwell	2.00
74-05	VFW	2.50
74-06	Robert Frost	3.50
74-07	Expo '74	4.00
74-08	Horse Racing	4.00
74-09	Skylab	4.50
74-10	UPU (8)	4.75
74-11	Mineral Heritage (4)	4.75
74-12	Fort Harrod	2.25
74-13	Continental Congress (4)	3.50
74-14	Chautauqua	2.50
74-15	Kansas Wheat	1.90
74-16	Energy Conservation	2.00
74-17	6.3¢ Liberty Bell coil (2)	2.25
74-18	Sleepy Hollow	3.00
74-19	Retarded Children	2.00
74-20	Christmas (3)	4.25

1975

75-01	Benjamin West	2.25
75-02	Pioneer/Jupiter	5.00
75-03	Collective Bargaining	2.25
75-04	8¢ Sybil Ludington	2.25
75-05	Salem Poor	3.00
75-06	Haym Salomon	2.25
75-07	18¢ Peter Francisco	2.25
75-08	Mariner 10	4.25
75-09	Lexington & Concord	2.50
75-10	Paul Dunbar	3.00
75-11	D.W. Griffith	2.50
75-12	Bunker Hill	2.50
75-13	Military Uniforms (4)	5.00
75-14	Apollo Soyuz (2)	5.00
75-15	International Women's Year	2.00
75-16	Postal Service Bicentennial (4)	3.00
75-17	World Peace Through Law	2.00
75-18	Banking & Commerce (2)	3.00
75-19	Christmas (2)	3.00
75-20	3¢ Francis Parkman	2.50
75-21	11¢ Printing Press	1.75
75-22	24¢ Old North Church	1.90

75-23	Flag over Independence Hall (2)	2.00
75-24	9¢ Freedom to Assemble (2)	1.75
75-25	Liberty Bell coil (2)	2.00
75-26	Eagle & Shield	2.50

1976

76-01	Spirit of '76 (3)	3.25
76-01E	Spirit of '76 with cancellation error Jan. 2, 1976 (3)	—
76-02	25¢ and 31¢ Plane and Globes airmails (2)	2.25
76-03	Interphil '76	2.50
76-04	State Flags, DE to VA (10)	5.50
76-05	State Flags, NY to MS (10)	5.50
76-06	State Flags, IL to WI (10)	5.50
76-07	State Flags, CA to SD (10)	5.50
76-08	State Flags, MT to HI (10)	5.50
76-09	9¢ Freedom to Assemble coil (2)	1.75
76-10	Telephone Centennial	1.75
76-11	Commercial Aviation	1.75
76-12	Chemistry	1.75
76-13	7.9¢ Drum coil (2)	1.90
76-14	Benjamin Franklin	1.75
76-15	Bicentennial souvenir sheet	7.00
76-15E	13¢ Bicentennial souvenir sheet with perforation and numerical errors	7.00
76-16	18¢ Bicentennial souvenir sheet	7.00
76-17	24¢ Bicentennial souvenir sheet	7.00
76-18	31¢ Bicentennial souvenir sheet	7.00
76-19	Declaration of Independence (4)	3.50
76-20	Olympics (4)	3.50
76-21	Clara Maass	2.75
76-22	Adolph S. Ochs	2.25
76-23	Christmas (3)	2.25
76-24	7.7¢ Saxhorns coil (2)	1.75

1977

77-01	Washington at Princeton	1.75
77-02	Flag over Capitol booklet pane (9¢ and 13¢)	

	Perf. 10 (8)	14.00
77-03	Sound Recording	2.00
77-04	Pueblo Pottery (4)	3.00
77-05	Lindbergh Flight	2.25
77-06	Colorado Centennial	1.90
77-07	Butterflies (4)	2.25
77-08	Lafayette	1.50
77-09	Skilled Hands (4)	2.25
77-10	Peace Bridge	1.60
77-11	Battle of Oriskany	1.60
77-12	Alta, CA, First Civil Settlement	1.60
77-13	Articles of Confederation	1.60
77-14	Talking Pictures	2.00
77-15	Surrender at Saratoga	2.25
77-16	Energy (2)	1.60
77-17	Christmas, Mailbox and Christmas, Valley Forge, Omaha cancel (2)	1.60
77-18	Same, Valley Forge cancel	—
77-19	10¢ Petition for Redress coil (2)	2.25
77-20	10¢ Petition for Redress sheet (2)	2.25
77-21	1¢-4¢ Americana (5)	2.00

1978

78-01	Carl Sandburg	2.00
78-02	Indian Head Penny	2.00
78-03	Captain Cook, Anchorage cancel (2)	2.00
78-04	Captain Cook, Honolulu cancel (2)	2.00
78-05	Harriet Tubman	3.00
78-06	American Quilts (4)	2.50
78-07	16¢ Statue of Liberty sheet and coil (2)	1.90
78-08	29¢ Sandy Hook Lighthouse	1.90
78-09	American Dance (4)	2.75
78-10	French Alliance	1.90
78-11	Early Cancer Detection	2.25
78-12	"A" (15¢) sheet and coil (2)	3.25
78-13	Jimmie Rodgers	3.00
78-14	CAPEX '78 (8)	5.50
78-15	Oliver Wendell Holmes coil	3.50
78-16	Photography	1.90
78-17	Fort McHenry Flag sheet and coil (2)	2.00

78-18	George M. Cohan	1.60
78-19	Rose booklet single	2.00
78-20	8.4¢ Piano coil (2)	2.00
78-21	Viking Missions	3.75
78-22	28¢ Ft. Nisqually	2.00
78-23	American Owls (4)	2.50
78-24	31¢ Wright Brothers airmails (2)	2.50
78-25	American Trees (4)	2.75
78-26	Christmas, Madonna	2.00
78-27	Christmas, Hobby Horse	2.00
78-28	$2 Kerosene Lamp	4.50

1979

79-01	Robert F. Kennedy	2.00
79-02	Martin Luther King, Jr.	3.50
79-03	International Year of the Child	2.00
79-04	John Steinbeck	2.50
79-05	Albert Einstein	3.00
79-06	21¢ Octave Chanute airmails (2)	2.50
79-07	Pennsylvania Toleware (4)	2.50
79-08	American Architecture (4)	2.25
79-09	Endangered Flora (4)	2.50
79-10	Seeing Eye Dogs	1.90
79-11	Candle & Holder	3.50
79-12	Special Olympics	1.90
79-13	$5 Lantern	9.00
79-14	30¢ Schoolhouse	2.50
79-15	10¢ Summer Olympics (2)	2.25
79-16	50¢ Whale Oil Lamp	3.00
79-17	John Paul Jones	2.00
79-18	Summer Olympics (4)	3.75
79-19	Christmas, Madonna	2.25
79-20	Christmas, Santa Claus	2.50
79-21	3.1¢ Guitar coil (2)	3.50
79-22	31¢ Summer Olympics airmail	3.00
79-23	Will Rogers	2.25
79-24	Vietnam Veterans	2.75
79-25	25¢ Wiley Post airmails (2)	3.00

1980

80-01	W.C. Fields	2.75
80-02	Winter Olympics (4)	3.50

85-49	Christmas, Madonna	1.50
85-50	Christmas, Poinsettias	2.50
85-51	18¢ Washington/ Washington Monument coil (2)	2.25

1986

86-01	Arkansas Statehood	1.50
86-02	25¢ Jack London	1.50
86-03	Stamp Collecting booklet pane (4)	3.00
86-04	Love	2.00
86-05	Sojourner Truth	2.50
86-06	5¢ Hugo L. Black (5)	2.25
86-07	Republic of Texas (2)	1.75
86-08	$2 William Jennings Bryan	2.25
86-09	Fish booklet pane (5)	3.00
86-10	Public Hospitals	1.50
86-11	Duke Ellington	3.25
86-12	Presidents, Washington- Harrison (9)	3.75
86-13	Presidents, Tyler-Grant (9)	3.75
86-14	Presidents, Hayes-Wilson (9)	3.75
86-15	Presidents, Harding- Johnson (9)	3.75
86-16	Polar Explorers (4)	2.75
86-17	17¢ Belva Ann Lockwood (2)	1.50
86-18	1¢ Margaret Mitchell (3)	2.50
86-19	Statue of Liberty	2.25
86-20	4¢ Father Flanagan (3)	1.60
86-21	17¢ Dog Sled coil (2)	2.25
86-22	56¢ John Harvard	2.00
86-23	Navajo Blankets (4)	2.75
86-24	3¢ Paul Dudley White, MD (8)	1.50
86-25	$1 Bernard Revel	1.75
86-26	T.S. Eliot	2.50
86-27	Wood-Carved Figurines (4)	2.75
86-28	Christmas, Madonna	1.75
86-29	Christmas, Village Scene	1.75
86-30	5.5¢ Star Route Truck coil (4)	3.00
86-31	25¢ Bread Wagon coil	3.00

1987

87-01	8.5¢ Tow Truck coil (5)	1.50
87-02	Michigan Statehood	2.50
87-03	Pan American Games	2.50
87-04	Love	2.00
87-05	7.1¢ Tractor coil (5)	2.50
87-06	14¢ Julia Ward Howe (2)	1.50
87-07	Jean Baptiste Pointe Du Sable	4.00
87-08	Enrico Caruso	2.25
87-09	2¢ Mary Lyon (3)	1.50
87-10	Reengraved 2¢ Locomotive coil (6)	2.25
87-11	Girl Scouts	3.50
87-12	10¢ Canal Boat coil (5)	1.75
87-13	Special Occasions booklet pane (10)	3.75
87-14	United Way	1.50
87-15	Flag with Fireworks	1.50
87-16	Flag over Capitol coil, prephosphored paper (2)	2.25
87-17	Wildlife, Swallow- Squirrel (10)	4.00
87-18	Wildlife, Armadillo- Rabbit (10)	4.00
87-19	Wildlife, Tanager- Ladybug (10)	4.00
87-20	Wildlife, Beaver- Prairie Dog (10)	4.00
87-21	Wildlife, Turtle-Fox (10)	4.00
87-22	Delaware Statehood	2.00
87-23	U.S./Morocco Friendship	1.50
87-24	William Faulkner	1.50
87-25	Lacemaking (4)	3.50
87-26	10¢ Red Cloud (3)	1.75
87-27	$5 Bret Harte	8.00
87-28	Pennsylvania Statehood	1.50
87-29	Drafting of the Constitution booklet pane (5)	2.50
87-30	New Jersey Statehood	1.75
87-31	Signing of Constitution	1.50
87-32	Certified Public Accountants	3.25

87-33	5¢ Milk Wagon and 17.5¢ Racing Car coils (4)	2.75
87-34	Locomotives booklet pane (5)	6.75
87-35	Christmas, Madonna	1.50
87-36	Christmas, Ornaments	1.50
87-37	Flag with Fireworks booklet-pair	2.25

1988

88-01	Georgia Statehood	1.75
88-02	Connecticut Statehood	1.75
88-03	Winter Olympics	1.75
88-04	Australia Bicentennial	1.75
88-05	James Weldon Johnson	2.75
88-06	Cats (4)	3.75
88-07	Massachusetts Statehood	2.25
88-08	Maryland Statehood	2.25
88-09	3¢ Conestoga Wagon coil (8)	2.50
88-10	Knute Rockne	5.00
88-11	"E" (25¢) Earth sheet and coil (3)	2.75
88-12	"E" (25¢) Earth booklet pane (10)	3.25
88-13	"E" (25¢) Penalty Mail coil (2)	2.25
88-14	44¢ New Sweden airmail	1.75
88-15	Pheasant booklet pane (10)	3.25
88-16	Jack London booklet pane (6)	2.25
88-17	Jack London booklet pane (10)	4.25
88-18	Flag with Clouds	1.50
88-19	45¢ Samuel Langley airmail	1.75
88-19A	20¢ Penalty Mail coil (2)	1.75
88-20	Flag over Yosemite coil (2)	1.75
88-21	South Carolina Statehood	1.50
88-22	Owl & Grosbeak booklet pane (10)	3.00
88-23	15¢ Buffalo Bill Cody (2)	1.75
88-24	15¢ and 25¢ Penalty Mail coils (4)	2.25
88-25	Francis Ouimet	4.00
88-26	45¢ Harvey Cushing, MD	1.50
88-27	New Hampshire Statehood	1.75

88-28	36¢ Igor Sikorsky airmail	2.00
88-29	Virginia Statehood	2.00
88-30	10.1¢ Oil Wagon coil, precancel (3)	2.25
88-31	Love	2.00
88-32	Flag with Clouds booklet pane (6)	3.00
88-33	16.7¢ Popcorn Wagon coil (2)	2.50
88-34	15¢ Tugboat coil (2)	2.50
88-35	13.2¢ Coal Car coil (2)	2.75
88-36	New York Statehood	2.00
88-37	45¢ Love	1.75
88-38	8.4¢ Wheelchair coil (3)	2.50
88-39	21¢ Railroad Mail Car coil (2)	3.00
88-40	Summer Olympics	1.75
88-41	Classic Cars booklet pane (5)	3.75
88-42	7.6¢ Carreta coil (4)	2.25
88-43	Honeybee coil (2)	3.00
88-44	Antarctic Explorers (4)	2.75
88-45	5.3¢ Elevator coil (5)	2.25
88-46	20.5¢ Fire Engine coil (2)	3.00
88-47	Carousel Animals (4)	3.00
88-48	$8.75 Eagle	15.00
88-49	Christmas, Madonna	1.50
88-50	Christmas, Snow Scene	1.50
88-51	21¢ Chester Carlson	1.50
88-52	Special Occasions booklet pane (6), Love You, Thinking of You	9.25
88-53	Special Occasions booklet pane (6), Happy Birthday, Best Wishes	14.00
88-54	24.1¢ Tandem Bicycle coil (2)	2.50
88-55	20¢ Cable Car coil (2)	2.50
88-56	13¢ Patrol Wagon coil (2)	2.75
88-57	23¢ Mary Cassatt	1.50
88-58	65¢ H.H. "Hap" Arnold	2.25

1989

89-01	Montana Statehood	2.00
89-02	A. Philip Randolph	3.00
89-03	Flag over Yosemite coil, prephosphored paper (2)	1.75
89-04	North Dakota Statehood	1.50
89-05	Washington Statehood	1.50
89-06	Steamboats booklet pane (5)	3.50
89-07	World Stamp Expo '89	1.50
89-08	Arturo Toscanini	2.00
89-09	U.S. House of Representatives	1.50
89-10	U.S. Senate	1.50
89-11	Executive Branch	1.50
89-12	South Dakota Statehood	1.50
89-13	7.1¢ Tractor coil, precancel (4)	2.25
89-14	$1 Johns Hopkins	2.25
89-15	Lou Gehrig	10.00
89-16	1¢ Penalty Mail	2.25
89-17	45¢ French Revolution airmail	2.25
89-18	Ernest Hemingway	2.50
89-19	$2.40 Moon Landing	11.00
89-20	North Carolina Statehood	2.00
89-21	Letter Carriers	1.50
89-22	28¢ Sitting Bull	1.75
89-23	Drafting of the Bill of Rights	1.50
89-24	Prehistoric Animals (4)	5.50
89-25	25¢ and 45¢ PUAS/ America (2)	2.00
89-26	Christmas, Madonna	4.25
89-27	Christmas, Antique Sleigh	4.25
89-28	Eagle and Shield, self-adhesive	1.75
89-29	World Stamp Expo '89 souvenir sheet	7.00
89-30	Classic Mail Transportation (4)	2.75
89-31	Future Mail Transportation souvenir sheet	3.25
89-32	45¢ Future Mail Transportation airmails (4)	3.25
89-33	Classic Mail Transportation souvenir sheet	3.50

1990

90-01	Idaho Statehood	1.50
90-02	Love sheet and booklet pane (10)	3.00
90-03	Ida B. Wells	3.00
90-04	U.S. Supreme Court	1.50
90-05	15¢ Beach Umbrella booklet pane (10)	3.00
90-06	5¢ Luis Muñoz Marín (5)	2.00
90-07	Wyoming Statehood	2.25
90-08	Classic Films (4)	4.25
90-09	Marianne Moore	1.50
90-10	$1 Seaplane coil (2)	5.00
90-11	Lighthouses booklet pane (5)	5.00
90-12	Plastic Flag stamp	2.75
90-13	Rhode Island Statehood	2.00
90-14	$2 Bobcat	4.00
90-15	Olympians (5)	4.75
90-16	Indian Headdresses booklet pane (10)	5.50
90-17	5¢ Circus Wagon coil (5)	3.25
90-18	40¢ Claire Lee Chennault	2.50
90-19	Federated States of Micronesia/ Marshall Islands (2)	2.25
90-20	Creatures of the Sea (4)	4.75
90-21	25¢ and 45¢ PUAS/America (2)	2.25
90-22	Dwight D. Eisenhower	2.50
90-23	Christmas, Madonna, sheet and booklet pane (10)	5.00
90-24	Christmas, Yule Tree, sheet and booklet pane (10)	5.00

1991

91-01	"F" (29¢) Flower sheet and coil (3)	2.50
91-02	"F" (29¢) Flower booklet panes (20)	8.00
91-03	4¢ Makeup	2.00
91-04	"F" (29¢) ATM booklet single	2.75
91-05	"F" (29¢) Penalty Mail coil (2)	2.50
91-06	4¢ Steam Carriage coil (7)	2.25
91-07	50¢ Switzerland	2.25
91-08	Vermont Statehood	2.50
91-09	19¢ Fawn (2)	2.25
91-10	Flag over Mount Rushmore coil (2)	2.25
91-11	35¢ Dennis Chavez	2.75
91-12	Flower sheet and booklet pane (10)	8.00
91-13	4¢ Penalty Mail (8)	2.00
91-14	Wood Duck booklet panes (10)	9.50
91-15	23¢ Lunch Wagon coil (2)	2.25
91-16	Flag with Olympic Rings booklet pane (10)	5.00
91-17	50¢ Harriet Quimby	2.25
91-18	Savings Bond	2.00
91-19	Love sheet and booklet pane, 52¢ Love (12)	6.00
91-20	19¢ Balloon booklet pane (10)	4.00
91-21	40¢ William Piper airmail	2.25
91-22	William Saroyan	2.50
91-23	Penalty Mail coil and 19¢ and 23¢ sheet (4)	2.50
91-24	5¢ Canoe and 10¢ Tractor Trailer coils (4)	2.25
91-25	Flags on Parade	2.50
91-26	Fishing Flies booklet pane (5)	5.25
91-27	52¢ Hubert H. Humphrey	2.00
91-28	Cole Porter	2.25
91-29	50¢ Antarctic Treaty airmail	2.75
91-30	1¢ Kestrel, 3¢ Bluebird and 30¢ Cardinal (3)	2.25
91-31	Torch ATM booklet single	2.50

91-32	Desert Shield/ Desert Storm sheet and booklet pane (11)	5.00
91-33	Flag over Mount Rushmore coil, gravure printing (darker, 3)	2.50
91-34	Summer Olympics (5)	4.00
91-35	Flower coil, slit perforations (3)	2.25
91-36	Numismatics	2.50
91-37	Basketball	5.25
91-38	through 91-47 are unassigned	
91-48	19¢ Fishing Boat coil (3)	2.50
91-49	Comedians booklet pane (10)	5.25
91-50	World War II miniature sheet (10)	6.50
91-51	District of Columbia	2.25
91-52	Jan Matzeliger	4.00
91-53	$1 USPS/ Olympic Logo	3.00
91-54	Space Exploration booklet pane (10)	6.75
91-55	50¢ PUASP/America airmail	2.25
91-56	Christmas, Madonna sheet and booklet pane (10)	5.00
91-57	Christmas, Santa Claus sheet and booklet pane (11)	11.00
91-58	5¢ Canoe coil, gravure printing (red, 6)	3.00
91-59	29¢ Eagle and Shield, self-adhesive (3)	4.00
91-60	23¢ Flag presort	2.50
91-61	$9.95 Express Mail	22.50
91-62	$2.90 Priority Mail	7.50
91-63	$14.00 Express Mail International	30.00

1992

92-01	Winter Olympic Games (5)	3.75
92-02	World Columbian Stamp Expo '92	2.50
92-03	W.E.B. DuBois	3.75
92-04	Love	2.50

92-05	75¢ Wendell Willkie	2.25
92-06	29¢ Flower coil, round perforations (2)	2.50
92-07	Earl Warren	3.00
92-08	Olympic Baseball	10.00
92-09	Flag over White House, coil (2)	2.50
92-10	First Voyage of Christopher Columbus (4)	3.75
92-11	New York Stock Exchange	2.50
92-12	Christopher Columbus	3.75
92-13	Columbus- Seeking Royal Support (3)	7.50
92-14	Columbus- First Sighting of Land (3)	7.50
92-15	Columbus- Claiming New World (3)	7.50
92-16	Columbus- Reporting Discoveries (3)	7.50
92-17	Columbus- Royal Favor Restored (3)	7.50
92-18	Space Adventures (4)	4.00
92-19	Alaska Highway	2.50
92-20	Kentucky Statehood	2.50
92-21	Summer Olympic Games (5)	3.75
92-22	Hummingbirds booklet pane (5)	5.00
92-22A	23¢ Presort USA (3)	2.50
92-23	Wildflowers (10)	6.50
92-24	Wildflowers (10)	6.50
92-25	Wildflowers (10)	6.50
92-26	Wildflowers (10)	6.50
92-27	Wildflowers (10)	6.50
92-28	World War II miniature sheet (10)	6.00
92-29	29¢ Variable Rate	2.75
92-30	Dorothy Parker	2.75
92-31	Theodore von Karman	3.50
92-32	Pledge of Allegiance (10)	7.00
92-33	Minerals (4)	4.00
92-34	Eagle and Shield (3)	3.75
92-35	Juan Rodriguez Cabrillo	2.50
92-36	Wild Animals booklet pane (5)	5.00
92-37	23¢ Presort (3)	2.75

92-38	Christmas Contemporary, sheet and booklet pane (8)	7.50
92-39	Christmas Traditional, sheet and booklet pane (11)	5.50
92-40	Pumpkinseed Sunfish	2.75
92-41	Circus Wagon	2.75
92-42	Year of the Rooster	7.75

1993

93-01	Elvis	10.00
93-02	Space Fantasy (5)	6.00
93-03	Percy Lavon Julian	3.50
93-04	Oregon Trail	2.75
93-05	World University Games	2.75
93-06	Grace Kelly	6.00
93-07	Oklahoma!	2.25
93-08	Circus	4.50
93-09	Thomas Jefferson	2.75
93-10	Cherokee Strip	3.50
93-11	Dean Acheson	3.00
93-12	Sporting Horses	5.50
93-13	USA Coil	2.50
93-14	Garden Flowers, booklet pane (5)	3.50
93-15	Eagle and Shield, coil	4.00
93-16	World War II miniature sheet (10)	5.50
93-17	Futuristic Space Shuttle	8.00
93-18	Hank Williams, sheet	5.00
93-19	Rock & Roll/ Rhythm & Blues, sheet single, booklet pane (8)	10.00
93-20	Joe Louis	7.50
93-21	Red Squirrel	2.75
93-22	Broadway Musicals, booklet pane (4)	4.50
93-23	National Postal Museum, strip (4)	3.25
93-24	Red Rose	2.50
93-25	American Sign Language, pair	2.75
93-26	Country & Western Music, sheet and booklet pane (4)	9.25
93-27	African Violets, booklet pane (10)	4.25
93-28	10¢ Official Mail	2.75
93-29	Contemporary Christmas, booklet pane (10), sheet and self-adhesive stamps	8.50

93-30	Traditional Christmas, sheet, booklet pane (4)	4.75
93-31	Classic Books, strip (4)	3.25
93-32	Mariana Islands	2.75
93-33	Pine Cone	2.50
93-34	Columbus' Landing in Puerto Rico	3.25
93-35	AIDS Awareness	4.75

1994

94-01	Winter Olympics	5.00
94-02	Edward R. Murrow	3.25
94-03	Love, self-adhesive	3.25
94-04	Dr. Allison Davis	4.50
94-05	29¢ Eagle, self-adhesive	3.50
94-06	Year of the Dog	4.00
94-07	Love, booklet pane (10), single sheet stamp	6.50
94-08	Postage and Mailing Center	5.00
94-09	Buffalo Soldiers	5.00
94-10	Silent Screen Stars	6.00
94-11	Garden Flowers, booklet pane (5)	6.00
94-12	Victory at Saratoga	4.75
94-13	10¢ Tractor Trailer gravure printing	5.00
94-14	World Cup Soccer	6.00
94-15	World Cup Soccer souvenir sheet	6.00
94-16	World War II miniature sheet (10)	5.50
94-17	Love, sheet stamp	3.25
94-18	Statue of Liberty	3.50
94-19	Fishing Boat, reissue	3.75
94-20	Norman Rockwell	9.00
94-21	$9.95 and 29¢ Moon Landing	15.00
94-22	Locomotives (5)	6.50
94-23	George Meany	3.25
94-24	$5.00 Washington/ Jackson	10.00
94-25	Popular Singers (5)	6.00
94-26	James Thurber	4.00
94-27	Jazz Singers/ Blues Singers (10)	9.00
94-28	Wonders of the Sea (4)	5.00

94-29	Chinese/Joint Issue (2)	4.00
94-30	Holiday Traditional (10)	8.50
94-31	Holiday Contemporary (4)	6.50
94-32	Holiday, self-adhesive	7.00
94-33	20¢ Virginia Apgar	4.50
94-34	BEP Centennial	15.00
94-35	Year of the Boar	4.50
94-G1	G1 (4) Rate Change	4.00
94-G2	G2 (6) Rate Change	4.00
94-G3	G3 (5) Rate Change	4.00
94-G4	G4 (2) Rate Change	8.00
94-36	Legends of West	12.00

1995

95-01	Love (2)	3.00
95-02	Florida State	2.75
95-03	Butte (7)	5.50
95-04	Automobile (4)	6.00
95-05	Flag Over Field, self-adhesive	2.75
95-06	Juke Box (2+2)	3.00
95-07	Tail Fin (2+2)	4.50
95-08	Circus Wagon (7)	5.00
95-09	Kids Care (4)	3.50
95-10	Richard Nixon	3.50
95-11	Bessie Coleman	4.50
95-12	Official Mail	3.00
95-13	Kestrel with cent sign	6.00
95-14	Love 1 oz. and 2 oz.	6.00
95-15	Flag Over Porch	5.50
95-16	Recreational Sports (5)	9.00
95-17	POW & MIA	4.50
95-18	Marilyn Monroe	12.00
95-19	Pink Rose	5.00
95-20	Ferry Boat (3)	4.00
95-21	Cog Railway Car (3)	4.00
95-22	Blue Jay (10)	6.00
95-23	Texas Statehood	4.00
95-24	Great Lake Lighthouses (5)	9.00
95-25	Challenger Shuttle	10.00
95-26	United Nations	2.75
95-27	Civil War (front and back)	14.00
95-28	Peach & Pear	4.50
95-29	Alice Hamilton	2.75
95-30	Carousel Horses	5.25
95-31	Endeavor Shuttle	22.50
95-32	Alice Paul	2.75
95-33	Women's Suffrage	2.75

95-34	Louis Armstrong	4.50
95-35	World War II	6.00
95-36	Milton Hershey	2.75
95-37	Jazz Musicians	7.00
95-38	Fall Garden Flowers (5)	6.00
95-39	Eddie Rickenbacker (airmail)	4.50
95-40	Republic of Palau	3.50
95-41	Holiday Contemporary/ Santa (4)	3.50
95-42	American Comic Strips	15.00
95-43	Naval Academy	4.50
95-44	Tennessee Williams	4.50
95-45	Holiday Children Sledding	4.75
95-46	Holiday Traditional sheet and booklet pane (10)	5.50
95-47	Holiday Midnight Angel	4.75
95-48	Ruth Bendict	3.25
95-49	James K. Polk	7.00
95-50	Antique Automobiles, strip (5)	6.00

1996

96-01	Utah Statehood	3.50
96-02	Garden Flowers	6.00
96-03	Love/Kestrel	16.00
96-04	Postage and Mailing Center (3)	5.00
96-05	Ernest E. Just	5.00
96-06	Woodpecker	6.00
96-07	Smithsonian Institution	3.75
96-08	Year of the Rat	6.00
96-09	Pioneers of Communication	7.00
96-10	Fulbright Scholarships	3.75
96-11	Jacqueline Cochran	3.75
96-12	Mountain	10.00
96-13	Bluebird	3.75
96-14	Marathon	3.75
96-15	Flag over Porch/ Eagle & Shield	4.50
96-16	Cal Farley	3.25
96-17	Classic Olympic Collection	8.00
96-18	Georgia O'Keefe Art	4.75
96-19	Tennessee	3.75
96-20	American Indian Dances	4.75
96-21	Prehistoric Animals	4.75
96-22	Breast Cancer Awareness	4.75

96-23	Flag over Porch/ Juke Box/Butte/ Tail Fin Automobile/ Mountain	9.00
96-24	James Dean	6.00
96-25	Folk Heroes	5.00
96-26	Olympic/Discus	5.00
96-27	Iowa	5.00
96-28	Blue Jay	5.00
96-29	Rural Free Delivery	4.00
96-30	Riverboats	5.50
96-31	Big Band Leaders	6.00
96-32	Songwriters	6.00
96-33	F. Scott Fitzgerald	4.00
96-34	Endangered Species	15.00
96-35	Computer Technology	4.00
96-36	Holiday Family Scenes	7.50
96-37	Skaters	6.00
96-38	Hanukkah	5.00
96-39	Madonna and Child	6.00
96-40	Yellow Rose	6.00
96-41	Cycling	6.00

1997

97-01	Year of the Ox	6.00
97-02	Flag Over Porch/ Juke Box/ Mountain	5.50
97-03	Benjamin O. Davis Sr.	6.00
97-04	Statue of Liberty	5.50
97-05	Love Swans	5.50
97-06	Helping Children Learn	5.00
97-07	Merian Botanical Plants	5.50
97-08	Pacific 97 - Stagecoach and Ship	6.00
97-09	Linerless Flag Over Porch/ Juke Box	5.50
97-10	Thornton Wilder	5.00
97-11	Raoul Wallenberg	5.00
97-12	Dinosaurs	12.50
97-13	Pacific '97 - Franklin	10.00
97-14	Pacific '97 - Washington	10.00
97-15	Bugs Bunny	10.00
97-16	The Marshall Plan	5.00
97-17	Humphrey Bogart	6.00
97-18	Classic Aircraft	12.50
97-19	Classic American Dolls	10.00
97-20	Football Coaches	10.00
97-20A	George Halas	8.00
97-20B	Vince Lombardi	8.00
97-20C	Pop Warner	8.00
97-20D	Bear Bryant	8.00

97-21	Yellow Rose	7.00
97-22	"Stars and Stripes Forever"	6.00
97-23	Padre Félix Varela	6.00
97-24	Composers and Conductors	9.00
97-25	Opera Singers	8.00
97-26	Air Force	8.00
97-27	Movie Monsters	10.00
97-28	Supersonic Flight	8.00
97-29	Women in Military	6.00
97-30	Kwanzaa	7.50
97-31	Holiday Traditional, Madonna and Child	7.50
97-32	Holly	7.50
97-33	Mars Pathfinder	12.00

1998

98-01	Year of the Tiger	6.00
98-02	Winter Sports	6.00
98-03	Madam C. J. Walker	6.00
98-03A	Celebrate The Century® 1900s	10.00
98-03B	Celebrate The Century® 1910s	10.00
98-04	"Remember the Maine"	6.00
98-05	Flowering Trees	8.00
98-06	Alexander Calder	8.00
98-07	Henry R. Luce	5.50
98-08	Cinco De Mayo	6.00
98-09	Sylvester & Tweety	6.00
98-09A	Celebrate The Century® 1920s	10.00
98-10	Wisconsin	6.00
98-11	Trans-Mississippi Reissue of 1898	10.00
98-12	Trans-Mississippi (single stamp)	6.00
98-13	Folk Musicians	8.00
98-14	Berlin Airlift	5.50
98-15	Diner/Wetlands coil	5.50
98-16	Spanish Settlement of the Southwest	6.00
98-17	Gospel Singers	7.50
98-18	The Wallaces	5.50
98-19	Stephen Vincent Benet	6.00
98-20	Tropical Birds	8.00
98-21	Breast Cancer Research (semi-postal)	6.00
98-22	Ring-Neck Pheasant	7.00
98-23	Alfred Hitchcock	6.00

98-24	Organ Donations	6.00
98-24A	Red Fox	7.00
98-24B	Green Bicycle coil	6.00
98-25	Bright Eyes	7.50
98-26	Klondike Gold Rush	6.00
98-26A	Celebrate The Century® 1930s	10.00
98-27	American Art	10.00
98-28	Ballet	6.00
98-28A	Diner coil	5.50
98-29	Space Discovery	7.50
98-30	Philanthropy	6.00
98-31	Holiday Traditional	6.00
98-32	Holiday Contemporary	7.50
98-33	Hat Rate Change "H" Series/ Makeup Rate	10.00
98-34	Uncle Sam — Rate Change	6.00
98-35	Hat Rate Change "H" Series	7.00
98-36	Hat Rate Change "H" Series	7.00
98-37	Mary Breckinridge	4.50
98-38	Space Shuttle Landing	9.00
98-39	Shuttle Piggyback	17.50
98-40	Wetlands non-denominated nonprofit coil and Eagle & Shield non-denominated presort coil	6.50

1999

99-01	Year of the Hare	6.00
99-02	Malcolm X	6.00
99-03	33¢ Victorian — Love	6.00
99-04	55¢ Victorian — Love	6.50
99-05	Hospice Care	6.00
99-06	Celebrate The Century® 1940s	10.00
99-07	City Flag	6.50
99-08	Irish Immigration	6.00
99-09	Alfred Lunt and Lynn Fontanne	6.00
99-10	Arctic Animals	7.50
99-10A	Classroom Flag	6.00
99-11	Nature of America Sonoran Desert	10.00
99-11A	Fruit Berries	7.50
99-12	Daffy Duck	8.00
99-13	Ayn Rand	6.50
99-14	Cinco de Mayo	6.00

99-15	Tropical Flowers	7.50
99-16	Niagara Falls	6.50
99-17	John and William Bartram	6.00
99-18	Celebrate The Century® 1950s	10.00
99-19	Prostate Cancer	6.00
99-20	California Gold Rush	6.00
99-20A	Woodpecker Stamp	—
99-21	Aquarium Fish	7.50
99-22	Xtreme Sports	7.50
99-23	American Glass	7.50
99-24	Justin Morrill	6.00
99-25	James Cagney	7.50
99-26	Billy Mitchell	7.50
99-27	Rio Grande	6.00
99-28	Pink Coral Rose	7.00
99-29	Honoring Those Who Served	6.00
99-29A	UPU	6.00
99-30	All Aboard!	7.50
99-31	Frederick Law Olmsted	6.00
99-32	Hollywood Composers	7.50
99-33	Celebrate The Century® 1960s	10.00
99-34	Broadway Songwriters	7.50
99-35	Insects and Spiders	10.00
99-36	Hanukkah	6.00
99-37	Official Mail	6.00
99-38	Uncle Sam	6.00
99-39	Nato	6.00
99-40	Holiday Traditional, Madonna & Child	6.00
99-41	Holiday Contemporary, Deer	7.50
99-42	Kwanzaa	6.00
99-43	Celebrate The Century® 1970s	10.00
99-44	Kestrel	6.50
99-45 through 99-49 are unassigned		
99-50	Year 2000	6.00

2000

00-01	Year of the Dragon	6.00
00-02	Celebrate The Century® 1980s	10.00
00-03	Grand Canyon	6.00
00-04	Patricia Roberts Harris	6.00
00-05	Fruit Berries	6.00
00-06	U.S. Navy Submarine – *Los Angeles* Class	6.00

00-07	Pacific Coast Rain Forest	10.00
00-08	Louise Nevelson	7.50
00-09	Coral Pink Rose	—
00-10	Edwin Powell Hubble	7.50
00-11	American Somoa	6.00
00-12	Library of Congress	6.00
00-13	Wile E. Coyote/ Road Runner	7.50
00-14	Celebrate The Century® 1990s	10.00
00-15	Summer Sports	6.00
00-16	Adoption	6.00
00-17	Youth Team Sports	6.50
00-18	Distinguished Soldiers	—
00-19	The Stars and Stripes	10.00
00-20	Legends of Baseball	10.00
00-21	Stampin' The Future™	6.50
00-22	Joseph Stilwell	6.00
00-23	Claude Pepper	6.00
00-24	California Statehood	6.00
00-25	Edward G. Robinson	6.00
00-26	Deep Sea Creatures	7.50
00-27	Thomas Wolfe	6.00
00-28	White House	6.00
00-29	New York Public Library Lion Presort	6.00

2001

01-01	Farm Flag (1 oz.)	6.00
01-02	Statue of Liberty	NDN
01-03	Flowers	7.50
01-04	Statue of Liberty	6.00
01-05	Love Letters (1 oz.)	6.00
01-06	Year of the Snake	6.00
01-07	Roy Wilkins	6.00
01-08	Washington Monument	20.00
01-09	U.S. Capitol	10.00
01-10	American Illustrators (front & back)	10.00
01-11	Farm Flag (1 oz.)	6.00
01-12	Statute of Liberty	7.50
01-13	Flowers	7.50
01-14	Love Letters (1 oz. & 2 oz.)	7.50
01-15	Hattie Caraway (3 oz.)	6.00
01-16	Bison (2 oz.)	6.00
01-17	George Washington	6.00
01-18	Art Deco Eagle (2 oz.)	6.00

01-19	Official Mail	6.00
01-20	Apple and Orange	6.00
01-21	Nine-Mile Prairie	6.00
01-22	Farm Flag (1 oz.)	6.00
01-23	Diabetes Awareness	6.00
01-24	The Nobel Prize	6.00
01-25	The Pan-American Inverts (front and back)	10.00
01-26	Mt. McKinley (Int'l PC)	7.50
01-27	Great Plains Prairie (front and back)	10.00
01-28	Peanuts	6.00
01-29	Honoring Veterans	6.00
01-30	Acadia National Park	7.50
01-31	Frida Kahlo	6.00
01-32	Baseball's Legendary Playing Fields (front and back)	12.50
01-33	Atlas Statue	6.00
01-34	Leonard Bernstein	6.00
01-35	Woody Wagon	6.00
01-36	Lucille Ball	6.00
01-37	The Amish Quilts	7.50
01-38	Carnivorous Plants	7.50
01-39	Holiday Celebration–Eid	6.00
01-40	Dr. Enrico Fermi	6.00
01-41	Bison (2 oz.)	6.00
01-42	George Washington	6.00
01-43	Art Deco Eagle (2 oz.)	6.00
01-44	"That's All Folks!"	6.00
01-45	Holiday Traditional: Lorenza Costa–Virgin and Child	6.00
01-46	Holiday Contemporary: Santas	7.50
01-47	Holiday Celebration: Thanksgiving	6.00
01-48	James Madison	6.00
01-49	Kwanzaa	6.00
01-50	Hanukkah	6.00
01-51	Farm Flag (1 oz.)	6.00
01-52	Love Letters (2 oz.)	6.00
01-53	United We Stand	7.50

2002

02-01	Winter Sports	—
02-02	Mentoring a Child	—
02-03	Langston Hughes	—
02-04	Happy Birthday	—
02-05	Year of the Horse	—
02-06	U.S. Military Academy	—
02-07	Greetings From America	—
02-08	Longleaf Pine Forest	—
02-09	American Toleware	—
02-10	U.S. Flag	—
02-11	Antique Toys	—
02-12	Star	—
02-13	U.S. Flag	—
02-14	George Washington	—
02-15	Heroes 2001	—
02-16	Masters of American Photography	—
02-17	John James Audubon	—
02-18	Harry Houdini	—
02-19	Eagle Coverlet	—
02-20	Antique Toys	—
02-21	Edna Ferber	—
02-22	Jefferson Memorial	—
02-23	Capitol at Dusk	—
02-24	Official Mail	—
02-25	Andy Warhol	—
02-26	Teddy Bears	—
02-27	Love (1 oz. & 2 oz.)	—
02-28	Ogden Nash	—
02-29	Duke Kahanamoku	—
02-30	American Bats	—
02-31	Women in Journalism	—
02-32	Irving Berlin	—
02-33	Neuter or Spay	—
02-34	Christmas: Gossaert	—
02-35	Eid	—
02-36	Kwanzaa	—
02-37	Hanukkah	—
02-38	Cary Grant	—
02-39	Sea Coast Nonprofit	—
02-40	Hawaiian Missionaries	—
02-41	Happy Birthday	—
02-42	Greetings From America	—
02-43	Holiday: Snowmen	—

Note: Numbers and prices may be changed without notice due to additional USPS stamp issues and/or different information that may become available on older issues.

American Commemorative Panels

The Postal Service offers American Commemorative Panels for each new commemorative stamp and special Holiday and Love stamp issued. The series began in 1972 with the Wildlife Commemorative Panel. The panels feature mint stamps complemented by fine reproductions of steel line engravings and the stories behind the commemorated subjects.

The identifying numbers used below are based on the Postal Service's numbering system for American Commemorative Panels; therefore, they do not follow the Scott numbering system.

1972

1	Wildlife	4.75
2	Mail Order	4.75
3	Osteopathic Medicine	6.50
4	Tom Sawyer	5.00
5	Pharmacy	6.00
6	Christmas, Angels	8.00
7	Santa Claus	8.00
7E	Same with error date (1882)	—
8	Stamp Collecting	5.50

1973

9	Love	6.75
10	Pamphleteers	5.50
11	George Gershwin	6.00
12	Posting a Broadside	5.50
13	Copernicus	5.50
14	Postal Employees	5.25
15	Harry S. Truman	6.50
16	Postrider	6.00
17	Boston Tea Party	15.00
18	Electronics	5.50
19	Robinson Jeffers	4.75
20	Lyndon B. Johnson	6.50
21	Henry O. Tanner	5.50
22	Willa Cather	5.00
23	Drummer	8.25
24	Angus Cattle	5.50
25	Christmas, Madonna	7.75
26	Christmas Tree, Needlepoint	7.75

1974

27	VFW	5.25
28	Robert Frost	5.25
29	Expo '74	6.00
30	Horse Racing	8.00
31	Skylab	8.50
32	Universal Postal Union	6.00
33	Mineral Heritage	7.00
34	First Kentucky Settlement	5.25
35	Continental Congress	7.00
35A	Same with corrected logo	—
36	Chautauqua	5.75
37	Kansas Wheat	5.75

38	Energy Conservation	5.00
39	Sleepy Hollow	5.75
40	Retarded Children	5.00
41	Christmas, Currier & Ives	7.50
42	Christmas, Angel Altarpiece	7.50

1975

43	Benjamin West	5.50
44	Pioneer	8.50
45	Collective Bargaining	4.75
46	Contributors to the Cause	6.25
47	Mariner 10	9.00
48	Lexington & Concord	5.50
49	Paul Laurence Dunbar	6.00
50	D.W. Griffith	5.75
51	Bunker Hill	5.75
52	Military Uniforms	5.00
53	Apollo Soyuz	8.25
54	World Peace Through Law	5.00
54A	Same with August 15, 1975 date	—
55	Women's Year	5.75
56	Postal Service Bicentennial	5.50
57	Banking and Commerce	6.25
58	Early Christmas, Card	7.00
59	Christmas, Madonna	7.00

1976

60	Spirit of '76	8.00
61	Interphil 76	7.00
62	State Flags	15.00
63	Telephone	6.75
64	Commercial Aviation	9.25
65	Chemistry	7.00
66	Benjamin Franklin	7.00
67	Declaration of Independence	7.00

68	12th Winter Olympics	7.50
69	Clara Maass	8.00
70	Adolph S. Ochs	9.00
70A	Same with charter logo	—
71	Christmas, Winter Pastime	8.00
71A	Same with charter logo	—
72	Christmas, Nativity	8.75
72A	Same with charter logo	—

1977

73	Washington at Princeton	9.00
73A	Same with charter logo	—
74	Sound Recording	16.00
74A	Same with charter logo	—
75	Pueblo Art	45.00
75A	Same with charter logo	—
76	Solo Transatlantic Lindbergh Flight	45.00
77	Colorado	11.00
78	Butterflies	12.00
79	Lafayette	10.50
80	Skilled Hands	10.50
81	Peace Bridge	10.50
82	Battle of Oriskany	10.50
83	Alta, CA, Civil Settlement	11.00
84	Articles of Confederation	15.00
85	Talking Pictures	13.50
86	Surrender at Saratoga	15.00
87	Energy	12.00
88	Christmas, Valley Forge	18.00
89	Christmas, Mailbox	24.00

1978

90	Carl Sandburg	6.50
91	Captain Cook	12.00
92	Harriet Tubman	9.50
93	Quilts	14.00

94	Dance	10.00
95	French Alliance	10.00
96	Early Cancer Detection	8.25
97	Jimmie Rodgers	11.00
98	Photography	8.00
99	George M. Cohan	12.50
100	Viking Missions	27.50
101	Owls	27.50
102	Trees	26.00
103	Christmas, Madonna	10.50
104	Christmas, Hobby Horse	10.50

1979

105	Robert F. Kennedy	7.25
106	Martin Luther King, Jr.	7.50
107	International Year of the Child	6.50
108	John Steinbeck	6.00
109	Albert Einstein	7.25
110	Pennsylvania Toleware	6.75
111	Architecture	7.50
112	Endangered Flora	7.00
113	Seeing Eye Dogs	6.25
114	Special Olympics	7.50
115	John Paul Jones	7.00
116	15¢ Olympics	8.50
117	Christmas, Madonna	8.50
118	Christmas, Santa Claus	8.50
119	Will Rogers	7.00
120	Vietnam Veterans	9.50
121	10¢, 31¢ Olympics	8.50

1980

122	W.C. Fields	7.50
123	Winter Olympics	7.50
124	Benjamin Banneker	7.25
125	Frances Perkins	5.50
126	Emily Bissell	6.00
127	Helen Keller/ Anne Sullivan	5.50
128	Veterans Administration	6.00
129	General Bernardo de Galvez	5.25
130	Coral Reefs	8.00
131	Organized Labor	5.50
132	Edith Wharton	5.25
133	Education	5.50
134	Indian Masks	8.00
135	Architecture	6.75
136	Christmas, Epiphany Window	8.00
137	Christmas, Toys	8.00

1981

138	Everett Dirksen	6.50
139	Whitney Moore Young	7.00
140	Flowers	7.00
141	Red Cross	7.00
142	Savings & Loans	6.75
143	Space Achievements	11.00
144	Professional Management	5.50

145	Wildlife Habitats	8.00
146	Int'l. Year of the Disabled	5.50
147	Edna St. Vincent Millay	6.00
148	Architecture	6.50
149	Babe Zaharias/ Bobby Jones	20.00
150	James Hoban	5.50
151	Frederic Remington	6.75
152	Battle of Yorktown/ Virginia Capes	5.25
153	Christmas, Madonna	7.00
154	Christmas, Bear and Sleigh	8.00
155	John Hanson	5.50
156	U.S. Desert Plants	8.00

1982

157	Roosevelt	8.25
158	Love	10.00
159	George Washington	9.50
160	State Birds & Flowers	27.50
161	U.S./Netherlands	10.00
162	Library of Congress	10.00
163	Knoxville World's Fair	8.50
164	Horatio Alger	8.75
165	Aging Together	9.50
166	The Barrymores	10.50
167	Dr. Mary Walker	9.00
168	Peace Garden	9.50
169	America's Libraries	8.00
170	Jackie Robinson	30.00
171	Touro Synagogue	9.50
172	Architecture	10.50
173	Wolf Trap Farm Park	10.00
174	Francis of Assisi	10.50
175	Ponce de Leon	10.50
176	Christmas, Madonna	13.50
177	Christmas, Season's Greetings	13.50
178	Kitten & Puppy	14.00

1983

179	Science and Industry	5.25
180	Sweden/USA Treaty	5.25
181	Balloons	6.00
182	Civilian Conservation Corps	5.25
183	40¢ Olympics	6.50
184	Joseph Priestley	5.25
185	Voluntarism	5.25
186	Concord/German Immigration	5.25
187	Physical Fitness	5.25
188	Brooklyn Bridge	6.00
189	TVA	5.25
190	Medal of Honor	8.00
191	Scott Joplin	7.25
192	28¢ Olympics	6.50
193	Babe Ruth	22.50
194	Nathaniel Hawthorne	5.25

195	13¢ Olympics	7.50
196	Treaty of Paris	5.50
197	Civil Service	5.50
198	Metropolitan Opera	6.50
199	Inventors	6.75
200	Streetcars	7.50
201	Christmas, Madonna	8.00
202	Christmas, Santa Claus	8.00
203	35¢ Olympics	8.00
204	Martin Luther	7.00

1984

205	Alaska	4.50
206	Winter Olympics	5.00
207	FDIC	4.75
208	Love	4.00
209	Carter G. Woodson	4.75
210	Soil and Water Conservation	4.75
211	Credit Union Act	4.75
212	Orchids	5.50
213	Hawaii	6.25
214	National Archives	4.50
215	20¢ Olympics	5.25
216	Louisiana World Exposition	5.00
217	Health Research	4.75
218	Douglas Fairbanks	4.75
219	Jim Thorpe	8.25
220	John McCormack	4.75
221	St. Lawrence Seaway	6.25
222	Preserving Wetlands	7.50
223	Roanoke Voyages	4.75
224	Herman Melville	4.75
225	Horace Moses	4.75
226	Smokey Bear	15.00
227	Roberto Clemente	25.00
228	Dogs	6.25
229	Crime Prevention	5.25
230	Family Unity	4.75
231	Christmas, Madonna	6.75
232	Christmas, Santa Claus	6.75
233	Eleanor Roosevelt	8.50
234	Nation of Readers	4.75
235	Hispanic Americans	4.50
236	Vietnam Veterans Memorial	8.25

1985

237	Jerome Kern	5.75
238	Mary McLeod Bethune	5.75
239	Duck Decoys	10.50
240	Winter Special Olympics	5.00
241	Love	5.00
242	Rural Electrification Administration	5.00
243	AMERIPEX '86	6.75
244	Abigail Adams	5.00
245	Frederic Auguste Bartholdi	6.50
246	Korean War Veterans	6.00
247	Social Security Act	5.00

248	World War I Veterans	5.00
249	Horses	9.00
250	Public Education	5.00
251	Youth	8.25
252	Help End Hunger	5.00
253	Christmas, Madonna	7.00
254	Christmas, Poinsettias	7.00

1986

255	Arkansas	5.25
256	Stamp Collecting Booklet	6.75
257	Love	6.00
258	Sojourner Truth	7.50
259	Republic of Texas	7.50
260	Fish Booklet	6.75
261	Public Hospitals	4.75
262	Duke Ellington	7.50
263	U.S. Presidents' Sheet #1	6.25
264	U.S. Presidents' Sheet #2	6.25
265	U.S. Presidents' Sheet #3	6.25
266	U.S. Presidents' Sheet #4	6.25
267	Polar Explorers	6.75
268	Statue of Liberty	7.50
269	Navajo Blankets	8.00
270	T.S. Eliot	6.25
271	Wood-Carved Figurines	6.75
272	Christmas, Madonna	5.75
273	Christmas, Village Scene	5.75

1987

274	Michigan	5.75
275	Pan American Games	3.50
276	Love	5.75
277	Jean Baptiste Pointe Du Sable	5.75
278	Enrico Caruso	5.50
279	Girl Scouts	7.50
280	Special Occasions Booklet	5.50
281	United Way	4.75
282	#1 American Wildlife	6.50
283	#2 American Wildlife	6.50
284	#3 American Wildlife	6.50
285	#4 American Wildlife	6.50
286	#5 American Wildlife	6.50
287	Delaware	5.75
288	Morocco/U.S. Diplomatic Relations	4.75
289	William Faulkner	4.75
290	Lacemaking	5.50
291	Pennsylvania	5.25
292	Constitution Booklet	5.00
293	New Jersey	5.25
294	Signing of the Constitution	5.00

295	Certified Public Accountants	20.00
296	Locomotives Booklet	7.50
297	Christmas, Madonna	6.25
298	Christmas, Ornaments	5.50

1988

299	Georgia	5.25
300	Connecticut	5.25
301	Winter Olympics	6.25
302	Australia	5.75
303	James Weldon Johnson	5.00
304	Cats	6.50
305	Massachusetts	5.25
306	Maryland	5.25
307	Knute Rockne	9.00
308	New Sweden	5.75
309	South Carolina	5.25
310	Francis Ouimet	14.00
311	New Hampshire	5.25
312	Virginia	5.25
313	Love	6.50
314	New York	6.25
315	Summer Olympics	6.25
316	Classic Cars Booklet	7.00
317	Antarctic Explorers	6.25
318	Carousel Animals	7.00
319	Christmas, Madonna, Sleigh	6.50
320	Special Occasions Booklet	6.50

1989

321	Montana	6.25
322	A. Philip Randolph	8.00
323	North Dakota	6.25
324	Washington	6.25
325	Steamboats Booklet	7.50
326	World Stamp Expo '89	5.50
327	Arturo Toscanini	6.25
328	U.S. House of Representatives	6.25
329	U.S. Senate	6.25
330	Executive Branch	6.25
331	South Dakota	6.25
332	Lou Gehrig	25.00
333	French Revolution	6.50
334	Ernest Hemingway	8.75
335	North Carolina	5.25
336	Letter Carriers	6.50
337	Drafting of the Bill of Rights	6.50
338	Prehistoric Animals	13.50
339	25¢ and 45¢ America/PUAS	7.25
340	Christmas, Traditional and Contemporary	8.50
341	Classic Mail Transportation	6.50
342	Future Mail Transportation	8.00

1990

343	Idaho	5.50
344	Love	7.25
345	Ida B. Wells	12.50
346	U.S. Supreme Court	6.00
347	Wyoming	6.25
348	Classic Films	13.00
349	Marianne Moore	5.50
350	Lighthouses Booklet	10.00
351	Rhode Island	5.25
352	Olympians	8.50
353	Indian Headdresses Booklet	10.00
354	Micronesia/ Marshall Islands	7.00
355	25¢ and 45¢ America/PUAS	7.50
356	Eisenhower	8.25
357	Creatures of the Sea	11.50
358	Christmas, Traditional and Contemporary	8.00

1991

359	Switzerland	8.00
360	Vermont	6.00
361	Savings Bonds	6.25
362	29¢ and 52¢ Love	8.00
363	Saroyan	8.50
364	Fishing Flies Booklet	10.00
365	Cole Porter	6.00
366	Antarctic Treaty	5.50
367	Desert Shield/ Desert Storm	25.00
368	Summer Olympics	7.50
369	Numismatics	6.50
370	Basketball	12.50
371	World War II Miniature Sheet	12.00
372	Comedians Booklet	9.50
373	District of Columbia	7.00
374	Jan Matzeliger	7.50
375	Space Exploration Booklet	11.50
376	America/PUAS	6.50
377	Christmas, Traditional and Contemporary	9.50

1992

378	Winter Olympics	8.50
379	World Columbian Stamp Expo '92	8.75
380	W.E.B. Du Bois	10.00
381	Love	8.75
382	Olympic Baseball	30.00
383	Columbus' First Voyage	10.00
384	Space Adventures	10.00
385	New York Stock Exchange	11.00
386	Alaska Highway	7.50
387	Kentucky Statehood	6.50
388	Summer Olympics	8.00
389	Hummingbirds Booklet	10.00

390	World War II	
	Miniature Sheet	10.00
391	Dorothy Parker	6.50
392	Theodore	
	von Karman	10.00
393	Minerals	9.50
394	Juan Rodriguez	
	Cabrillo	10.50
395	Wild Animals	
	Booklet	10.00
396	Christmas,	
	Traditional and	
	Contemporary	9.25
397	Columbus	
	Souvenir Sheets	40.00
398	Columbus	
	Souvenir Sheets	40.00
399	Columbus	
	Souvenir Sheets	40.00
400	Wildflowers #1	27.50
401	Wildflowers #2	27.50
402	Wildflowers #3	27.50
403	Wildflowers #4	27.50
404	Wildflowers #5	27.50
405	Happy New Year	15.00

1993

406	Elvis	20.00
407	Space Fantasy	11.00
408	Percy Julian	10.00
409	Oregon Trail	9.00
410	World Univ.Games	9.00
411	Grace Kelly	17.50
412	Oklahoma!	8.50
413	Circus	9.00
414	Cherokee Strip	8.50
415	Dean Acheson	10.50
416	Sport Horses	10.00
417	Garden Flowers	8.50
418	World War II	12.00
419	Hank Williams	15.00
420	Rock & Roll/R&B	20.00
421	Joe Louis	27.50
422	Broadway Musicals	11.00
423	National Postal	
	Museum	9.00
424	Deaf	
	Communication	9.00
425	Country Western	15.00
426	Christmas,	
	Traditional	10.00
427	Youth Classics	10.00
428	Mariana Islands	8.75
429	Columbus Landing	
	In Puerto Rico	10.50
430	AIDS Awareness	10.00

1994

431	Winter Olympics	15.00
432	Edward R. Murrow	9.00
433	Dr. Allison Davis	10.00
434	Year of the Dog	14.00
435	Love	9.50
436	Buffalo Soldiers	13.00
437	Silent ScreenStars	14.00
438	Garden Flowers	11.00
439	World Cup Soccer	12.50
440	World War II	15.00
441	Norman Rockwell	13.00
442	Moon Landing	16.00
443	Locomotives	12.00
444	George Meany	8.00

445	Popular Singers	12.50
446	James Thurber	8.00
447	Jazz/Blues	15.00
448	Wonders of the Sea	11.00
449	Birds (Cranes)	11.00
450	Christmas, Madonna	8.00
451	Christmas, Stocking	8.00
452	Year of the Boar	13.00

1995

453	Florida	10.00
454	Bessie Coleman	14.50
455	Kids Care!	10.00
456	Richard Nixon	15.00
457	Love	14.00
458	Recreational Sports	14.00
459	POW & MIA	12.50
460	Marilyn Monroe	22.50
461	Texas	12.50
462	Great Lakes	
	Lighthouses	14.00
463	United Nations	11.00
464	Carousel Horses	14.00
465	Jazz Musicians	17.50
466	Women's Suffrage	11.00
467	Louis Armstrong	16.00
468	World War II	15.00
469	Fall Garden Flowers	11.00
470	Republic of Palau	11.00
471	Christmas,	
	Contemporary	14.00
472	Naval Academy	14.00
473	Tennessee Williams	12.50
474	Christmas,	
	Traditional	14.00
475	James K. Polk	10.00
476	Antique	
	Automobiles	17.50

1996

477	Utah	10.00
478	Garden Flowers	10.00
479	Ernest E. Just	12.50
480	Smithsonian	
	Institution	10.00
481	Year of the Rat	17.50
482	Pioneers of	
	Communication	14.00
483	Fulbright	
	Scholarships	10.00
484	Summer Olympics	30.00
485	Marathon	13.50
486	Georgia O'Keefe	10.00
487	Tennessee	10.00
488	James Dean	17.50
489	Prehistoric	
	Animals	17.50
490	Breast Cancer	
	Awareness	11.00
491	American Indian	
	Dances	17.50
492	Folk Heroes	17.50
493	Centennial	
	Games (Discus)	11.50
494	Iowa Statehood	10.00
495	Rural Free Delivery	10.00
496	Riverboats	17.50
497	Big Band Leaders	17.50
498	Songwriters	17.50
499	Endangered	
	Species	27.50

500	Family Scenes	
	(4 designs)	14.00
501	Hanukkah	15.00
502	Madonna and Child	13.50
503	Cycling	15.00
503A	F. Scott Fitzgerald	19.00
503B	Computer	
	Technology	19.00

1997

504	Year of the Ox	19.00
505	Benjamin O. Davis	14.00
506	Love	12.00
507	Helping Children	
	Learn	10.50
508	Pacific 97	
	Triangle Stamps	14.00
509	Thornton Wilder	12.00
510	Raoul Wallenberg	12.00
511	Dinosaurs	20.00
512	Bugs Bunny	16.00
513	Pacific 97	
	Franklin	40.00
514	Pacific 97	
	Washington	40.00
515	The Marshall Plan	10.00
516	Classic Aircraft	27.50
517	Football Coaches	17.50
518	Dolls	25.00
519	Humphrey Bogart	14.00
520	Stars and Stripes	13.00
521	Opera Singers	14.00
522	Composers and	
	Conductors	14.00
523	Padre Varela	13.00
524	Air Force	13.50
525	Movie Monsters	16.00
526	Supersonic Flight	16.00
527	Women in the	
	Military	13.00
528	Holiday Kwanzaa	14.00
529	Holiday, Traditional	18.00
530	Holiday Holly	18.00

1998

531	Year of the Tiger	13.00
532	Winter Sports	13.00
533	Madam C.J. Walker	13.00
533A	Celebrate The	
	Century® 1900s	20.00
533B	Celebrate The	
	Century® 1910s	20.00
534	Spanish	
	American War	14.00
535	Flowering Trees	16.00
536	Alexander Calder	16.00
537	Cinco de Mayo	13.00
538	Sylvester & Tweety	17.00
538A	Celebrate The	
	Century® 1920s	20.00
539	Wisconsin	13.00
540	Trans-Mississippi	20.00
541	Folk Singers	14.00
542	Berlin Airlift	13.00
543	Spanish Settlement	
	of the Southwest	14.00
544	Gospel Singers	13.00
545	Stephen Vincent	
	Benet	13.00
546	Tropical Birds	13.00

546A	Breast Cancer Research	17.50
547	Alfred Hitchcock	13.00
548	Organ Donations	13.00
549	Bright Eyes	13.50
550	Klondike Gold Rush	13.00
551	American Art	20.00
551A	Celebrate The Century® 1930s	20.00
552	Ballet	13.00
553	Space Discovery	13.50
554	Philanthropy	13.00
555	Holiday, Traditional	18.00
556	Holiday, Contemporary	13.00

1999

557	Year of the Hare	15.00
558	Malcolm X	15.00
559	33¢ Victorian - Love	20.00
560	55¢ Victorian - Love	15.00
561	Hospice Care	15.00
562	Celebrate The Century® 1940s	20.00
563	Irish Immigration	15.00
564	Alfred Lunt and Lynn Fontanne	15.00
565	Arctic Animals	15.00
566	Nature of America Sonoran Desert	22.50
567	Daffy Duck	22.50
568	Ayn Rand	15.00
569	Cinco de Mayo	15.00
570	John and William Bartram	15.00
571	Celebrate The Century® 1950s	20.00
572	Prostate Cancer	15.00
573	California Gold Rush	15.00
574	Aquarium Fish	15.00
575	Xtreme Sports	15.00
576	American Glass	15.00
577	James Cagney	15.00
578	Honoring Those Who Served	15.00
579	All Aboard!	16.00
580	Frederick Law Olmsted	15.00
581	Hollywood Composers	16.00
582	Celebrate The Century® 1960s	20.00
583	Broadway Songwriters	16.00
584	Insects and Spiders	22.50
585	Hanukkah	15.00
586	Nato	15.00
587	Holiday Traditional, Bartolomeo Vivarini	15.00
588	Holiday Contemporary, Deer	15.00
589	Kwanzaa	15.00
590	Celebrate The Century® 1970s	20.00
591	Year 2000	16.00

2000

592	Year of the Dragon	15.00
593	Celebrate The Century® 1980s	20.00
594	Patricia Roberts Harris	15.00
595	U.S. Navy Submarines – Los Angeles Class	10.00
596	Pacific Coast Rain Forest	25.00
597	Louise Nevelson	10.00
598	Edwin Powell Hubble	10.00
599	American Samoa	10.00
600	Library of Congress	10.00
601	Wile E. Coyote/ Road Runner	10.00
602	Celebrate The Century® 1990s	20.00
603	Summer Sports	10.00
604	Adoption	10.00
605	Youth Team Sports	10.00
606	Distinguished Soldiers	10.00
607	The Stars and Stripes	25.00
608	Legends of Baseball	25.00
609	Stampin' The Future™	10.00
610	Edward G. Robinson	10.00
611	California Statehood	10.00
612	Deep Sea Creatures	10.00
613	Thomas Wolfe	10.00
614	The White House	10.00

2001

615	Love Letters	12.00
616	Lunar New Year— Year of the Snake	12.00
617	Roy Wilkins	12.00
618	American Illustrators	30.00
619	Love Letters (1 oz)	12.00
620	Love Letters (2 oz)	12.00
621	Nine-Mile Prairie	12.00
622	Diabetes Awareness	16.00
623	The Nobel Prize	12.00
624	Mt. McKinley	12.00
625	The Pan-American Inverts	30.00
626	Great Plains Prairie	30.00
627	Peanuts	12.00
628	Honoring Veterans	12.00
629	Frida Kahlo	12.00
630	Baseball's Legendary Playing Fields	30.00
631	Leonard Bernstein	12.00
632	Lucille Ball	12.00
633	The Amish Quilts	12.00
634	Carnivorous Plants	12.00
635	Holiday Celebration: EID	12.00
636	Dr. Enrico Fermi	12.00
637	That's All Folks!	12.00
638	Holiday Traditional: Lorenzo Costa's Virgin and Child	12.00
639	Holiday Contemporary: Santas	12.00
640	James Madison	12.00
641	Holiday Celebration: Thanksgiving	12.00
642	Kwanzas	12.00
643	Hanukkah	12.00
644	Love Letters	12.00

2002

645	Winter Sports	—
646	Mentoring a Child	—
647	Langston Hughes	—
648	Happy Birthday	—
649	Year of the Horse	—
650	U.S. Military Academy	—
651	Greetings From America	—
652	Longleaf Pine Forest	—
653	Heroes 2001	—
654	Masters of American Photography	—
655	John James Audubon	—
656	Harry Houdini	—
657	Andy Warhol	—
658	Teddy Bears	—
659	Love (1 oz.)	—
660	Love (2 oz.)	—
661	Ogden Nash	—
662	Duke Kahanamoku	—
663	American Bats	—
664	Women in Journalism	—
665	Irving Berlin	—
666	Neuter or Spay	—
667	Christmas: Gossaert	—
668	Hanukkah	—
669	Eid	—
670	Kwanzaa	—
671	Cary Grant	—
672	Hawaiian Missionaries	—
673	Happy Birthday	—
674	Greetings From America	—
675	Holiday: Snowmen	—

Glossary

Accessories
The tools used by stamp collectors, such as tongs, hinges, etc.

Aerophilately
Stamp collecting that focuses on stamps or postage relating to airmail.

Airmail
Mail which has been transported by air, as distinct from "surface" mail. Most long-distance mail is now transported by air; in the U.S., the distinction (and premium) for domestic airmail ceased in the late 1970s, and for foreign mail in the mid-1990s (now generically called "international rate").

Approvals
Stamps sent by a dealer to a collector for examination.

Block
An unseparated group of stamps, at least two stamps high and two stamps wide.

Bogus
A completely fictitious, worthless "stamp," created only for sale to collectors. Bogus stamps include labels for nonexistent values added to regularly issued sets, issues for nations without postal systems, etc.

Booklet Pane
A small sheet of stamps specially cut to be sold in booklets.

Bourse
A marketplace, such as a stamp exhibition, where stamps are bought, sold or exchanged.

Cachet (ka-shay')
A design on an envelope describing an event.

Cancellation
A mark placed on a stamp by a postal authority to show that it has been used.

Centering
The position of the design on a postage stamp.

Cinderella
Any stamp-like label without an official postal value.

Classic
An early stamp issue.

Coils
Stamps issued in rolls (one stamp wide) for use in dispensers or vending machines.

Commemoratives
Stamps that honor anniversaries, important people, special events or aspects of national culture.

Compound Perforations
Different gauge perforations on different (normally adjacent) sides of a single stamp.

Condition
Refers to the state of a stamp regarding such details as centering, color and gum.

Cover
An envelope that has been sent through the mail.

Cracked Plate
A term used to describe stamps which show evidence that the plate from which they were printed was cracked.

Definitives
Regular issues of postage stamps, usually sold over long periods of time.

Denomination
The postage value appearing on a stamp, such as 5 cents.

Die Cut
Scoring of self-adhesive stamps that allows stamp separation from liner.

Directory Markings
Postal markings that indicate a failed delivery attempt, stating reasons such as "No Such Number" or "Address Unknown."

Double Transfer
The condition on a printing plate that shows evidence of a duplication of all or part of the design.

Duplicates
Extra copies of stamps that can be sold or traded. Duplicates should be examined carefully for color and perforation variations.

Entire
An intact piece of postal stationery, in contrast to a cut-out of the printed design.

Error
A stamp with some-thing incorrect in its design or manufacture.

Exploded (booklet)
A stamp booklet that has been separated into its various components for display.

Face Value
The monetary value or denomination of a stamp.

Fake
A genuine stamp that has been altered in some way to make it more attractive to collectors. It may be repaired, reperfed or regummed to resemble a more valuable variety.

First Day Cover (FDC)
An envelope with a new stamp and cancellation showing the date the stamp was issued.

Foreign Entry
When original transfers are erased incompletely from a plate, they can appear with new transfers of a different design which are subsequently entered on the plate.

Franks
Marking on the face of a cover, indicating it is to be carried free of postage. Franks may be written, hand-stamped, imprinted or represented by special adhesives. Such free franking is usually limited to official correspondence, such as the President's mail.

Freak
An abnormal variety of stamps occurring because of paper fold, over-inking, perforation shift, etc., as opposed to a continually appearing variety or a major error.

Grill
A pattern of small, square pyramids in parallel rows impressed or embossed on the stamp to break paper fibers, allowing cancellation ink to soak in and preventing washing and reuse.

Gum
The coating of glue on the back of an unused stamp.

Hinges
Small strips of gummed material used by collectors to affix stamps to album pages.

Imperforate
Indicates stamps without perforations or separating holes.

Label
Any stamp-like adhesive that is not a postage stamp.

Laid Paper
When held to the light, the paper shows alternate light and dark crossed lines.

Line Pairs (LP)
Most coil stamp rolls prior to 1981 freature a line of ink (known as a "joint line") printed between two stamps at various intervals, caused by the joining of two or more curved plates around the printing cylinder.

Liner
The backing paper for self-adhesive stamps.

Linerless Coil
Self-adhesive roll of coil stamps without a liner.

Miniature Sheet
A single stamp or block of stamps with a margin on all sides bearing some special wording or design.

On Paper
Stamps "on paper" are those that still have portions of the original envelope or wrapper stuck to them.

Overprint
Additional printing on a stamp that was not part of the original design.

Packet
A presorted unit of all different stamps. One of the most common and economical ways to begin a collection.

Pane
A full "sheet" of stamps as sold by a Post Office.

Par Avion
French for mail transported "by air."

Perforations
Lines of small holes or cuts between rows of stamps that make them easy to separate.

Philately
The collection and study of postage stamps and other postal materials.

Pictorials
Stamps with a picture of some sort, other than portraits or static designs such as coats of arms.

Plate Block (PB) (or Plate Number Block)
A block of stamps with the margin attached that bears the plate number used in printing that sheet.

Plate Number Coils (PNC)
For most coil stamp rolls beginning with #1891, a small plate number appears at varying intervals in the roll in the design of the stamp.

Postage Due
A stamp issued to collect unpaid postage.

Postal Stationery
Envelopes, postal stamped cards and aerogrammes with stamp designs printed or embossed on them.

Postal Cards
See "stamped cards."

Postcards
Commercially-produced mailable cards, but without imprinted postage (postage must be affixed).

Postmark
A mark put on envelopes or other mailing pieces showing the date and location of the post office where it was mailed.

Precancels
Cancellations applied to stamps before the stamps were affixed to mail.

Presort Stamp
A discounted stamp used by qualified mailers who presort mail.

Prestige Booklet
A stamp booklet with oversized panes, descriptive information and images, commemorating a special topic.

Registered Mail
First-Class mail with a numbered receipt, including a valuation of the registered item. This guarantees customers will get their money back if an item is lost in the mail.

Reissue
An official reprinting of a stamp that was no longer being printed.

Replicas
Reproductions of stamps sold during the early days of collecting. Usually printed in one color on a sheet containing a number of different designs. Replicas were never intended to deceive either the post office or the collector.

Reprint
A stamp printed from the original plate after the issue is no longer valid for postage. Official reprints are sometimes made for presentation purposes, official collections, etc., and are often distinguished in some way from the "real" ones.

Revenue Stamps
Stamps not valid for postal use but issued for collecting taxes.

Ribbed Paper
Paper which shows fine parallel ridges on one or both sides of a stamp.

Rouletting
The piercing of the paper between stamps to facilitate their separation. No paper is actually removed from the sheet, as is the case in the punchin method used in most perforating. Instead, rouletting often gives the appearance of a series of dashes.

Se-tenant
An attached pair, strip or block of stamps that differ in design, value or surcharge.

Secret Marks
Many stamps have included tiny reference points in their designs to foil attempts at counterfeiting and to differentiate issues.

Self-Adhesive Stamp
A stamp with a pressure sensitive adhesive.

Selvage
The unprinted paper around panes of stamps, sometimes called the margin.

Semipostal Stamp
A stamp priced above the First-Class Mail rate plus an addtional charge earmarked for some charitable purpose.

Series
A number of individual stamps or sets of stamps having a common purpose or theme, issued over an extended period of time (generally a year or more), including all variations of design and/or denomination.

Set
A group of stamps with a common design or theme issued at one time for a common purpose or over a limited period of time (generally less than a year).

Souvenir Sheet
A small sheet of stamps with a commemorative inscription of some sort.

Special Issues
Stamps which supplement definitives, while meeting specific needs and having a more commemorative appearance. These include Christmas, Love, Holiday Celebration, airmail, international rate, Express Mail and Priority Mail stamps.

Speculative
A stamp or issue released primarily for sale to collectors, rather than to meet any legitimate postal need.

Stamped Cards
The current term for postal cards, which are mailable cards with postage imprinted directly on them.

Stamped Envelopes
Mailable envelopes with postage embossed and/or imprinted on them.

Strip
Three or more un-separated stamps in a row.

Surcharge
An overprint that changes the denomin-ation of a stamp from its original face value.

Sweatbox
A closed box with a grill over which stuck-together unused stamps are placed. A wet, sponge-like material under the grill creates humidity so the stamps can be separated with-out removing the gum.

Tagging
The marking of stamps with a phosphor or similar coating (which may be in lines, bars, letters, overall design area or entire stamp surface), done by many countries for use with automatic mail-handling equipment. When a stamp is issued both with and without this marking, catalogs will often note varieties as "tagged" or "untagged."

Thematic
A stamp collection that relates to a specific theme.

Tied On
Indicates a stamp whose postmark touches the envelope.

Tongs
A tool, used to handle stamps, that resembles a tweezers with rounded or flattened tips.

Topicals
Indicates a group of stamps with the same theme—space travel, for example.

Unhinged
A stamp without hinge marks, but not necessarily with original gum.

Unused
The condition of a stamp that has no cancellation or other sign of use.

Used
The condition of a stamp that has been canceled.

Variety
A stamp which varies in some way from its standard or original form. Varieties can include missing colors or perforations, constant plate flaws, changes in ink or paper, differences in printing method or in format, such as booklet and coil "varieties" of the same stamp.

Want List
A list of philatelic material needed by a collector.

Watermark
A design pressed into stamp paper during its manufacture.

Water Activated Gum
Water soluable adhesives such as sugar based starches on back of unused stamps.

Wove Paper
A uniform paper which, when held to the light, shows no light or dark figures.

Organizations

Please enclose a stamped, self-addressed envelope when writing to these organizations.

American Air Mail Society
Rudy Roy
PO Box 5367
Virginia Beach, VA 23471-0367
(p) 757/499-5234
AAMSinformation@aol.com
http://www.americanairmail
society.org

Specializes in all phases of aerophilately. Membership services include Advance Bulletin Service, Auction Service, free want ads, Sales Department, monthly journal, discounts on Society publications, translation service.

American First Day Cover Society
Douglas Kelsey
Executive Director
PO Box 65960
Tucson, AZ 85728-5960
(p) 520/321-0880
520/321-0879
AFDCS@aol.com
http://www.afdcs.org

A full-service, not-for-profit, noncommercial society devoted exclusively to First Day Covers and First Day Cover collecting. Publishes 90-page magazine, First Day, eight times a year. Offers information on 300 current cachet producers, expertizing, foreign covers, translation service, color slide programs and archives covering First Day Covers.

American Ceremony Program Society
John E. Peterson
ACPS Secretary/Treasurer
6987 Coleshill Drive
San Diego, CA 92119-1953
jkpete@pacbell.net
www.webacps.org

The American Ceremony Program Society is a place to learn about First Day and Supplemental (Second Day or later) stamp Ceremonies and Ceremony Programs. The Society publishes a journal, The Ceremonial, can be sent to members in a hard copy format at $2.50 per issue. The Society dues are $7 a year.

American Philatelic Society
Robert E. Lamb
Department PG
PO Box 8000
State College, PA
16803-8000
(p) 814/237-3803
(f) 814/237-6128
apsinfo@stamps.org
http://www.stamps.org
Moving in 2004, check web site for date, address and phone.

America's national stamp society. Membership benefits include various publications, services, and more. Sponsors national stamp exhibitions annually in partnership with the ASDA and USPS. 50,000+ members worldwide.

American Philatelic Research Library
aprl@stamps.org
www.stamplibrary.org

The largest philatelic library in the US, the APRL receives more than 400 periodicals, and houses extensive collections of philatelic literature.

American Society for Philatelic Pages and Panels
Gerald Blankenship
PO Box 475
Crosby, TX 77532-0475
(p) 281/324-2709
asppp134@aol.com
www.asppp.org

The only society with a focus on commemorative cancellations (formerly souvenir pages) and commemorative panels. Free ads, member auction, quarterly publica-tion sent to all members with reports on new issues, varieties, errors, oddities and dis-coveries. Active web site.

American Stamp Dealers Association
Joseph B. Savarese
3 School St., Suite 205
Glen Cove, NY 11542-2548
(p) 516/759-7000
(f) 516/759-7014
asda@erols.com
http://www.asdaonline.com

Association of dealers engaged in every facet of philately, with 6 regional chapters nationwide. Sponsors national and local shows. Will send you a com-plete listing of dealers in your area or collecting spe-cialty. A #10 SASE must accompany your request.

American Topical Association
Executive Director
PO Box 50820
Albuquerque, NM 87181-0820
(p) 505/323-8595
(f) 505/323-8795
ATAStamps@juno.com
http://home.prcn.org/~pauld/
ata

A service organization concentrating on the specialty of topical stamp collecting. Offers handbooks and checklists on specific topics; exhibition awards; Topical Time, a bimonthly publication dealing with topical interest areas; a slide loan service, and information, translation and sales services.

Ebony Society of Philatelic Events and Reflections
Manuel Gilyard
800 Riverside Drive, Apt. 4H
New York, NY 10032-7412
(p) 212-928-5165
(f) 212-928-1477
gilyardmani@aol.com
http://www.esperstamps.org

Junior Philatelists of America

Jennifer Arnold
Executive Secretary
PO Box 2625
Albany, OR 97321-0643
Exec.sec@jpastamps.org
http://www.jpastamps.org/

Member services include: pen pals, philatelic library, stamp identification, contests, study groups, and other services to young collectors. Members receive a bimonthly newsletter, The Philatelic Observer. Adult supporting membership and gift memberships are available. The JPA also publishes various brochures on stamp collecting.

Mailer's Postmark Permit Club

Charles F. Myers
Central Office
PO Box 3
Portland, TN 37148-0003
(p) 615/325-9478
(f) 615/451-7930
cfmyers@mindspring.com

Publishes bimonthly newsletter, Permit Patter, which covers all aspects of mailer's precancel postmarks. Also available, an 8-page step by step brochure "How to obtain a Mailer's Postmark Permit...a basic guide."

Plate Number Coil Collectors Club

Thomas McFarland
PNC3 Secretary
PO Box 756
Princeton Jct, NJ 08550-0756
www.pnc3.org

The Plate Number Coil Collectors Club (PNC[3]) is an organization that studies the plate numbers and plate varieties of United States coil stamps issued since 1981. The PNC[3] publishes a monthly newsletter, Coil Line. The website includes a membership application and discusses plate number coils and PNC[3] at length.

Postal History Society

Kalman V. Illyefalvi
8207 Daren Court
Pikesville, MD 21208-2211
(p) 410/653-0665
kalphyl@juno.com

Devoted to the study of various aspects of the development of the mails and local, national and international postal systems; UPU treaties; and means of transporting mail.

The Souvenir Card Collectors Society, Inc.

Dana M. Marr
PO Box 4155
Tulsa, OK 74159-0155
(p) 918/664-6724
DMARR5569@aol.com

Provides member auctions, a quarterly journal and access to limited-edition souvenir cards.

Compilation of U.S. Souvenir Cards

United Postal Stationery Society

UPSS Central Office
Cora Collins
Executive Director
PO Box 1792
Norfolk, VA 23501-1792
poststat@juno.com
www.upss.org

Postal stationary is made up of the post office-issued postal cards, envelopes, letter sheets and other postal products having the stamp already printed. The UPSS is the largest society devoted to the collecting and study of postal stationery of the world with members throughout the U.S. and many foreign countries.

19th Century Envelopes Catalog

20th Century Envelopes Catalog

U.S. Postal Card Catalog

U.S. Commemorative Stamped Envelopes, 1867-1965

Universal Ship Cancellation Society

Steve Shay
747 Shard Court
Fremont, CA 94539-7419
e-mail: Shaymur@flash.net
http://www.uscs.org

Specializes in naval ship postmarks and cachets.

U.S. Postal Service Stamp Services

475 L'Enfant Plaza SW
Washington, D.C. 20260-2437

U.S. Stamp Society

Executive Secretary
PO Box 6634
Katy, TX 77491-6634
http://www.usstamps.org

An association of collectors to promote the study of all postage and revenue stamps and stamped paper of the United States and U.S.-administered areas produced by the Bureau of Engraving and Printing and other contract printers.

Durland Plate Number Catalog

Expertisers

American Philatelic Expertizing Service (APEX)

Mercer Bristow
Director of Expertizing
PO Box 8000
State College, PA 16803-8000
Ambristo@stamps.org

Krystal Harter
Expertizing Coordinator
Krharter@stamps.org
(p) 814/237-3803
(f) 814/237-6128
http://www.stamps.org

A member service of the American Philatelic Society and the ASDA, APEX utilizes the outstanding reference collections at APS headquarters in conjunction with the nation's best philatelic scholars to pass judgement on the identification, authenticity and condition of stamps from around the world.

Philatelic Foundation
Attention: Chairman
70 W 40th Street
New York, NY 10018
(p) 212/221-6555
(f) 212/221-6208
www.philatelicfoundation.org

A nonprofit organization known for its excellent expertization service. The Foundation's broad resources, including extensive reference collections, 5,000-volume library and Expert Committee, provide collectors with comprehensive consumer protection. Book series include expertizing case histories in Opinions, *Foundation seminar subjects in "textbooks" and specialized U.S. subjects in monographs.*

Professional Stamp Experts, Inc.
PO Box 6170
Newport Beach, CA 92658
(p) 877/782-6788
http://www.psestamp.com
pse@collectors.com

Organization specializing in identification, expertization and grading of U.S. Postage Stamps, Covers, Revenues etc.... PSE issues a Certificate of Authenticity accepted by all auction firms, dealers and collectors.

PSE publishes a Guide to the Grading of U.S. Stamps and The Stamp Market Quarterly Price Guide. Either is free upon request.

Periodicals

The following publications will send you a free copy of their magazine or newspaper upon request.

Global Stamp News
PO Box 97
Sidney, OH 45365-0097
(p) 937/492-3183
global@bright.net

America's largest-circulation monthly stamp magazine featuring U.S. and foreign issues.

Linn's Stamp News
PO Box 29
Sidney, OH 45365-0097
(p) 937/498-7273
(f) 937/498-0876
(f) 937/498-0814 (outside US)
linns@linns.com
www.linns.com

Linn's Stamps News, the world's largest weekly stamp newspaper, contains breaking news stories of major importance to stamp collectors, features on a variety of stamp-collecting topics, the monthly U.S. Stamp Market Index, Stamp Market Tips and much more. A sample copy of the weekly newspaper is available upon request.

Linn's U.S. Stamp Yearbook
(p) 937/498-0802
(f) 800/572-6885 (US only)
(f) 937/498-0807 (outside US)
linns@linns.com
www.linns.com

Linn's World Stamp Almanac

Stamp Collecting Made Easy

Mekeel's & Stamps Magazine-fa
John Dunn
175R Proctor Hill Road
Hollis, NH 03049
stampnews@aol.com
http://www.stampnews.com

Weekly magazine for collectors of U.S. & worldwide stamps & covers.

U.S. Stamp News-fb
Monthly magazine for all collectors of U.S. stamps, covers and postal history.

Stamp Collector
Wayne Youngblood
Publisher, Stamps Dept.
700 E. State St.
Iola, WI 54990-0001
(p) 715/445-2214
youngbloodw@krause.com

For beginning and advanced collectors of all ages.

Stamp Wholesaler
For dealers of all levels and those interested in the stamp business. (Published monthly as part of Stamp Collector.)

Basic Philately

USA Philatelic Information Fulfillment
Dept. 6270
U.S. Postal Service
PO Box 219010
Kansas City, MO 64121-9014
(p) 1 800 STAMP-24

Scott Specialized Catalogue of U.S. Stamps and Covers
PO Box 828
Sidney, OH 45365-0828
(p) 937/498-0802
(p) 800/572-6885
(f) 937/498-0807
ssm@scottonline.com
http://www.scottonline.com

Scott Stamp Monthly

Scott Standard Postage Stamp Catalogue

Scott Classic Specialized Catalogue of U.S. Stamps and Covers (World from 1840-1940)

Museums, Libraries and Displays

Please contact the institutions before visiting to confirm hours and any entry fees.

The Collectors Club
Irene Bromberg
Executive Secretary
22 E. 35th Street
New York, NY
10016-3806
(p) 212/683-0559
(f) 212/481-1269
collectorsclub@nac.net
http://www.collectorsclub.org

Bimonthly journal, publication of various reference works, one of the most extensive reference libraries in the world, reading and study rooms. Regular meetings on the first and third Wednesdays of each month at 6:30 p.m., except July and August.

National Postal Museum
Smithsonian Institution
Washington, D.C. 20560-0570
(p) 202/633-9360
http://www.si.edu/postal/

*Located in the Old City Post
Office building at
2 Massachusetts Avenue, NE
National Postal Museum
houses more than 16 million
items for exhibition and
study purposes. Collections
research may be conducted
separately or jointly with
library materials. Call the
museum and its library
(202/633-9370) separately to
schedule an appointment.*

**The Postal History
Foundation**
Betsy Towle
PO Box 40725
Tucson, AZ 85717-0725
(p) 520/623-6652
(f) 520/623-6652
phf3@mindspring.com
Hours: M-F 8 a.m.-3 p.m.

*Located at 920 N. First Ave
in Tucson, the Foundation,
established in 1960, has
been a specialist in youth
philatelic education in the
classroom. Regular services
include a library, USPS contract post office, philatelic
sales, archives, artifacts and
collections and a Youth
Department.*

**San Diego County
Philatelic Library**
Al Kish, Library Manager
7403C Princess View Drive
San Diego, CA 92120
(p) 619/229-8813
Hours:
M & T & Th 6:30 p.m.-9:30
p.m. and Sat noon-3 p.m.
Other hours available by
appointment. Please call for
confirmation of hours.

**Spellman Museum of
Stamps and Postal History**
Executive Director
235 Wellesley Street
Weston, MA 02493-1538
(p) 781/768-8367
(f) 781/768-7332
info@spellman.org
www.spellman.org

*America's first fully accred-
ited museum devoted to the
display, collection and
preservation of stamps and
postal history. Exhibitions
feature rarities, U.S., and
worldwide collections.
Philatelic library and family
activity center open with
admission. School and scout
programs by appointment.
Museum store and post
office carries gifts, collecting
supplies, and stamps.*

Western Philatelic Library
PO Box 2219
Sunnyvale, CA 94087-2219
(p) 408/733-0336
stulev@ix.netcom.com
http://www.pbbooks.com/w
pl.htm
http://www.fwpl.org

**Friends of the Western
Philatelic Library**

**Wineburgh Philatelic
Research Library**
Erik D. Carlson, Ph.D.
McDermott Library
University of Texas at Dallas
PO Box 830643
Mailstation: MC33
Richardson, TX 75083-0643
(p) 972/883-2570
http://www.utdallas.edu/libr
ary/special/wprl.html
Hours: M-Th 9 a.m.–6 p.m.;
Fri 9 a.m.-5 p.m.

Exchange Service

Stamp Master
Charles Bergeron
PO Box 17
Putnam Hall, FL 32185-0017
Cbergero@bellsouth.net

*An "electronic connection"
for philatelists via modem
and computer to display/
review members' stamp
inventories for trading purposes, etc.*

Literature

**ArtCraft First Day Cover
Price List**
Washington Press
2 Vreeland Road
Florham Park, NJ 07932-1501
(p) 877/966-0001 (toll free)
info@washpress.com
http://www.washpress.com

*Includes Presidential
Inaugural covers.*

Legends of the West
Washington Press
*How some collectors struck
it rich!*

The Hammarskjold Invert
*Tells the story of the Dag
Hammarskjold error/invert.*

**The 24¢ 1918 Air Mail
Invert**
*Tells all there is to know
about this famous stamp.*

**The U.S. Transportation
Coils**
*How some collectors struck
it rich!*

*ALL ABOVE FREE for
#10 SASE.*

**Brookman's 1st Edition
Black Heritage First Day
Cachet Cover Catalog**
Arlene Dunn
Brookman/Barrett &
Worthen
10 Chestnut Drive
Bedford, NH 03110-5566
(p) 603/472-5575
(f) 603/472-8795

*Illustrated 176-page perfect
bound book.*

Brookman's 2nd Edition Price Guide for Disney Stamps
Illustrated 256-page perfect bound book.

2003 Brookman Price Guide of U.S., U.N. and Canada Stamps and Postal Collectibles
Illustrated 384-page catalog.

Postmark Advisory
Paul Brenner
General Image, Inc.
PO Box 335
Maplewood, NJ 07040-0335
Postmark1@earthlink.net
http://home.earthlink.net/
~postmark1
(How-to-do-it is excellent for beginners)

A weekly newsletter is available which provides descriptive information on U.S. pictorial postmarks that you can send away for. A free sample newsletter is available if you send a SASE and ask for a copy. If you are interested in postmarks, you might like to visit the web site.

Fleetwood's Standard First Day Cover Catalog
Fleetwood
Unicover Corporation
1 Unicover Center
Cheyenne, WY 82008-0001
(p) 307/771-3000
(p) 800/443-4225
http://www.unicover.com

Precancel Stamp Society Catalogs
Dick Laetsch
108 Ashwamp Road
Scarborough, ME 04070
(p) 207/883-2505
precancel@aol.com
www.precanceledstamps.com

Stamp Collecting Made Easy
PO Box 29
Sidney, OH 45365-0097
(p) 937/498-0802
(p) 800/572-6885 (US only)
(f) 937/498-0807 (outside US)

An illustrated, easy-to-read, 96-page booklet for beginning collectors.

International Agents

Japan Philatelic Agency
PO Box 96 Toshima
Tokyo 170-8668
JAPAN

Max Stern
234 Flinders Street
Box 997 H
GPO Melbourne 3001
AUSTRALIA

Harry Allen
PO Box 5
Watford Herts WD2 5SW
UNITED KINGDOM

Nordfrim
DK 5450 Otterup
DENMARK

DeRosa S.P.A.
Via Privata Maria Teresa 11
I-20123 Milan
ITALY

Hermann Sieger GMBH
Venusberg 32-34
D73545 Lorch Wurttemberg
GERMANY

Alberto Bolaffi
Via Cavour 17
10123 Torino
ITALY

International House of Stamps
98/2 Soi Tonson
Langsuan Rd
Lumpinee, Pathumwan
Bangkok 10330
THAILAND

Philatelic Centers

In addition to the more than 20,000 postal facilities authorized to sell philatelic products, the Postal Service also maintains Philatelic Centers located in major population centers. These Philatelic Centers have been established to serve stamp collectors and make it convenient for them to acquire an extensive range of current postage stamps, postal stationery and philatelic products issued by the Postal Service.

Please note that Philatelic Centers in this listing include offices that may have only one philatelic window or limited hours dedicated to philatelic services.

For questions, location and hours of operation about a Philatelic Center near you, please call 800-275-8777.

Alabama
Birmingham
Decatur
Dothan
Huntsville
Mobile
Montgomery

Alaska
Fairbanks
Anchorage

Arizona
Flagstaff
Phoenix
Tucson

Arkansas
Little Rock

California
Bakersfield
Cerritos
Concord
Downey
El Cajon
Eureka
Fresno
Glendale
Long Beach
Los Angeles
Napa
Oakland
Pasadena
Pleasanton
Redondo Beach
San Bernadino
San Diego
San Francisco
San Jose
San Ramon
Santa Ana
Santa Barbara

Santa Maria
Santa Rosa
Van Nuys
West Covina

Colorado
Aurora
Boulder
Colorado Springs
Denver
Durango
Fort Collins
Grand Junction
Littleton
Longmont

Connecticut
Hartford
Middletown
New Haven
Ridgefield
Waterbury

Delaware
Dover
New Castle
Wilmington

District of Columbia
Washington, DC

Florida
Altamonte Springs
W. Bradenton
Brooksville
Deland
Fort Lauderdale
Fort Myers
Fort Pierce
Hollywood
Lakeland
Leesburg
Longwood

Miami
Naples
Orange Park
Orlando
Sebring
St. Petersburg
Tampa
Titusville
W. Palm Beach

Georgia
Atlanta
Duluth
Gainesville
Marietta

Hawaii
Honolulu

Idaho
Boise
Moscow
Pocatello

Illinois
Arlington Heights
Aurora
Bridgeview
Chicago
Des Plaines
Evanston
Granite City
Joliet
Naperville
Park Forest
River Forest
Rockford
Rock Island
Schaumburg
Springfield
Waukegan

Indiana
Evansville
Fort Wayne
Lafayette
South Bend

Iowa
Cedar Rapids
Des Moines
Sioux City

Kansas
Shawnee Mission
Topeka
Wichita

Kentucky
Lexington
Louisville

Louisiana
Alexandria
Baton Rouge
Lafayette
Lake Charles
Metairie
Monroe
New Orleans
Shreveport

Maine
*There are no locations
in this area.*

Maryland
Annapolis
Baltimore
Cumberland
Fredrick
Riverdale
Salisbury

Massachusetts
Boston
Brockton
Fall River
Fitchburg
New Bedford
Pittsfield
Springfield
Turner Falls

*For questions, location
and hours of operation
about a Philatelic
Center near you, please
call 800-275-8777.*

Michigan
Ann Arbor
Battle Creek
Dearborn Hgts
Flint
Grand Rapids
Jackson
Kalamazoo
Lansing
Midland
Pontiac
Port Huron
Roseville
Royal Oak
Saginaw

Minnesota
Duluth
Rochester
Minneapolis

Mississippi
Jackson

Missouri
Chillicothe
Columbia
Kansas City
St. Joseph
St. Louis
Springfield

Montana
Billings
Great Falls
Missoula

Nebraska
Grand Island
Lincoln
North Platte
Omaha

Nevada
Las Vegas
Reno

New Hampshire
North Salem

New Jersey
Atlantic City
Bellmawr
Bergenfield
Cranford
Edison
Flemington
Fort Lee
Hazlet

Island Heights
Jersey City
Maplewood
Morristown
Nutley
Trenton
Wayne
W. Caldwell
Woodbury
Wyckoff

New Mexico
Albuquerque

New York
Albany
Baldwin
Bethpage
Binghamton
Brooklyn
Buffalo
Cedarhurst
Crompond
East Northport
Elmira
Flushing
Garden City
Glen Falls
Glenham
Hicksville
Holbrook
Huntington
Huntingon Station
Jamaica
Jamestown
Lindenhurst
New York
Oneonta
Pearl River
Plattsburgh
Poughkeepsie
Rochester
Schenectady
Smithtown
Staten Island
Syosset
Syracuse
Warwick
White Plains
Yonkers

North Carolina
Asheville
Charlotte
Raleigh

North Dakota
Bismarck
Fargo

Ohio
Akron
Cincinnati
Cleveland
Columbus
Dayton
Elyria
Mansfield
Steubenville
Toledo
Warren
Youngstown

Oklahoma
Muskogee

Oregon
Portland

Pennsylvania
Allentown
Bethlehem
Bradford
Du Bois
Erie
Greensburg
Harrisburg
Johnstown
Lancaster
Langhorne
Lehigh Valley
New Castle
New Kensington
Pittsburgh
Philadelphia
Southeastern
State College
Stroudsburg
Wilkes Barre
Williamsport

Puerto Rico
San Juan

Rhode Island
Newport
Pawtucket
Providence

South Carolina
Charleston
Columbia

South Dakota
Rapid City
Sioux Falls

Tennessee
Chattanooga
Jackson
Johnson City
Knoxville
Memphis

Texas
Abilene
Amarillo
Arlington
Austin
Beaumont
Bryan
College State
Corpus Christi
Dallas
Denton
El Paso
Fort Worth
Houston
Killeen
McAllen
Midland
Richardson
San Angelo
San Antonio
Spring
Waco
Tyler
Wichita Falls

Utah
Ogden
Prove
Salt Lake City

Vermont
Brattleboro
Burlington
White River Junction

Virginia
Bristol, VA
Charlottesville
Danville
Lynchburg
Merrifield
N. Chesapeake
Norfolk
Petersburg
Portsmouth
Radford
Roanoke
Staunton

Washington
Auburn
Bellevue
Bellingham
Pasco
Port Angeles
Seattle
Spokane
Tacoma
Yakima

West Virginia
Bluefield
Charleston
Clarksburg
Huntington
Martinsburg

Wisconsin
Eau Claire
Green Bay
La Crosse
Madison
Milwaukee
Oshkosh
Wausau

Wyoming
Cheyenne

*For questions, location
and hours of operation
about a Philatelic
Center near you, please
call 800-275-8777.*

Index

The Numbers listed next to the stamp description are the Scott numbers, and the numbers in the parentheses are the numbers of the pages on which the stamps are listed.

J

N

Providence, RI, 1164 (127)
Pteranodon, 2423 (268)
PUAS, America, 2426 (268),
    2512 (279), C121 (470),
    C127 (473), C131 (473)
Public
    Education, 2159 (236)
    Hospitals, 2210 (243)
    Schools, Desegregating,
    3187f (379)
Pueblo Pottery, 1706–1709 (187)
Puerto Rico
    Arecibo Observatory, Radio tel-
    escope, 3409f (427)
    Clemente, Roberto,
    2097 (228)
    Columbus Landing in, 2805
    (315)
    De Leon, Ponce, 2024 (220)
    Election, 983 (107)
    Marin, Luis Munoz, 2173 (239)
    San Juan, 1437 (152)
    Territory, 801 (91)
Pulaski, General, 690 (80)
Pulitzer, Joseph, 946 (103)
Puma, 1881 (204)
Pumper, Fire, 1908 (208)
Pumpkinseed Sunfish, 2481 (275)
Puppy and Kitten, 2025 (220)
Pure Food and Drugs, Act, 1906,
    3182f (375)
    Laws, 1080 (119)
Purple
    Deer, 3358 (415), 3362 (415),
    3366 (415)
    Flower, 3454 (431), 3465 (431),
    3481 (435), 3487 (435)
    Heart (21)
Pushcart, 2133 (232)
Putnam, Rufus, 795 (91)
Pyle
    Ernie, 1398 (148)
    Howard, 3502h (436)

Q

Quail, Gambel, 3293d (404)
Quarter
    Horse, 2155 (236)
    Seated, 1578 (168)
Quill
    Inkwell and, 1535 (163), 1581
    (168), 1811 (199)
    Pen, 1099 (120), 1119 (123),
    1230 (131), 1250 (132), 2360
    (259), 2421 (268)
Quilts
    American, 1745–1748 (191)
    Amish, 3524–3527 (443)
    Basket Design, 1745–1748
    (191)
Quimbly, Harriet, C128 (473)

R

Raccoon, 1757h (192)
Racing
    Car, 2262 (248)

Horse, 1528 (163), 3189g (380)
Stock Car, 3187n (379)
Radiator, Airplane, and Wooden
    Propeller, C4 (461)
Radio
    Amateur, 1260 (135)
    Entertains America, 3184i (376)
    interferometer very large array,
    New Mexico, 3409b (427)
    telescope, Arecibo
    Observatory, Puerto Rico,
    3409f (427)
    Waves, 1260 (135), 1274 (135),
    1329 (140)
"Raggedy Ann," 3151c (367)
Railroad
    Baltimore & Ohio, 1006 (108)
    Engineers, 993 (108)
    Lantern, 1612 (171)
    Mail Car, 2265 (248)
    Transcontinental, 922 (100)
Railway
    Car, Cog, 2463 (272)
    Mail Car, 2781 (312)
Rain Forest, Pacific Coast, 3378
    (419), 3378a-j (419)
Rainey, Ma, 2859 (323)
Rand, Ayn, 3308 (407)
Randolph, A. Philip, 2402 (267)
Range Conservation, 1176 (128)
Raphael Semmes, 2975i (336)
Raspberries, 3295 (404),
    3299 (404), 3303 (404),
    3407 (424)
Rat, Ord's Kangaroo, 3506j (439)
Ratification of the Constitution,
    835 (95), 2336–2348 (256)
Rattlesnake, Western
    Diamondback, 3293i (404)
Raven Dance, 3075 (351)
Ray, Man, 3649i (452)
Rayburn, Sam, 1202 (131)
Read, George, 1687e (180), 1694
    (184)
Readers, A Nation of, 2106 (231)
Reality, Virtual, 3191j (384)
Rearing Stallion, 3200 (387)
Rebecca Everingham, 3094 (355)
Rebecca of Sunnybrook Farm,
    2785 (312)
Recognizing Deafness, 2783
    (312)
Records, New Baseball, 3191a
    (384)
Recovering Species, 3191g (384)
Recreational Sports, 2961–2965
    (332)
Red
    Bat, 3661 (455)
    -bellied Woodpecker, 3611c
    (451)
    -breasted Merganser, RW61
    (480)
    Cloud, 2175 (239)
    Cross, American, 702 (80), 967
    (104), 1910 (208)
    Cross, International, 1016
    (111), 1239 (132)
    Deer, 3356 (415), 3360 (415),
    3364 (415)

Fish, 3317 (407), 3319 (407)
Flower, 3457 (431), 3463 (431),
    3479 (435), 3490 (435)
Fox, 1757g (192), 3036 (347)
    -Headed Woodpecker, 3032
    (347), 3045 (347)
    -Nosed Reindeer, 2792 (315),
    2797 (315), 2802 (315)
Rose, 2490 (276)
Squirrel, 2489 (276)
Redding, Otis, 2728 (307), 2735
    (307)
Redhead Decoy, 2141 (235)
Redhead Ducks, RW13 (479),
    RW27 (479)
Redheads, RW54 (480)
Redwood Library & Athenaeum,
    UX303 (506)
Reed, Dr. Walter, 877 (96)
Refuge National Park, City of,
    C84 (466)
Register and Vote, 1249 (132),
    1344 (143)
Religious Freedom in America,
    1099 (120)
"Remember the Maine," 3192,
    (387)
Remington, Frederic, 888 (96),
    1187 (128), 1934 (211),
    3502p (436)
Renwick, James, 1838 (200)
Representatives, House of, 2412
    (267)
Reptiles and Amphibians (19)
Republic of
    China, 1188 (128)
    Palau, 2999 (340)
    Texas, 776 (88), 778 (88), 2204
    (240)
    the Marshall Islands, 2507 (279)
Research, Breast Cancer, B1
    (399)
    Health, 2087 (227)
    Resolution, 1733 (188)
Restaurationen, 620 (75)
Retarded Children, 1549 (164)
Reticulate collared lizard (19)
Reticulated Helmet, 2118 (232)
Retriever, Chesapeake Bay, 2099
    (228)
Return to Space, 3191h (384)
Reuben James, Destroyer, 2559f
    (284)
Reuter, Ernst, 1136–1137 (124)
Revel, Bernard, 2193 (240)
Revere, Paul, 1048 (115), 1059A
    (115)
Rhode Island, 1645 (175), 1991
    (216), 3599 (448), 3734 (459)
    Flag, 1349 (143)
    Settlement, 777 (88)
    Statehood, 2348 (256)
    Windmill, 1739 (191)
Rhodochrosite, 1541 (164)
Rhythm & Blues/Rock & Roll
    Musicians, 2724–2737 (307)
Ribalt Monument, Jan, 616 (72)
Ribbon Star, U649 (492)
Richardson, Henry Hobson, 1839
    (200)

X

Y

Z

Postmasters General of the United States

Acknowledgments

This stamp collecting catalog was produced by Stamp Services, Government Relations, United States Postal Service.

UNITED STATES POSTAL SERVICE
John E. Potter
Postmaster General and Chief Executive Officer

Ralph J. Moden
Senior Vice President, Government Relations and Public Policy

David E. Failor
Executive Director, Stamp Services

Terrence W. McCaffrey
Manager, Stamp Development

Sonja D. Edison
Project Manager and Editor

Priscilla Simms-Pryor
Project Assistant

Betty Zelkowitz
Project Assistant

HARPERCOLLINS PUBLISHERS
Megan Newman
Editorial Director, HarperResource

Greg Chaput
Editor, HarperResource

Lucy Albanese
Design Director, General Books Group

DESIGN SERVICES
Roberta Wojtkowski Design
10992 Thrush Ridge Road
Reston, VA 20191

Night & Day Design
41 River Terrace #2104
New York, NY 10282

RESEARCH AND WRITING SERVICES
PhotoAssist, Inc.
7735 Old Georgetown Road
Bethesda, MD 20814

COLOR SEPARATION AND DIGITAL PREPRESS SERVICES
Dodge Color
4827 Rugby Avenue
Bethesda, MD 20814

PRINTING AND BINDING
Quebecor/World Taunton
MA, 02780